MW00398170

The Pearson
Custom Program for CIS

GO! with Office 2010 Integrated Projects

PEARSON

Cover Art: Jerry Driendl/Getty Images, Inc.; Steve Bloom/Getty Images, Inc.; "Cheetah" courtesy of Marvin Mattelson/ Getty Images; "Tabs" courtesy of Andrey Prokhorov/iStockphoto; "Open Doors" courtesy of Spectral-Design/iStockphoto; "Compass" courtesy of Laurent Hamels/Getty Images; "Fortune Teller" courtesy of Ingvald Kaldhussaeter/iStockphoto; "Ladder of Success" courtesy of iStockphoto; "Global Communication in Blue" courtesy of iStockphoto. Additional images courtesy of Photodisc/Getty Images, Photodisc, Stockbyte/Getty Images, Digital Vision/Getty Images, Pearson Learning Solutions, and brandXpictures.

Copyright © 2013 by Pearson Learning Solutions
All rights reserved.

Permission in writing must be obtained from the publisher before any part of this work may be reproduced or transmitted in any form or by any means, electronic or mechanical, including photocopying and recording, or by any information storage or retrieval system.

Additional copyright information is included, where applicable, as a footnote at the beginning of each chapter.

The information, illustration, and/or software contained in this book, and regarding the above mentioned programs, are provided "as is," without warranty of any kind, express or implied, including without limitation any warranty concerning the accuracy, adequacy, or completeness of such information. Neither the publisher, the authors, nor the copyright holders shall be responsible for any claims attributable to errors, omissions, or other inaccuracies contained in this book. Nor shall they be liable for direct, indirect, special, incidental, or consequential damages arising out of the use of such information or material.

Microsoft and/or its respective suppliers make no representations about the suitability of the information contained in the documents and related graphics published as part of the services for any purpose. All such documents and related graphics are provided "as is" without warranty of any kind. Microsoft and/or its respective suppliers hereby disclaim all warranties and conditions with regard to this information, including all warranties and conditions of merchantability, whether express, implied or statutory, fitness for a particular purpose, title and non-infringement. In no event shall Microsoft and/or its respective suppliers be liable for any special, indirect or consequential damages or any damages whatsoever resulting from loss of use, data or profits, whether in an action of contract, negligence or other tortious action, arising out of or in connection with the use or performance of information available from the services.

The documents and related graphics contained herein could include technical inaccuracies or typographical errors. Changes are periodically added to the information herein. Microsoft and/or its respective suppliers may make improvements and/or changes in the product(s) and/or the program(s) described herein at any time.

Microsoft® and Windows® are registered trademarks of the Microsoft Corporation in the U.S.A. and other countries. This book is not sponsored or endorsed by or affiliated with the Microsoft Corporation.

This special edition published in cooperation with Pearson Learning Solutions.

Printed in the United States of America.

V092

Please visit our website at *www.pearsonlearningsolutions.com*.

Attention bookstores: For permission to return any unsold stock, contact us at *pe-uscustomreturns@pearson.com*.

Pearson Learning Solutions, 501 Boylston Street, Suite 900, Boston, MA 02116
A Pearson Education Company
www.pearsoned.com

ISBN 10: 1-256-54124-9
ISBN 13: 978-1-256-54124-0

Table of Contents

Integrating Word and Excel

OUTCOMES
At the end of this chapter you will be able to:

OBJECTIVES
Mastering these objectives will enable you to:

PROJECT 1A
Create an Excel workbook that includes data copied from a Word document.

1. Create a Word Document
2. Copy Word Text into an Excel Workbook
3. Modify an Excel Worksheet
4. Preview and Print Word and Excel Files

PROJECT 1B
Create and format an Excel chart and link the chart to a Word document.

5. Work with an Existing Word Document
6. Create and Format a Chart in Excel
7. Link Excel Data and an Excel Chart to a Word Document

Patricia Malina/Shutterstock

In This Chapter

In this chapter, you will create documents using Word's tab and table features to insert and format text. You will create workbooks in Excel by pasting information from a Word document, entering data, creating formulas, inserting functions, and creating and formatting a chart. Finally, you will link the chart to a Word document.

The projects in this chapter relate to **Adamantine Jewelry**. This company is based in Milan, Italy, one of the world's leading centers for fashion and design. Adamantine Jewelry's designers take inspiration from nature, cultural artifacts, and antiquities to produce affordable, fashionable jewelry that is sold through major retailers in the United States. With a 40-year history, the company is well respected among its retail customers and has expanded to online and television retailers in recent years. In addition to women's bracelets, rings, and earrings, the company also produces sport and fashion watches for men and women.

From Chapter 1 of *GO! with Microsoft® Office 2010 Integrated Projects Comprehensive*, First Edition, Shelley Gaskin, Carol L. Martin. Copyright © 2012 by Pearson Education, Inc. Published by Pearson Prentice Hall. All rights reserved.

Project 1A Sales Memo

In Activities 1.01 through 1.10, you will enter sales data for Adamantine Jewelry into a Word document. You will copy and paste the Word data into an Excel workbook. In Excel, you will create formulas and functions. Additionally, you will format numbers and text. Your completed files will look similar to Figure 1.1.

Project Files

For Project 1A, you will need the following files:

New blank Word document
New blank Excel workbook
i01A_Memo_Headings

You will save your files as:

Lastname_Firstname_1A_Sales_Memo
Lastname_Firstname_1A_Adamantine_Sales

Project Results

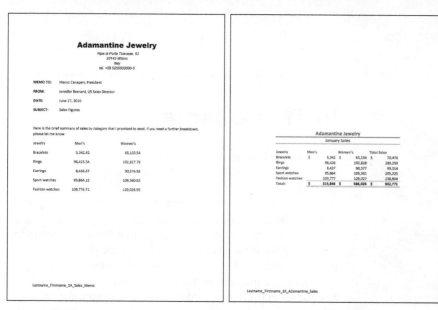

Figure 1.1
Project 1A Sales Memo

Objective 1 | Create a Word Document

When you create a Word document, there are times when you might want to use some of the information that you enter in a different application. If you enter the information in the proper format, you will be able to reuse the data without having to do any retyping. In the following activities, you will review how to create a Word document, set tab stops, and insert the document name in the footer.

Activity 1.01 | Starting Word and Setting Tabs

To move data from Word to Excel, you must format the information properly. One way to format a block of data is to separate each item in each row with a tab.

1 **Start** Word, and then display a new blank document. If necessary, on the Home tab, in the Paragraph group, click the **Show/Hide** button ¶ to display the formatting marks. On the status bar, use the **Zoom Slider** to adjust the page width to display both the left and right margins.

> *Print Layout view* is a view of a document that looks like a sheet of paper and displays margins, headers, footers, and graphics. Because formatting marks guide your eyes in a Word document—just as map and road signs guide you along a highway—these marks will display throughout this instruction.

2 On the **Home tab**, in the **Paragraph group**, in the lower right corner, click the **Dialog Box Launcher** ⓘ.

3 At the bottom of the **Paragraph** dialog box, click the **Tabs** button.

4 In the **Tabs** dialog box, in the **Tab stop position** box, type **2** Under **Alignment**, click the **Decimal** option button, and then click **Set**. In the **Tab stop position** box, type **4** Under **Alignment**, click the **Decimal** option button, and then click **Set**. Compare your screen with Figure 1.2.

> *Tab stops* mark specific locations on a line of text, indicated on the Word ruler, to which you can move the insertion point by pressing the ⟨Tab⟩ key. Tab stops are used to align and indent text. A *decimal tab stop* causes the text to align with the decimal point at the tab stop location.

Figure 1.2

Tab stop position

Decimal option button

Set button

5 At the bottom of the **Tabs** dialog box, click **OK**. Notice the tab stop indicators display on the horizontal ruler.

> **Alert! | What if the ruler does not display?**
>
> If the horizontal and vertical rulers do not display, at the top of the vertical scroll bar, click the View Ruler button.

Activity 1.02 | Entering and Formatting Text

1 With the insertion point blinking in the upper left corner of the document, to the left of the default first paragraph mark, type **Adamantine Jewelry** and then press Enter. Type the following text, pressing Enter after each line:

> **Ripa di Porta Ticenese, 53**
> **20143 Milano**
> **Italy**
> **tel. +39 0255500000–5**

2 Select the entire first line of text—*Adamantine Jewelry*. On the displayed Mini toolbar, click the **Font button arrow** [Calibri (Body) ▾], and then click **Arial Black**. With the Mini toolbar still displayed, click the **Font Size button arrow** [11 ▾], and then click **20**. If the Mini toolbar disappears, right-click on the selected text.

> The *Mini toolbar* is a small toolbar containing frequently used formatting commands that displays as a result of selecting text or objects.

3 Select the next four lines of text, beginning with *Ripa* and ending with the telephone number. On the Mini toolbar, click the **Font button arrow** [Calibri (Body) ▾], and then click **Arial**. Click the **Font Size arrow** [11 ▾], click **10**, and then apply **Italic** [*I*].

4 Select all five lines of text, being careful not to select the blank line below the text. On the Mini toolbar, click **Center** [≡]. Click the **Page Layout tab**, and then in the **Paragraph group**, under **Spacing**, click the **After spin box down arrow** two times to change the value to **0 pt**. Click to the left of the text *Adamantine Jewelry*, and then compare your screen with Figure 1.3.

Figure 1.3

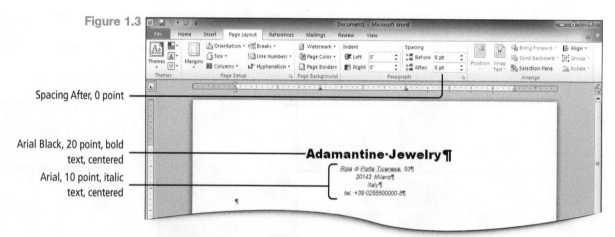

Spacing After, 0 point

Arial Black, 20 point, bold
text, centered

Arial, 10 point, italic
text, centered

5 Press Ctrl + End to move to the end of the document, and then press Enter two times. Type the following text: **Here is the brief summary of sales by category that I promised to send. If you need a further breakdown, please let me know.**

6 Press Enter, and then type the following company sales data pressing Tab to separate the columns. Press Enter one time at the end of each row. Note: The arrow that indicates a tab is a nonprinting formatting mark.

Jewelry	Men's	Women's
Bracelets	5,342.41	65,133.54
Rings	96,425.54	192,827.79
Earrings	8,436.67	90,576.92
Sport watches	95,864.22	109,360.63
Fashion watches	109,776.71	129,026.95

7 Compare your screen with Figure 1.4.

Figure 1.4

Tab stop indicators

Tab marks

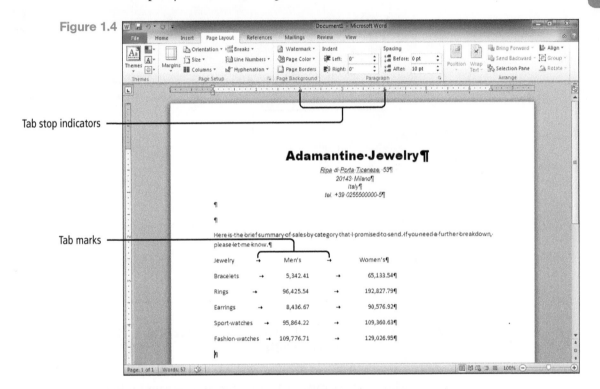

Activity 1.03 | Inserting Text from Another Word Document

1 In the second blank line below the centered text, click to position the insertion point.

2 Click the **Insert tab**, and then in the **Text group**, click the **Object button arrow**, and then click **Text from File**.

3 In the **Insert File** dialog box, navigate to the location where your student data files are stored. Locate the file **i01A_Memo_Headings**, click the file name to select it, and then click **Insert**.

Text from the Word document *i01A_Memo_Headings* is inserted in the current Word document.

4 In the *MEMO TO* line, select [**Name, Title**], and then type **Marco Canaperi, President**

5 Use the same procedure to replace the data after the three memo headings with the following:

FROM	**Jennifer Bernard, US Sales Director**
DATE	**June 17, 2016**
SUBJECT	**Sales Figures**

6 Compare your screen with Figure 1.5.

Figure 1.5

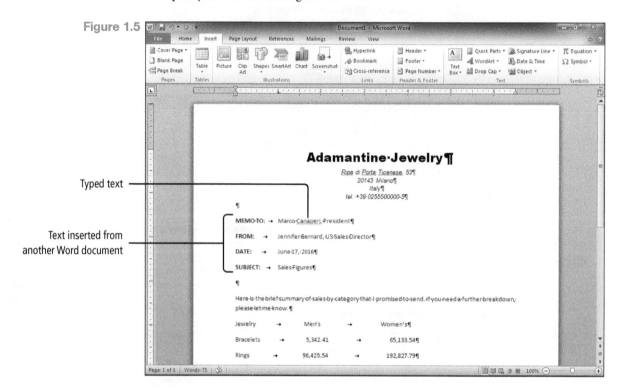

Typed text

Text inserted from another Word document

Activity 1.04 | Saving a Document, Creating a Footer, and Inserting Quick Parts

1 On the Quick Access Toolbar, click the **Save** button. In the **Save As** dialog box, navigate to the location where you are storing your projects for this chapter, and then on the toolbar, click the **New folder** button.

In the file list, a new folder is created, and the text *New folder* is selected.

2 Type **Integrated Projects Chapter 1** to replace the selected text, and then press Enter.

In Windows-based programs, the Enter key confirms an action.

3 With the Integrated Projects Chapter 1 folder selected, at the bottom right of the **Save As** dialog box, click **Open**. Compare your screen with Figure 1.6.

The name of your folder displays in the address bar. In the File name box, Word inserts the text at the beginning of the document as a suggested file name.

Figure 1.6

New folder button

Folder name displays in address bar

File name box with default name

Here is the brief summary of sales by category that I promised to send. If you need a further breakdown, please let me know.¶

Jewelry	→	Men's	→	Women's¶
Bracelets	→	5,342.41	→	65,133.54¶
Rings	→	96,425.54	→	192,827.79¶

4 In the lower portion of the **Save As** dialog box, click in the **File name** box to select the existing text.

5 With the text selected, using your own first and last name, type **Lastname_Firstname_1A_Sales_Memo** being sure to include the underscore—Shift + - —instead of spaces between words.

> The Microsoft Windows operating system recognizes file names with spaces; however, some Internet file transfer programs do not. In this instruction, underscores are used instead of spaces in file names.

6 In the lower right corner, click **Save**; or press Enter.

> Your new file name displays in the title bar, indicating that the file has been saved to the location that you have specified. The file extension .docx may or may not display, depending on your Windows settings.

Another Way

Right-click near the bottom edge of the page, and then from the shortcut menu, click Edit Footer.

7 On the **Insert tab**, in the **Header & Footer group**, click the **Footer** button to display the **Footer** gallery. At the bottom of the **Footer** gallery, click **Edit Footer**.

> A *gallery* displays a list of potential results instead of just the command name.

8 On the **Design tab**, in the **Insert group**, click the **Quick Parts** button, and then click **Field**. In the **Field** dialog box, under **Field names**, locate and then click **FileName**. Click **OK**, and then compare your screen with Figure 1.7.

> A *field* is a placeholder that displays preset content, such as the current date, the file name, a page number, or other stored information.

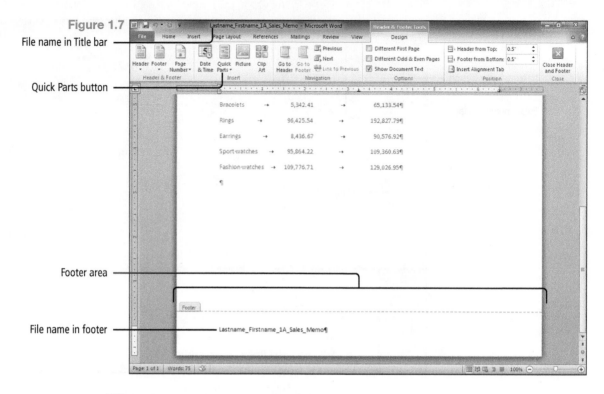

Figure 1.7

File name in Title bar

Quick Parts button

Footer area

File name in footer

Bracelets	→	5,342.41	→	65,133.54¶
Rings	→	96,425.54	→	192,827.79¶
Earrings	→	8,436.67	→	90,576.92¶
Sport-watches	→	95,864.22	→	109,360.63¶
Fashion-watches	→	109,776.71	→	129,026.95¶

Footer

Lastname_Firstname_1A_Sales_Memo¶

9 Double-click anywhere in your document to close the footer. Notice that the file name displays in the footer as light gray.

10 **Save** 🖫 your document.

Objective 2 | Copy Word Text into an Excel Workbook

After you have started a Word document, you may realize that you can manipulate the data more easily in another application, such as Excel. Instead of starting over and retyping all of your data, you can copy the data from Word and paste it into Excel.

Activity 1.05 | Starting Excel, Saving a Workbook, and Inserting a Footer

1 **Start** Excel, and then display a new blank workbook.

2 In cell **A1**, type **Adamantine Jewelry** and then press Enter.

After you type data into a cell, you must confirm the entry. One way to complete the entry is to press Enter which moves the active cell to the cell directly below.

3 In cell **A2**, type **January Sales** and then press Enter.

4 On the Quick Access Toolbar, click the **Save** button 🖫. In the **Save As** dialog box, navigate to your **Integrated Projects Chapter 1** folder, and then click **Open**.

5 In the **File name** box, using your own first and last name, type **Lastname_Firstname_1A_Adamantine_Sales** and then click **Save**. Compare your screen with Figure 1.8.

The new file name displays in the title bar. The file extension .xlsx may or may not display, depending on your Windows settings.

Figure 1.8

File name in Title bar

6 Click the **Insert tab**, and then in the **Text group**, click the **Header & Footer** button to switch to Page Layout view.

Page Layout view is a screen view in which you can use the rulers to measure the width and height of data, set margins for printing, hide or display the numbered row headings and lettered column headings, and change the page orientation. This view is useful in preparing your worksheet for printing.

7 On the **Design tab**, in the **Navigation group**, click the **Go to Footer** button.

The insertion point displays in the center section of the footer area.

8 In the **Footer** area, click just above the word *Footer*, and then in the **Header & Footer Elements group**, click the **File Name** button. Compare your screen with Figure 1.9.

Notice the file name field displays on the left side of the footer area.

Figure 1.9

File Name button

Footer area

File name field in the footer

9 Click any cell in the workbook to exit the footer.

The file name field in the footer area is replaced with the file name.

10 Near the right side of the status bar, click the **Normal** button ⊞ to return to Normal view.

Normal view maximizes the number of cells visible on your screen and keeps the column letters and row numbers close to the columns and rows.

11 Press Ctrl + Home to display the top of your worksheet and to make cell A1 the active cell.

Activity 1.06 | Copying and Pasting Word Text into an Excel File

1 On the taskbar, click the **Lastname_Firstname_1A_Sales_Memo** button to make the Word document window active.

2 In the first tabbed paragraph, move the pointer to the left of the word *Jewelry* to display the 🔄 pointer. Drag down to select the six rows of tabbed text, as shown in Figure 1.10.

Project 1A: Sales Memo | **Integrated Projects**

Figure 1.10

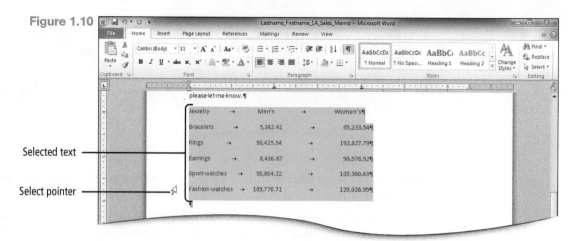

Selected text

Select pointer

Another Way

Press Ctrl + C.

3 On the **Home tab**, in the **Clipboard group**, click the **Copy** button.

4 On the taskbar, click the **Lastname_Firstname_1A_Adamantine_Sales** button to make the Excel window active.

5 Click in cell **A4** to make it the active cell.

Another Way

Press Ctrl + V.

6 On the **Home tab**, in the **Clipboard group**, click the **Paste** button. Notice that your Word data is pasted into the Excel worksheet, starting in cell A4—the cell that contained the insertion point. Compare your screen with Figure 1.11.

Because some of the numbers are too wide for the column, they are displayed as a series of pound signs (#).

Figure 1.11

Word text pasted into the worksheet

Columns too narrow

7 **Save** your workbook.

Objective 3 | Modify an Excel Worksheet

In Excel, you can create and analyze data with formulas and functions. A *formula* is a mathematical expression that contains functions, operators, constants, and properties, and returns a value to a cell. A *function* is a predefined formula—a formula that Excel has already built for you—that performs calculations by using specific values in a particular order. Text and numbers can be formatted to present data in a professional manner.

Activity 1.07 | Creating a Formula, Using the SUM Function to Calculate Totals, and Using AutoFill

1 Click cell **D4** to make it the active cell. Type **Total Sales** and then press Enter.

2 In cell **D5**, type **=B5+C5** and then press Enter.

The result of the formula calculation displays in cell D5.

3 Click cell **D5** to make it the active cell.

The *fill handle*—a small black square in the lower right corner of a selected cell—displays.

4 Point to the fill handle to display the ⊞ pointer. Hold down the left mouse button, and then drag down to cell **D9**. Release the mouse button, and then compare your screen with Figure 1.12.

Excel copies the formula from cell D5 into cells D6 through D9 using a *relative cell reference*. In a formula, a relative cell reference is the address of a cell based on the relative position of the cell that contains the formula and the cell referred to. The *AutoFill* feature extends values into adjacent cells based on the values of selected cells.

Figure 1.12

Formulas copied to adjacent cells

Fill handle

5 Click cell **B10**. On the **Home tab**, in the **Editing group**, click the **Sum** button Σ and then press Enter. Note: Depending upon your screen resolution, the *Sum* button may display as the *AutoSum* button; the Sum button is also referred to as the AutoSum button.

The *SUM function* is a predefined formula that adds all the numbers in a selected range of cells.

6 Click cell **B10**. Point to the fill handle to display the ⊞ pointer, hold down the left mouse button, and then drag right to cell **D10**. Release the mouse button.

The Sum function from cell B10 is copied into cells C10 and D10.

7 Click cell **A10**, type **Totals** and then press Enter. Compare your screen with Figure 1.13.

Figure 1.13

Formulas copied to adjacent cells

8 Save 🖫 your workbook.

Activity 1.08 | Formatting Numbers and Text

1 Select cells **A1:D1**. On the **Home tab**, in the **Alignment group**, click the **Merge & Center** button 🔳.

The *Merge & Center* command joins selected cells into one large cell and then centers the contents in the new cell.

2 In the **Styles group**, click the **Cell Styles** button. In the **Cell Styles** gallery, under **Titles and Headings**, click **Heading 1**.

3 Select cells **A2:D2**. In the **Alignment group**, click the **Merge & Center** button 🔳. In the **Styles group**, click the **Cell Styles** button. In the **Cell Styles** gallery, under **Titles and Headings**, click **Heading 2**.

4 Select cells **A4:A10**. Hold down Ctrl and select cells **B4:D4**.

The titles should all be selected. By holding down Ctrl while selecting cells, you can select nonadjacent cells.

5 In the **Styles group**, click the **Cell Styles** button. In the **Cell Styles** gallery, under **Titles and Headings**, click **Heading 4**, and then compare your screen with Figure 1.14.

Figure 1.14

Titles merged and centered

Heading 1 style

Heading 2 style

Heading 4 style

6 Select cells **B6:D9**. On the **Home tab**, in the **Number group**, click the **Comma Style** button.

> The *Comma Style* inserts thousand comma separators where appropriate, applies two decimal places, and leaves space at the right to accommodate a parenthesis for negative numbers. The columns are also widened to make room for the new number format.

7 In the **Number group**, click the **Decrease Decimal** button two times.

8 Select cells **B5:D5**. Hold down Ctrl and select cells **B10:D10**.

9 On the **Home tab**, in the **Number group**, click the **Accounting Number Format** button $.

> The *Accounting Number Format* applies a thousand comma separator where appropriate, inserts a fixed U.S. dollar sign aligned at the left edge of the cell, applies two decimal places, and leaves a small amount of space at the right edge of the cell to accommodate a parenthesis for negative numbers. By leaving the dollar sign off the other rows, the worksheet looks less cluttered.

10 Point to either of the selected ranges, and then right-click to display a shortcut menu and the Mini toolbar. On the Mini toolbar, click the **Decrease Decimal** button two times.

> A *shortcut menu* is a context-sensitive menu that displays commands and options relevant to the selected object.

11 Select cells **B10:D10**. In the **Styles group**, click the **Cell Styles** button. In the **Cell Styles** gallery, under **Titles and Headings**, click **Total**.

12 Select **columns A:D**. On the **Home tab**, in the **Cells group**, click the **Format** button. Under **Cell Size**, click **Column Width**, and then in the **Column Width** dialog box, type **15** Click **OK**, and then compare your screen with Figure 1.15.

> Columns A through D become wider. The column width number represents the number of characters that can be displayed across the width of a cell.

Figure 1.15

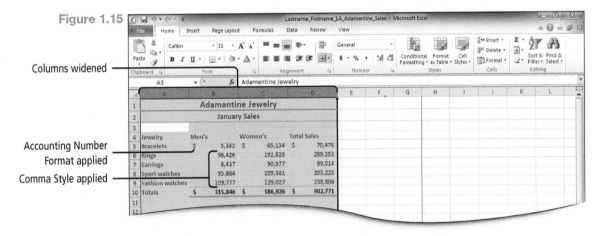

Columns widened

Accounting Number Format applied

Comma Style applied

13 Hold down Ctrl and press Home to make cell **A1** the active cell.

14 **Save** your workbook.

Objective 4 | Preview and Print Word and Excel Files

Excel and Word enable you to preview the printed page before you actually print the file. You will preview your files, center the worksheet on the page, and then print the files.

Activity 1.09 | Previewing and Printing an Excel Workbook

1 With the Excel workbook still active, click the **Page Layout tab**, and then in the **Page Setup group**, click the **Dialog Box Launcher** ⬚.

2 In the **Page Setup** dialog box, click the **Margins tab**. Under **Center on page**, select both the **Horizontally** check box and the **Vertically** check box, and then click **OK**.

3 Click the **File tab** to display **Backstage** view. With the **Info tab** selected, on the right, click **Properties**, and then click **Show Document Panel**. In the **Author** box, type your firstname and lastname, in the **Subject** box, type your course name and section number, and then in the **Keywords** box, type **sales worksheet** Above and to the right of the **Status** box, click the **Close** button ⊠ to close the Document Information Panel.

4 **Save** 🖫 your workbook.

5 In the upper left corner of your screen, click the **File tab** to display **Backstage** view, and then click the **Print tab** to display the **Print Preview**. Compare your screen with Figure 1.16

> *Print Preview* displays information exactly as it will print based on the options that are selected. Your data is centered horizontally and vertically on the page, and the file name displays on the left edge of the footer area.

Figure 1.16

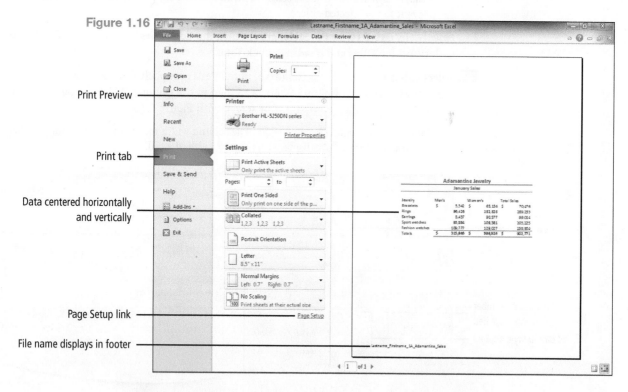

Print Preview
Print tab
Data centered horizontally and vertically
Page Setup link
File name displays in footer

6 If your instructor directs you to submit your files electronically, go to Step 8.

7 To print your worksheet, under **Print**, click the **Print** button.

Another Way
Press Ctrl + `.

8 Click the **Formulas tab**, and then in the **Formula Auditing group**, click the **Show Formulas** button.

> Your formulas display on the worksheet. When viewing formulas, the Show Formulas button doubles the width of every column.

9 Click the **File tab** to display **Backstage** view, and then click the **Print tab** to display the **Print Preview**. Below the Print Preview, notice a navigation bar indicates you are viewing page 1 of 2.

If printed with the current settings, your worksheet will print on two pages.

10 At the bottom of the screen, to the left of the **Print Preview**, under **Settings**, click the **Page Setup** link to display the Page Setup dialog box.

11 In the **Page Setup** dialog box, on the **Page tab**, under **Orientation**, click the **Landscape** option button. Under **Scaling**, click the **Fit to** option button. Verify the options are *1 page(s) wide by 1 tall*, and then click **OK**. Compare your screen with Figure 1.17.

Your worksheet will print on one page.

Figure 1.17

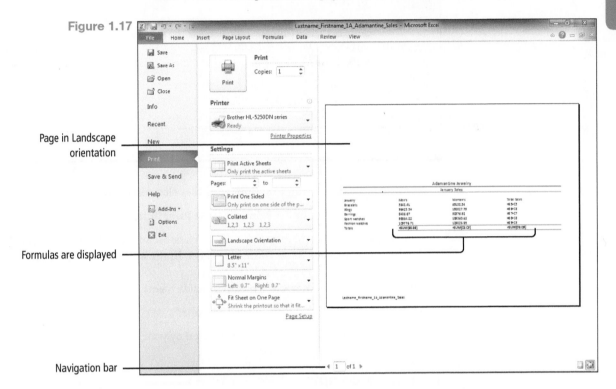

Page in Landscape orientation

Formulas are displayed

Navigation bar

12 If your instructor directs you to submit your files electronically, go to Step 14.

13 To print your worksheet, under **Print**, click the **Print** button.

14 In the upper right corner of the Excel window, click the **Close** button to close Excel. When asked *Do you want to save the changes you made?*, click **Don't Save**.

Saving your worksheet now would save the view displaying your formulas.

Activity 1.10 | Previewing and Printing a Word Document

1 On the taskbar, click the **Lastname_Firstname_1A_Sales_Memo** button to make your Word document active. Press Ctrl + Home.

Another Way
Press Ctrl + F2.

2 Click the **File tab** to display **Backstage** view, and then click the **Print tab** to display the **Print Preview**. Notice the file name displays in the footer. Compare your screen with Figure 1.18.

Figure 1.18

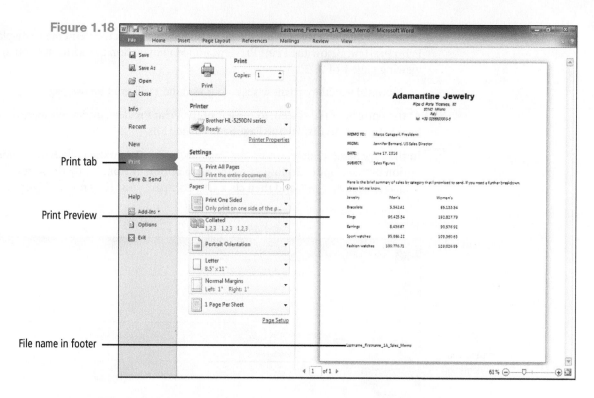

Print tab

Print Preview

File name in footer

3 If your instructor directs you to submit your files electronically, go to Step 5.

4 To print your document, under **Print**, click the **Print** button.

5 Display **Backstage** view, and then if necessary, click the **Info tab**. On the right, click **Properties**, and then click **Show Document Panel**. In the **Author** box, type your firstname and lastname, in the **Subject** box, type your course name and section number, and then in the **Keywords** box, type **sales memo**

6 **Save** the document, and then **Close** Word.

7 Submit your printed or electronic files as directed by your instructor.

End **You have completed Project 1A**

Project 1B Sales Chart

Project Activities

In Activities 1.11 through 1.21, you will create a table in a Word document that lists the different designers who create the fashionable jewelry sold by Adamantine Jewelry. You will create and format a chart in Excel, and then link the Excel data and chart into the Word document. Claudio Lenti, Creative Director of Adamantine Jewelry, will provide you with new sales data. You will update the Excel data to reflect the new information. You will review the Word document to see that the changes made in Excel are updated in both files. Your completed files will look similar to Figure 1.19.

Project Files

For Project 1B, you will need the following files:

> i01B_US_Sales
> i01B_Sales_Chart

You will save your files as:

> Lastname_Firstname_1B_US_Sales
> Lastname_Firstname_1B_Sales_Chart

Project Results

Figure 1.19
Project 1B Sales Chart

Objective 5 | Work with an Existing Word Document

A *table* is a format for information that organizes and presents text and data in columns and rows. You can insert a table by choosing from a selection of preformatted tables or by selecting the number of rows and columns that you want. After you create a table, you can format the table using a *Table Style*—a predefined set of formatting characteristics, including font, alignment, and cell shading—or you can apply your own custom formatting.

Activity 1.11 | Creating a Table in Word

1 **Start** Word, and then navigate to the location of the student data files for this instruction. Locate and open the document **i01B_US_Sales**. If necessary, display formatting marks, and be sure your screen displays both the left and right document edges. Display the **Save As** dialog box, navigate to your **Integrated Projects Chapter 1** folder, and then save the document as **Lastname_Firstname_1B_US_Sales**

2 Click the **Insert tab**, and then in the **Header & Footer group**, click the **Footer** button to display the **Footer** gallery. At the bottom of the **Footer** gallery, click **Edit Footer**. On the **Design tab**, in the **Insert group**, click the **Quick Parts** button, and then click **Field**. In the **Field** dialog box, under **Field names**, locate and click **FileName**, and then click **OK**. Double-click in your document to close the footer. Compare your screen with Figure 1.20.

Figure 1.20

File name in Title bar

3 Press Ctrl + End to place the insertion point at the end of the document, and then press Enter two times.

Another Way

Click the Insert Table option, and then type the number of columns and rows.

4 Click the **Insert tab**, and then in the **Tables group**, click the **Table** button. In the **Table** grid, move the pointer down to the cell in the eighth row and the fourth column. Compare your screen with Figure 1.21.

The cells are selected, and the table size—4x8 Table—displays at the top of the menu.

Figure 1.21

Table button

Table size

Selected cells

5 Click the selected cell.

A table with eight rows and four columns is inserted. A *cell* is the small box formed by the intersection of a column and a row. The insertion point is positioned in the upper left cell of the table. The *contextual tabs* Design and Layout display on the Ribbon. Contextual tabs are tabs that are added to the Ribbon when a specific object, such as a table, is selected and that contain commands relevant to the selected object.

6 With the insertion point in the first cell, type **Designer Name** and then press [Tab] to move to the second column in the first row of the table.

The [Tab] key is used to move from cell to cell in a Word table. Pressing [Enter] will create another line in the same cell.

7 Type the following data in your table.

Designer Name	Bracelets	Earrings	Watches
Logan Garron	9,634.08	12,942.32	13,492.89
Mano Gauthier	7,452.23	9,994.13	18,448.01
Cameron Mathers	10,863.77	9,356.44	5,793.15
Kim Ngan	6,210.89	13,301.02	6,493.22
Sammie Tate	4,700.76	7,535.50	25,985.39
Miguel Torres	10,745.34	12,994.36	19,091.07
Hayden Vaught	7,311.12	4,929.68	29,783.23

8 Press [Ctrl] + [End], and then press [Enter].

[Ctrl] + [End] will place the insertion point below the table.

More Knowledge | Navigating in a Table

You can move to a previous cell in a table by pressing [Shift] + [Tab]. This action selects the contents of the previous cell. The selection moves back one cell at a time each time you press [Tab] while holding down [Shift]. You can also use the up or down arrow keys to move up or down a column. The left and right arrow keys, however, move the insertion point one character at a time within a cell.

---

9 Type the following paragraph, including any misspelled words or grammatical errors:

We believe watches are an upcoming fashion trend. Adamantine Jewelry will be focusing on all the special watch lines during the next six months and selected designers will introduce a number of new watch styles in both the sport and fashion areas for men and women. The following designers will apply there unique emphasis on these watch styles:

10 Press [Enter] two times. Click the **Insert tab**. In the **Tables group**, click the **Table** button, and then at the bottom of the list, point to **Quick Tables**. In the **Quick Tables** gallery, under **Built-In**, scroll down and locate **Tabular List**. Compare your screen with Figure 1.22.

Inserting a table using *Quick Tables* enables you to choose from a selection of preformatted tables.

Figure 1.22

Quick Tables —

Tabular list —

11 Click **Tabular List**. In the first cell of the inserted table, delete the word *ITEM*. Type **Watch Styles** press Tab, and then type **Designer**

> Pressing Tab moves the insertion point to the next cell and selects the contents of the cell. Because the cell contents are selected, the content in those cells will be deleted when you begin to type. You do not have to delete the contents before you begin to type your data.

12 Type the following information in the table using Tab to move between the cells.

Men's Sport	Lydia Barnes
Men's Fashion	Trent Gaston
Women's Sport	Sammie Tate
Women's Fashion	Hayden Vaught

13 Save 💾 your Word document.

Activity 1.12 | Inserting and Deleting Table Rows and Table Columns

To change the size of a table, you can add or delete rows or columns at the beginning, middle, or end of a table.

1 In the first table you created, in the fourth row, click the first cell containing the text *Cameron Mathers* to position the insertion point in that cell.

2 Click the **Layout tab**, and then in the **Rows & Columns group**, click the **Insert Above** button. Compare your screen with Figure 1.23.

> A blank row is inserted above the *Cameron Mathers* row.

Figure 1.23

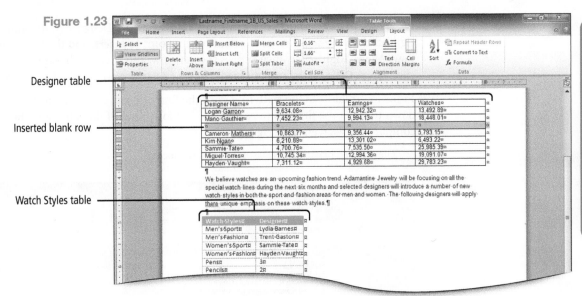

Designer table

Inserted blank row

Watch Styles table

3 Type the following information in the new blank row:

Noel Jamison   5,012.53   8,900.03   3,221.43

4 In the same table, in the second column, right-click in the first cell containing the text *Bracelets*. On the shortcut menu, point to **Insert**, and then click **Insert Columns to the Right**. Compare your screen with Figure 1.24.

A blank column is inserted to the right of the *Bracelets* column.

Figure 1.24

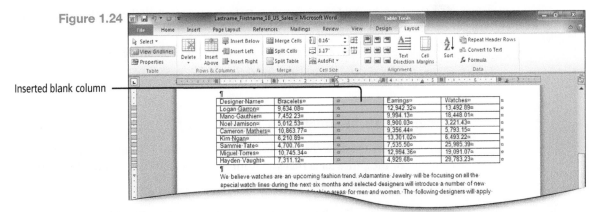

Inserted blank column

5 Click in the first cell of the new column. Type the following information in the new blank column, using the ↓ key to move down to the next cell.

Rings
18,654.67
20,312.11
25,569.54
12,690.03
10,240.56
20,978.60
17,964.88
27,643.45

6 Locate the first cell of the same table containing the text *Designer Name*, and then right-click in the cell. On the shortcut menu, point to **Insert**, and then click **Insert Rows Above**. Right-click anywhere in the new row, and then on the shortcut menu, click **Merge Cells**. In the new merged cell, type **Adamantine Jewelry Designers**

7 In the lower table, in the sixth row, click the first cell containing the text *Pens*. Drag down to select the first cell in each of the last four rows of the table, and then compare your screen with Figure 1.25.

> The first cell in each of the last four rows is selected.

Figure 1.25

Watch Styles table

Cells in last four rows are selected

8 On the **Layout tab**, in the **Rows & Columns group**, click the **Delete** button, and then click **Delete Rows**.

> The four extra rows of the preformatted Quick Table are deleted.

9 Save your document.

Activity 1.13 | Formatting a Table

Formatting a table will make the information easier to read. Select the text, rows, columns, or the entire table that you want to format, and then choose the formats you want to apply.

1 Click in any cell in the upper table. Click the **Design tab**, and then in the **Table Styles group**, click the **More** button ⏷. In the **Table Style** gallery, under **Built-In**, in the first row, point to the third style—**Light Shading - Accent 2**. Notice that the Live Preview temporarily changes your table. Compare your screen with Figure 1.26.

> *Live Preview* is a technology that shows the result of applying an editing or formatting change as the pointer is moved over the results presented in the gallery.

Figure 1.26

Live Preview displays
in table

Light Shading – Accent 2

Table Style gallery

2 In the second row, click the fourth style—**Light List - Accent 3**.

The table style is applied to the entire table.

3 In the same table, position the insertion point to the left of the second row to display the 🔄 pointer. Click one time to select all the cells in the second row. In the **Table Styles group**, click the **Shading** button, and then in the seventh column, click the first color—**Olive Green, Accent 3**. With the second row still selected, click the **Home tab**, and then in the **Font group**, click the **Bold** button B two times.

4 With the second row still selected, in the **Font group**, click the **Font Color button arrow** A·, and then under **Theme Colors**, in the first column, click the first color—**White, Background 1**. Compare your screen with Figure 1.27.

Figure 1.27

Light List – Accent 3
style applied to table

Column headings
formatted with bold and
white font color

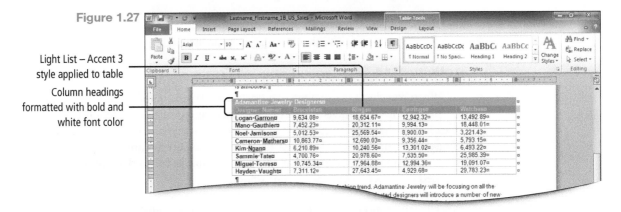

5 With the second row still selected, click the **Layout tab**, and then in the **Alignment group**, click the **Align Center** button ▦. In the same table, select all the cells that contain numbers. In the **Alignment group**, click the **Align Center Right** button ▦.

Each column heading is centered in the columns, and the numbers are right-aligned.

6 In the **Cell Size group**, click the **AutoFit** button, and then click **AutoFit Contents**.

AutoFit adjusts the width of the columns in a table to fit the cell content of the widest cell in each column.

7 In the **Table group**, click the **Properties** button. In the **Table Properties** dialog box, click the **Table tab**. Under **Alignment**, click **Center**, and then click **OK**.

The Designer table is centered horizontally on the page.

Project 1B: Sales Chart | **Integrated Projects**

8 Click in any cell in the lower table. Using the techniques you practiced, **Align Center** the headings in the first row, and then **Center** the table. Compare your screen with Figure 1.28.

Figure 1.28

AutoFit applied to table ———

Tables centered
horizontally on the page ———

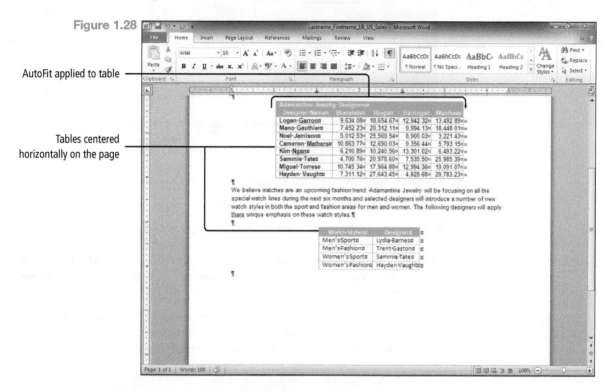

9 Press ⎇Ctrl + ⎇Home, and then **Save** 🖫 your document.

Activity 1.14 | Correcting Spelling Errors

When you check the spelling of a document, Word compares your words to those in the Word dictionary and compares your phrases and punctuation to a list of grammar rules. Words that are not in the Word dictionary are marked with a wavy red underline. Phrases and punctuation that differ from the grammar rules are marked with a wavy green underline. The *contextual spelling* feature marks words that are spelled correctly but used incorrectly with a wavy blue underline.

1 Click the **File tab** to display **Backstage** view, and then click the **Options tab**.

2 In the **Word Options** dialog box, click the **Proofing tab**. Under **When correcting spelling and grammar in Word**, verify that the **Use contextual spelling** check box is selected. If necessary, click to select the check box. Compare your screen with Figure 1.29.

Figure 1.29

Proofing tab

Use contextual spelling
check box selected

3 In the **Word Options** dialog box, click **OK**.

4 Press Ctrl + Home. Click the **Review tab**, and then in the **Proofing group**, click the **Spelling & Grammar** button to check the spelling in your document. Compare your screen with Figure 1.30.

> The first identified error—*Ripa*—is highlighted in the Spelling and Grammar dialog box. This word is a proper noun, and it is spelled correctly. You can add this word to your dictionary or choose to ignore it. If a word is added to the dictionary, in the future, Microsoft Word will consider it to be spelled correctly and will no longer flag the word.

Figure 1.30

Spelling and Grammar
dialog box

Proper noun

5 Click the **Ignore Once** button.

6 The next two errors—*Porta* and *Ticenese*—are both proper nouns. As each displays in the **Spelling and Grammar** dialog box, click the **Ignore Once** button. For each designer name that is identified as an error, check the spelling, and if the name is spelled correctly, click **Ignore All**. Correct the spelling if the name is not correct.

7 The next error—*there*—is a contextual spelling error. In the **Spelling and Grammar** dialog box, under **Suggestions**, select *their*, and then click the **Change** button. In the message box indicating that the spelling and grammar check is complete, click **OK**.

8 **Save** 💾 your document.

Project 1B: Sales Chart | **Integrated Projects**

Integrated Projects

Objective 6 | Create and Format a Chart in Excel

When looking at numbers in an Excel worksheet, analyzing the data may be difficult. A chart is a visual way to illustrate your Excel data in an understandable manner. You will create a chart from existing Excel data, and then copy the data and the chart to your Word document.

Activity 1.15 | Inserting an AutoSum

Before creating the chart, you will add totals to the worksheet.

1 **Start** Excel, and then navigate to the location of the student data files for this instruction. Locate and open the workbook **i01B_Sales_Chart**. Display the **Save As** dialog box, navigate to your **Integrated Projects Chapter 1** folder, and then save the workbook as **Lastname_Firstname_1B_Sales_Chart**

2 Click the **Insert tab**, and then in the **Text group**, click the **Header & Footer** button. On the **Design tab**, in the **Navigation group**, click the **Go to Footer** button. In the **Footer** area, click just above the word *Footer*, and then in the **Header & Footer Elements group**, click the **File Name** button.

> The file name field displays on the left side of the footer area.

3 Click in the cell above the file name field to exit the footer, and then notice that the file name replaces the file name field. Near the right side of the status bar, click the **Normal** button 🔳, and then press Ctrl + Home to display the top of the worksheet.

4 Click cell **F2** to make it the active cell. Click the **Formulas tab**. In the **Function Library group**, click the **AutoSum** button, and then press Enter.

> The sum of cells B2 through E2 is shown in cell F2. AutoSum will add contiguous cells in a column or a row. The AutoSum function will first look above the active cell for a range of cells to sum. If no range is above the active cell, such as in F2, Excel will look to the left for a range of cells to sum. Because the Sum function is frequently used, it has its own button on the Home tab in the Editing group.

5 Cell **F3** is currently the active cell. Click the **AutoSum** button, and then press Enter.

> The sum of cells B3:E3 is displays in cell F3.

6 Cell **F4** is currently the active cell. Click the **AutoSum** button, and then compare your screen with Figure 1.31.

> The *AutoSum* function automatically looks above the active cell to add a range of numbers. The AutoSum function sees numbers *above* cell F4 and will add the numbers in cells F2 and F3. This would be an incorrect answer because the sum of row 4 should display in cell F4. The incorrect formula displays in cell F4 and in the *Formula Bar*. The Formula Bar displays the value or formula contained in the active cell and permits you to enter or edit the values or formulas.

Figure 1.31

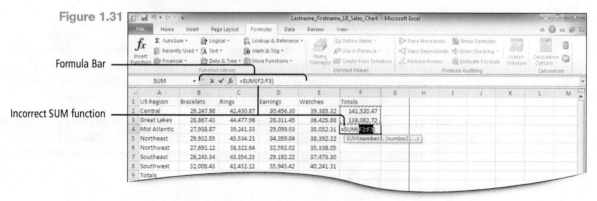

Formula Bar

Incorrect SUM function

---

7 Press [Esc] to cancel the function.

8 Click cell **F3** to make it the active cell. Point to the fill handle to display the ⊞ pointer. Hold down the left mouse button, drag down to cell **F8**, and then release the mouse button. Compare your screen with Figure 1.32.

The formula in cell F3 is copied with a relative cell reference to cells F4 through F8.

Figure 1.32

Totals in cells F2:F8

9 Click cell **B9** to make it the active cell. On the **Formulas tab**, in the **Function Library group**, click the **AutoSum** button, and then in the **Formula Bar**, click the **Enter** button ✔.

Clicking the Formula Bar Enter button will accept the change and leave the current cell as the active cell.

10 Point to the **B9** fill handle to display the ⊞ pointer, drag to the right to cell **F9**, and then release the mouse button. Compare your screen with Figure 1.33.

The formula in cell B9 is copied with a relative cell reference to cells C9 through F9.

Figure 1.33

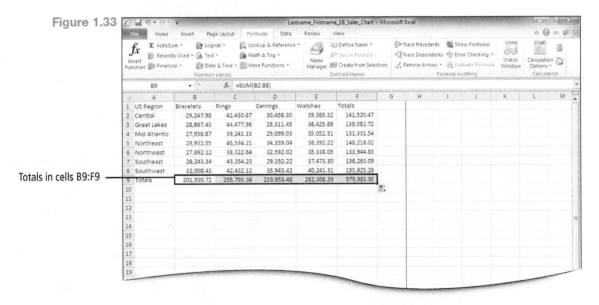

Totals in cells B9:F9

11 **Save** 🖫 your workbook.

Project 1B: Sales Chart | **Integrated Projects**

Activity 1.16 | Creating and Formatting a Chart in Excel

1 Select cells **A1:F1**. Hold down Ctrl, and then select cells **A2:A9**. Click the **Home tab**, and then in the **Font group**, click the **Fill Color button arrow** 🖊. Under **Theme Colors**, in the seventh column, click the first color—**Olive Green, Accent 3**. In the **Font group**, click the **Font Color button arrow** A, and then under **Theme Colors**, in the first column, click the first color—**White, Background 1**. In the **Font group**, click the **Bold** button B.

Another Way
To create an embedded chart, select the data, and then press Alt + F1.

2 Select cells **A1:E8**. On the **Insert tab**, in the **Charts group**, click the **Column** button. Under **3-D Column**, click the first chart—**3-D Clustered Column**—to create an embedded chart on your worksheet. Compare your screen with Figure 1.34.

An *embedded chart* is a chart that displays as an object within a worksheet.

Figure 1.34

Formatted headings

Source data

Embedded 3-D clustered column chart

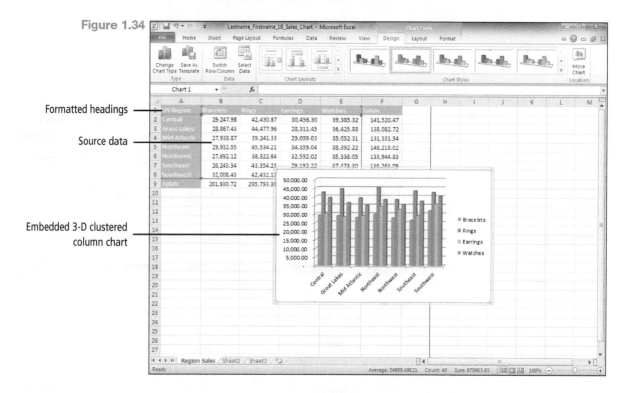

3 If necessary, click the chart to select it and to display the Chart Tools contextual tabs. On the **Design tab**, in the **Location group**, click the **Move Chart** button. In the **Move Chart** dialog box, click the **New sheet** option button, and then click **OK**.

The chart is moved to a new *chart sheet*. A chart sheet is a workbook sheet that contains only a chart and is useful when you want to view a chart separately from the worksheet data.

4 Click the **Insert tab**, and then in the **Text group**, click the **Header & Footer** button. In the **Page Setup** dialog box, on the **Header/Footer tab**, click the **Footer down arrow**, scroll down, and then click on the file name **Lastname_Firstname_1B_Sales_Chart**. Click **OK**.

The footer can be seen in Print Preview and will print, but the footer is not displayed on the Excel chart sheet.

5 Click the **Design tab**, and then in the **Chart Styles group**, click the **More** button ⏷. In the fifth row, click the fifth style—**Style 37**.

Integrated Projects | Integrating Word and Excel

28

6 Click the **Layout tab.** In the **Labels group**, click the **Chart Title** button, and then select **More Title Options**. In the **Format Chart Title** dialog box, if necessary, click **Fill**, and then click **Gradient fill** to display various fill options. Click the **Preset colors** button, and then in the **Preset colors** gallery, in the fifth column, click the second color—**Fog**. Compare your screen with Figure 1.35.

Figure 1.35

Gradient fill

Preset colors button

Style 37 applied to chart

7 On the left side of the **Format Chart Title** dialog box, click **3-D Format**. Under **Bevel**, click the **Top** button, and then under **Bevel**, in the second row, click the second style—**Soft Round**. Click **Close**.

8 Click on the **Chart Title**, and then delete the words *Chart Title*. Type **Adamantine Jewelry**

9 On the **Layout tab**, in the **Labels group**, click the **Axis Titles** button, point to **Primary Horizontal Axis Title**, and then click **Title Below Axis**. Click the **Axis Title**, select and delete the existing text, and then type **US Regions**

10 In the **Labels group**, click the **Axis Titles** button, point to **Primary Vertical Axis Title**, and then click **Vertical Title**. Click the **vertical Axis Title**, select and delete the existing text, and then type **US Sales** Compare your screen with Figure 1.36.

Figure 1.36

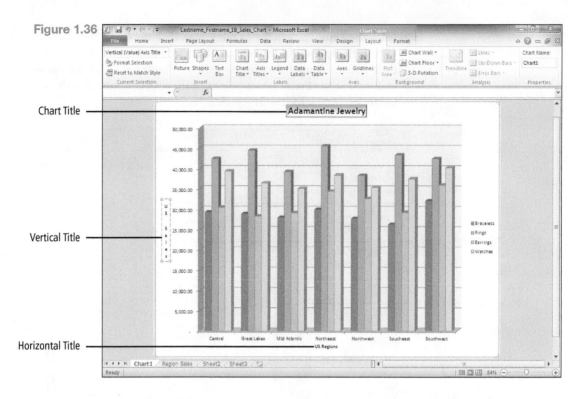

Chart Title —

Vertical Title —

Horizontal Title —

11 Click on the horizontal axis title to select the title. In the **Current Selection group**, click the **Format Selection** button. In the **Format Axis Title** dialog box, click **Border Color**. Under **Border Color**, click **Solid line**, and then click the **Color** button. Under **Theme Colors**, in the seventh column, click the fourth color—**Olive Green, Accent 3, Lighter 40%**. Click **Border Styles**. Under **Border Styles**, in the **Width** box, select the current number, and then type **3** Click **Close**.

12 Click on the vertical axis title to select the title. In the **Current Selection group**, click the **Format Selection** button. In the **Format Axis Title** dialog box, click **Border Color**. Under **Border Color**, click **Solid line**, and then click the **Color** button. Under **Theme Colors**, in the seventh column, click the fourth color—**Olive Green, Accent 3, Lighter 40%**. Click **Border Styles**. Under **Border Styles**, in the **Width** box, select the current number, and then type **3** Click **Close**.

13 In the **Current Selection group**, at the top of the group, click the **Chart Elements button arrow**, and then on the displayed list, click **Back Wall**. In the **Current Selection group**, click the **Format Selection** button. In the **Format Wall** dialog box, under **Fill**, click **Gradient fill**, and then click **Close**. Compare your screen with Figure 1.37.

Integrated Projects | Integrating Word and Excel

Figure 1.37

Legend at right side of chart

Back Wall, gradient fill

Horizontal and Vertical Titles—Olive Green border

14 Save 🔲 your workbook.

Objective 7 | Link Excel Data and an Excel Chart to a Word Document

You can connect the contents of one file to another file by linking the files. *Linking* is the process of inserting information from a source file into a destination file, while maintaining a connection between the two files. The *source file* is the file where the data or object is created. The *destination file* is the file where the linked data or object is inserted. When linked, the changes that are made in the source file are reflected in the destination file.

Activity 1.17 | Copying Excel Data

1 Right-click the **Chart1 sheet tab**, and then on the shortcut menu, point to **Tab Color**. Under **Theme Colors**, in the fifth column, click the first color—**Blue, Accent 1**. Right-click the **Chart1 sheet tab**, and then on the shortcut menu, click **Rename**. Type **US Sales Chart** and then press Enter.

2 Right-click the **Region Sales sheet tab**, and then point to **Tab Color**. Under **Theme Colors**, in the seventh column, click the first color—**Olive Green, Accent 3**.

3 Click to select the **Sheet2 tab**, hold down Ctrl, and then click the **Sheet3 tab** to select the two unused sheets. Right-click on the selected sheet tabs, and then on the shortcut menu, click **Delete**.

Another Way

Press Ctrl + C.

4 On the **Region Sales** sheet, select the range **A1:F9**. On the **Home tab**, in the **Clipboard group**, click the **Copy** button 📋. Compare your screen with Figure 1.38.

Figure 1.38

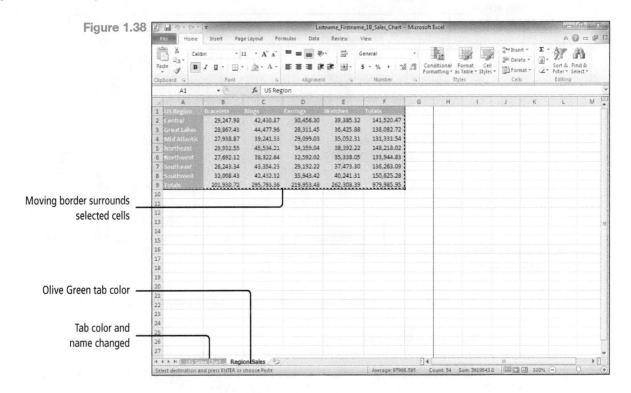

Moving border surrounds selected cells

Olive Green tab color

Tab color and name changed

Activity 1.18 │ Accessing Paste Special and Pasting Excel Data into a Word Document

1 On the taskbar, click the Word document **Lastname_Firstname_1B_US_Sales** button to make the Word window active. Press Ctrl + End to move to the end of the document. Click the **Insert tab**, and then in the **Pages group**, click the **Blank Page** button to create a blank page at the insertion point.

2 Type the following paragraph in your Word document:

> **We are pleased with our current sales volume in the United States, but as always, we believe sales increases are possible. Following are the sales numbers broken down by US region.**

3 Press Enter two times. Click the **Home tab**. In the **Clipboard group**, click the **Paste button arrow**, and then click **Paste Special**. In the **Paste Special** dialog box, click the **Paste link** option button, and then under **As**, click **Microsoft Office Excel Worksheet Object**. Compare your screen with Figure 1.39.

Figure 1.39

Paste Special dialog box

Microsoft Office Excel
Worksheet Object selected

Paste link option
button selected

4 Click **OK**, and then press Enter two times.

The linked data from Excel is pasted into the Word document.

5 Save 🔲 your Word document.

6 Double-click the pasted data in your Word document to access the Excel source file. Notice Excel becomes the active window.

7 Press Esc to remove the moving border around the copied Excel cells. If necessary, maximize the Excel workbook window.

Activity 1.19 | Copying and Linking an Excel Chart into a Word Document

1 Click on the **US Sales Chart tab** to make it the active Excel worksheet.

2 On the **Home tab**, in the **Clipboard group**, click the **Copy** button 📋.

3 On the taskbar, click the Word document **Lastname_Firstname_1B_US_Sales** button to make the Word window active. Press Ctrl + End to move to the end of the document.

4 On the **Home tab**, in the **Clipboard group**, click **Paste**. At the bottom right corner of the chart, click on the **Smart Tag** button to view the Smart Tag options. Under **Paste Options**, point to the third button—*Use Destination Theme & Link Data (L).* Compare your screen with Figure 1.40.

Figure 1.40

Smart Tag Paste Options

5 Under **Paste Options,** click the third option— **Use Destination Theme & Link Data (L).**

6 In the Word document, click on the chart to make it the active object. On the **Format tab**, in the **Arrange group**, click the **Position** button. Under **With Text Wrapping**, in the third row, click the second option—**Position in Bottom Center with Square Text Wrapping**.

The chart moves independently of the surrounding text.

7 With the chart still selected, at the top right corner of the chart, move the pointer to the sizing handle until the ⟋ pointer displays. Drag the sizing handle down and to the left until the chart is about 5 1/2 inches wide and 4 1/2 inches high. Compare your screen with Figure 1.41.

Sizing handles are the small squares or circles that display on each corner and in the middle of each side of a chart or graphic. Sizing handles are used to increase or decrease the size of the chart or graphic.

Figure 1.41

Sizing handles

Chart about 5 ½ inches wide and 4 ½ inches high

Chart positioned at bottom center of document

Integrated Projects

8 Check the spelling in your document, and correct any spelling errors.

9 **Save** your document.

Activity 1.20 | Modifying Excel Data

Data often changes after you have completed your documents. In this case, Claudio Lenti, Creative Director of Adamantine Jewelry, has provided you with updated sales data.

1 On the taskbar, click the Excel file **Lastname_Firstname_1B_Sales_Chart** button to make the Excel window active. Click on the **Region Sales sheet tab**.

2 Click cell **B3** to make it the active cell, type **24,700.01** and then press Enter. Click cell **D7** to make it the active cell, type **30,989.89** and then press Enter.

> You have updated the data for *Bracelets* in the *Great Lakes* region and the data for *Earrings* in the *Southeast* region.

3 Click on the Excel chart sheet **US Sales Chart** to make it the active worksheet. Notice the columns representing the updated data have been automatically updated to reflect the new data. Compare your screen with Figure 1.42.

Figure 1.42

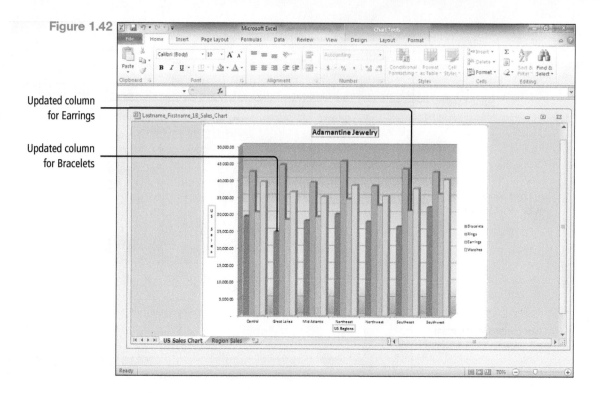

Updated column for Earrings

Updated column for Bracelets

4 **Save** 🔲 your workbook.

5 If your instructor directs you to submit your files electronically, go to Step 7.

6 To print your entire workbook, click the **File tab** to display **Backstage** view. Click the **Print tab**, and then under **Settings**, click the **Print Active Sheets** button, and then click **Print Entire Workbook**. Click the **Print** button.

7 Display **Backstage** view. With the **Info tab** selected, on the right, click **Properties**, and then click **Show Document Panel**. In the **Author** box, type your firstname and lastname, in the **Subject** box, type your course name and section number, and then in the **Keywords** box, type **sales chart, linked Close** ❌ the Document Information Panel.

8 **Save** 🔲 the workbook, and then **Close** ❌ Excel.

Activity 1.21 | Viewing Data and Chart Changes in a Word Document

1 If necessary, on the taskbar, click the Word document **Lastname_First_1B_US_Sales** button to make the Word window active.

2 If necessary, press Ctrl + End, and then click in the chart. Press F9. Notice that the changes made to the regional sales numbers in Excel are reflected in the linked chart.

3 Scroll up as necessary, and at the top of the second page, click anywhere in the table. Press F9, and then compare your screen with Figure 1.43.

The changes made to the regional sales numbers in Excel are reflected in the linked table.

Figure 1.43

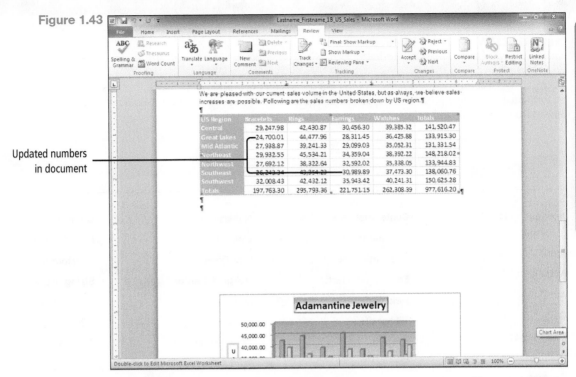

Updated numbers
in document

4 Save 🖫 your document.

5 If your instructor directs you to submit your files electronically, go to Step 7.

6 To print your document, click the **File tab** to display **Backstage** view. Click the **Print tab**, and then click the **Print** button.

7 Display **Backstage** view, on the right, click **Properties**, and then click **Show Document Panel**. In the **Author** box, type your firstname and lastname, in the **Subject** box, type your course name and section number, and then in the **Keywords** box, type **designers, jewelry, linked Close** ☒ the Document Information Panel.

8 Save 🖫 the document, and then **Close** ☒ Word.

9 Submit your printed or electronic files as directed by your instructor.

End **You have completed Project 1B** ——————————

Content-Based Assessments

Summary

Microsoft Word and Excel include features you can use to enter data and create charts. The files can be formatted to create a professional appearance. The data from the source file can be linked to or embedded in the destination file.

Key Terms

Accounting Number Format

AutoFill

AutoFit

AutoSum

Cell

Chart sheet

Comma Style

Contextual spelling

Contextual tabs

Decimal tab stop

Destination file

Embedded chart

Field

Fill handle

Formula

Formula Bar

Function

Gallery

Linking

Live Preview

Merge & Center

Mini toolbar

Normal view

Page Layout view

Print Layout view

Print Preview

Quick Tables

Relative cell reference

Shortcut menu

Sizing handles

Source file

SUM function

Tab stop

Table

Table style

Matching

Match each term in the second column with its correct definition in the first column by writing the letter of the term on the blank line in front of the correct definition.

_____ 1. A specific location on a line of text to which you can move the insertion point by pressing the Tab key, and which is used to align and indent text.

_____ 2. A placeholder that displays preset content, such as the current date, the file name, a page number, or other stored information.

_____ 3. A mathematical expression that contains functions, operators, constants, and properties, and returns a value to a cell.

_____ 4. A predefined formula that performs calculations by using specific values in a particular order.

_____ 5. A small black square located in the lower right corner of a selected cell.

_____ 6. The address of a cell based on the relative position of the cell that contains the formula and the cell referred to.

_____ 7. A context-sensitive menu that displays commands and options relevant to the selected object.

_____ 8. A format for information that organizes and presents text and data in columns and rows.

_____ 9. A predefined set of formatting characteristics, including font, alignment, and cell shading.

_____ 10. A small box formed by the intersection of a column and a row.

_____ 11. A Word feature that adjusts the width of the columns in a table to fit the cell content of the widest cell in each column.

A AutoFit

B Cell

C Chart sheet

D Destination file

E Field

F Fill handle

G Formula

H Function

I Relative cell reference

J Shortcut menu

K Sizing handles

L Source file

M Tab stop

N Table

O Table style

Content-Based Assessments

_____ 12. A workbook sheet that contains only a chart and is useful when you want to view a chart separately from the worksheet data.

_____ 13. The file where the data or object is created.

_____ 14. The file where the linked data or object is inserted.

_____ 15. The small squares or circles that display on each corner and in the middle of each side of a chart or graphic.

Multiple Choice

Circle the correct answer.

1. A small toolbar containing frequently used formatting commands that display as a result of selecting text or objects is the:
   A. Formatting toolbar   **B.** Mini toolbar   **C.** Quick Access Toolbar

2. An Office feature that displays a list of potential results instead of just the command name is:
   A. a gallery   **B.** a shortcut menu   **C.** the Ribbon

3. A screen view that maximizes the number of cells visible on your screen and keeps the column letters and row numbers close to the columns and rows is:
   A. Normal view   **B.** Page Layout view   **C.** Print Layout view

4. An Excel feature that extends values into adjacent cells based on the values of selected cells is called:
   A. AutoComplete   **B.** AutoCorrect   **C.** AutoFill

5. A predefined formula that adds all the numbers in a selected range of cells is the:
   A. COUNT function   **B.** SUM function   **C.** TOTAL function

6. The Excel number format that applies a thousand comma separator where appropriate, inserts a fixed U.S. dollar sign aligned at the left edge of the cell, applies two decimal places, and leaves a small amount of space at the right edge of the cell to accommodate a parenthesis for negative numbers is called:
   A. Accounting Number   **B.** Currency   **C.** General

7. Tabs that are added to the Ribbon when a specific object is selected and that contain commands relevant to the object are called:
   A. action tabs   **B.** content tabs   **C.** contextual tabs

8. The element in the Excel window that displays the value or formula contained in the active cell is the:
   A. Address bar   **B.** Formula bar   **C.** Function bar

9. A chart that displays as an object within a worksheet is called:
   A. a copied chart   **B.** an embedded chart   **C.** a pasted chart

10. The process of inserting information from a source file into a destination file, while maintaining the connection between the two files is called:
    A. embedding   **B.** linking   **C.** pasting

Apply 1A skills from these Objectives:

1. Create a Word Document
2. Copy Word Text into an Excel Workbook
3. Modify an Excel Worksheet
4. Preview and Print Word and Excel Files

Skills Review | Project **1C Television Sales**

In the following Skills Review, you will develop a proposal to expand sales in the television direct sales market. Your completed files will look similar to Figure 1.44.

Project Files

For Project 1C, you will need the following files:

New blank Word document
New blank Excel workbook
i01C_Company_Memo

You will save your files as:

Lastname_Firstname_1C_TV_Gemstones
Lastname_Firstname_1C_Gemstones_Sales

Project Results

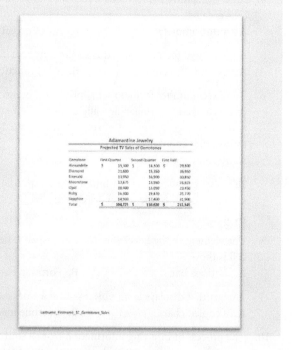

Figure 1.44

Integrating Word and Excel

1. **Start** Word, and then display a new blank document. If necessary, click the **Show/Hide** button to display the formatting marks. On the **Home tab**, in the **Paragraph group**, click the **Dialog Box Launcher**, and then click the **Tabs** button.

   a. In the **Tabs** dialog box, in the **Tab stop position** box, type **3** under **Alignment**, click the **Decimal** option button, and then click **Set**. In the **Tab stop position** box, type **5** under **Alignment**, click the **Decimal** option button, and then click **Set**. Click **OK**.

   b. With the insertion point in the upper left corner of the document, type **Adamantine Jewelry** and then press Enter two times.

   c. Select *Adamantine Jewelry*, and then on the Mini toolbar, click the **Font button arrow**, and then click **Cambria**. Click the **Font Size button arrow**, click **24**, apply **Bold**, and then click **Center**.

2. Press Ctrl + End, and then press Enter. Type the text: **Adamantine Jewelry has been pleased with our jewelry sales through our television retailers. We want to explore the possibility of expanding our marketing efforts of gemstones in the television direct sales market area. I have been researching this market and following are the projected sales figures for the first two quarters**: Press Enter two times.

   a. Type the following data pressing Tab to separate the columns. Press Enter one time at the end of each row.

Gemstone	First Quarter	Second Quarter
Alexandrite	15,300	14,500
Diamond	21,600	15,350
Emerald	13,950	16,900
Moonstone	12,675	13,950
Opal	10,400	13,050
Ruby	16,300	19,470
Sapphire	14,500	17,400

   b. Near the top of the document, in the second blank line, click to position the insertion point.

3. Click the **Insert tab**. In the **Text group**, click the **Object button arrow**, and then click **Text from File**.

   a. In the **Insert File** dialog box, locate and click the file **i01C_Company_Memo**, and then click **Insert**.

   b. In the *MEMO TO* line, select **[Name, Title]**, and then type **Wattana Dithasaro, International Sales Director**

   c. Use the same procedure to replace the data after the memo headings with the following:

FROM	Jennifer Bernard, US Sales Director
DATE	June 17, 2016
SUBJECT	Gemstone Sales

   d. Click the **Save** button. In the **Save As** dialog box, navigate to your **Integrated Projects Chapter 1** folder, click in the **File name** box, and then type **Lastname_Firstname_1C_TV_Gemstones** Click the **Save** button.

   e. On the **Insert tab**, in the **Header & Footer group**, click the **Footer** button, and then click **Edit footer**.

Integrating Word and Excel

f.   On the **Design tab**, in the **Insert group**, click the **Quick Parts** button, and then click **Field**. In the **Field** dialog box, under **Field names**, click **File Name**, and then click **OK**. Double-click in the document to close the footer, and then **Save** your document.

4.   **Start** Excel, and then display a new blank workbook. In cell **A1**, type **Adamantine Jewelry** In cell **A2**, type **Projected TV Sales of Gemstones**

a.   Click the **Save** button. In the **Save As** dialog box, navigate to your **Integrated Projects Chapter 1** folder. In the **File name** box, type **Lastname_Firstname_1C_Gemstones_Sales** and then click **Save**.

b.   Click the **Insert tab**, and then in the **Text group**, click the **Header & Footer** button. On the **Design tab**, in the **Navigation group**, click the **Go to Footer** button.

c.   In the Footer area, click just above the word *Footer*, and then in the **Header & Footer Elements group**, click the **File Name** button.

d.   Click in any cell to exit the footer, and then click the **Normal** button to return to Normal view. Press ⌃Ctrl + ⌂Home. **Save** your changes.

5.   On the taskbar, click the **Lastname_Firstname_1C_TV_Gemstones** button. In the tabbed list, click to position the insertion point to the left of *Gemstone*, and then drag down to select the eight rows of tabbed text. On the **Home tab**, in the **Clipboard group**, click the **Copy** button.

a.   On the taskbar, click the **Lastname_Firstname_1C_Gemstones_Sales**. Click cell **A4**, and then on the **Home tab**, in the **Clipboard group**, click the **Paste** button.

b.   Click cell **D4**, type **First Half** and then press ⏎Enter. In cell **D5**, type **=B5+C5** and then press ⏎Enter. Click cell **D5** to make it the active cell, point to the fill handle, and then drag down to cell **D11**.

c.   Click cell **A12**. Type **Total** and then click cell **B12**. On the **Home tab**, in the **Editing group**, click the **Sum** button, and then press ⏎Enter. Click cell **B12**, point to the fill handle, and then drag right to cell **D12**. **Save** your changes.

6.   Select cells **A1:D1**. On the **Home tab**, in the **Alignment group**, click the **Merge & Center** button. In the **Styles group**, click the **Cell Styles** button. In the **Cell Styles** gallery, under **Titles and Headings**, click **Heading 1**.

a.   Select cells **A2:D2**. On the **Home tab**, in the **Alignment group**, click the **Merge & Center** button. In the **Styles group**, click the **Cell Styles** button. In the **Cell Styles** gallery, under **Titles and Headings**, click **Heading 2**.

b.   Select cells **A4:D4**. hold down ⌃Ctrl and select cells **A5:A12**. In the **Styles group**, click the **Cell Styles** button. In the **Cell Styles** gallery, under **Titles and Headings**, click **Heading 4**.

c.   Select cells **B6:D11**. On the **Home tab**, in the **Number group**, click the **Comma Style** button, and then click the **Decrease Decimal** button two times.

d.   Select cells **B5:D5**. Hold down ⌃Ctrl and select cells **B12:D12**. On the **Home tab**, in the **Number group**, click the **Accounting Number Format** button, and then click the **Decrease Decimal** button two times.

e. Select cells **B12:D12**. In the **Styles group**, click the **Cell Styles** button. In the **Cell Styles** gallery, under **Titles and Headings**, click **Total**.

f. Select columns **A:D**. On the **Home tab**, in the **Cells group**, click the **Format** button. Under **Cell Size**, click **Column Width**. In the **Column Width** dialog box, type **15** and then click **OK**.

g. Hold down Ctrl and press Home to make cell **A1** the active cell. **Save** your changes.

7. With the Excel workbook still active, click the **Page Layout tab**, and then in the **Page Setup group**, click the **Dialog Box Launcher**.

a. In the **Page Setup** dialog box, click the **Margins tab**. Under **Center on page**, select the **Horizontally** check box and the **Vertically** check box, and then click **OK**.

b. Click the **File tab** to display **Backstage** view. With the **Info tab** selected, on the right, click **Properties**, and then click **Show Document Panel**. In the **Author** box, type your firstname and lastname, in the **Subject** box, type your course name and section number, and then in the **Keywords** box, type **sales, worksheet. Close** the Document Information Panel. **Save** your changes.

c. Click the **Formulas tab**, and then in the **Formula Auditing group**, click the **Show Formulas** button.

d. Click the **File tab** to display **Backstage** view, and then click the **Print tab** to display **Print Preview**. At the bottom of the screen to the left of the **Print Preview**, under **Settings**, click the **Page Setup** link.

e. In the **Page Setup** dialog box, on the **Page tab**, under **Orientation**, click the **Landscape** option button. Under **Scaling**, click the **Fit to** option button. Verify the options are *1 page(s) wide by 1 tall*, and then click **OK**. If you are submitting your files electronically, go to Step 8.

f. To print your worksheet, under **Print**, click the **Print** button.

8. **Close** Excel. When asked *Do you want to save the changes you made?* click **Don't Save**.

a. On the taskbar, click the **Lastname_Firstname_1C_TV_Gemstones** button to make the document active. Ctrl + Home

b. Click the **File tab** to display **Backstage** view, click **Properties,** and then click **Show Document Panel.** In the **Author** box, type your firstname and lastname, in the **Subject** box, type your course name and section number, and then in the **Keywords** box, type gemstone memo **Close** the Document Information Panel.

c. **Save** the document, and then **Close** Word.

d. Submit your printed or electronic files as directed by your instructor.

You have completed Project 1C

Apply 1B skills from these Objectives:

1. Work with an Existing Word Document
2. Create and Format a Chart in Excel
3. Link Excel Data and an Excel Chart to a Word Document

Skills Review | Project **1D Travel Tours**

In the following Skills Review, you will prepare a proposal for Adamantine Jewelry to expand travel opportunities into Italy. Your completed files will look similar to Figure 1.45.

Project Files

For Project 1D, you will need the following files:

> i01D_Travel_Tours
> i01D_Travel_Chart

You will save your files as:

> Lastname_Firstname_1D_Travel_Tours
> Lastname_Firstname_1D_Travel_Chart

Project Results

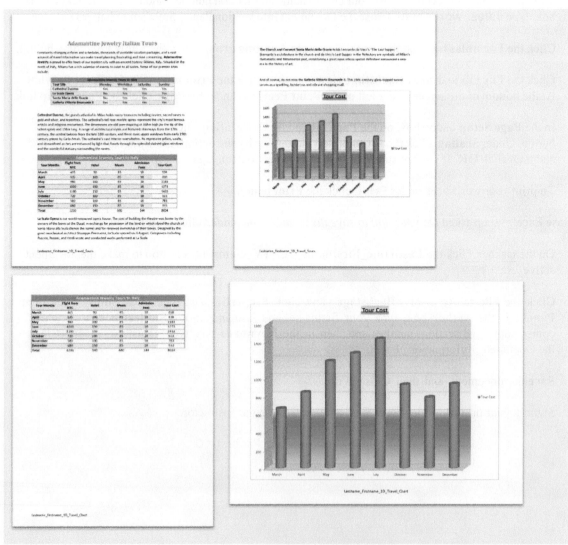

Figure 1.45

Integrating Word and Excel

1. **Start** Word. Locate and open the file **i01D_Travel_Tours**. If necessary, click the **Show/Hide** button to display the formatting marks. **Save** the document in your **Integrated Projects Chapter 1** folder as **Lastname_Firstname_1D_Travel_Tours**

   a. On the **Insert tab**, in the **Header & Footer group**, click the **Footer** button, and then click **Edit footer**.

   b. On the **Design tab**, in the **Insert group**, click the **Quick Parts** button, and then click **Field**. In the **Field** dialog box, under **Field names**, click **File Name**, and then click **OK**.

   c. Near the top of the document, locate the paragraph beginning *Cathedral Duomo*. Immediately above that paragraph, click in the blank paragraph to position the insertion point.

2. Click the **Insert tab**. In the **Tables group**, click the **Table** button, and then point to **Quick Tables**. In the **Quick Tables** gallery, under **Built-In**, scroll down, and then click **Matrix**.

   a. In the first row, click the fifth cell—*Point D*. Drag right to select the last two column headings of the table—*Point D* and *Point E*.

   b. On the **Layout tab**, in the **Rows & Columns group**, click the **Delete** button, and then click **Delete Columns**.

   c. In the fifth row, click the first cell—*Point D*. Drag down to select the last two row headings of the table—*Point D* and *Point E*.

   d. On the **Layout tab**, in the **Rows & Columns group**, click the **Delete** button, and then click **Delete Rows**.

3. In the first cell of the table, select and delete the text *City or Town*. Type the following information in the table using the ⌨Tab key to move between the cells.

Tour Site	Weekdays	Saturday	Sunday
Cathedral Duomo	Yes	Yes	Yes
La Scala Opera	Yes	Yes	Yes
Galleria Vittorio Emanuelell	Yes	Yes	Yes

   a. In the fourth row, click the first cell containing the text that begins **Galleria**. On the **Layout tab**, in the **Rows & Columns group**, click the **Insert Above** button.

   b. In the new blank row, type the following information:

SantaMariadelleGrazie	Yes	Yes	Yes

   c. In the first row, right-click the second cell containing *Weekdays*. On the shortcut menu, point to **Insert**, and then click **Insert Columns to the Left**.

   d. Click in the first cell of the new column. Type the following information in the new blank column, using the ⬇ to move down to the next cell.

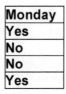

Monday
Yes
No
No
Yes

    e. Right click in the first cell of the table—*Tour Site*, on the shortcut menu, point to **Insert**, and then click **Insert Rows Above**.

    f. Right-click anywhere in the new row, and then on the shortcut menu, click **Merge Cells**. In the new merged cell, type **Adamantine Jewelry Tours to Italy**

4. Click the **Design tab**, and then in the **Table Styles group**, click the **More** button. In the **Table Style** gallery, under **Built-In**, in the tenth row, click the fourth style—**Medium Shading 1 – Accent 2**.

    a. On the **Layout tab**, in the **Table group**, click **Properties**. In the **Table Properties** dialog box, on the **Table tab**, under **Alignment**, click **Center**, and then click **OK**.

    b. Click the **File tab** to display **Backstage** view, and then click the **Options tab**.

    c. In the **Word Options** dialog box, click the **Proofing tab**. If necessary, under **When correcting spelling and grammar in Word**, click to select the **Use contextual spelling** check box, and then click **OK**.

    d. On the **Review tab**, in the **Proofing group**, click the **Spelling & Grammar** button. The Italian proper names in the original document are spelled correctly. Correct any misspelled or contextually incorrect words.

    e. **Save** your changes.

5. **Start** Excel. Locate and open the workbook **i01D_Travel_Chart**. Display the **Save As** dialog box, navigate to the **Integrated Projects Chapter 1** folder, and then save the workbook as **Lastname_Firstname_1D_Travel_Chart**

    a. Click the **Insert tab**, and then in the **Text group**, click the **Header & Footer** button. On the **Design tab**, in the **Navigation group**, click the **Go to Footer** button.

    b. In the **Footer** area, click just above the word *Footer*, and then in the **Header & Footer Elements group**, click the **File Name** button.

    c. Click in the cell above the file name, click the **Normal** button, and then press Ctrl + Home

6. Click cell **F2**, type **Tour Cost** and then press Enter

    a. On the **Formulas tab**, in the **Function Library group**, click the **AutoSum** button, and then in the **Formula Bar**, click the **Enter** button. In cell **F3**, point to the fill handle, and then drag down to cell **F10**.

    b. Click cell **B11**. On the **Formulas tab**, in the **Function Library group**, click the **AutoSum** button, and then in the **Formula Bar**, click the **Enter** button. In cell **B11**, point to the fill handle, and then drag right to cell **F11**.

Integrating Word and Excel

c. With cells **B11:F11** selected, on the **Home tab**, in the **Alignment group**, click the **Center** button.

7. Select cells **A2:A10**. Hold down Ctrl, and then select cells **F2:F10**. On the **Insert tab**, in the **Charts group**, click the **Column** button. Under **Cylinder**, click the first chart—**Clustered Cylinder**.

  a. On the **Design tab**, in the **Location group**, click the **Move Chart** button. In the **Move Chart** dialog box, click the **New Sheet** option button, and then click **OK**.

  b. On the **Insert tab**, in the **Text group**, click the **Header & Footer** button. In the **Page Setup** dialog box, on the **Header/Footer tab**, click the **Footer arrow**, scroll down, and then click on the file name **Lastname_Firstname_1D_Travel_Chart**. Click **OK**.

  c. On the **Design tab**, in the **Chart Styles** group, click the **More** button. In the fifth row, click the fourth style—**Style 36**.

  d. On the **Layout tab**, in the **Labels group**, click the **Chart Title** button, and then select **More Title Options**. In the **Format Chart Title** dialog box, under **Fill**, click **Gradient fill**. Click the **Preset colors** button, and then in the **Preset colors** gallery, in the first column, click the second color—**Desert**. Click the **Close** button.

  e. On the **Layout tab**, in the **Current Selection group**, click the **Chart Elements button arrow**, and then on the displayed list, click **Back Wall**. In the **Current Selection group**, click the **Format Selection** button. In the **Format Wall** dialog box, under **Fill**, click **Gradient fill**, and then click **Close**.

  f. **Save** your Excel workbook.

8. Right-click the **Chart1 sheet tab**, and then on the shortcut menu, point to **Tab Color**. Under **Theme Colors**, in the fourth column, click the first color—**Dark Blue, Text 2**. Right-click the **Chart1 sheet tab**, and then on the shortcut menu, click **Rename**. Type **Cost Chart** and then press Enter.

  a. Click to select the **Sheet2 tab**, hold down Ctrl, and then click the **Sheet3 tab**. Right-click on the selected sheet tabs, and then on the shortcut menu, click **Delete**.

  b. On the **Tour Cost sheet tab**. Select the range **A1:F11**, and then on the **Home tab**, in the **Clipboard group**, click the **Copy** button.

  c. On the taskbar, click the **Lastname_Firstname_1D_Travel_Tours** button. Immediately above the paragraph that begins *La Scala Opera*, click to position the insertion point in the blank paragraph.

  d. On the **Home tab**, in the **Clipboard group**, click the **Paste button arrow**, and then click **Paste Special**. In the **Paste Special** dialog box, click the **Paste link** option button, and then under **As**, click **Microsoft Excel Worksheet Object**. Click **OK**.

  e. On the taskbar, click the **Lastname_Firstname_1D_Travel_Chart** button. Press Esc. Click the **Cost Chart sheet tab**. On the **Home tab**, in the **Clipboard group**, click the **Copy** button.

  f. On the taskbar, click the **Lastname_Firstname_1D_Travel_Tours** button. Press Ctrl + End, and then press Enter. On the **Home tab**, in the **Clipboard group**, click **Paste**. At the bottom right corner of the chart, click the **Smart Tag** button. Under **Paste Options**, click the third option—**Use Destination Theme & Link Data (L)**. **Save** your changes.

Integrating Word and Excel

9. On the taskbar, click the **Lastname_Firstname_1D_Travel_Chart** button. Click the **Tour Cost sheet tab**. Click cell **B6** to make it the active cell, type **1020** and then press [Enter]. Click cell **B10**, type **680** and then press [Enter].

   a. Display **Backstage** view, click **Properties**, and then click **Show Document Panel**. In the **Author** box, type your firstname and lastname, in the **Subject** box, type your course name and section number, and then in the **Keywords** box, type **tourchart, linked** Close the Document Information Panel. Press [Ctrl] + [Home].

   b. **Save** your changes, and then **Close** the workbook.

   c. With the **Lastname_Firstname_1D_Travel_Tours** document displayed, click in the Excel data, and then press [F9] to update the data. Click in the Excel chart, and then press [F9]. Press [Ctrl] + [Home].

   d. Display **Backstage** view, click **Properties**, and then click **Show Document Panel**. In the **Author** box, type your firstname and lastname, in the **Subject** box, type your course name and section number, and then in the **Keywords** box, type **linked data, chart** Close the Document Information Panel.

   e. **Save** the document, and then **Close Word**.

   f. Submit your printed or electronic files as directed by your instructor.

You have completed Project 1D

<table>
<tr><td>

Apply 1A skills from these Objectives:

1. Create a Word Document
2. Copy Word Text into an Excel Workbook
3. Modify an Excel Worksheet
4. Preview and Print Word and Excel Files

</td></tr>
</table>

In the following Mastering Integration project, you will create a proposal for Adamantine Jewelry to expand into China. Your completed files will look similar to Figure 1.46.

Project Files

For Project 1E, you will need the following files:

New blank Word document
New blank Excel workbook
i02E_Company_Headings

You will save your files as:

Lastname_Firstname_1E_China_Expansion
Lastname_Firstname_1E_Chinese_Expenses

Project Results

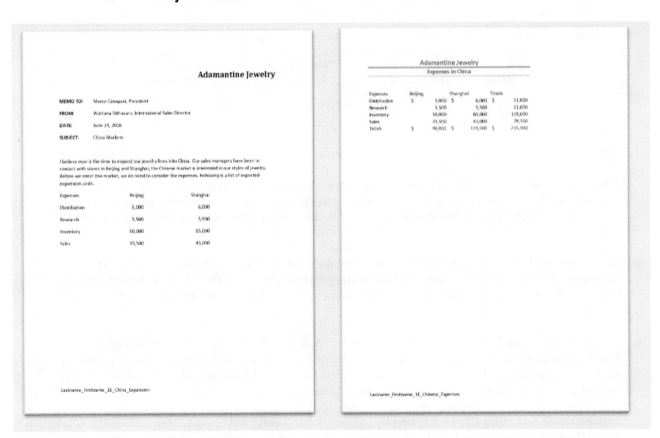

Figure 1.46

1. **Start** Word. If necessary, display formatting marks. **Save** the document in your **Integrated Projects Chapter 1** folder as **Lastname_Firstname_1E_China_Expansion** Insert the file name in the footer. Insert **Decimal Tab stops** at **2.5** inches and **4.5** inches. At the top of the document, type **Adamantine Jewelry** and then press Enter three times. Select the first paragraph, change the **Font** to **Cambria**, change the **Font Size** to **18**, apply **Bold**, and then **Align Text Right**.

2. Press Ctrl + End. Type **I believe now is the time to expand our jewelry lines into China. Our sales managers have been in contact with stores in Beijing and Shanghai; the Chinese market is interested in our styles of jewelry. Before we enter this market, we do need to consider the expenses. Following is a list of expected expansion costs:** Press Enter, and then type the following:

Expenses	Beijing	Shanghai
Distribution	5,000	6,000
Research	5,500	5,500
Inventory	50,000	65,000
Sales	35,500	43,000

3. Near the top of the document, in the second blank line, click to position the insertion point. Insert **Text from File**, using the data file **i02_E_Company_Headings**. To the right of each heading, replace the existing text with the following:

TO	Marco Canaperi, President
FROM	Wattana Dithasaro, International Sales Director
DATE	June 24, 2016
SUBJECT	China Markets

4. **Start** Excel. In cell **A1**, type **Adamantine Jewelry** and then in cell **A2**, type **Expenses in China** Save the workbook in the **Integrated Projects Chapter 1** folder as **Lastname_Firstname_1E_Chinese_Expenses** Make your Word document window active. Select and copy the five lines of tabbed text. Make the Excel workbook window active, move the insertion point to cell **A5**, and then **Paste** the Word data. Insert the file name in the footer, and then return to **Normal** view.

5. In cells **D5** and **A10**, type **Totals** and then **Sum** all of the rows in the range **D6:D9. Sum** all of the columns in the range **B10:D10**. Apply the **Accounting Style** to the ranges **B6:D6** and **B10:D10**, and then **Decrease Decimals** to zero decimals. Apply the **Comma Style** to the range **B7:D9**, and then **Decrease Decimals** to zero decimals.

6. **Merge & Center** the first worksheet title over columns **A:D**, and then format the title by changing the **Cell Style** to **Heading 1**. **Merge & Center** the second worksheet title over columns **A:D**, ad then format the title by changing the **Cell Style** to **Heading 2**. Select the ranges **A5:D5** and **A6:A10**, and then change the **Cell Style** to **Heading 4**. Change the **Column Width** of columns **A:D** to **15**.

7. Rename the **Sheet1** tab as **China Expenses** and then delete **Sheet2** and **Sheet3**. Press Ctrl + Home . Click **Show Document Panel**. In the **Author** box, type your firstname and lastname, in the **Subject** box, type your course name and section number, and then in the **Keywords** box, type **expensetotals** Close the Document Information Panel. **Save** your workbook, and then **Close** Excel.

8. In your Word document, press ⌈Ctrl⌉ + ⌈Home⌉.Click **Show Document Panel**. In the **Author** box, type your firstname and lastname, in the **Subject** box, type your course name and section number, and then in the **Keywords** box, type **China expenses totals**. **Close** the Document Information Panel. **Save** your document, and then **Close** Word.

9. Submit your printed or electronic files as directed by your instructor.

You have completed Project 1E

Apply 1B skills from these Objectives:	

1. Work with an Existing Word Document
2. Create and Format a Chart in Excel
3. Link Excel Data and an Excel Chart to a Word Document

In the following Mastering Integration project, you will prepare a proposal for Adamantine Jewelry to hire Brazilian designers. Your completed files will look similar to Figure 1.47.

Project Files

For Project 1F, you will need the following files:

> i01F_Brazil_Proposal
> i01F_Brazil_Chart

You will save your files as:

> Lastname_Firstname_1F_Brazil_Proposal
> Lastname_Firstname_1F_Brazil_Chart

Figure 1.47

1. **Start** Word. Open the document **i01F_Brazil_Proposal**. Display formatting marks. **Save** the document in your **Integrated Projects Chapter 1** folder as **Lastname_Firstname_1F_Brazil_Proposal** Insert the file name in the footer.

2. Click to position the insertion point in the second blank paragraph immediately below the paragraph that begins *Following is a list*. Insert a table that is **6 rows** by **4 columns**, and then type the following data:

Brazilian Designer	Bracelets	Rings	Earrings
Rosa Afonso	No	Yes	Yes
Luis Alvares	Yes	Yes	Yes
Joana Dias	Yes	No	No
Mariade Lurdes	No	Yes	No
Rodolfo Peltier	No	No	Yes

3. In the last row of the table, click in the first cell, and then insert a new row above. Type the following data in the new row:

Paulo Mata	Yes	Yes	Yes

4. Apply the Table Style **Medium Shading 1–Accent 4**. **AutoFit Contents** to adjust column width, and then **Center** align the table between the left and right margins.

5. **Start** Excel. Open the workbook **i01F_Brazil_Chart**. **Save** the workbook in the **Integrated Projects Chapter 1** folder as **Lastname_Firstname_1F_Brazil_Chart**. Insert the file name in the footer, return to **Normal** view, and then click cell **A1**. **Sum** all of the rows in the range **E6:E11**. **Sum** all of the columns in the range **B12:E12**. **Merge & Center** the range **A2:E2**. Format the title by changing the **Fill Color** to **Purple, Accent 4**, the **Font Color** to **White, Background 1**, the **Font Size** to **18**, and applying **Bold** emphasis.

6. Select the range **A5:D11**. Insert a **3-D Clustered Column** chart on a new sheet, and then insert the file name on the footer of the new sheet. Apply **Chart Style 6**. Insert a chart title **Above Chart** with the **Gradient fill**, **Preset color** format **Calm Water**. In the chart title, delete the existing text, and then type **Sales by Designer**. Rename the **Chart1 sheet tab** as **Designer Sales Chart** and then delete **Sheet2** and **Sheet3**. **Save** your changes.

7. On the **Brazilian Sales** sheet, copy cells **A5:E12**, and then in the Word document, below the Brazilian Designer table, in the blank paragraph, press ⏎ . **Paste link** the cells. In Excel, copy the **Designer Sales Chart** sheet, and then in the Word document, at the top of **page 2**, in the first blank paragraph, paste the chart with the option **Use Destination Theme & Link Data (L)**. Press ⏎ three times. **Save** your changes.

8. In Excel, change the *Earrings* sales for *Joana Dias* to **8,509** and then change the *Rings* sales for *Paulo Mata* to **7,656** In your workbook, press Ctrl + Home. Click **Show Document Panel**. In the **Author** box, type your firstname and lastname, in the **Subject** box, type your course name and section number, and then in the **Keywords** box, type **Brazil, sales** Close the Document Information Panel. **Save** your changes, and then **Close** Excel. In your Word document, **Update** the linked Excel data and chart. Press Ctrl + Home. Click **Show Document Panel**. In the **Author** box, type your firstname and lastname, in the **Subject** box, type your course name and section number, and then in the **Keywords** box, type **Brazil, designers** Close the Document Information Panel. **Save** your document, and then **Close** Word.

9. Print your printed or electronic files as directed by your instructor.

You have completed Project 1F

Integrating Word and Excel

Rubric

The following outcomes-based assessments are open-ended assessments. That is, there is no specific correct result; your result will depend on your approach to the information provided. Make Professional Quality your goal. Use the following scoring rubric to guide you in how to approach the problem and then to evaluate how well your approach solves the problem.

The *criteria*—Software Mastery, Content, Format and Layout, and Process—represent the knowledge and skills you have gained that you can apply to solving the problem. The *levels of performance*—Professional Quality, Approaching Professional Quality, or Needs Quality Improvements—help you and your instructor evaluate your result.

	Your completed project is of **Professional Quality**	Your completed project is of **Approaching Professional Quality**	Your completed project **Needs Quality Improvements**
1-Software Mastery	Chooses and applies the most appropriate skills, tools, and features and identifies efficient methods to solve the problem.	Chooses and applies some appropriate skills, tools, and features, but not in the most efficient manner.	Chooses inappropriate skills, tools, or features, or is inefficient in solving the problem.
2-Content	Constructs a solution that is clear and well organized, containing content that is accurate, appropriate to the audience and purpose, and complete. The solution contains no errors of spelling, grammar, or style.	Constructs a solution in which some components are unclear, poorly organized, inconsistent, or incomplete. May misjudge the needs of the audience. May contain some errors in spelling, grammar, or style, but the errors do not detract from comprehension.	Constructs a solution that is unclear, incomplete, or poorly organized, containing some inaccurate or inappropriate content. May contain many errors of spelling, grammar, or style. May fail to solve the problem.
3-Format and Layout	Formats and arranges all elements to communicate information and ideas, clarify function, illustrate relationships, and indicate relative importance.	Applies appropriate format and layout features to some elements, but not others. Or, overuses features, causing minor distraction.	Applies format and layout that fails to communicate information or ideas or clearly. May fail to use format and layout features to clarify function, illustrate relationships, or indicate relative importance. Or, may use available features excessively, causing distraction.
4-Process	Uses an organized approach that integrates planning, development, self-assessment, revision, and reflection.	Demonstrates an organized approach in some areas, but not others. Or, uses an insufficient process of organization throughout.	Does not use an organized approach to solve the problem.

Integrating Word and Excel

<table>
<tr><td>

Apply a combination of the 1A and 1B skills.

</td><td>

GO! Think | **Project 1G Web Proposal**

Project Files

For Project 1G, you will need the following files:

</td></tr>
</table>

i01G_Web_Proposal
i01G_Web_Chart

You will save your files as:

Lastname_Firstname_1G_Web_Proposal
Lastname_Firstname_1G_Web_Chart

Adamantine Jewelry is considering an expansion of the company Web site to sell more merchandise. Jennifer Bernard, US Sales Director, has asked you to complete the proposal.

Complete the Excel worksheet by inserting totals, merging and centering the titles, and creating a column chart. The chart should display on a separate sheet. Modify the chart style and format appropriate chart elements. In the Word document include the linked Excel data and chart. In both files, insert the file name in the footer and add appropriate document properties. Save the Word document as **Lastname_Firstname_1G_Web_Proposal** and then save the Excel workbook as **Lastname_Firstname_1G_Web_Chart** Submit your printed or electronic files as directed by your instructor.

You have completed Project 1G

GO! Think | Project 1H Watch Sales

Project Files

For Project 1H, you will need the following files:

New blank Word document
i01H_Watch_Sales

You will save your files as:

Lastname_Firstname_1H_Watches_Memo
Lastname_Firstname_1H_Watch_Sales

Adamantine Jewelry wants to introduce its fashion watches lines into the Miami, New York City, and San Francisco markets. You have been asked to create a memo that includes charts with sales forecasts, low-end sales, expected sales, and high-end sales that will be sent to all sales representatives from Jennifer Bernard, US Sales Director.

Create a letterhead that includes the title **Adamantine Jewelry** Include a paragraph explaining that the new watch lines have sold well in Europe and will be introduced in the three new markets over the next year. Insert and format the data displayed below. In the Excel workbook, insert appropriate totals, format the worksheet, and create an Excel chart. Include the Excel data and chart in the Word document. In both files, insert the file name in the footer and add appropriate document properties. Save the Word document as **Lastname_Firstname_1H_Watches_Memo** and then save the Excel workbook as **Lastname_Firstname_1H_Watch_Sales** Submit your printed or electronic files as directed by your instructor.

Introduction Timeline			
Watch Lines	Miami	New York City	San Francisco
Men's Sport	Quarter3	Quarter1	Quarter1
Men's Fashion	Quarter2	Quarter3	Quarter2
Women's Sport	Quarter2	Quarter2	Quarter1
Women's Fashion	Quarter2	Quarter3	Quarter2
Children's Sport	Quarter4	Quarter2	Quarter1

You have completed Project 1H

GO! Think | **Project 1I Airport Store**
Project Files

For Project 1I, you will need the following files:

i01I_Airport_Store
i01I_Airport_Chart

You will save your files as:

Lastname_Firstname_1I_Airport_Store
Lastname_Firstname_1I_Airport_Chart

You will finish a request to open a retail store in the duty free area of an airport. In the Excel workbook, insert totals, adjust column widths, format the titles, and create an appropriate chart. Format the chart title, axis titles, and chart background. Copy the chart to the Word document. Adjust the size and position of the chart. Complete the last sentence of the document, based on the Excel data, recommending at which airport a store should be located. In both files, insert the file name in the footer and add appropriate document properties. Save the Word document as **Lastname_Firstname_1I_Airport_Store** and then save the Excel workbook as **Lastname_Firstname_1I_Airport_Chart** Submit your printed or electronic files as directed by your instructor.

You have completed Project 1I

Integrating Word and PowerPoint

OUTCOMES
At the end of this chapter you will be able to:

OBJECTIVES
Mastering these objectives will enable you to:

PROJECT 2A
Create a PowerPoint presentation that includes data imported from a Word document.

1. Create an Outline in Word
2. Import a Word Outline into a PowerPoint Presentation
3. Modify a PowerPoint Presentation
4. Create a Footer and Save a PowerPoint Presentation
5. Preview and Print a Presentation, Slide Handouts, and Speaker Notes

PROJECT 2B
Create a PowerPoint presentation from a template and save it as an RTF file to be modified in Word.

6. Create a PowerPoint Presentation with a Template
7. Save a Presentation as an Outline/RTF File
8. Modify a Word Document in Outline View
9. Create a New Presentation from a Modified Word Outline

Stephen Coburn/Shutterstock

In This Chapter

In this chapter, you will create an outline in Word. You can promote and demote the outline levels and move levels from one location to another in the outline. When the outline is imported into PowerPoint, slides are created automatically based on the assigned outline levels. In PowerPoint, you can modify the presentation. You can insert and delete slides, change the slide layout and design themes, and add SmartArt graphics and shapes. Notes can be added to the presentation for the speaker to refer to as the presentation is delivered. In PowerPoint, you will use a template to create a presentation. The preformatted presentation contains fonts, bullets, placeholders, background colors, text, pictures, and shapes, all of which can be modified to better suit your needs. When the presentation is completed, you can save it in the Outline/RTF format in Word.

The projects in this chapter refer to **Skyline Bakery & Café**, a chain of casual dining restaurants and bakeries based in Boston. Each restaurant has its own in-house bakery, which produces a wide variety of high-quality specialty breads, breakfast sweets, and desserts. Breads and sweets are sold by counter service along with coffee drinks, gourmet teas, fresh juices, and sodas. The full-service restaurant area features a menu of sandwiches, salads, soups, and light entrees. Fresh, high-quality ingredients and a professional and courteous staff are the hallmarks of every Skyline Bakery & Café.

From Chapter 2 of *GO! with Microsoft® Office 2010 Integrated Projects Comprehensive*, First Edition, Shelley Gaskin, Carol L. Martin. Copyright © 2012 by Pearson Education, Inc. Published by Pearson Prentice Hall. All rights reserved.

Project 2A Franchise Presentation

In Activities 2.01 through 2.13, you will create a Word outline for Samir Taheri, the CEO of Skyline Bakery & Café. He has decided to expand the company by offering franchise locations to interested chefs and business people. You will open and modify a Word document, and then import the Word document into PowerPoint. You will modify the PowerPoint presentation by inserting slides, changing slide layouts, and changing the design theme. You will also create speaker's notes to accompany the slides. Your completed files will look similar to Figure 2.1.

Project Files

For Project 2A, you will need the following files:

New blank PowerPoint presentation
i02A_Franchisee_Information

You will save your files as:

Lastname_Firstname_2A_Franchisee_Information
Lastname_Firstname_2A_Franchisee_Presentation

Project Results

Figure 2.1
Project 2A Franchisee Presentation

Objective 1 | Create an Outline in Word

In Word, Outline view shows the headings of a document as a representation of their level in the document structure. The outline can be collapsed to make it easier to view and reorganize the levels, or it can be expanded to view all levels. Many students find Word to be an easy program to learn. Students find that they can create and modify a Word document quickly, and then they can import the Word document into another software application such as PowerPoint. PowerPoint will use the outline levels to set up the slides in a presentation.

Activity 2.01 | Changing to Outline View in Word

1 **Start** Word, and then navigate to the location of the student files for this instruction. Locate and open the document **i02A_Franchisee_Information**. Display formatting marks and the rulers if they are not visible.

2 Click the **File tab** to display **Backstage** view, click **Save**. In the **Save As** dialog box, navigate to the location where you are saving your files for this chapter, and then on the toolbar, click the **New folder** button. Type **Integrated Projects Chapter 2** and then press [Enter] two times. In the **File name** box, select the existing text, type **Lastname_Firstname_2A_Franchisee_Information** and then click **Save**.

3 On the **Insert tab**, in the **Header & Footer group**, click the **Footer** button, and then click **Edit Footer**. On the **Design tab**, in the **Insert group**, click the **Quick Parts** button, and then click **Field**. Under **Field names**, click **FileName**, and then click **OK**. Double-click in the document to exit the Footer area.

> **Another Way**
> On the status bar, click the Outline button.

4 Click the **View tab**, and then in the **Document Views group**, click the **Outline** button to display the document in Outline view. Compare your screen with Figure 2.2.

> *Outline view* is a document view that shows headings and subheadings, which can be expanded or collapsed. Each paragraph is treated as a separate topic or level in the outline. All paragraphs are preceded by an *outline symbol*—a small gray circle that identifies heading and body text paragraphs in an outline. In Outline view, the Outlining tab displays on the Ribbon.

Figure 2.2

Outlining tab ———

Outline symbol ———

5 On the status bar, use the **Zoom slider** to adjust the zoom level to **100%**.

> *Zooming* is the action of increasing or decreasing the viewing area on the screen.

6 **Save** the document.

Activity 2.02 | Promoting and Demoting Levels in an Outline

In Outline view, levels are identified in a document and can be promoted or demoted using the Outlining tools.

1 At the beginning of the document, move the pointer to the left of the first paragraph, *The People Behind Skyline Bakery & Café*. When the ⟨⟩ point displays, click one time to select the paragraph. On the **Outlining tab**, in the **Outline Tools group**, click the **Promote to Heading 1** button ⟨⟩. Compare your screen with Figure 2.3.

> The first paragraph is formatted with the built-in Level 1 style, the highest outline level. A *plus outline symbol* displays to the left of the paragraph indicating there are subordinate heading or body text paragraphs.

Figure 2.3

Promote to Heading 1 button

Paragraph formatted with Level 1 style

Plus outline symbol

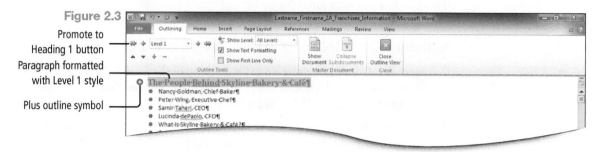

2 Select the sixth paragraph, *What Is Skyline Bakery & Café?*, and then click the **Promote to Heading 1** button ⟨⟩.

3 Select the paragraph *Bakeries Produce High-Quality*. Hold down ⟨Ctrl⟩, and then select the following paragraphs: *Full-Service Restaurant, Franchisee Advantages*, and *Available Locations*. Click the **Promote to Heading 1** button ⟨⟩.

> The four paragraphs are formatted with the Level 1 style. You can hold down ⟨Ctrl⟩ to select multiple items and then promote or demote them all at once.

4 Near the end of the document, move the insertion point to the end of the paragraph *Training*, and then press ⟨Enter⟩. Type **Staff Training** press ⟨Enter⟩, and then type **Chef Training** Move the insertion point to the end of the paragraph *Pricing Discounts*, and then press ⟨Enter⟩. Type **Lower Failure Rate** press ⟨Enter⟩, and then type **Continuous Support**

5 At the top of the document, below the paragraph *The People Behind Skyline Bakery & Café*, select the four paragraphs containing the names and titles of employees. In the **Outline Tools group**, click the **Demote** button ⟨⟩.

> The four paragraphs are demoted to the Level 2 style. A *minus outline symbol* displays, indicating there are no subordinate heading or body text paragraphs.

6 Below the paragraph *What Is Skyline Bakery & Café?*, select the next two paragraphs, and then press ⟨Tab⟩.

> The paragraphs are demoted to the Level 2 style. At the beginning of a paragraph, you can press ⟨Tab⟩ to demote a paragraph. Pressing ⟨Shift⟩ + ⟨Tab⟩ will promote a paragraph.

7 Below the paragraph *Bakeries Produce High-Quality*, select the seven paragraphs listing the baked goods. Hold down ⟨Ctrl⟩. Below *Full-Service Restaurant*, select the next four paragraphs, below *Franchisee Advantages*, select the next seven paragraphs, and then below *Available Locations*, select the remaining four paragraphs. Release ⟨Ctrl⟩, and then in the **Outline Tools group**, click the **Demote** button ⟨⟩.

8 Locate the Level 1 heading *Franchisee Advantages*. Below the Level 2 heading *Training*, select the two paragraphs *Staff Training* and *Chef Training*, and then click the **Demote** button ⟨⟩.

> The two paragraphs are demoted to the Level 3 style.

9 Locate the Level 1 heading *Bakeries Produce High-Quality*. Below the Level 2 heading *Specialty Breads*, select the four paragraphs *Rye*, *Pumpkin*, *Banana*, and *Rhubarb*, and then click the **Demote** button ⬛. Compare your screen with Figure 2.4.

Figure 2.4

Level 3 indicated as Outline Level

Paragraphs formatted with Level 3 style

Paragraph formatted with Level 1 style

Paragraphs formatted with Level 2 style

10 **Save** ⬛ the document.

Activity 2.03 | Moving Outline Levels in Word

In Outline view, the entire document or parts of a document can be collapsed in order to see an overview of the document. When parts of the document are collapsed, it is easy to move or delete sections of the document.

1 To the left of the paragraph *Franchisee Advantages*, click the **plus outline symbol**.

The Level 1 heading as well as all the subtopics are selected.

2 On the **Outlining tab**, in the **Outline Tools group**, click the **Collapse** button ⬛ two times.

Collapsing an outline level hides all subordinate heading and body text paragraphs. In this case, you must click twice to hide both the Level 2 and Level 3 headings.

3 To the left of the paragraph *Franchisee Advantages*, point to the **plus outline symbol** until the ⬛ pointer displays. Hold down the left mouse button and drag the paragraph up above the paragraph *Full-Service Restaurant*. Without releasing the mouse button, compare your screen with Figure 2.5.

Dragging a paragraph causes a black horizontal line to display.

Figure 2.5

Black horizontal line

Pointer

Level 1 paragraph highlighted

Project 2A: Franchise Presentation | **Integrated Projects**

4 Drag up until the black horizontal line is above the paragraph *Bakeries Produce High-Quality*, and then release the mouse button.

The selected Level 1 paragraph and all of its subtopics are moved.

5 With the paragraph *Franchisee Advantages* still selected, in the **Outline Tools group**, click the **Expand** button ⊞ two times to display the sublevels.

6 Below the Level 1 heading *Full-Service Restaurant*, to the left of the paragraph *Light Entrees*, click the **minus outline symbol**. In the **Outline Tools group**, click the **Move Up** button ▲ three times.

The paragraph is moved above the other three Level 2 paragraphs below the Level 1 heading.

7 To the left of the paragraph *Salads*, click the **minus outline symbol**, and then in the **Outline Tools group**, click the **Move Down** button ▼ one time. Compare your screen with Figure 2.6

Figure 2.6

Light Entrees is the first subtopic
Salads is the highlighted and the last subtopic

8 Display **Backstage** view, on the right, click **Properties**, and then click **Show Document Panel**. In the **Author** box, type your firstname and lastname, in the **Subject** box, type your course name and section number, and then in the **Keywords** box, type **franchisee, outline**

9 **Save** 🖫 your document. If your instructor directs you to submit your files electronically go to Step 10. If you are instructed to print your files, under **Print**, click the **Print** button.

10 **Close** Word.

Objective 2 | Import a Word Outline into a PowerPoint Presentation

PowerPoint slides can be automatically created by importing a Word outline. Each Word paragraph formatted with Level 1 will become the title of a new PowerPoint slide. Each Word paragraph formatted with Level 2 will become a bullet point on a PowerPoint slide.

Activity 2.04 | Importing a Word Outline into a PowerPoint Presentation

1 **Start** PowerPoint. If necessary, display the rulers.

2 On the **Home tab**, in the **Slides group**, click the **New Slide button arrow**, and then click **Slides from Outline**.

In the **Insert Outline** dialog box, navigate to your **Integrated Projects Chapter 2** folder, select your Word document **Lastname_Firstname_2A_Franchisee_Information**, and then click **Insert**. Compare your screen with Figure 2.7.

> Seven slides are created based on the outline levels you designated in the outline. Heading 1 style paragraphs display as the title for each slide. Subordinate paragraphs display as bulleted items.

Figure 2.7

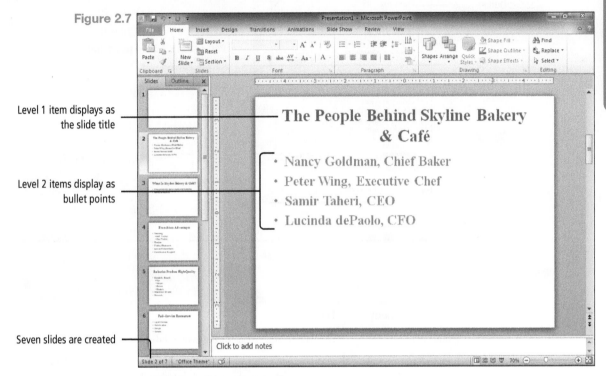

From **Backstage** view, display the **Save As** dialog box, and then navigate to your **Integrated Projects Chapter 2** folder. *Save* the file as **Lastname_Firstname_2A_Franchisee_Presentation**

In the **Slides/Outline pane**, click the **Outline tab** to view your imported Word outline. Compare your screen with Figure 2.8, and then take a moment to study the table in Figure 2.9.

> The presentation displays in *Normal view*—the primary editing view in PowerPoint where you write and design your presentation.

Figure 2.8

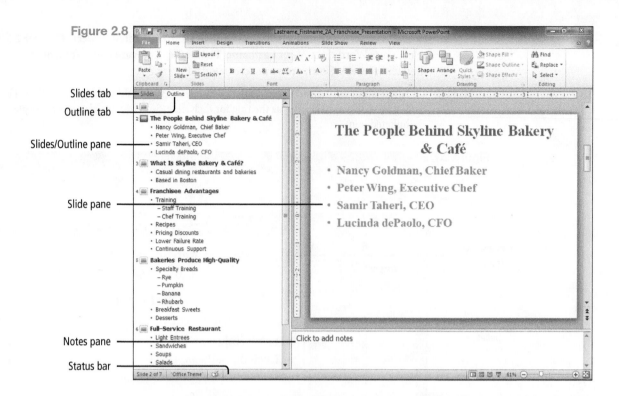

Slides tab
Outline tab
Slides/Outline pane
Slide pane
Notes pane
Status bar

Microsoft PowerPoint Screen Elements	
Screen Element	**Description**
Slide pane	Displays a large image of the active slide.
Slides/Outline pane	Displays either the presentation outline (Outline tab) or all of the slides in the presentation in the form of thumbnails (Slides tab).
Notes pane	Displays below the Slide pane and allows you to type notes regarding the active slide.
Status bar	A horizontal bar at the bottom of the presentation window that displays the current slide number, number of slides in a presentation, the applied theme, View buttons, Zoom slider, and Fit slide to current window button.
View buttons	A set of commands that control the look of the presentation window.

Figure 2.9

6 Click the **Slides tab** to return to the slide thumbnails.

> **More Knowledge** | **Using Body Text in an Outline**
>
> When you use a Word outline to create slides in PowerPoint, heading styles must be applied to all paragraphs. Body text paragraphs will not display in the slides.

Objective 3 | Modify a PowerPoint Presentation

In PowerPoint, you start with a basic design, and then you can modify a presentation by inserting and deleting slides, modifying the slide layout, and changing the design theme and color to give the presentation a professional appearance.

Integrated Projects | Integrating Word and PowerPoint

Activity 2.05 | Inserting and Deleting Slides

Slide layouts may contain a *placeholder*, which is a slide element that reserves a portion of a slide and serves as a container for text, graphics, and other slide elements.

1 In the **Slides/Outline pane**, click **Slide 1** to make it the active slide. In the **Slide pane**, click in the text *Click to add title*, the title placeholder, and then type **Skyline Bakery & Caf** being careful not to type the final *e*.

2 Click the **Insert tab**, and then in the **Symbols group**, click the **Symbols** button. In the **Symbol** dialog box, click the **Font arrow**, scroll to the top of the list, and then click **(normal text)**. In the eleventh row, click the ninth symbol—**é**. Click **Insert**, and then click **Close**. Compare your screen with Figure 2.10.

> The name of the bakery, including the *é*, displays on the first slide. You should insert this symbol any time you type the bakery name in this instruction.

Figure 2.10

First slide selected

é included in company name

3 On the **Slides/Outline tab**, click **Slide 2**—*The People Behind Skyline Bakery & Café*, and then press Del.

> Slide 2 is deleted. Slide 3 becomes the new Slide 2, and all subsequent slides are automatically renumbered. There are six slides in the presentation.

4 Click **Slide 3**—*Franchisee Advantages*. Click the **Home tab**, and then in the **Slides group**, click the **New Slide** button.

> A new slide is added below the current slide; all subsequent slides are automatically renumbered.

5 On **Slide 4**—the new slide, click the title placeholder, and then type **What Is Behind Our Success?** Click the bottom placeholder—the content placeholder, and then type **Excellent food** Press Enter, and then type **Exceptional people** Press Enter, and then type **Great ambiance**

> The text you typed displays as a bulleted list.

6 **Save** 🖫 the presentation.

Project 2A: Franchise Presentation | **Integrated Projects**

Activity 2.06 | Changing Slide Layouts

1 Click **Slide 5**—*Bakeries Produce High-Quality*. On the **Home tab**, in the **Slides group**, click the **Layout** button, and then click **Two Content**. Compare your screen with Figure 2.11.

A new content placeholder displays to the right of the existing placeholder.

Figure 2.11

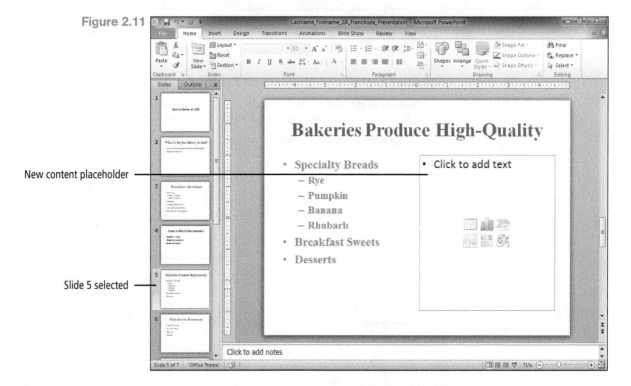

New content placeholder

Slide 5 selected

2 In the left placeholder, select the last two bullet points, *Breakfast Sweets* and *Desserts*. Point to the selection, hold down the left mouse button, and drag the selection to the top of the right placeholder—*Click to add text*. Release the mouse button.

The two bullet points are moved to the right placeholder.

3 Click at the end of the paragraph *Breakfast Sweets*, press Enter, and then press Tab. Type **Apple Spice Muffins** and then press Enter. Compare your screen with Figure 2.12

Pressing Tab at the beginning of a bullet point increases the indent.

Figure 2.12

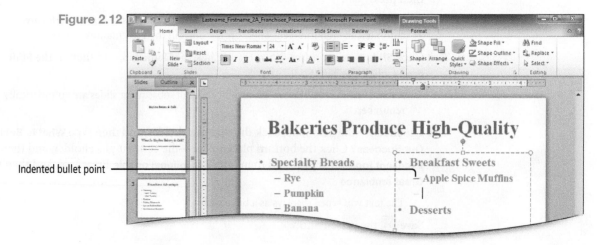

Indented bullet point

Integrated Projects | Integrating Word and PowerPoint

4 Type **Cherry Scones** press Enter, and then type **Blueberry Bars**

5 Click at the end of the bullet point *Desserts*. Press Enter, and then press Tab. Type **Carrot Cake** press Enter, and then type **Chocolate Cookies**

6 In the left placeholder, click at the end of the bullet point *Rhubarb*, and then press Enter. Type **Sourdough** press Enter, and then type **Dusted Wheat**

7 Click **Slide 1**. On the **Home tab**, in the **Slides group**, click the **Layout** button, and then click **Title and Content**. Click in the content placeholder below the title, and then click the **Insert Clip Art** button 🖼 to display the the **Clip Art** task pane on the right of your screen.

8 In the **Clip Art** task pane, click in the **Search for** box, and then replace any existing text with **seeded wholegrain loaves** In the **Results should be** box, verify **All media file types** is selected and that the **Include Office.com content** check box is selected. Click the **Go** button. Locate the image of bread. Click the image to insert it, and then compare your screen with Figure 2.13.

> The picture is inserted in the center of the placeholder, and the Format contextual tab displays on the Ribbon.

Figure 2.13

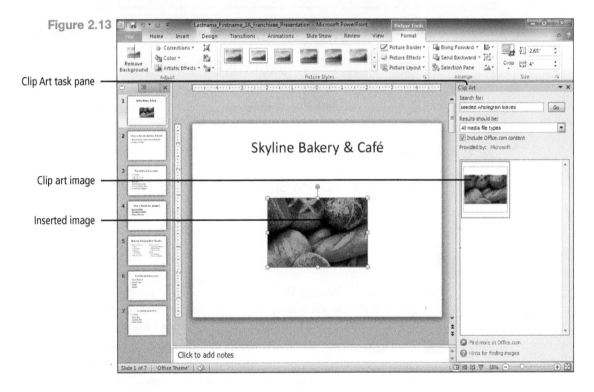

Clip Art task pane

Clip art image

Inserted image

9 **Save** 🖫 the presentation.

Activity 2.07 | Changing the Design Theme

You can quickly format an entire PowerPoint presentation by applying a document *theme*. A theme is a predefined set of colors, fonts, lines, and fill effects that are professionally designed.

1 Click the **Design tab**, and then in the **Themes group**, click the **More** button ⊡. In the **Themes** gallery, under **Built-In**, point to several different themes and use Live Preview to view how the slides will display. Under **Built-In**, in the third row, click the second theme—**Flow**.

> **Alert!** | **What if I don't see the Flow theme?**
>
> The Themes gallery may display differently depending on your screen resolution. Themes are arranged in alphabetical order; point to each theme and read the ScreenTip until you find Flow.

2 In the **Themes group**, click the **Colors** button, and then click **Module**. Notice that the presentation color scheme is changed, as shown in Figure 2.14.

Figure 2.14

Flow theme selected

Colors button

3 **Save** 🖫 the presentation.

Activity 2.08 | Adding Speaker's Notes

You can insert *speaker's notes* into each slide of a PowerPoint presentation. Speaker's notes are notes that are printed for the speaker to refer to as the presentation is being delivered. The audience will not view the speaker's notes unless they are printed on the handouts.

1 Click **Slide 2**—*What Is Skyline Bakery & Café?*—to make it the active slide. Below the slide, click in the **Notes pane**, and then type **Introduce Samir Taheri, our Chief Executive Officer, and Lucinda dePaolo, our Chief Financial Officer.**

2 Click **Slide 5**—*Bakeries Produce High-Quality.* Click the **View tab**, and then in the **Presentation Views group**, click the **Notes Page** button. Below the slide, click the **Notes pane**, and then type **Mention that we use fresh, high-quality ingredients in all our baked goods including our specialty breads, our breakfast sweets, and our cakes. Remember to emphasize that our repeat business is very high.**

> In *Notes Page view* you can work with your notes in a full page format. Speaker's notes are printed in this format—with a copy of the slide at the top of the page and the speaker's notes at the bottom of the page.

3 In the **Notes pane**, select the text. On the Mini toolbar, click the **Font Size button arrow** ⌷, and then click **28**. Compare your screen with Figure 2.15.

> The presenter will refer to the notes during the slide show. A large font size makes the notes easier to read, especially in low light conditions.

Integrated Projects | Integrating Word and PowerPoint

Figure 2.15

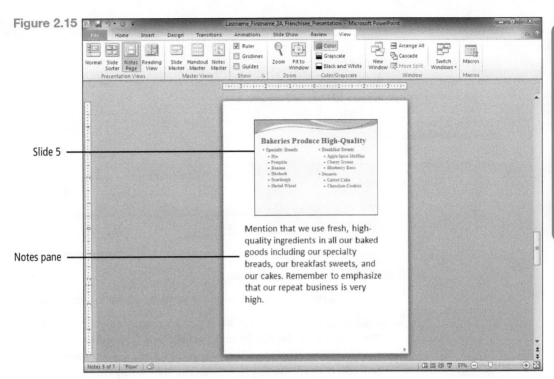

Slide 5

Notes pane

4 Below the vertical scroll bar, locate and then click the **Next Slide** button ⬇ to make **Slide 6**—*Full-Service Restaurant*—the active slide. Click in the **Notes pane**, and then type **Mention that Nancy Goldman, our Chief Baker, trains all our chefs and then introduce Nancy to the group.**

5 Using the technique you practiced in Step 3, change the **Font Size** of the note to **28**.

6 On the **View tab**, in the **Presentation Views group**, click the **Normal** button, and then **Save** 🔲 the presentation.

Objective 4 | Create a Footer and Save a PowerPoint Presentation

A PowerPoint presentation can be printed as Slides, Handouts, Notes Pages, or in Outline view. Depending on how you are planning to print the presentation, you may want to add footers to these different views. When the footer is created, it can be added to one slide or applied to all the slides in the presentation.

Activity 2.09 | Inserting a Footer in a Presentation

1 Click the **Insert tab**, and then in the **Text group**, click the **Header & Footer** button. In the **Header and Footer** dialog box, on the **Slide tab**, under **Include on slide**, select the **Slide number** check box. Select the **Footer** check box, and then in the **Footer** box, type **Lastname_Firstname_2A_Franchisee_Presentation** Compare your screen with Figure 2.16.

Figure 2.16

Slide number check box

Footer check box

Footer box

2 Click the **Apply to All** button.

The *Apply to All* option displays the footer on all slides of the presentation.

3 Click **Slide 7**—*Available Locations*. On the **Insert tab**, in the **Text group**, click the **Date & Time** button. In the **Header and Footer** dialog box, under **Include on slide**, select the **Date and Time** check box. If necessary, click the **Update automatically** option button to select it. Click the **Apply** button, and then compare your screen with Figure 2.17.

The Apply button displays the date in the footer only on the selected slide. The Update automatically option causes the date to be updated to the current date each time the presentation is opened.

Figure 2.17

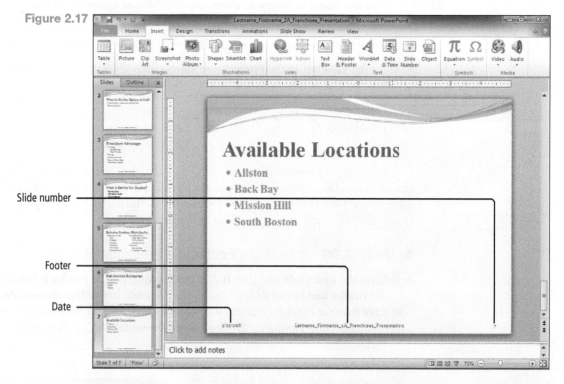

Slide number

Footer

Date

Activity 2.10 | Inserting a Footer in Slide Handouts

Your presentation can be printed as a handout. The handout enables your audience to follow along as you deliver your presentation and can be saved for future reference.

Integrated Projects | Integrating Word and PowerPoint

1 On the **Insert tab**, in the **Text group**, click the **Header & Footer** button. In the **Header and Footer** dialog box, click the **Notes and Handouts tab**.

2 Under **Include on page**, select the **Date and time** check box, and then click the **Fixed** option button. If necessary, insert the current date if it does not display.

> Each time you open the presentation, a fixed date will remain the date entered in the Fixed box and display on the handout. By default the Page number check box is selected.

3 Select the **Footer** check box, and then in the **Footer** box, type **Lastname_Firstname_ 2A_Franchisee_Presentation** Compare your screen with Figure 2.18.

Figure 2.18

Notes and Handouts tab

Fixed date option (your date will differ)

4 Click **Apply to All**, and then **Save** the presentation.

Objective 5 | Preview and Print a Presentation, Slide Handouts, and Speaker Notes

Previewing your presentation should always be part of your preparation process, in order to see how your graphics and effects will look during the actual presentation. The PowerPoint presentation, slide handouts, and speaker's notes can all be previewed before printing.

Activity 2.11 | Previewing and Printing a Presentation

1 Click the **Slide Show tab**, and then in the **Start Slide Show group**, click the **From Beginning** button to open Slide Show view.

> In *Slide Show view*, the slides fill the computer screen, which enables you to view your presentation the way your audience will see it.

Another Way

Press Spacebar, Enter, or ↓ to advance to the next slide

2 Click the left mouse button to advance to the second slide.

3 Continue to click to advance through the slides. When a black slide displays, click one more time to display the presentation in **Normal view**.

> After the last slide in a presentation, a *black slide* displays, indicating that the presentation is over.

4 Click the **File tab** to display **Backstage** view, and then click the **Print tab**. Under **Settings**, in the **Slides** box, type **3** and then compare your screen with Figure 2.19. Note: If you do not have a color printer connected to your computer, the Print Preview will display in grayscale.

The *Custom Range* option allows you to indicate what slides to print. Because you typed 3, only Slide 3 will print. The default setting—*Full Page Slides*—will print each slide on a separate page. The Print Preview of Slide 3 displays on the right.

Figure 2.19

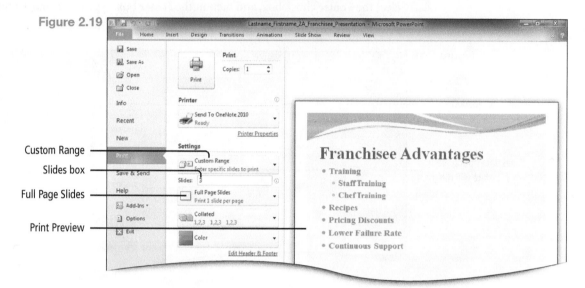

5 Under **Print**, in the **Copies** box, verify that **1** displays.

Activity 2.12 | Previewing and Printing Slide Handouts

1 Under **Settings**, click **Custom Range**, and then click **Print All Slides**. Click **Full Page Slides**, and then under **Handouts**, click **9 Slides Horizontal**.

The setting *9 Slides Horizontal* will print nine slides on a single page, with slides 1, 2, and 3 displayed in the first row. In this case, because your presentation only has seven slides, all seven slides will print on one page.

2 If your instructor directs you to submit your files electronically, go to Activity 2.13.

3 To print the handout, under **Print**, click the **Print** button.

4 Display **Backstage** view, and then click the **Print tab**.

Activity 2.13 | Previewing and Printing Speaker Notes

Speaker notes are referenced by the speaker during a presentation. When speaker notes are printed, the slide is printed on the top half of the page, and the speaker notes are printed on the bottom half of the page.

1 Under **Settings**, click **9 Slides Horizontal**, and then under **Print Layout**, click **Notes Pages**.

2 At the bottom of the **Print Preview**, click the **Next Page** button ▶ four times so that **Page 5** displays.

Indicated below the Notes page are the current slide number and the number of pages that will print when Notes Pages is selected. You can use the Next Page and Previous Page arrows to display each Notes page in the presentation.

Integrated Projects | Integrating Word and PowerPoint

3 In the **Slides** box, type **5** and then compare your screen with Figure 2.20.

Figure 2.20

Print Preview —

Slides box —

Notes Pages —

Next Page button —

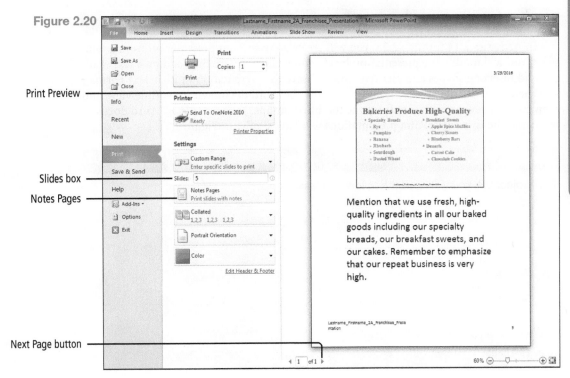

4 If your instructor directs you to submit your files electronically, go to Step 6.

5 Under **Print**, click the **Print** button.

6 Display **Backstage** view, on the right, click **Properties**, and then click **Show Document Panel**. In the **Author** box, type your firstname and lastname, in the **Subject** box, type your course name and section number, and then in the **Keywords** box, type **franchisee presentation**

7 **Save** 🖫 the presentation, and then **Close** ⊠ PowerPoint.

8 Submit your printed or electronic files as directed by your instructor.

End You have completed Project 2A ———————————————

Project 2B Restaurant Presentation

Project Activities

In Activities 2.14 through 2.23, you will create a PowerPoint presentation from a template. You will modify the presentation by changing character spacing, adding a text shadow, and inserting shapes and pictures. You will save the presentation in Rich Text Format, and then open the file in Word. You will modify the Word document in Outline view, and then create a new presentation from the modified outline. Your completed Word document and the two PowerPoint presentations will look similar to Figure 2.21.

Project Files

For Project 2B, you will need the following files:

New blank PowerPoint presentation
i02B_Skyline_Template
i02B_Bakery1
i02B_Bakery2
i02B_Bakery3
i02B_Entree1
i02B_Entree2
i02B_Entree3
i02B_Taheri

You will save your files as:

Lastname_Firstname_2B_Restaurant_Presentation
Lastname_Firstname_2B_Menu_Outline
Lastname_Firstname_2B_Menu_Presentation

Project Results

Figure 2.21
Project 2B Restaurant Presentation
Corbis Premium RF/Alamy

Objective 6 | Create a PowerPoint Presentation with a Template

A PowerPoint template is a preformatted presentation containing the size and type of fonts and bullets, placeholder sizes and position, and background styles and colors. You can preview and change suggested text, pictures, and shapes in the template to fit your content. Various templates are installed on your computer, or you may search online for many additional template options. In this project, you will use a template designed by Jasmine Turner, Marketing Director of Skyline Bakery & Café.

Activity 2.14 | Opening a PowerPoint Template

In this activity, you will open a PowerPoint template to create a new presentation.

1 **Start** PowerPoint. Display **Backstage** view, and then click the **New tab**. Under **Available Templates and Themes**, in the first row, click **New from Existing**. In the **New from existing Presentation** dialog box, navigate to the location of the student data files, select **i02B_Skyline_Template**, and then click **Create New**. Compare your screen with Figure 2.22.

> An 8-slide PowerPoint presentation is created. Because this presentation was created from a template, the presentation opens unsaved with the name Presentation followed by a number. This ensures that you won't make changes and then overwrite the template file.

Figure 2.22

Presentation created from template

2 Display **Backstage** view, and then click the **Save As tab**. In the **Save As** dialog box, navigate to your **Integrated Projects Chapter 2** folder, and then save the PowerPoint presentation with the file name **Lastname_Firstname_2B_Restaurant_Presentation**

3 Click the **Insert tab**, and then in the **Text group**, click the **Header & Footer** button. In the **Header and Footer** dialog box, click the **Notes and Handouts tab**. Select the **Footer** check box, in the **Footer** box, type **Lastname_Firstname_2B_Restaurant_Presentation** and then click **Apply to All**.

> The footer will print on the handouts or notes pages but will not display on the slides.

4 Click the **Design tab**, and then in the **Themes group**, click the **More** button ⏷. In the **Themes** gallery, under **Built-In**, in the second row, click the first theme—**Civic**. If necessary, point to each theme and use the ScreenTips to locate the Civic theme.

> The Civic theme is applied to all slides in the presentation.

Activity 2.15 | Changing Character Spacing and Text Shadow

1 In the **Slide pane**, with **Slide 1** displayed, in the title placeholder, click to the right of **Skyline**. Press Spacebar, and then type **Bakery & Caf** Insert the symbol **é** to complete the name of the bakery. Select the title. On the **Home tab**, in the **Font group**, click the **Character Spacing** button ⏷, and then click **Very Loose**. Compare your screen with Figure 2.23.

> *Character spacing* increases or decreases the space between characters. In this case, the space is increased and the title is spaced across the slide.

Figure 2.23

Character Spacing button

Title spaced across the slide

2 In the bottom subtitle placeholder, delete the existing text, type **Restaurant Menu** and then select the text. In the **Font group**, click the **Character Spacing** button ⏷, and then click **Loose**. In the **Font group**, click the **Font Size button arrow** ⏷, and then click **24**.

> The text in the subtitle placeholder displays as capital letters because the Font Effect for the All Caps option has been applied in the template.

3 Display **Slide 2**. Delete the title, and then type **What's For Lunch?** In the left content placeholder, delete the existing text, and then type **Our chain of casual full-service restaurants with our in-house bakeries feature fresh, high-quality ingredients.** Select the text you just typed. From the Mini toolbar, click the **Font Size button arrow** ⏷, and then click **32**. Select the word *fresh*. In the **Font group**, click the **Text Shadow** button ⏷.

> Text Shadow adds a shadow behind the selected text to make it stand out from the surrounding text.

4 In the right content placeholder, a SmartArt graphic displays. Click in the first text box of the **SmartArt** graphic.

SmartArt graphics are designer-quality visual representations of your information that you can create by choosing from the many different layouts to effectively communicate your message or ideas.

5 In the **SmartArt Tools**, click the **Design tab**—the Design tab on the right side of the Ribbon. In the **Layouts group**, click the **More** button, and then in the fifth row, click the first layout—**Vertical Block List**. If the Text Pane does not display, on the Design tab, in the Create Graphic group, click the Text Pane button. Compare your screen with Figure 2.24.

The *Text Pane*—the pane where text that displays in the graphic can be entered and edited—displays to the left of the SmartArt graphic. The description of the selected graphic may not display in the SmartArt task pane.

Figure 2.24

SmartArt Tools contextual Design tab

Text Pane – description may not display

SmartArt graphic

6 In the **Text Pane**, under **Type your text here**, delete the first line of text, and then type **Sandwiches** Delete the second line of text, and then type **Salads** Delete the third line of text, and then type **Soups** Delete the fourth line of text, and then type **Light Entrees** Press [Enter] to add a fifth box to the SmartArt graphic, and then type **Desserts**

7 In the **Create Graphic group**, click the **Text Pane** button to close the Text Pane, and then compare your screen with Figure 2.25.

Project 2B: Restaurant Presentation | **Integrated Projects**

Figure 2.25

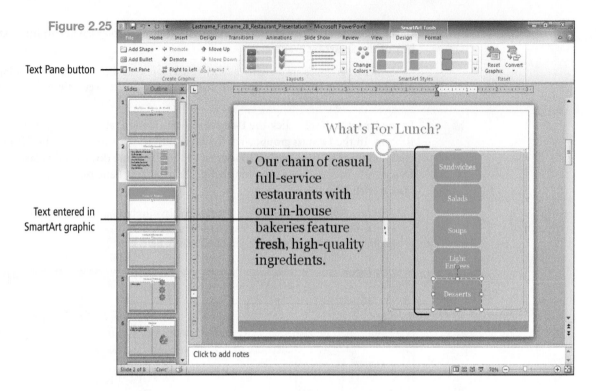

Text Pane button

Text entered in SmartArt graphic

---

8 Display **Slide 3**. Click in the title placeholder, delete the existing text, and then type **Sandwiches**

9 In the **Slides/Outline pane**, right-click **Slide 4**, and then from the shortcut menu, click **Delete Slide**.

> Slide 4 is deleted. Slide 5 becomes Slide 4, and all subsequent slides are renumbered.

10 **Save** 🖫 the presentation.

Activity 2.16 | Inserting and Modifying a Shape

The appearance of a shape can be modified by adjusting the fill or by adding effects, such as shadows, glows, and bevels.

1 On **Slide 4**, click in the title placeholder, delete the existing text, and then type **Our Sandwiches** In the left content placeholder, delete the existing text, and then type **Our sandwiches are prepared with our own specialty breads, which are baked daily in our own bakery. After finishing your meal, we would be pleased to offer you a tour of our bakery next door. Favorite sandwiches include:**

2 On the right side of the slide, click the top shape—*Sun*. Hold down Ctrl, and then click each of the other two shapes. Press Del to delete the three shapes.

> By holding down Ctrl, you can select more than one shape at a time. When multiple shapes are selected, any formatting changes are applied to all selected shapes.

3 Click the **Insert tab**. In the **Illustrations group**, click the **Shapes** button, and then under **Basic Shapes**, in the first row, click the sixth shape—**Trapezoid**. On the right side of the slide, below the title placeholder, click one time to insert a trapezoid shape.

4 With the shape selected, on the **Format tab**, in the **Size group**, click in the **Shape Width** box [⊞ 1.37″ ⇕], type **3** and then press ⏎. In the **Shape Styles group**, click the **Shape Effects** button. Point to **Bevel**, and then under **Bevel**, in the first row, click the fourth bevel—**Cool Slant**. Use the arrow keys to nudge the shape so the top middle sizing handle displays at **approximately 2.5 inches on the right side of the horizontal ruler** and the top of the trapezoid is aligned with the top of the content placeholder. Compare your screen with Figure 2.26.

Figure 2.26

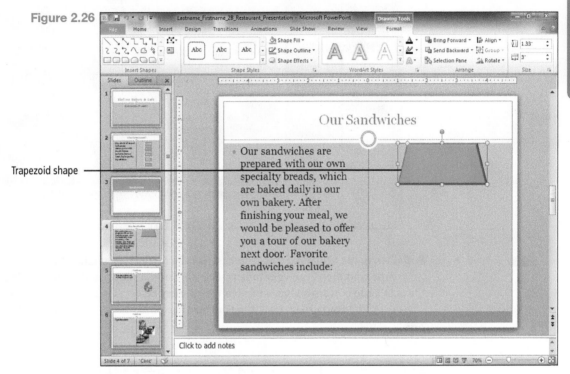

Trapezoid shape

5 With the shape selected, press Ctrl + D.

The Trapezoid shape is copied in the same area as the original shape.

6 Drag the selected shape down until the bottom middle sizing handle displays at **approximately 2.5 inches on the right side of the horizontal ruler** and at **approximately 3.5 inches on the lower portion of the vertical ruler**.

7 Press Ctrl + D. Drag the selected shape up until the top middle sizing handle displays at **approximately 2.5 inches on the right side of the horizontal ruler** and the shape is approximately in the middle of the other two trapezoids.

8 Click the top trapezoid, hold down Ctrl and then click the other two shapes. On the **Format tab**, in the **Arrange group**, click the **Align** button [▤], and then click **Align Left**. Click the **Align** button [▤] and then click **Distribute Vertically**. Compare your screen with Figure 2.27.

The left borders of the shapes are aligned and the spaces are equally spaced vertically.

Figure 2.27

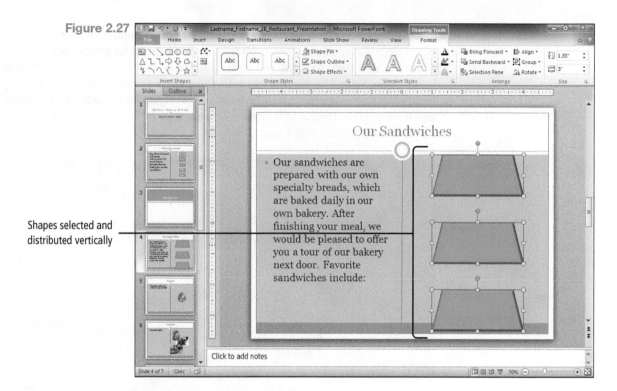

Shapes selected and distributed vertically

9 Click in the title placeholder to deselect the three shapes. Click the top trapezoid shape, and then type **Vegetarian** Click the middle shape, and then type **Cheese Steak** Click the bottom shape, and then type **Turkey** Select all three shapes. Click the **Home tab**, in the **Font group**, click the **Font Size button arrow** `44 ▾`, and then click **28**.

10 **Save** 💾 the presentation.

Activity 2.17 | Inserting and Modifying a SmartArt Graphic

Inserting SmartArt graphics will visually present your information in a professionally designed manner. The appearance of SmartArt graphics can be customized by changing edges or shadows or applying a three-dimensional perspective. In this activity, you will insert and modify a SmartArt graphic.

1 In the **Slides/Outline pane**, click **Slide 3** to make it the active slide. On the **Home tab**, in the **Clipboard group**, click the **Copy** button 📋. Click **Slide 4** to make it the active slide, and then in the **Clipboard group**, click the **Paste** button.

A copy of Slide 3 is pasted after Slide 4. You now have eight slides in your presentation.

2 With **Slide 5** selected, click in the title placeholder, delete the existing text, and then type **Salads**

3 Click **Slide 6**. In the title placeholder, delete the existing text, and then type **Our Salads**

4 In the left content placeholder, delete the existing text, and then type **In our hectic lives, salads are a healthy alternative to fast food. At Skyline Bakery & Café, our chefs use only the freshest ingredients brought in daily by farmers. We are proud to support the growers in the local Boston area.**

5 In the right content placeholder, click the picture, and then press ⌨Del. In the middle of the right placeholder, click the **Insert SmartArt Graphic** button 📊. In the **Choose a SmartArt Graphic** dialog box, click **List**, and then in the first row, click the first graphic—**Basic Block List**. Click **OK**.

6 In the SmartArt Graphic, click in the top left box, and then type **Snap Bean** In the top row, click in the second box, and then type **Antipasto Pasta** In the middle left box, type **Cranberry and Walnuts** In the middle row, in the second box, type **Garden Pasta** and then in the last box, type **Herb Chicken**

7 In the **SmartArt Tools**, on the **Design tab**, and then in the **Create Graphic group**, click the **Add Shape** button. In the new box, type **Fresh Fruit** and then compare your screen with Figure 2.28.

Figure 2.28

Add Shape button —

Text inserted in text boxes —

Text box added —

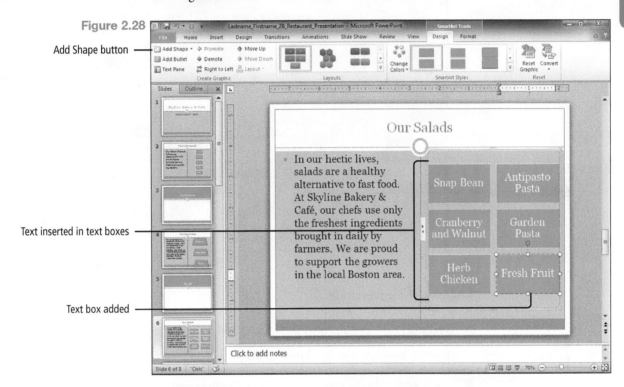

8 In the **SmartArt tools**, on the **Design tab**, in **the SmartArt Styles group**, click the **More** button 🔽. Under **3-D**, in the first row, click the first style—**Polished**.

9 In the **Slides/Outline pane**, click **Slide 5**, hold down ⌨Ctrl, and then click **Slide 6**. On the **Home tab**, in the **Clipboard group**, click the **Copy** button 📋. Click **Slide 6** to make it the active slide, and then in the **Clipboard group**, click the **Paste** button two times.

> Two copies of Slides 5 and Slide 6 are pasted after Slide 6. You now have twelve slides in your presentation.

10 Click **Slide 7**, delete the text *Salads*, and then type **Soups**

11 Click **Slide 8**. In the title placeholder, delete the existing text, and then type **Our Soups** In the left content placeholder, delete the existing text, and then type **We are proud to serve our delicious homemade soups with our salads. Our soups change seasonally depending on the availability of fresh ingredients. Our chefs are always combining various ingredients to surprise you with a scrumptious new soup.**

12 In the right content placeholder, click above the top row of shapes, to display the thick border that surrounds the SmartArt graphic and to select the graphic. In the **SmartArt Tools**, on the **Design tab**, in the **Layouts group**, click the **More** button ⏷, and then click **More Layouts**. In the **Choose a SmartArt Graphic** dialog box, click **Matrix**, and then click the first layout—**Basic Matrix**. Click **OK**.

13 In the **Text Pane**, in the first bullet point, delete the text, and then type **Homemade** In a similar manner, in the second bullet point, type **Great Chefs** in the third bullet point, type **Full Flavored** and then in the fourth bullet point, type **Prepared Daily** **Close** ⊠ the **Text Pane**, and then compare your screen with Figure 2.29.

Figure 2.29

Matrix layout applied

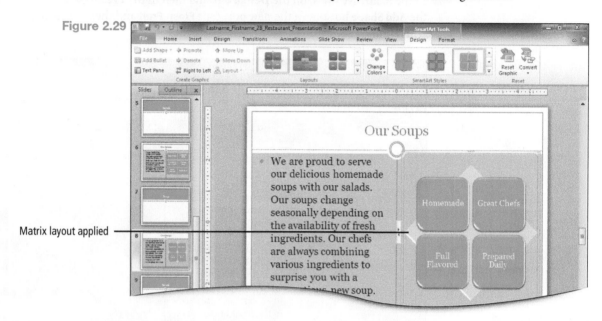

14 Save 💾 the presentation.

Activity 2.18 | Replacing and Modifying Pictures

You can insert personal or business pictures in a PowerPoint presentation.

1 Click **Slide 9**, in the title placeholder, delete the existing text, and then type **Light Entrees**

2 Click **Slide 10**, and then press ⌈Del⌋.

Slide 10 is deleted. You now have eleven slides in your presentation.

3 On **Slide 10**, in the title placeholder, delete the existing text, and then type **Our Light Entrees** In the left content placeholder, delete the existing text, and then type **Immediately as you enter Skyline Bakery & Café you know you are in for a pleasurable eating experience. The aroma that greets you is warm and welcoming. Our Light Entrees are as delicious to look at as they are to eat.**

4 On the right side of the slide, click the top picture to select it. On the **Format tab**, in the **Adjust group**, click the **Change Picture** button 🖼. In the **Insert Picture** dialog box, navigate to the location of the student data files and locate the file **i02B_Entree1**, and then click **Insert**. In the **Size group**, click in the **Shape Height** box, type **2.1** and then press ⌈Enter⌋.

5 Click one time on the bottom picture to select it, and then change the picture to **i02B_Entree2**. In the **Size group**, click in the **Shape Height** box, type **2.1** and then press Enter.

6 Click the middle picture to select it, and then change the picture to **i02B_Entree3**. Press ↓ two times, and then press → five times. In the **Arrange group**, click the **Bring Forward** button. Compare your screen with Figure 2.30.

Figure 2.30

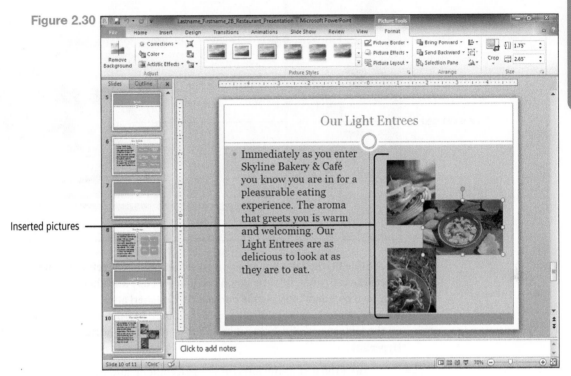

Inserted pictures

7 In the **Slides/Outline pane**, click **Slide 9**, hold down Ctrl, and then click **Slide 10**. On the **Home tab**, in the **Clipboard group**, click the **Copy** button. Click to make **Slide 10** the active slide, and then in the **Clipboard group**, click the **Paste** button.

Slide 9 and Slide 10 are pasted after Slide 10. You now have thirteen slides in your presentation.

8 Click **Slide 11**. In the title placeholder, delete the existing text, and then type **In-House Bakery**

9 Click **Slide 12**. In the title placeholder, delete the existing text, and then type **Our In-House Bakery** In the left content placeholder, delete the existing text, and then type **A delightful way to conclude your visit to the Skyline Bakery & Café is a stop at our in-house bakery. Our pastry chefs are pleased to serve you a wondrous selection of desserts.**

10 On the right side of the slide, using the skills you practiced previously, change the top and bottom pictures using the files **i02B_Bakery1** for the top picture, **i02B_Bakery2** for the bottom picture. With the bottom picture selected, hold down Ctrl and then click the top picture. With both pictures selected, in the **Size group**, click the **Shape Height** box, type **1.6** and then press Enter. Change the middle picture using the file **i02B_Bakery3**. In the **Arrange group**, click the **Bring Forward** button. Press ↓ six times. Compare your screen with Figure 2.31.

Figure 2.31

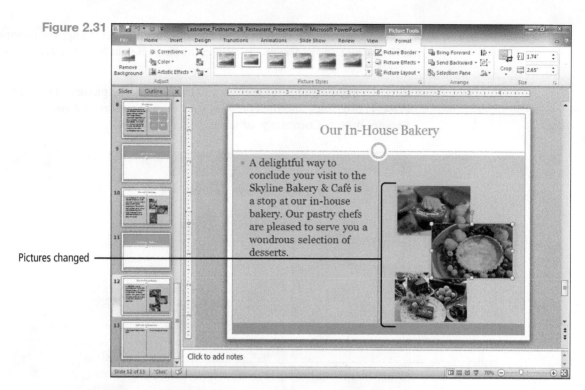

Pictures changed

11 Click **Slide 13**, the last slide of your presentation. In the left content placeholder, delete the existing text, type **When can you visit us?** and then press Enter. Type **For your own personal tour, please contact Samir Taheri** and then press Enter. Type **www.skylinebakery.biz** press Enter, and then type **617-555-0037** Right-click anywhere on the text *www.skylinebakery.biz*, and then from the shortcut menu, click **Remove Hyperlink**.

12 Select all of the text in the left content placeholder, and then on the **Home tab**, in the **Font group**, click the **Increase Font Size** button A. In the **Paragraph group**, click the **Bullets** button to turn off the bulleted formatting. With the text still selected, in the **Paragraph group**, click the **Center** button, click the **Line Spacing** button, and then click **Line Spacing Options**. In the **Paragraph** dialog box, under **Spacing**, click the **Before spin box up arrow** and change to **12 pt**. Click the **After spin box up arrow** and change to **12 pt**, and then click **OK**.

13 In the right content placeholder, delete the existing text, and then in the middle of the placeholder, click the **Insert Picture from File** button. In the **Insert Picture** dialog box, navigate to your student files for this chapter, select the file **i02B_Taheri**, and then click **Insert**. Compare your screen with Figure 2.32.

Integrated Projects | Integrating Word and PowerPoint

Figure 2.32

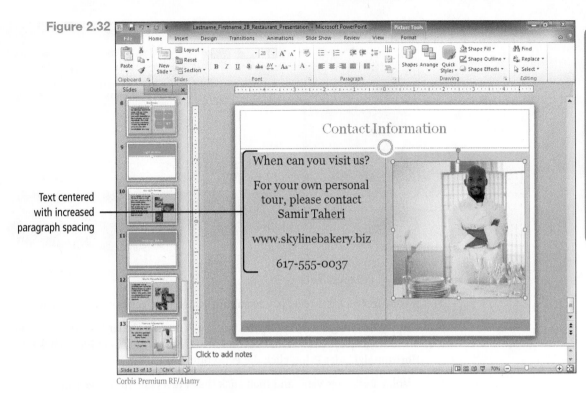

Text centered with increased paragraph spacing

Corbis Premium RF/Alamy

14 Click the **Review tab**, and then in the **Proofing group**, click the **Spelling** button. Check the spelling in the presentation and correct any misspelled words.

> The spelling tool will check the spelling of the words on the slides, as well as the words in the footer.

15 **Save** 🖫 the presentation.

Objective 7 | Save a Presentation as an Outline/RTF File

You can save a PowerPoint presentation as a text-only document by saving it in the Outline/RTF format. You may open the file in another software application, such as Word, or in an older version of PowerPoint. When a presentation is saved as an Outline/RTF file, the graphical content of the presentation and any text in the Notes pane will not be saved.

Activity 2.19 | Saving a File as an Outline/RTF File

1 Click the **Slide Show tab**, and then in the **Start Slide Show group**, click the **From Beginning** button to view your presentation. Notice that the background colors are not consistent from slide to slide.

2 Click **Slide 1**. Click the **Design tab**, and then in the **Background group**, click the **Background Styles** button. In the displayed list, in the third row, click the third style— **Style 11**. Compare your screen with Figure 2.33.

> The background style is changed on all slides in the presentation.

Project 2B: Restaurant Presentation | **Integrated Projects**

Figure 2.33

Background
Style 11 applied

3 **Save** 🔲 the presentation.

4 If your instructor directs you to submit your files electronically, go to Step 6.

5 Display **Backstage** view, and then click the **Print tab**. Under **Settings**, verify **Print All Slides** displays. Click **Full Page Slides**, and then under **Handouts**, click **9 Slides Horizontal**. Under **Print**, click the **Print** button.

6 Display **Backstage** view, and then click the **Save As tab**. In the **Save As** dialog box, navigate to your **Integrated Projects Chapter 2** folder, and then type the file name **Lastname_Firstname_2B_Menu_Outline** Click the **Save as type arrow**, scroll down near the bottom of the list, and then click **Outline/RTF**. Click **Save**.

> *Rich Text Format*, or *RTF*, is a universal document format that can be read by nearly all word processing programs and that retains most text and paragraph formatting. A PowerPoint presentation saved as an RTF file will include only the text of the presentation in an outline format. This allows you to share the information in the presentation with others who may not have the same version of PowerPoint.

7 Display **Backstage** view, on the right, click **Properties**, and then click **Show Document Panel**. In the **Author** box, type your firstname and lastname, in the **Subject** box, type your course name and section number, and then in the **Keywords** box, type **menu, bakery template**

8 **Save** 🔲 your presentation, and then **Close** ❌ PowerPoint.

Activity 2.20 | Opening an Outline/RTF in Word

Nancy Goldman, the Chief Baker, has asked you to modify the PowerPoint presentation to emphasize the soups and salads. You can open an Outline/RTF file in Word, modify the document, and then create a new PowerPoint presentation from the modified Word document.

1 **Start** Word. From **Backstage** view, click **Open**, navigate to your **Integrated Projects Chapter 2** folder, and then open the RTF file **Lastname_Firstname_2B_Menu_Outline**. Insert the file name in the footer.

2 Click the **View tab**, and then in the **Document Views group**, click **Outline**.

Another Way
Press Ctrl + A.

3 Click the **Home tab**, and then in the **Editing group**, click **Select**, and then click **Select All** to select the entire document.

4 In the **Font group**, click the **Font Color button arrow** [A▾], and then click **Automatic**. Compare your screen with Figure 2.34.

> The text in the document is the same font color as in the presentation. Because some of your presentation text was white, by changing the font color to automatic—black—all document text is now visible. The text you typed in the SmartArt and the shapes is not part of the Word document.

Figure 2.34
Outlining tab displays, but is not active
Document text displays

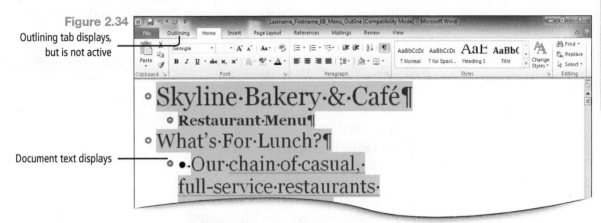

5 From **Backstage** view, click the **Convert** button. In the message box, click **OK**.

> Your document is changed from an RTF file to a Word document. The message box warns you that you are changing your document from .rtf format to .docx format and that the file format change may cause differences in the layout of the document.

Objective 8 | Modify a Word Document in Outline View

Typing text and keeping track of slides in a PowerPoint presentation can sometimes be difficult. Opening the presentation in Word and making modifications to the Word outline enables you to see more text and to modify it more easily.

Activity 2.21 | Collapsing Outline Levels

Recall that in Outline view, parts of a Word document can be collapsed or expanded to view or move sections of the document.

1 Click the **Outlining tab**. In the **Outline Tools group**, click the **Show Level arrow**, and then click **Level 1**.

2 To the left of *Our Salads*, click the **plus outline symbol**, and then in the **Outline Tools group**, click the **Expand** button [+]. To the left of *Our Soups*, click the **plus outline symbol**, and then click the **Expand** button [+].

3 To the left of the paragraph that begins *We are proud*, click the **minus outline symbol**, and then type **Fire Roasted Tomato** Press [Enter].

> Clicking the minus outline symbol selects all the text for that item. When you begin to type, the selected text is automatically deleted.

4 Press `Tab` and then type **Enhanced by the rustic character of flame roasted tomatoes, our creamy tomato soup is served with roasted garlic and sour cream.** Press `Enter`.

> Instead of clicking the Demote and Promote buttons in the Outline Tools group, you can press `Tab` to demote a paragraph and press `Shift` + `Tab` to promote a paragraph. In this case, the paragraph you typed is demoted.

5 Press `Shift` + `Tab`, type **Minestrone** and then press `Enter`. Press `Tab`, and then type **Our minestrone soup is a favorite of our customers.** Press `Enter`, and then compare your screen with Figure 2.35.

Figure 2.35

New text entered and formatted

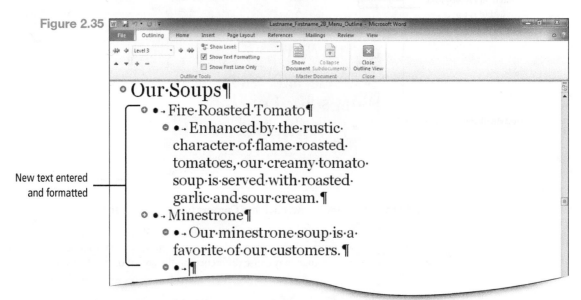

6 Press `Shift` + `Tab`, type **Classic French Onion** and then press `Enter`. Press `Tab`, and then type **Enriched by caramelized onions, our rich beef broth is served with garlic croutons and gruyere cheese.** Press `Enter`.

7 Press `Shift` + `Tab`, type **Corn Chowder** and then press `Enter`. Press `Tab`, and then type **Roasted corn is featured in this creamy chowder. A bit of wild rice and roasted red pepper garnish this soup.**

8 To the left of the paragraph that begins *In our hectic lives*, click the **minus outline symbol**. Type **Spinach Salad** and then press `Enter`. Press `Tab`, and then type **Fresh garden spinach, hard boiled eggs, bacon, and tomatoes are topped with a sweet honey mustard dressing.** Press `Enter`.

9 Press `Shift` + `Tab`, type **Fresh Fruit** and then press `Enter`. Press `Tab`, and then type **Fresh fruits are sliced and displayed in a dish made from a uniquely carved watermelon.** Press `Enter`.

10 Press `Shift` + `Tab`, type **Cold Pasta Salad** and then press `Enter`. Press `Tab`, and then type **Rainbow pasta is boiled, chilled, and then mixed with carrots, celery, and our secret ingredients, which make this salad exceptional.**

11 In the **Outline Tools group**, click the **Show Level button arrow**, and then click **Level 1**.

12 To the left of the paragraph *Soups*, click the **minus outline symbol**. Hold down Shift, and then to the left of the paragraph *Our Soups*, click the **plus outline symbol**. In the **Outline Tools group**, click the **Move Up** button ▲ two times, and then compare your screen with Figure 2.36.

> The *Soup* and *Our Soups* outline levels, and related text, are moved above *Salads*. Holding down Shift enables you to select consecutive levels.

Figure 2.36

Soups and *Our Soups* display above *Salads*

13 **Save** 💾 the document.

Activity 2.22 | Deleting Outline Levels

With the levels collapsed in a Word outline, more of the document can be selected and deleted at one time.

1 Press Ctrl + Home to move to the beginning of the document. Select the outline levels *Sandwiches* and *Our Sandwiches*, and then press Del.

2 Select the outline level *Light Entrees*. Hold down Shift, and then select the outline level *Our In-House Bakery*. Press Del to delete the four paragraphs in the outline.

3 **Save** 💾 the document. If your instructor directs you to submit your files electronically, go to Step 5.

4 Display **Backstage** view, click the **Print tab**, and then under **Print**, click the **Print** button.

5 Display **Backstage** view, and then click the **Info tab**. On the right, click **Properties**, and then click **Show Document Panel**. In the **Author** box, type your firstname and lastname, in the **Subject** box, type your course name and section number, and then in the **Keywords** box, type **menu, soups, salads**

6 **Save** 💾 the document, and then **Close** ✖ Word.

Objective 9 | Create a New Presentation from a Modified Word Outline

After you have modified a Word outline, you can create a new PowerPoint presentation from the outline.

Activity 2.23 | Creating a Modified PowerPoint Presentation

1 **Start** PowerPoint. On the **Home tab**, in the **Slides group**, click the **New Slide button arrow**, and then click **Slides from Outline**. Navigate to your **Integrated Projects Chapter 2** folder, click **Lastname_Firstname_2B_Menu_Outline**, and then click **Insert**.

2 Display **Backstage** view, and then click the **Save As tab**. In the **Save As** dialog box, navigate to your **Integrated Project Chapter 2** folder, and then save the presentation with the file name **Lastname_Firstname_2B_Menu_Presentation**

3 Click the **Insert tab**, and then in the **Text group**, click the **Header & Footer** button. In the **Header and Footer** dialog box, click the **Notes and Handouts tab**, and then under **Include on page**, select the **Page number** check box. Select the **Footer** check box, type **Lastname_Firstname_2B_Menu_Presentation** and then click **Apply to All**.

4 Click the **Design tab**, and then in the **Themes group**, click the **More** button ⏷. In the **Themes** gallery, under **Built-In**, in the first row, click the fourth theme—**Apex**.

5 Click **Slide 1**, and then press ⌈Del⌉.

There are seven slides in the presentation.

6 Click **Slide 7**. In the bottom content placeholder, delete the text *When can you visit us?* and then type **For more information about our Soups and Salads** To the right of the second bullet, delete the existing text that begins *For your own*, and then type **Contact Nancy Goldman, our Chief Baker**

7 Select all of the text in the bottom content placeholder. Click the **Home tab**, and then in the **Paragraph group**, click the **Bullets** button ⌈≣ ▾⌉. Click the **Center** button ⌈≣⌉. Click the **Align Text** button ⌈⊟⌉, and then click **Middle**. Compare your screen with Figure 2.37.

Figure 2.37

Bullets button deselected

Text centered and middle-aligned

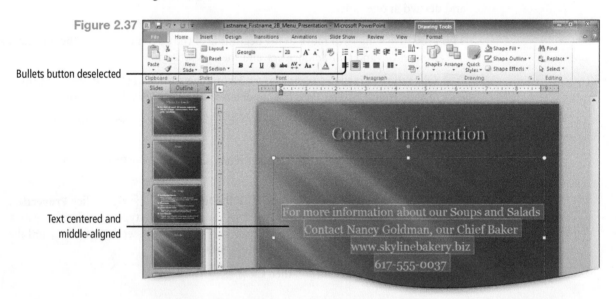

8 Click **Slide 1**, and then click in the bottom content placeholder. On the **Home tab**, in the **Paragraph group**, click the **Bullets** button ⌈≣ ▾⌉, and then click the **Center** button ⌈≣⌉.

9 Click **Slide 3**—*Soups*, hold down ⌈Ctrl⌉, click **Slide 5**—*Salads*, and then press ⌈Del⌉.

There are five slides in your presentation.

10 Click the **Slide Show tab**, and then in the **Start Slide Show group**, click the **From Beginning** button. View your presentation.

11 Click the **Review tab**, and then in the **Proofing group**, click the **Spelling** button. Check the spelling of the presentation and correct any misspelled words.

12 **Save** 🖫 the presentation. If your instructor directs you to submit your files electronically, go to Step 14.

13 Display **Backstage** view, and then click the **Print tab**. Under **Settings**, be sure **Print All Slides** displays. Click **Full Page Slides**, and then under **Handouts**, click **6 Slides Horizontal**. Under **Print**, click the **Print** button.

14 Display **Backstage** view, and then click the **Info tab**. On the right, click **Properties**, and then click **Show Document Panel**. In the **Author** box, type your firstname and lastname, in the **Subject** box, type your course name and section number, and then in the **Keywords** box, type **soups, salads, presentation**

15 **Save** 🖫 the presentation, and then **Close** ⌧ PowerPoint.

16 Submit your printed or electronic files as directed by your instructor.

End **You have completed Project 2B** ————————————————

Content Based Assessments

Summary

You can create and modify the text in a Word outline, and then import the outline into PowerPoint. You can customize a PowerPoint presentation by inserting and deleting slides, changing text formats, and modifying the theme. Insert SmartArt graphics, pictures, and shapes to add interest to the presentation. You can save a PowerPoint presentation as an outline in Rich Text Format. The RTF outline can be modified in Word.

Key Terms

Black slide

Character spacing

Minus outline symbol

Normal view

Notes Page view

Notes pane

Outline view

Outline symbol

Placeholder

Plus outline symbol

Rich Text Format (RTF)

Slide pane

Slide Show view

Slides/Outline pane

Speaker's notes

SmartArt

Status bar

Text Pane

Theme

View buttons

Zooming

Matching

Match each term in the second column with its correct definition in the first column by writing the letter of the term on the blank line in front of the correct definition.

_____ 1. A document view that shows headings and subheadings, which can be expanded or collapsed.

_____ 2. The action of increasing or decreasing the viewing area on the screen.

_____ 3. A formatting mark that indicates there are subordinate heading or body text paragraphs.

_____ 4. A formatting mark that indicates there are no subordinate heading or body text paragraphs.

_____ 5. The primary editing view in PowerPoint where you write and design your presentation.

_____ 6. A PowerPoint screen element that displays a large image of the active slide.

_____ 7. A set of commands that control the look of the presentation window.

_____ 8. A slide element that reserves a portion of a slide and serves as a container for text, graphics, and other slide elements.

_____ 9. A predefined set of colors, fonts, lines, and fill effects that are professionally designed.

_____ 10. A view where you can work with notes in a full page format.

_____ 11. A view where slides fill the computer screen, which enables you to view the presentation the way your audience will see it.

_____ 12. A slide that displays at the end of a PowerPoint presentation indicating that the slide show is over.

A Black slide

B Character spacing

C Minus outline symbol

D Normal view

E Notes Page view

F Outline view

G Placeholder

H Plus outline symbol

I RTF

J Slide pane

K Slide Show view

L SmartArt

M Theme

N View buttons

O Zooming

Content Based Assessments

_____ 13. An Office feature that allows you to increase or decrease the space between characters.

_____ 14. A designer-quality representation of your information that you can create by choosing from many different layouts to effectively communicate your message or ideas.

_____ 15. A universal document format that can be read by nearly all word processing programs and that retains most text and paragraph formatting.

Multiple Choice

Circle the correct answer.

1. A small gray circle that identifies heading and body text paragraphs in an outline is called:
   A. a bullet   **B.** a level indicator   **C.** an outline symbol

2. A PowerPoint screen element that displays either the presentation outline or all of the slides in the form of thumbnails is called the:
   A. Slide Sorter   **B.** Slides/Outline pane   **C.** Slide pane

3. A PowerPoint element that displays below the Slide pane and allows you to type notes regarding the active slide is the:
   A. Message pane   **B.** Notes pane   **C.** Notes placeholder

4. A horizontal bar at the bottom of the presentation window that displays the current slide number, number of slides in a presentation, the applied theme, and other elements is called the:
   A. status bar   **B.** Taskbar   **C.** Slides pane

5. In an outline, a paragraph that is assigned Level 1:
   A. has been demoted   **B.** is designated as the highest outline level   **C.** is a subordinate paragraph

6. In the Themes gallery, built-in themes are arranged:
   A. in alphabetical order   **B.** by color   **C.** in order of use

7. Notes that are printed for the speaker to refer to as a presentation is being delivered are called:
   A. a speaker's handout   **B.** presentation notes   **C.** speaker's notes

8. When a shape is selected, you can automatically copy the shape in the same area of a slide by pressing:
   A. Alt + C   **B.** Alt + D   **C.** Ctrl + D

9. A SmartArt element where text that displays in the graphic can be entered and edited is the:
   A. Text Pane   **B.** SmartArt dialog box   **C.** SmartArt Design tab

10. RTF is another term for:
    A. Real Text Format   **B.** Rich Text Format   **C.** Rich Type Format

Apply 2A skills from these Objectives:

1. Create an Outline in Word
2. Import a Word Outline into a PowerPoint Presentation
3. Modify a PowerPoint Presentation
4. Create a Footer and Save a PowerPoint Presentation
5. Preview and Print a Presentation, Slide Handouts, and Speaker Notes

Skills Review | Project **2C Franchisee Advantages**

In the following Skills Review, you will create a PowerPoint presentation from a Word outline to explain the advantages of becoming a Skyline Bakery and Café franchisee. Your completed files will look similar to Figure 2.38.

Project Files

For Project 2C, you will need the following files:

New blank PowerPoint presentation
i02C_Advantages_Outline

You will save your files as:

Lastname_Firstname_2C_Advantages_Outline
Lastname_Firstname_2C_Advantages_Presentation

Project Result

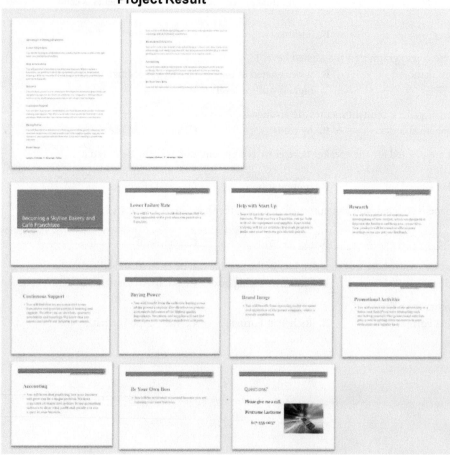

Integrating Word and PowerPoint

1. **Start** Word, and then from your data files, open the document **i02C_Advantages_Outline**. **Save** the document in your **Integrated Projects Chapter 2** folder with the file name **Lastname_Firstname_2C_Advantages_Outline** Insert the file name in the footer.

   a. On the **View tab**, in the **Document Views group**, click the **Outline** button to display the document in Outline view.

   b. Press Ctrl + Home

   c. Select the first paragraph—*Advantages of Buying a Franchise*. On the **Outlining tab**, in the **Outline Tools group**, click the **Promote to Heading 1** button. Use the **Promote to Heading 1** button to promote the following paragraphs: *Lower Failure Rate, Help with Start Up, Continuous Support, Buying Power, Brand Image, Promotional Activities, Accounting, Research, and Be Your Own Boss.*

   d. Below the paragraph *Lower Failure Rate*, select the paragraph that begins *You will*, and then in the **Outline Tools group**, click the **Demote** button. Select and **Demote** each of the following eight paragraphs that begin with *You will*.

2. To the left of the paragraph *Research*, click the **plus outline symbol** to select the heading and the related subtopics.

   a. On the **Outlining tab**, in the **Outline Tools group**, click the **Collapse** button.

   b. To the left of the paragraph *Research*, point to the **plus outline symbol**, hold down the left mouse button, drag up until the black horizontal line is above the paragraph *Continuous Support*, and then release the mouse button.

   c. With the paragraph *Research* selected, in the **Outline Tools group**, click the **Expand** button to display the sublevel.

   d. On the **Outlining tab**, in the **Close group**, click the **Close Outline View** button.

   e. Display **Backstage** view, click **Properties**, and then click **Show Document Panel**. In the **Author** box, type your firstname and lastname, in the **Subject** box, type your course name, and section number, and then in the **Keywords** box, type **franchise outline** Save your document, and then **Close** Word.

3. **Start** PowerPoint. On the **Home tab**, in the **Slides group**, click the **New Slide button arrow**, and then click **Slides from Outline**.

   a. Navigate to your **Integrated Projects Chapter 2** folder, select the document **Lastname_Firstname_2C_Advantages_Outline**, and then click **Insert**.

   b. From **Backstage** view, display the **Save As** dialog box, navigate to your **Integrated Projects Chapter 2** folder, and then **Save** the PowerPoint presentation as **Lastname_Firstname_2C_Advantages_Presentation**

4. In the **Slides/Outlines pane**, click **Slide 1** to make it the active slide. In the title placeholder, type **Becoming a Skyline Bakery and Café Franchisee**

a. Click **Slide 2**—*Advantages of Buying a Franchise*, and then press Delete

b. In the **Slides/Outline pane**, scroll down and click **Slide 10**—*Be Your Own Boss*. On the **Home tab**, in the **Slides group**, click the **New Slide** button.

c. On **Slide 11**, click the title placeholder, and then type **Questions?** Click the lower placeholder, and then type **Please give me a call**. Press Enter, and then using your first name and last name, type **Firstname Lastname** Press Enter, and then type **617-555-0037**

d. On **Slide 11**, select the three lines of bulleted text. In the **Paragraph group**, click the **Bullets button arrow**, and then click **None**. In the **Paragraph group**, click the **Center** button. In the **Paragraph group**, click the **Line Spacing** button, and then click **2.0**.

5. Be sure **Slide 11** is the active slide. On the **Home tab**, in the **Slides group**, click the **Layout** button, and then click **Two Content**.

a. In the right placeholder, click the **Insert Clip Art** button.

b. In the **Clip Art** task pane, click in the **Search for** box, and then replace any existing text with **cell phone, calls**

c. In the **Results should be** box, verify **All media file types** is selected, and that the **Include Office.com content** check box is selected. Click the **Go** button.

d. In the first row, click the second image as shown in Figure 2.38. **Close** the **Clip Art** task pane.

e. On the **Design tab**, in the **Themes group**, click the **More** button. Under **Built-In**, in the fourth row, click the second theme—**Urban**. In the **Themes group**, click the **Colors** button, and then click **Executive**.

6. In the **Slides/Outline pane**, scroll up and click **Slide 1**. Click in the subtitle placeholder, and then type **Advantages** Click **Slide 3**—*Help with Start Up*.

a. Below the slide, click in the **Notes pane**, and then type **Mention that the five-week program will focus on counter service, food preparation, food ordering, and managing the business.**

b. In the **Notes pane**, select the text. On the Mini toolbar, click the **Font Size button arrow**, and then click **28**.

c. Click the **Insert tab**, and then in the **Text group**, click the **Header & Footer** button.

d. In the **Header and Footer** dialog box, on the **Notes and Handouts tab**, select the **Footer** check box, and then in the **Footer** box, type **Lastname Firstname 2C Advantages Presentation** Click the **Apply to All** button.

e. Display **Backstage** view, click **Properties**, and then click **Show Document Panel**. In the **Author** box, type your firstname and lastname, in the **Subject** box, type your course name and section number, and then in the Keywords box, **type promotion, advantages**

f. **Save** the presentation, and then **Close** PowerPoint. Submit your printed or electronic files as directed by your instructor.

You have completed Project 2C

Integrating Word and PowerPoint

Apply 2B skills from these Objectives:

6. Create a PowerPoint Presentation with a Template
7. Save a Presentation as an Outline/RTF File
8. Modify a Word Document in Outline View
9. Create a New Presentation from a Modified Word Outline

In the following Skills Review, you will create two PowerPoint presentations—one based on a template and the other using an imported Word outline—to promote the products sold at Skyline Bakery and Café. Your completed files will look similar to Figure 2.39.

Project Files

For Project 2D, you will need the following files:

New blank PowerPoint presentation
i02D_Bakery_Template
i02D_Dessert1
i02D_Dessert2
i02D_Dessert3
i02D_Bakery_Logo

You will save your files as:

Lastname_Firstname_2D_Bakery_Products
Lastname_Firstname_2D_Product_Outline
Lastname_Firstname_2D_Specialty_Presentation

Project Results

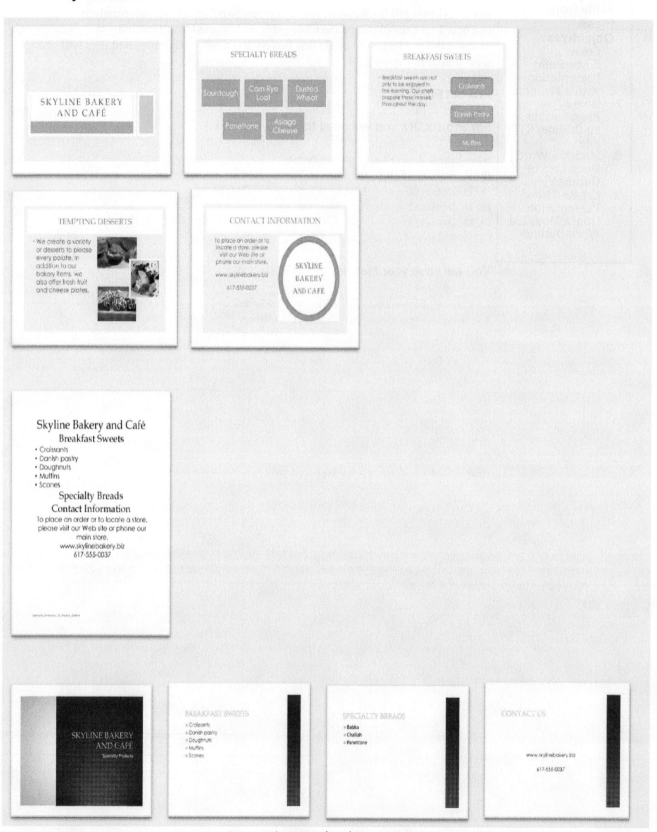

Figure 2.39 Integrating Word and PowerPoint

1. **Templates and Themes**, in the first row, click **New from Existing**. In the **New from existing Presentation** dialog box, navigate to your data files, select **i02D_Bakery_Template**, and then click **Create New**. **Save** the presentation in your **Integrated Projects Chapter 2** folder with the file name **Lastname_Firstname_2D_Bakery_Products**

   a. On the **Insert tab**, in the **Text group**, click the **Header & Footer** button. In the **Header and Footer** dialog box, click the **Notes and Handouts tab**. Select the **Footer** check box, type **Lastname_Firstname_2D_Bakery Products** and then click the **Apply to All** button.

   b. Click the **Design tab**, and then in the **Themes group**, click the **More** button. In the **Themes** gallery, under **Built-In**, in the first row, click the fifth theme—**Apothecary**.

   c. On **Slide 1**, in the title placeholder, delete the existing text, and then type **Skyline Bakery and Caf** Insert the symbol é to complete the name of the bakery.

   d. Select the title. On the **Home tab**, in the **Font group**, click the **Character Spacing** button, and then click **Very Loose**.

2. Click **Slide 2**. In the title placeholder, delete the text, and then type **Specialty Breads**

   a. In the content placeholder, in the **SmartArt** graphic, click in the first text box.

   b. In the **SmartArt Tools**, click the **Design tab**. In the **Layouts group**, click the **More** button, and then in the first row, click the first layout—**Basic Block List**. If the text pane does not display, on the Design tab, in the Create Graphic group, click the Text Pane button.

   c. In the **Text Pane**, With the insertion point to the right of the first bullet, type **Sourdough** Click to the right of the second bullet, and then type **Corn Rye Loaf** In a similar manner, in the third line, type **Dusted Wheat** in the fourth line, type **Panettone** and then in the fifth line, type **Asiago Cheese**

   d. In the **Create Graphic group**, click the **Text Pane** button to close the Text Pane.

   e. In the **Slides/Outline pane**, right-click **Slide 3**, and then on the shortcut menu, click **Delete Slide**. **Save** the presentation.

3. On **Slide 3**, in the title placeholder, type **Breakfast Sweets** In the left content placeholder, type **Breakfast sweets are not only to be enjoyed in the morning. Our chefs prepare these morsels throughout the day.**

   a. On the right side of the slide, click the top shape—*Star*. Hold down Ctrl, and then click each of the other two shapes. Press Delete to delete the three shapes. Click the **Insert tab**. In the **Illustrations group**, click the **Shapes** button, and then under **Basic Shapes**, in the first row, click the sixth shape—**Rounded Rectangle**. On the right side of the slide, below the title, click one time to insert the shape.

   b. With the shape selected, on the **Format tab**, in the **Size group**, click the **Shape Width box**, type **3** and then press Enter. Drag the shape to the left so the top middle sizing handle displays at approximately **2.5 inches on the right side of the horizontal ruler** and at **2.5 inches on the upper portion of the vertical ruler**.

Integrating Word and PowerPoint

c. With the shape selected, press `Ctrl` + `D`. Drag the selected shape down until the bottom middle sizing handle displays at **approximately 2. 5 inches on the right side of the horizontal ruler and at approximately 3 inches on the lower portion of the vertical ruler.**

d. Press `Ctrl` + `D`. Drag the selected shape up until the top middle siding handle displays at **approximately 2.5 inches on the right side of the horizontal ruler** and the shape is approximately in the middle of the other two rectangles.

e. Click the top rectangle, hold down `Ctrl`, and then click the other two shapes. On the **Format tab**, in the **Arrange group**, click the **Align** button, and then click **Align Left**. Click the **Align** button, and then click **Distribute Vertically**.

f. Click in the title placeholder to deselect the three shapes. Click the top shape, and then type **Croissants** Click the middle shape, and then type **Danish Pastry** Click the bottom shape, and then type **Muffins** Select all three shapes. On the **Home tab**, in the **Font group**, click the **Font Size button arrow**, and then click **28**.

4. Click **Slide 4**, and then in the title placeholder, type **Tempting Desserts**

   a. In the left content placeholder, type **We create a variety of desserts to please every palate. In addition to our bakery items, we also offer fresh fruit and cheese plates.**

   b. On the right side of the slide, click the top picture to select it. On the **Format tab**, in the **Adjust group**, click the **Change Picture** button. In the **Insert Picture** dialog box, navigate to your data files, select the file **i02D_Dessert1**, and then click **Insert**.

   c. Click the bottom picture, change the picture to **i02D_Dessert2**. On the **Format tab**, in the **Size group**, click the **Shape Height** box, type **2** and then press `Enter`.

   d. Click the middle picture, and then change the picture to **i02D_Dessert3**. In the **Size group**, click the **Shape Height** box, type **2.3** and then press `Enter`.

5. Click **Slide 5**.In the title placeholder, type **Contact Information** In the left placeholder, delete the existing text, and then type **To place an order or to locate a store, please visit our Web site or phone our main store.** Press `Enter`, and then type **www.skylinebakery.biz** Press `Enter`, and then type **617-555-0037** Right-click anywhere on the text *www.skylinebakery.biz*, and then on the shortcut menu, click **Remove Hyperlink**.

   a. Select all the text in the left placeholder, and then on the **Home tab**, in the **Font group**, click the **Font Size button arrow**, and then click **24**. In the **Paragraph group**, click the **Bullets** button to turn off the bulleted formatting. In the **Paragraph group**, click the **Center** button.

   b. With the text still selected, click the **Line Spacing** button, and then click **Line Spacing Options**. In the **Paragraph** dialog box, under **Spacing**, click the **Before spin box up arrow** and change to **12 pt**. Click the **After spin box up arrow** and change to **12 pt**, and then click **OK**.

   c. In the right content placeholder, delete the existing text, and then in the middle of the placeholder, click the **Insert Picture from File** button. In the **Insert Picture** dialog box, navigate to your data file, select the file **i02D_Bakery_Logo**, and then click **Insert**. **Save** your presentation.

Integrating Word and PowerPoint

d. Click **Slide 1**. Display **Backstage view**, and then click the **Save As tab**. In the **Save As** dialog box, navigate to your **Integrated Projects Chapter 2** folder, and then type the file name **Lastname_Firstname_2D_Product_Outline** Click the **Save as type arrow**, scroll down near the bottom of the list, and then click **Outline/RTF**. Click **Save**.

e. e. Display **Backstage** view, click **Properties**, and then click **Show Document Panel**. In the **Author** box, type your firstname and lastname, in the **Subject** box, type your course name and section number, and then in the **Keywords** box, type **breakfast, dessert**

f. f. **Save** your presentation, and then **Close** PowerPoint.

6. **Start** Word. From **Backstage** view, click **Open**, navigate to your **Integrated Projects Chapter 2** folder, and then open the RTF file **Lastname_Firstname_2D_Product_Outline**. Insert the file name in the footer. Click the **View tab**, and then in the **Document Views group**, click **Outline**.

a. Click the **Home tab**, and then in the **Editing group**, click **Select**, and then click **Select All**. In the **Font group**, click the **Font Color button arrow**, and then click **Automatic**. From **Backstage** view, click the **Convert** button. In the message box, click **OK**.

b. Click the **Outlining tab**. In the **Outline Tools group**, click the **Show Level** arrow, and then click **Level 1**.

c. To the left of **Breakfast Sweets**, click the **plus outline symbol**, and then in the **Outline Tools group**, click the **Expand** button.

d. To the left of the paragraph that begins *Breakfast sweets are not only*, click the **minus outline sign**, and then type **Croissants** Press ⏎, and then type **Danish pastry** Press ⏎, and then type **Doughnuts** Press ⏎, and then type **Muffins** Press ⏎, and then type **Scones**

e. To the left of the paragraph *Breakfast Sweets*, click the **plus outline symbol**. In the **Outline Tools group**, click the **Show Level** arrow, and then click **Level 1**. With *Breakfast Sweets* selected, in the **Outline Tools group**, click the **Move Up** button. Select the outline level *Tempting Desserts*, and then press ⟨Delete⟩. In the **Close group**, click the **Close Outline View** button.

f. Display **Backstage** view, click **Properties**, and then click **Show Document Panel**. In the **Author** box, type your firstname and lastname, in the **Subject** box, type your course name and section number, and then in the **Keywords** box, type **breads, breakfast** Save the document, and then **Close** Word.

7. **Start** PowerPoint. On the **Home tab**, in the **Slides group**, click the **New Slide button arrow**, and then click **Slides from Outline**. Navigate to your **Integrated Projects Chapter 2** folder, click **Lastname_Firstname_2D_Product_Outline**, and then click **Insert**.

a. Display **Backstage** view, click the **Save As tab**, and then **Save** the presentation in your **Integrated Projects Chapter 2** folder with the file name **Lastname_Firstname_2D_Specialty_Products** On the **Insert tab**, in the **Text group**, click the **Header & Footer** button. In the **Header and Footer** dialog box, click the **Notes and Handouts tab**, select the **Footer** check box, type **Lastname_Firstname_2D_Specialty_Presentation** and then click **Apply to All**.

Integrating Word and PowerPoint

b. Click the **Design tab**, and then in the **Themes group**, click the **More** button. In the **Themes** gallery, under **Built-In**, in the third row, click the third theme—**Opulent**.

c. Click **Slide 1**, and then press Delete. With the new Slide 1 selected, click the **Home tab**. In the **Slides group**, click the **Layout** button, and then click **Title Slide**. Click in the subtitle placeholder, and then type **Specialty Products**

d. Click **Slide 3**. Click in the content placeholder, type **Babka** and then press Enter. Type **Challah** press Enter, and then type **Panettone** Click **Slide 4**. In the title placeholder, select the text *Information*, and then type **US** In the left placeholder delete the first paragraph that begins *To place an order*. Select the remaining text. On the **Home tab**, in the **Paragraph group**, click the **Bullets** button, and then click the **Center** button. click the **Line Spacing** button, and then click **2.0**. Click the **Align Text** button, and then click **Middle**.

e. Display **Backstage** view, click **Properties**, and then click **Show Document Panel**. In the **Author** box, type your firstname and lastname, in the **Subject** box, type your course name and section number, and then in the **Keywords** box, type **product outline**

f. **Save** the presentation, and then **Close** PowerPoint. Submit your printed or electronic files as directed by your instructor,

You have completed Project 2D

Apply 2A skills from these Objectives:

1. Create an Outline in Word
2. Import a Word Outline into a PowerPoint Presentation
3. Modify a PowerPoint Presentation
4. Create a Footer and Save a PowerPoint Presentation
5. Preview and Print a Presentation, Slide Handouts, and Speaker Notes

Mastering Integration | Project 2E Advertising Budget

In the following Mastering Integration project, you will create a Word outline for Skyline Bakery and Café promoting an increase in the company advertising budget. You will import the outline into a PowerPoint presentation and make modifications. Your completed files will look similar to Figure 2.47.

Project Files

For Project 2E, you will need the following files:

> New blank PowerPoint presentation
> i02E_Advertising_Budget

You will save your files as:

> Lastname_Firstname_2E_Advertising_Budget
> Lastname_Firstname_2E_Advertising_Presentation

Project Results

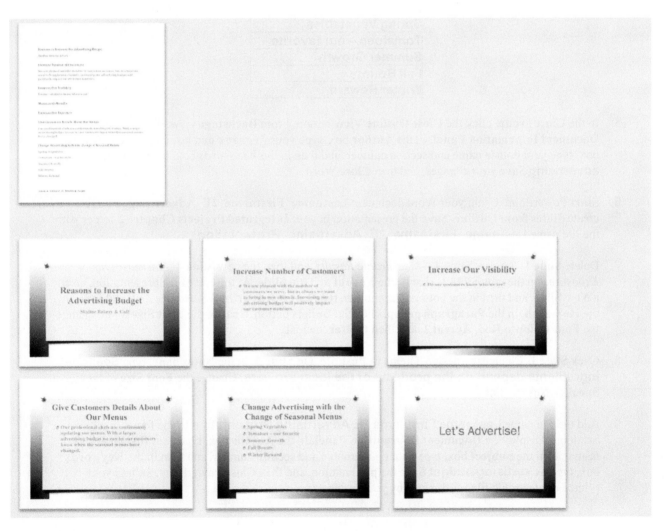

Figure 2.40

Integrating Word and PowerPoint

1. **Start** Word. Locate and open the document **i02E_Advertising_Budget**. **Save** the document in your **Integrated Projects Chapter 2** folder with the file name **Lastname_Firstname_2E_Advertising_Budget** Insert the file name in the footer, and then change to **Outline** view.

2. Change the style of all seven paragraphs to **Level 1**. At the end of the first paragraph, press ⎆, type **Skyline Bakery & Café** and then **Demote** this paragraph to **Level 2**. After the paragraph *Increase Number of Customers*, insert a **Level 2** paragraph, and then type **We are pleased with the number of customers we serve, but as always we want to bring in new clientele. Increasing our advertising budget will positively impact our customer numbers.**

3. After the paragraph *Increase Our Visibility*, insert a **Level 2** paragraph, and then type **Do our customers know who we are?** After the paragraph *Give Customers Details About Our Menus*, insert a **Level 2** paragraph, and then type **Our professional chefs are continuously updating our menus. With a larger advertising budget we can let our customers know when the seasonal menus have changed.**

4. Select the paragraph *Measurable Results*, and then move the paragraph above *Increase Our Exposure*. Move to the end of the document, insert a new paragraph, and then **Demote** the paragraph. Type the following, pressing ⎆ after each item except the last.

Spring Vegetables
Tomatoes – our favorite
Summer Growth
Fall Bounty
Winter Reward

5. In the **Close group**, click the **Close Outline View** button. From **Backstage** view, display the **Document Information Panel**. In the **Author** box, type your firstname and lastname, in the **Subject** box, type your course name and section number, and then in the **Keywords** box, type **outline, advertising** Save your changes, and then **Close** Word.

6. **Start** PowerPoint. Using your Word document **Lastname_Firstname_2E_Advertising_Budget**, create **Slides from Outline**. **Save** the presentation in your **Integrated Projects Chapter 2** folder with the file name **Lastname_Firstname_2E_Advertising_Presentation**

7. Delete **Slide 1**, the new **Slide 4**—*Measurable Results*, and then the new **Slide 4**—*Increase Our Exposure*. On the new **Slide 1**, change the **Layout** to **Title Slide**. At the end of the presentation, insert a **New Slide**, and then in the bottom placeholder, type **Let's Advertise!** Select the text, and then on the **Home tab**, in the **Paragraph group**, click the **Bullets** button. Change the **Font Size** to **60**, change the **Font Color** to **Red, Accent 2**, and then **Center** the text.

8. Click **Slide 1**. Change the design **Theme** to **Pushpin**. On **Slide 5**, in the **Notes pane**, type **Seasonal ingredients depend on the products of the local growers.** Change the **Font Size** of the **Speaker Note** to **28**.

9. Add the file name **Lastname Firstname 2E Advertising Presentation** to the footer in all handouts. Display the **Document Information Panel**. In the **Author** box, type your firstname and lastname, in the **Subject** box, type your course name and section number, and then in the **Keywords** box, type **advertising budget** Save the presentation, and then **Close** PowerPoint. Submit your printed or electronic files as directed by your instructor.

You have completed Project 2E

Integrating Word and PowerPoint

Apply 2B skills from these Objectives:

1. Create a PowerPoint Presentation with a Template
2. Save a Presentation as an Outline/RTF File
3. Modify a Word Document in Outline View
4. Create a New Presentation from a Modified Word Outline

In the following Mastering Integration project, you will create a PowerPoint presentation from a template to persuade the management of Skyline Bakery and Café to upgrade the equipment so that the products can be sold in local health food stores. You will create an outline based on the presentation, make modifications in Word, and then import the outline into PowerPoint to create a second version of the presentation. Your completed files will look similar to Figure 2.41.

Project Files

For Project 2F, you will need the following files:

New blank PowerPoint presentation
i02F_Equipment_Template
i02F_Breads
i02F_Muffins
i02F_Kitchen

You will save your files as:

Lastname_Firstname_2F_Equipment_Presentation
Lastname_Firstname_2F_Equipment_Outline
Lastname_Firstname_2F_Store_Presentation

Integrating Word and PowerPoint

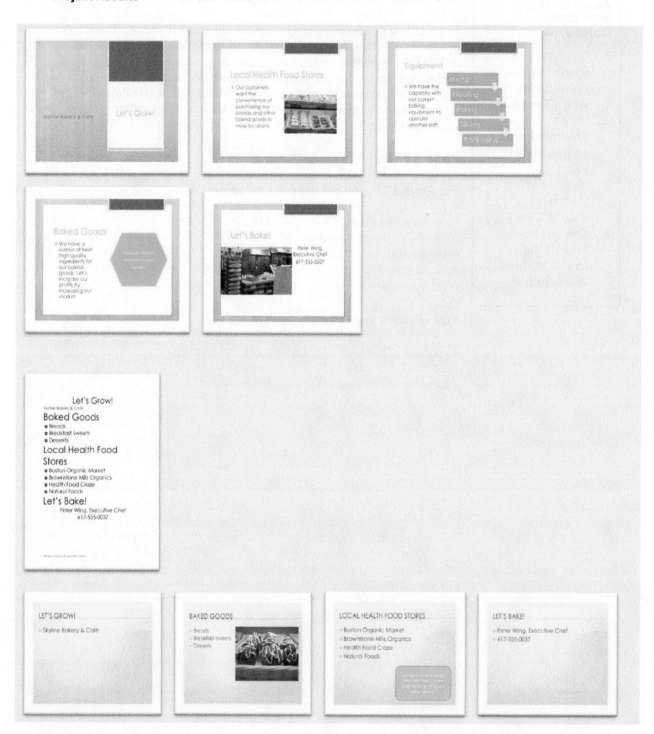

Figure 2.41

Integrating Word and PowerPoint

Rubric

The following outcomes-based assessments are open-ended assessments. That is, there is no specific correct result; your result will depend on your approach to the information provided. Make Professional Quality your goal. Use the following scoring rubric to guide you in how to approach the problem and then to evaluate how well your approach solves the problem.

The *criteria*—Software Mastery, Content, Format and Layout, and Process—represent the knowledge and skills you have gained that you can apply to solving the problem. The *levels of performance*—Professional Quality, Approaching Professional Quality, or Needs Quality Improvements—help you and your instructor evaluate your result.

	Your completed project is of Professional Quality	Your completed project is of Approaching Professional Quality	Your completed project Needs Quality Improvements if you:
1-Software Mastery	Chooses and applies the most appropriate skills, tools, and features and identifies efficient methods to solve the problem.	Chooses and applies some appropriate skills, tools, and features, but not in the most efficient manner.	Chooses inappropriate skills, tools, or features, or is inefficient in solving the problem.
2-Content	Constructs a solution that is clear and well organized, containing content that is accurate, appropriate to the audience and purpose, and complete. The solution contains no errors of spelling, grammar, or style.	Constructs a solution in which some components are unclear, poorly organized, inconsistent, or incomplete. May misjudge the needs of the audience. May contain some errors in spelling, grammar, or style, but the errors do not detract from comprehension.	Constructs a solution that is unclear, incomplete, or poorly organized, containing some inaccurate or inappropriate content. May contain many errors of spelling, grammar, or style. May fail to solve the problem.
3-Format and Layout	Formats and arranges all elements to communicate information and ideas, clarify function, illustrate relationships, and indicate relative importance.	Applies appropriate format and layout features to some elements, but not others. Or, overuses features, causing minor distraction.	Applies format and layout that fails to communicate information or ideas or clearly. May fail to use format and layout features to clarify function, illustrate relationships, or indicate relative importance. Or, may use available features excessively, causing distraction.
4-Process	Uses an organized approach that integrates planning, development, self-assessment, revision, and reflection.	Demonstrates an organized approach in some areas, but not others. Or, uses an insufficient process of organization throughout.	Does not use an organized approach to solve the problem.

Integrating Word and PowerPoint

<table>
<tr><td>

Apply a combination of the 2A and 2B skills.

</td><td>

GO! Think | **Project 2G Bagels Menu**

Project Files

For Project 2G, you will need the following files:

</td></tr>
</table>

New blank PowerPoint presentation
i02G_Bagels_Menu
i02G_Bagels

You will save your files as:

Lastname_Firstname_2G_Bagels_Menu
Lastname_Firstname_2G_Bagels_Presentation

Nancy Goldman, the Chief Baker for the Skyline Bakery and Café, wants to add bagels to the menu. She has asked you to complete a Word document listing the reasons why bagels would be a good addition to the menu. When the document is completed, she wants you to create a PowerPoint presentation to present to the management team. Ms. Goldman has indicated bagel varieties would include sesame see d, poppy seed, cinnamon raisin, blueberry, caraway, pumpernickel, and cheddar cheese.

In the Word document, promote or demote paragraphs and move at least one level to a different location so that the items display in a more logical order. Save the file as **Lastname_Firstname_2G_Bagels_Menu** Import the Word document into PowerPoint. Modify the presentation by inserting or deleting slides, applying a different theme, changing the slide layout, adding character spacing, adding text shadow, inserting and modifying at least one SmartArt graphic, and inserting the picture i02G_Bagels. Add speaker notes to at least two slides. Save the presentation as **Lastname_Firstname_2G_Bagels_Presentaton** In both files, insert the file name in the footer and add appropriate information to the Document Panel. Submit both files as directed.

You have completed Project 2G

Integrating Word and PowerPoint

<table>
<tr><td>

Apply a combination of the 2A and 2B skills.

</td><td>

Project Files

</td></tr>
</table>

For Project 2H, you will need the following files:

New blank PowerPoint presentation
i02H_Staff_Orientation

You will save your files as:

Lastname_Firstname_2H_Staff_Orientation
Lastname_Firstname_2H_Orientation_Presentation

Because the company is growing and adding more staff, Lucinda dePaolo—the CFO for Skyline Bakery and Café—wants all staff orientations to be more consistent than they have been in the past. She has started a list of topics to be covered. Ms. dePaolo has asked you to complete the list and create a PowerPoint presentation. She also wants you to include a new profit-sharing benefit—five percent of net profits will now be shared with all employees.

Open the Word document i02H_Staff_Orientation. Promote, demote, and move items so that the items display in a more logical order. Save the file as **Lastname_Firstname_2H_Staff_Orientation** Import the Word document into PowerPoint. Modify the presentation by inserting or deleting slides, applying a theme, changing the slide layout, applying character spacing, applying text shadow, and inserting and modifying at least one SmartArt graphic or shape. Add speaker notes to at least two slides. Save the presentation as **Lastname_Firstname_2H_Orientation_Presentation** In both files, insert the file name in the footer and add appropriate document properties. Submit both files as directed.

You have completed Project 2H

Integrating Word and PowerPoint

Apply a combination of the 2A and 2B skills.

For Project 2I, you will need the following files:

New blank PowerPoint presentation
i02I_Pet_Template
i02I_Dog_Treats

You will save your files as:

Lastname_Firstname_2I_Pet_Presentation
Lastname_Firstname_2I_Pet_Outline
Lastname_Firstname_21_Dog_Products

Peter Wing, the Executive Chef of Skyline Bakery and Café, has learned that people are willing to spend extra dollars on their pets. After researching pet treats, he has discovered that the company could produce dog biscuits and treats. He wants to propose to management that they support a dog food line for the family pets. He has asked you to create a new name for the product line and create a PowerPoint presentation that includes the following information. Dog treats will:

Be made with the highest quality bakery ingredients
Be made with all natural flavors
Contain no animal by-products
Contain no artificial preservatives or artificial colors
Be produced in large and small animal shapes

Create a new presentation from the i02_Pet_Template data file. Include the new dog food line name on the title slide, add appropriate text, modify the SmartArt graphic, and insert the picture i02I_Dog_Treats. Delete any unnecessary slides, text, or objects. Save the file as **Lastname_Firstname_2I_Pet_Presentation** Insert the file name in the footer and add appropriate information to the Document Panel. Save the presentation in the Rich Text Format as **Lastname_Firstname_2I_Pet_Outline** Open the document in Word, and then convert it to a Word document. Insert the file name in the footer and add appropriate information to the Document Panel. Add a new Level 1 item Product Categories. Below this paragraph, add several items, such as Gift Baskets, Holiday Specials, Monthly Deliveries, Samplers, and Celebration Cakes. Delete any unnecessary paragraphs. Import the Word document into a PowerPoint presentation. In the presentation change the theme and make any other modifications to create a professional appearance. Add speaker notes to at least two slides. Save the presentation as **Lastname_Firstname_2I_Dog_Products** Insert the file name in the footer and add document properties. Submit the two PowerPoint presentations and the Word document as directed.

You have completed Project 2I

Integrating Word and Access

OUTCOMES
At the end of this chapter you will be able to:

OBJECTIVES
Mastering these objectives will enable you to:

PROJECT 3A
Create an Access database from a template and export Access data to Word.

1. Create an Access Database Using a Template
2. Use an Access Form to Enter and Edit Records
3. Export an Access Table to a Word Document
4. Format a Word Document

PROJECT 3B
Use Mail Merge to generate letters and envelopes.

5. Use Mail Merge in Word to Complete Letters Using Access Data
6. Use Mail Merge in Word to Create Envelopes Using Access Data
7. Create and Modify a Query in Access
8. Use Mail Merge in Access

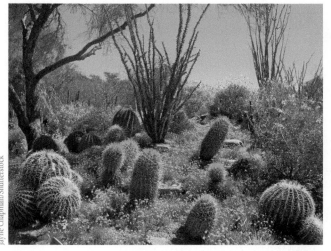

Jayne Chapman/Shutterstock

In This Chapter

In this chapter, you will create an Access database using a template. Access provides a variety of installed templates, or you can go online and download a wide range of templates to suit your needs. In Access, you can enter data in a table or form. You can also create a query or report to display specific data from the table. You can export data to a Word document in a variety of ways. For example, a database may contain contact information—such as names and addresses of customers. Using the Mail Merge feature in Word, you can create personalized letters and envelopes.

The projects in this chapter relate to **Southwest Gardens**, a television show produced by Media Southwest Productions. The southwest style of gardening is popular in many areas of the country, not just in the yards and gardens of Arizona and New Mexico. The stylish simplicity and use of indigenous, hardy plants that are traditional in the southwest United States make for beautiful, environmentally friendly gardens in any part of the country. The show, which is broadcast nationwide, and its Web site provide tips and tricks for beautiful gardens and highlight new tools and techniques. The show's hosts present tours of public and private gardens that showcase the southwest style.

From Chapter 3 of *GO! with Microsoft® Office 2010 Integrated Projects Comprehensive*, First Edition, Shelley Gaskin, Carol L. Martin.
Copyright © 2012 by Pearson Education, Inc. Published by Pearson Prentice Hall. All rights reserved.

Project 3A Walks List

In Activities 3.01 through 3.11, you will create a list of gardeners who tend gardens that Southwest Gardens want to feature on their Garden Walks section of the show. You will enter and update the gardeners' contact information using an Access table and an Access form. You will export the table to a Rich Text Format (RTF) file, and then open the file in Word. You will modify the Word document by using the Page Layout features, adding borders, and inserting and modifying a text box. Your completed documents will look similar to Figure 3.1.

Project Files

For Project 3A, you will need the following files:

> New blank Access database
> i03A_Garden_Walk

You will save your files as:

> Lastname_Firstname_3A_Garden_Contacts
> Lastname_Firstname_3A_Gardeners
> Lastname_Firstname_3A_Garden_Walk

Project Results

Figure 3.1
Project 3A Walks List

Objective 1 | Create an Access Database Using a Template

An Access **database** is an organized collection of facts about people, events, things, or ideas related to a particular topic or purpose. You can use a **template** to create a database or begin with a new blank database. An Access template is a preformatted database designed for a specific purpose. A wide variety of templates are provided when Access is installed. Additional templates can be downloaded from the Internet. A template contains the tables, queries, forms, and reports needed to perform a specific task.

Activity 3.01 | Creating a Database Using a Template

In this activity, you will create an Access database using a template.

1 **Start** Access. Under **Available Templates**, click **Sample templates**. If necessary, scroll down to locate and then click **Students**. Compare your screen with Figure 3.2.

> Sample templates are stored on your computer; they are included with the Access program.

Figure 3.2

Students template selected

2 On the right side of the screen, to the right of the **File Name** box, click the **Browse** button. In the **File New Database** dialog box, navigate to the location where you are saving your files for this chapter, click the **New folder** button, type **Integrated Projects Chapter 3** and then press Enter. Notice that *Students* displays as the default file name.

3 In the **File Name** box, replace the existing text with **Lastname_Firstname_3A_Garden_Contacts** and then click **OK**.

> On the right, the name of your database displays in the File Name box, and the drive and folder where the database is stored displays under the File Name box. An Access database has the file extension *.aacdb*.

4 Under the **File Name** box, click the **Create** button to create the new database.

> Access creates a new database and opens a form *object* named Student List. Objects are the basic parts of a database that you create to store your data and to work with your data; for example, *tables*, forms, queries, and reports. A table is the Access object that stores data organized in an arrangement of columns and rows, and which is the foundation of an Access database.

5 Directly below the Ribbon, on the **Message Bar**, check to see if a Security Warning displays. Compare your screen with Figure 3.3. If the Security Warning does not display, go to Step 7.

> When you open an Access file, you may see a Security Warning in the *Message Bar*. The Message Bar is the area directly below the Ribbon that displays information such as security alerts when there is potentially unsafe, active content in an Office 2010 document that you open. All databases provided by Microsoft and the student Access files that accompany this textbook are safe to use on your computer.

Figure 3.3

Message Bar – Security Warning

Enable Content button

Student List form object

6 On the **Message Bar**, click the **Enable Content** button.

7 Right-click the **Student List form tab**, and then on the shortcut menu, click **Close**.

8 If necessary, on the left side of the window, click the **Open** button ⟩⟩ to expand the **Navigation Pane**.

> The *Navigation Pane* is the area of the Access window that displays and organizes the names of the objects in a database. From the Navigation Pane, you can open objects for use.

9 In the **Navigation Pane**, click the **Students Navigation arrow** ⊙, and then click **Object Type**.

> The objects listed in the Navigation Pane indicate that the Students template includes a number of objects for you.

10 In the **Navigation Pane**, under **Tables**, right-click **Guardians**, and then on the shortcut menu, click **Delete**. In the message box asking if you want to delete the table *Guardians*, click **Yes**, and then in the next message box asking if you want to delete the relationships now, click **Yes**.

> The Guardian table and its relationship to other objects in the database are deleted. In this project, you will not use any of the existing objects displayed under Queries, Forms, or Reports.

11 Under **Tables**, right-click **Students**, and then on the shortcut menu, click **Rename**. Type the new table name **Lastname Firstname 3A Gardeners** and then press Enter. Double-click the new table name **Lastname Firstname 3A Gardeners** to open the table, and then compare your screen with Figure 3.4.

The Lastname Firstname 3A Gardeners table displays in *Datasheet view*—the Access view that displays data organized in columns and rows similar to an Excel worksheet. In a table object, each row is a *record*—all of the categories of data pertaining to one person, place, thing, event, or idea. Each column is a *field*—a single piece of information that is stored in every record.

Figure 3.4

12 On the **Home tab**, in the **Views group**, click the **View button arrow**, and then click **Design View**. Compare your screen with Figure 3.5.

The table opens in *Design view*—an Access view that displays the detailed structure of a table, query, form, or report; and the view in which some tasks must be performed. The first field name—ID— is the *primary key* in this table, noted with a key in the row selector box. A primary key is a field that uniquely identifies a record in a table. A *data type* is the characteristic that defines the kind of data that can be entered into a field, such as numbers, text, or dates. The ID field has the data type **AutoNumber**—an Access feature that creates a unique number for each record.

Figure 3.5

Project 3A: Walks List | **Integrated Projects**

119

13 To the left of the **E-mail Address** field, click the small gray square—the row selector box. Hold down Shift, point to the row selector box until the → pointer displays, hold down the left mouse button, and then drag down to select all the fields beginning with **E-mail Address**, and ending with **Business Phone**. With all eight fields selected, on the **Design tab**, in the **Tools group**, click the **Delete Rows** button. In the message box, click **Yes** to delete the rows. In a similar manner, delete the fields **Mobile Phone** and **Fax Number**, and then beginning with **Country/Region**, delete the last 12 fields in the table.

> Your table should have nine fields beginning with ID and ending with ZIP/Postal Code.

14 Click the **State/Province** field name, and then delete the text **/Province**. Click the **ZIP/Postal Code** field name, and then delete **/Postal Code**.

15 Click the row selector box for the **Home Phone** field. Point to the row selector box, hold down the left mouse button, and then drag the field down below the **ZIP** field name. In the same manner, drag the **Company** field below the **Home Phone** field. On the Quick Access Toolbar, click **Save** 🖫.

16 On the **Design tab**, in the **Views group**, click the **View** button to display the table in Datasheet view.

Activity 3.02 | Adding Records to a Table

A new database is not useful until you have **populated** it by entering data in the **cells** of a table. To populate the database means to fill the table with records. Recall that a cell is the intersection of a row and column in a table.

1 Click the **Close** button ≪ to close the **Navigation Pane**. Right-click the **Company** name field, and then on the shortcut menu, click **Hide Fields**. **Save** 🖫 the table.

> **Another Way**
> Press Enter to move to the next field.

2 In the first record, below **Last Name**, click in the cell, and then type **Balentine** Press Tab, in the **First Name** cell, type **Alejandra** and then press Tab. In the **Address** cell, type **2409 W Voltaire Ave** press Tab, in the **City** cell, type **Phoenix** and then press Tab. In the **State** cell, type **AZ** press Tab, in the **ZIP** cell, type **85016** press Tab and then in the **Home Phone** cell type **480-555-0185** Press Tab two times and then compare your screen with Figure 3.6.

> Pressing Tab two times moves you to the next row—the next record. As soon as you move to the next row, the record for the first gardener is saved in the Lastname Firstname 3A Gardeners table.

Figure 3.6

First record entered ⟶

Active cell in second row ⟶

3 Press Tab to move to the **Last Name** field.

> You can skip the ID field because it is an AutoNumber field.

4 Using the technique you just practiced, enter the contact information for two additional gardeners.

Last Name	First Name	Address	City	State	ZIP	Home Phone
Delgado	Anita	4221 E Ray Rd	Scottsdale	AZ	85255	480-555-5832
Fisler	Maricela	3438 E Tonto Ln	Mesa	AZ	85208	480-555-5332

Note | Correct Typing Errors

Correct typing errors by using the techniques you have practiced in other Office applications. For example, use
Backspace to remove characters to the left, Del to remove characters to the right, or select the text you want to
replace and type the correct information. Press Esc to exit out of a record that has not been completely entered.

---

5 Right-click the **Lastname Firstname 3A Gardeners table tab**, and then on the shortcut menu, click **Close** to close the table.

Objective 2 | Use an Access Form to Enter and Edit Records

An Access *form* is a database object used to enter data, edit data, or display data from a table or *query*. A query is a database object that retrieves specific data from one or more database objects—either tables or other queries—and then, in a single datasheet, displays only the data you specify. Most forms are *bound*—a term used to describe objects and controls that are based on data stored in one or more tables or queries in the database. Although a form is based on a table or query, it does not need to include all of the fields in the underlying objects.

Activity 3.03 | Adding Records Using a Form

There are various ways to create a form in Access. The quickest way is to use the Form command, which creates a form that displays all of the fields from the underlying data source (table) one record at a time. Records that you create or edit in a form are automatically added to or updated in the underlying table.

1 Open » the **Navigation Pane**.

2 In the **Navigation Pane**, be sure the **Lastname Firstname 3A Gardeners** table is selected. Click the **Create tab**, and then in the **Forms group**, click the **Form** button. Compare your screen with Figure 3.7.

> Access creates a form based on the selected table—the Lastname Firstname 3A Gardeners table. The form displays in *Layout view*—the Access view in which you can make changes to a form or to a report while the object is running—the data from the underlying data source display. Each field displays data for the first record—*Alejandra Balentine*—from the underlying table.

Figure 3.7

Lastname Firstname 3A
Gardeners table selected

Form displays in
Layout view

3 On the Quick Access Toolbar, click **Save** 📙. In the **Save As** dialog box, type **Lastname Firstname 3A Gardeners Form** and then click **OK**.

The form is saved and the new name displays on the form tab.

4 On the **Design tab**, in the **Views group**, click the **Views** button.

The form displays in *Form view*—the view in which you can view the records, but you cannot change the layout or design of the form.

5 At the bottom of the form, in the navigation area, click the **New (blank) record** button ▶.

A new blank form displays, indicated in the navigation area by *4 of 4*.

6 Press [Tab]. In the **Last Name** field, type **Lopez** and then press [Tab].

Use the [Tab] key to move from field to field in a form. This is known as *tab order*—the order in which the insertion point moves from one field to the next in a form when you press [Tab].

7 Type **Fernando** and then press [Tab]. Continue to enter the following data, pressing [Tab] to move to the next field, and then compare your screen with Figure 3.8.

Address	City	State	ZIP	Home Phone
4019 E Devonshire Ave	Phoenix	AZ	85029	480-555-4772

Figure 3.8

Data entered for
Fernando Lopez

Navigation area indicates
Record 4 of 4

8 Press Tab

By pressing Tab or Enter at the end of a record, the record is entered into the table, and the form moves to a new blank record.

9 Using the technique you just practiced, enter the contact information for five additional gardeners, and then compare your screen with Figure 3.9.

Last Name	First Name	Address	City	State	ZIP	Home Phone
Gerhard	Rae	21062 N 33rd Ave	Phoenix	AZ	85031	480-555-0031
Herrmann	Heidi	18417 N 30th St	Phoenix	AZ	85016	480-555-5831
Levens	Noreen	619 E Briles Rd	Chandler	AZ	85226	480-555-0992
Maciejewski	Jamie	4126 W Mercer Ln	Gilbert	AZ	85297	480-555-5351
Perez	Olivia	5048 E Via Montoya Dr	Phoenix	AZ	85017	480-555-8156

Figure 3.9

Completed form for
Olivia Perez

Navigation area indicates
Record 9 of 9

10 Press `Tab` to accept the record for Olivia Perez and to display a new blank form.

11 Enter the following data using your own **First Name** and **Last Name**, and then press `Tab`.

Last Name	First Name	Address	City	State	ZIP	Home Phone
Lastname	**Firstname**	**3931 W Las Palmaritas Dr**	**Phoenix**	**AZ**	**85016**	**480-555-4821**

The navigation area, located below the form, indicates Record 11 of 11, which is a blank form.

12 In the **Navigation Pane**, double-click the **Lastname Firstname 3A Gardeners** table to display the table. Verify that your record displays in the table.

13 At the top of the object window, click the **Lastname Firstname 3A Gardeners Form tab** to display the form. In the navigation area, click the **First record** button ⏮. To view the records, click the **Next record** button ▶ until your record is visible.

14 If your instructor directs you to submit your files electronically, go to Activity 3.04.

15 Click the **File tab**, click the **Print tab**, and then click the **Print** button. In the **Print** dialog box, in the lower left corner, click **Setup**. Click the **Columns tab**, change the **Width** to **7.5** so that the form prints on one page, and then click **OK**. In the lower left corner of the **Print** dialog box click the **Selected Record(s)** option button, and then click **OK**.

Activity 3.04 | Finding and Editing a Record Using a Form

A form can be used to find specific occurrences of a value in a field, find blank fields, or edit a specific record in the Access database. Adding, deleting, and editing records using a single-record form helps to prevent data entry errors.

1 In the **Lastname Firstname 3A Gardeners Form**, click in the **Address** field. On the **Home tab**, in the **Find group**, click the **Find** button. In the **Find and Replace** dialog box, in the **Find What** box, type **21062** Click the **Match arrow**, click **Any Part of Field**, and then click **Find Next**. Compare your screen with Figure 3.10.

The information for Rae Gerhard displays in the form.

Figure 3.10

Form for Rae Gerhard

Match box changed to Any Part of Field

Address field includes Find What entry

2 In the **Address** field, select the address, type **2103 E Sapium Way** and then press Tab three times. In the **ZIP** field, type **85009** and then press Tab to update the record in the table.

3 Click the **Home Phone** field. Click the **Find and Replace** dialog box to make it active, in the **Find What** box, type **480-555-8156** and then click **Find Next**. **Delete** the last four digits of the phone number, type **2081** and then press Tab to update the phone number. Keep the Find and Replace dialog box open for the next activity.

Activity 3.05 | Deleting Records Using a Form

Once a record has been located by using a form, the form can be used to delete the record from the table.

1 Click in the **Last Name** field. In the **Find and Replace** dialog box, in the **Find What** box, type **Levens** and then click **Find Next**.

The information for Noreen Levens displays.

2 **Close** [X] the **Find and Replace** dialog box. On the **Home tab**, in the **Records group**, click the **Delete button arrow**, and then compare your screen with Figure 3.11.

Figure 3.11

Delete button arrow

Form for Noreen Levens

3 In the displayed list, click **Delete Record**.

A message displays alerting you that you are about to delete *1 record*. In Access, if you click Yes and delete a record, you cannot use the Undo button to reverse the action.

4 Click **Yes** to delete the record. Notice the navigation area indicates that there are nine records.

Because the ID field is an AutoNumber data type, the ID number for each existing record does not change.

5 Right-click the **Lastname Firstname 3A Gardeners Form tab**. On the shortcut menu, click **Close All**.

Activity 3.06 | Printing an Access Table

Although you might choose to print a table for proofreading, you usually create a report to display the contents of a table in a professional manner. In this activity, you will simply print the table.

1 In the **Navigation Pane**, click the **Lastname Firstname 3A Gardeners** table. Click the **File tab**, click the **Print** tab, and then click **Print Preview**. Compare your screen with Figure 3.12. Notice that the Address column is too narrow to display all the information.

The name of the table displays at the top of the page. If a table will print on more than one page, at the bottom of the window, in the navigation area, you can click the Next Page button to view the subsequent pages.

Figure 3.12

Table name
Row of field names
Column too narrow

Next page button
Navigation area

---

2 On the **Print Preview tab**, in the **Close Preview group**, click the **Close Print Preview** button.

3 In the **Navigation Pane**, double-click the **Lastname Firstname 3A Gardeners** table. In the row of field names, point to the right boundary of the **ID** field to display the ⊞ pointer, and then double-click.

> Double-clicking the right border of a column changes the column width to fully display the field name and the longest entry in the column.

4 Click the **Last Name** field, hold down Shift, display the ↓ pointer, hold down the left mouse button, and then drag to the right to the **Home Phone** field.

> The fields Last Name through Home Phone are selected.

5 Point to the **Home Phone** field, and then right-click. On the shortcut menu, click **Field Width**, and then in the **Column Width** dialog box, click **Best Fit**. Compare your screen with Figure 3.13.

> The column widths of all the selected columns are adjusted to best fit the existing data.

Figure 3.13

Column widths adjusted

Project 3A: Walks List | **Integrated Projects**

6 Display **Backstage** view, click the **Print** tab, and then click **Print Preview**. On the **Print Preview tab**, in the **Page Layout group**, click the **Landscape** button.

> In the navigation area, notice that the Next Page button is dimmed, indicating that this is a one-page document.

7 **Save** 🖫 the changes you have made to the design of the table. If your instructor directs you to submit your files electronically, go to Step 9.

8 On the **Print Preview tab**, in the **Print group**, click the **Print** button, and then click **OK**. In the **Close Preview group**, click the **Close Print Preview** button.

9 Right-click the **Lastname Firstname 3A Gardeners table tab**, and then on the shortcut menu, click **Close**.

10 Display **Backstage** view, and then click **View and edit database properties**. In the **Properties** dialog box, on the **Summary tab**, in the **Subject** box, type your course name and section number, in the **Author** box, type your firstname and lastname and then in the **Keywords** box, type **gardener contacts** Click **OK** to close the dialog box, and then click the **Home tab**.

Objective 3 | Export an Access Table to a Word Document

Exporting, similar to copying and pasting, is a way to output data and database objects to another database, worksheet, or file format to be used in another file or application. For example, you can export an Access table to Word instead of retyping the information. Exporting can save you time and reduce the number of errors.

Activity 3.07 | Exporting an Access Table to an RTF File

1 With the **Navigation Pane** open, be sure the **Lastname Firstname 3A Gardeners** table is selected. Click the **External Data tab**. In the **Export group**, click the **More** button, and then click **Word**. Compare your screen to Figure 3.14.

> The export *wizard*—a feature that walks you step by step through a process—starts, and the Export - RTF File dialog box opens. Recall from the previous chapter that a Rich Text Format (RTF) file is a universal document format that can be read by nearly all word processing programs and that retains most text and paragraph formatting.

Figure 3.14

Export – RTF File
dialog box

Lastname Firstname 3A
Gardeners table selected

2 In the **Export – RTF File** dialog box, click the **Browse** button, and then navigate to your **Integrated Projects Chapter 3** folder. In the **File Save** dialog box, in the **File name** box, select the existing text, type **Lastname_Firstname_3A_Gardeners** and then click the **Save** button.

3 In the **Export – RTF File** dialog box, click the **OK** button. In the next dialog box, when asked *Do you want to save these export steps?*, the **Save export steps** check box should not be selected. Click the **Close** button.

> The Access table has been saved as Lastname Firstname 3A Gardeners.rtf. If you plan to repeat an export operation, you can save the settings used in an Import or Export wizard.

4 Close [ ] Access.

Activity 3.08 | Inserting Access Data in a Word Document

David Tang is the manager of the Garden Walks segment of the show. He has been in contact with local gardeners whom he would like to feature on his segment. Mr. Tang has started a memo to Toni Jones, President of Southwest Gardens. He has asked you to complete the memo by include the list of gardeners.

1 **Start** Word, and then navigate to the student data files. Locate and open the document **i03A_Garden_Walk**.

2 From **Backstage** view, display the **Save As** dialog box, and then navigate to your **Integrated Projects Chapter 3** folder. In the **File Name** box, select the existing text, type **Lastname_Firstname_3A_Garden_Walk** and then click **Save**.

3 Click the **Insert tab**. In the **Header & Footer group**, click the **Footer** button, and then click **Edit Footer**. On the **Design tab**, in the **Insert group**, click the **Quick Parts** button, and then click **Field**. Under **Field names**, click **FileName**, and then click **OK**. Double-click in the document to close the footer area. If necessary, click the Show/Hide button [¶] to display formatting marks.

4 Press Ctrl + End to move to the end of the document. Click the **Insert tab**. In the **Text group**, click the **Insert Object button arrow**, and then click **Text from File**. In the **Insert File** dialog box, verify your **Integrated Projects Chapter 3** folder displays, click the file name **Lastname_Firstname_3A_Gardeners.rtf** and then click **Insert**. Compare your screen with Figure 3.15.

The exported Access table has been inserted into the Word document.

> **Alert!** | **What if the .rtf extension does not display?**
>
> The file extension may or may not display on your system, depending on the computer settings.

Figure 3.15

Exported Access table
inserted in Word document

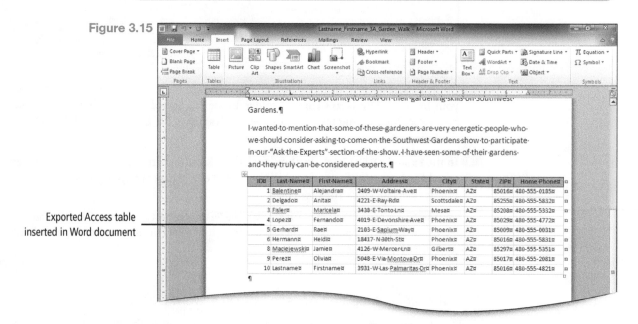

5 In the first row of the new table, click in the first cell **ID** to make the cell active. Click the **Layout tab**, in the **Rows & Columns group**, click the **Delete** button, and then click **Delete Columns**.

The ID column is deleted from the table.

6 Click the **Design tab**, and then in the **Table Styles group**, click the **More** button ▾. In the **Table Styles** gallery, under **Built-In**, in the second row, click the second style—**Light List – Accent 1**. In the **Table Styles group**, click the **Borders button arrow**, and then click **Borders and Shading**. In the **Borders and Shading** dialog box, on the **Borders tab**, click the **Color arrow**, and then in the tenth column, click the first color—**Orange, Accent 6**. Click the **Width arrow**, click 1½ pt, and then click **OK**.

7 Click the **Layout tab**. In the **Cell Size group**, click the **AutoFit** button, and then click **AutoFit Contents**. In the **Table group**, click the **Properties** button. In the **Table Properties** dialog box, on the **Table tab**, under **Alignment**, click **Center**, and then click **OK**. Compare your screen with Figure 3.16.

The columns are automatically resized to fit the contents of the cells, and the table is centered in the document.

Figure 3.16

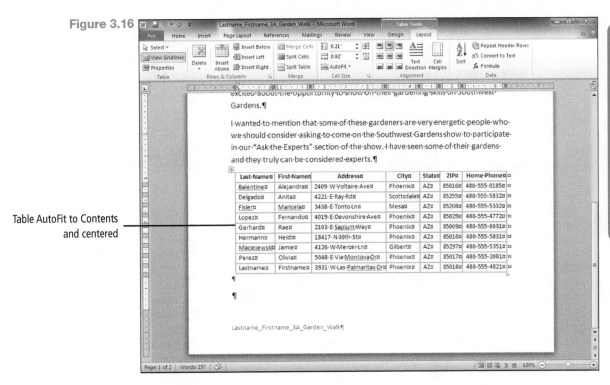

Table AutoFit to Contents
and centered

8 Save the document.

Objective 4 | Format a Word Document

Word galleries display predefined style and graphics that can be used to create a more polished document. You can add text boxes, page color, and page borders. Recall that modifying a document theme changes the appearance of text, tables, and graphics throughout the document.

Activity 3.09 | Formatting a Word Document Using Page Layout

1 Press Ctrl + Home to move to the top of the document. Select the first paragraph—*Southwest Gardens*. On the **Home tab**, in the **Styles group**, click the **More** button . In the **Quick Styles** gallery, click **Intense Reference**. In the **Font group**, click the **Font Size button arrow** , and then click **26**.

2 Select the second, third, and fourth paragraphs beginning with *41122 N 23rd St*. In the **Styles group**, click the **More** button , and then click **Subtle Reference**. In the **Font group**, click the **Font Size button arrow** , and then click **14**.

3 Select the first four paragraphs, and then in the **Paragraph group**, click the **Align Text Right** button . Click the **Line and Paragraph Spacing** button , and then click **Remove Space After Paragraph**. In the **Font group**, click the **Font Color button arrow** , and then in the tenth column, click the fifth color—**Orange, Accent 6, Darker 25%**. Compare your screen with Figure 3.17.

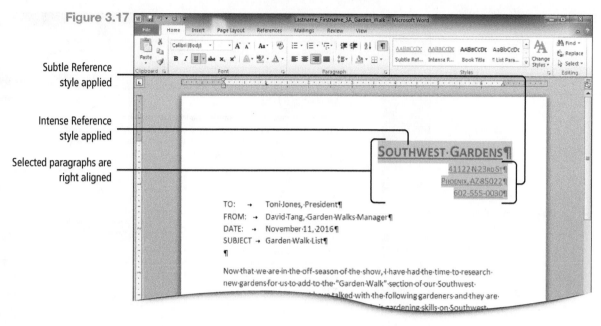

Figure 3.17

Subtle Reference style applied

Intense Reference style applied

Selected paragraphs are right aligned

SOUTHWEST·GARDENS¶

41122·N·23RD·ST¶
PHOENIX,·AZ·85022¶
602-555-0030¶

TO: →   Toni·Jones,·President¶
FROM: →   David·Tang,·Garden·Walks·Manager¶
DATE: →   November·11,·2016¶
SUBJECT →   Garden·Walk·List¶
¶

Now·that·we·are·in·the·off-season·of·the·show,·I·have·had·the·time·to·research·
new·gardens·for·us·to·add·to·the·"Garden·Walk"·section·of·our·Southwest·
...·talked·with·the·following·gardeners·and·they·are·
...·gardening·skills·on·Southwest...

4 Click anywhere in your document to deselect the text, and then **Save** 🖫 your document.

Activity 3.10 | Inserting and Modifying a Text Box

A *text box* is a movable, resizable container for text or graphics. You can use text boxes to position several blocks of text on a page or to give text a different orientation from other text in the document.

1 Click the **Insert tab**, in the **Text group**, click the **Text Box** button, and then click **Annual Quote**.

The text box is displayed on the right side of your document.

2 Type **Garden Walk** and then press ⌨Enter. Type **The Garden Walk segment of Southwest Gardens is always one of the highest rated segments of the program.**

3 Select all of the text in the text box. On the Mini toolbar, click the **Grow Font** button 🅰 two times. Click the **Font Color button arrow** 🅰▾, and then in the tenth column, click the sixth color—**Orange, Accent 6, Darker 50%**. Select the first paragraph *Garden Walk*, and then on the Mini toolbar, click the **Bold** button 🅱.

4 On the **Format tab**, in the **Size group**, if necessary, click the **Size** button. Use the spin box arrows to change the **Shape Height** 📏 1.5" ↕ to **2.1** and the **Shape Width** 📐 1.37" ↕ to **2.6**. In the **Shape Styles group**, click the **More** button ▾, and then in the fourth row, click the seventh style—**Subtle Effect – Orange, Accent 6**. Click the **Shape Outline** button 🖉, and then in the tenth column, click the fifth color—**Orange, Accent 6, Darker 25%**.

5 Point to any border on the text box until the 🔀 pointer displays. Hold down the left mouse button, and then drag the text box to the right of the paragraph that begins *Now that we are*. If necessary, use the arrow keys to nudge the text box to the location shown in Figure 3.18.

Figure 3.18

Integrated Projects

Annual Quote text box
formatted

Inserted and
formatted text

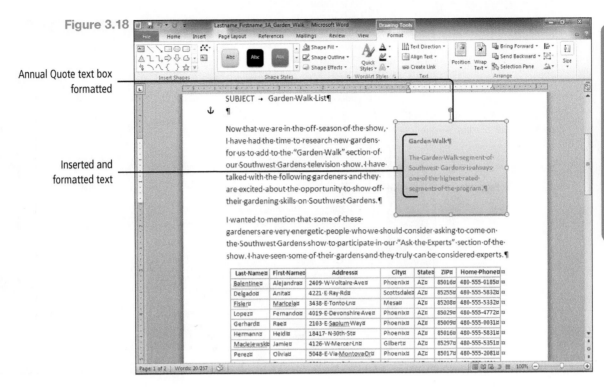

6 Save your changes.

Activity 3.11 | Adding Page Borders and Page Color

Page borders can add interest and emphasis to your document pages. You can add page borders to all pages, only specific pages, sides of pages, or sections. Page borders include many line styles and colors, as well as a variety of graphical borders.

1 Press [Ctrl] + [Home]. Click the **Page Layout tab**, and then in the **Page Background group**, click the **Page Borders** button. In the **Borders and Shading** dialog box, on the **Page Border tab**, under **Setting**, click **Shadow**. Click the **Color arrow**, and then in the tenth column, click the fifth color—**Orange, Accent 6, Darker 25%**. Click the **Width arrow**, and then click **2¼ pt**. Under **Apply to**, be sure **Whole document** displays, and then click **OK**.

2 In the **Page Background group**, click the **Page Color** button. Under **Theme Colors**, in the tenth column, click the third color—**Orange, Accent 6, Lighter 60%**. Compare your screen with Figure 3.19.

Figure 3.19

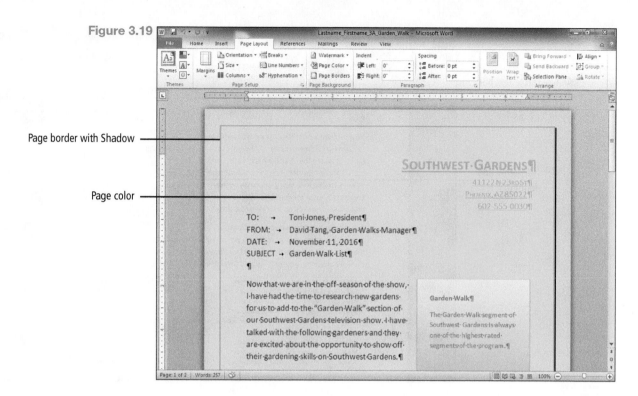

Page border with Shadow

Page color

3 Display **Backstage** view, and then click the **Info tab**. Click **Properties**, and then click **Show Document Panel**. In the **Author** box, type your firstname and lastname, in the **Subject** box, type your course name and section number, and then in the **Keywords** box, type **gardener memo, contacts Close** ☒ the Document Information Panel.

4 Press ⎡Ctrl⎤ + ⎡End⎤. If your document displays a second page, press ⎡Backspace⎤ to delete the paragraph mark.

5 Press ⎡Ctrl⎤ + ⎡Home⎤, and then **Save** 🖫 your document.

6 If your instructor directs you to submit your files electronically, go to step 7. To print your document, display **Backstage** view, click the **Print tab**, and then click **Print**.

7 **Close** ⎡☒⎤ Word. Submit your printed or electronic files as directed by your instructor.

End **You have completed Project 3A**

Project 3B Southwest Letter

Project Activities

In Activities 3.12 through 3.20, you will use the mail merge feature in Word to complete a letter and envelope for each supplier using the names and addresses listed in an Access database. In Access, you will create a query that will filter the supplier list. You will use the results of the query to complete an invitation using the mail merge feature. Your completed documents will look similar to Figure 3.20.

Project Files

For Project 3B, you will need the following files:

New blank Word document
i03B_New_Tools
i03B_Open_House
i03B_Tool_Suppliers

You will save your files as:

Lastname_Firstname_3B_Tool_Suppliers
Lastname_Firstname_3B_New_Tools
Lastname_Firstname_3B_Supplier_Letters
Lastname_Firstname_3B_Envelopes
Lastname_Firstname_3B_Supplier_Envelopes
Lastname_Firstname_3B_Invitations
Lastname_Firstname_3B_Supplier_Invitations

Project Results

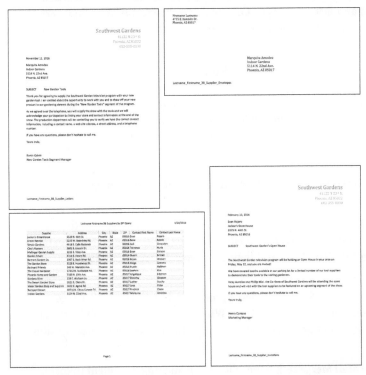

Figure 3.20
Project 3B Supplier Letter

Objective 5 | Use Mail Merge in Word to Complete Letters Using Access Data

It is common for a business to send out identical letters to its contacts. In order to personalize the letters, the business may use *mail merge*, a Microsoft Word feature that joins a main document and a data source to create customized letters, envelopes, or labels. Mail merge enables you to select data from various sources, such as an Access database. You can sort or filter the data before it is merged into the document.

Activity 3.12 | Starting Mail Merge in Word

You can start the mail merge feature in either Word or Access. Karen Galvin has created the letter that you will use for the *main document* in your mail merge. In a mail merge, the main document is the document that contains the text and formatting that remains constant. Karen knows the contact information for tool suppliers is located in an Access database. For this activity, you will use a table in the database as the *data source*—a list of variable information, such as names and addresses—that is merged with a main document to create customized form letters, envelopes, or labels.

1 From the **Start** menu, navigate to the location where your student data files are located, and then click one time to select the Access file **i03B_Tool_Suppliers**. Right-click the file, and then on the shortcut menu, click **Copy**.

2 Navigate to and then open your **Integrated Projects Chapter 3** folder. In an open area, right-click, and then on the shortcut menu, click **Paste**.

The database file is copied to your folder.

3 Right-click the selected file name, and then on the shortcut menu, click **Rename**. Using your own first and last name, type **Lastname_Firstname_3B_Tool_Suppliers** Press Enter to save the file with the new name. **Close** ✖ the window.

> **Alert!** | **Does a Confirm File Rename message display?**
>
> If the file you have copied has a Read-only property applied, a message box will display to alert you when you attempt to rename a file. In the message box, click Yes to rename the file. Right-click the file name, and then on the shortcut menu, click Properties. In the Properties dialog box, on the General tab, under Attributes, click to clear the Read-only check mark, click OK to accept the change, and then close the dialog box.

---

4 **Start** Word. From your student data files, locate and open the document **i03B_New_Tools**.

5 From **Backstage** view, display the **Save As** dialog box, and then navigate to the **Integrated Projects Chapter 3** folder. In the **File name** box, select the existing text, type **Lastname_Firstname_3B_New_Tools** and then click **Save**. If necessary, display formatting marks.

6 Click the **Mailings tab**. In the **Start Mail Merge group**, click the **Start Mail Merge** button, and then click **Step by Step Mail Merge Wizard** to display the **Mail Merge** task pane. In the task pane, under **Select document type**, confirm that the **Letters** option button is selected.

7 At the bottom of the **Mail Merge** task pane, click **Next: Starting document** to display **Step 2 of 6**. Under **Select starting document**, confirm that the **Use the current document** option button is selected, and then at the bottom of the task pane, click **Next: Select recipients** to display **Step 3 of 6**.

8 Under **Select recipients**, confirm that the **Use an existing list** option button is selected. Under **Use an existing list**, click **Browse**. Navigate to your **Integrated Projects Chapter 3** folder, select your **Lastname_Firstname_3B_Tool_Suppliers** file, and then click **Open**. Compare your screen with Figure 3.21.

> The Select Table dialog box displays. This allows you to select the table, or query, that contains the names and address of the recipients for this letter. This database contains more than one object—tables or queries.

Figure 3.21

Select Table dialog box ——

List of objects ——

9 In the **Select Table** dialog box, be certain **Supplier Contacts** is selected, and then click **OK**.

> In the Mail Merge Recipients dialog box you can add or edit data in a table—in this case, the names and addresses.

10 In the **Mail Merge Recipients** dialog box, scroll to the right to view the **Contact Last Name** field. Click the **Contact Last Name** field column heading. Compare your screen with Figure 3.22.

> You can *sort* on any of the fields by clicking the field column heading. Sorting is the process of arranging data in a specific order based on the value in each field. In this case, the records are sorted in ascending order by last name.

Figure 3.22

Mail Merge Recipients dialog box

Contact Last Name field column heading

List of tool suppliers ——

Last names in ascending order

11 At the bottom of the **Mail Merge Recipients** dialog box, click **OK**.

Activity 3.13 | Adding Merge Fields

1 At the bottom of the task pane, click **Next: Write your letter** to display **Step 4 of 6**. Click in the first blank line below the date to position the insertion point.

This is the location in the letter when you want to insert the address of the recipient.

2 In the **Mail Merge** task pane, under **Write your letter**, click **Address block**. In the **Insert Address Block** dialog box, under **Specify address elements**, verify that the **Joshua Randall Jr.** format is selected. Compare your screen with Figure 3.23.

On the right side of the Insert Address Block dialog box, under Preview, notice that the Supplier business name and the contact name are not listed.

Figure 3.23

Insert Address Block dialog box

Preview area

3 Near the bottom of the **Insert Address Block** dialog box, click **Match Fields**. Under **Required for Address Block**, click the **First Name arrow**, and then click **Contact First Name**. Click the **Last Name arrow**, and then click **Contact Last Name**. Click the **Company arrow**, click **Supplier**, and then compare your screen with Figure 3.24.

Word did not recognize the Contact First Name, Contact Last Name, and Supplier fields in the table, so it was necessary to associate them with the corresponding predefined fields. You can use the Match Fields feature to choose the correct fields to display.

Figure 3.24

First Name field

Last Name field

Company field

4 At the bottom of the **Match Fields** dialog box, click **OK**. A message box may display telling you that the data may be read by others. In the message box, click **Yes**. In the **Insert Address Block** dialog box, under **Preview**, confirm that the **Contact First Name**, **Contact Last Name**, and **Supplier** name display in the address, and then click **OK**.

> A mail merge field—the address block—is inserted in your letter. When you insert a mail merge field into the main document, the field name is surrounded by double angle brackets (<< >>). These double angle brackets help distinguish the fields in the main document and will not display in the final document.

5 In the document, select the <<**AddressBlock**>> field, being sure to include the paragraph mark. Click the **Page Layout tab**, and then in the **Paragraph group**, under **Spacing**, use the **down spin box arrow** to set the **After** box to **0 pt**.

6 At the bottom of the **Mail Merge** task pane, click **Next: Preview your letters** to display **Step 5 of 6**. Under **Preview your letters**, click the **Next** button ▶ three times to preview some of the letters. The letters are the same except for the address block.

7 At the bottom of the **Mail Merge** task pane, click **Next: Complete the merge**. Under **Merge**, click **Edit individual letters**. In the **Merge to New Document** dialog box, verify that the **All** option button is selected, and then click **OK**. Compare your screen with Figure 3.25.

> A new document with 29 letters has been created.

Figure 3.25

New document name

Merged address

29 pages in document

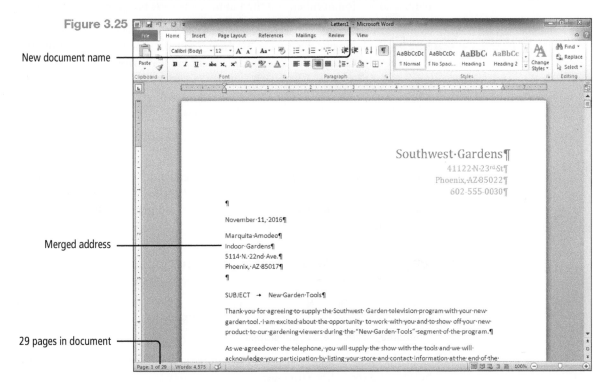

8 From **Backstage** view, display the **Save As** dialog box, and then navigate to your **Integrated Projects Chapter 3** folder. In the **File name** box, delete the existing text, type **Lastname_Firstname_3B_Supplier_Letters** and then click **Save**.

9 In your **Lastname_Firstname_3B_Supplier_Letters** document, display **Backstage** view, and then click the **Info** tab. Click **Properties**, and then click **Show Document Panel**. In the **Author** box, type your firstname and lastname, in the **Subject** box, type your course name and section number, and then in the **Keywords** box, type **supplier letter, merged Close** ☒ the Document Information Panel.

Project 3B: Supplier Letter | **Integrated Projects**

139

10 Near the bottom of the document, double-click to display the footer area. Using **Quick Parts**, insert the **FileName** field, and then double-click in the document to close the footer area.

Activity 3.14 | Printing Letters

Your document contains all the customized letters to the suppliers. Because the merged document has been saved, you have the ability to print one, several, or all of the letters.

1 If your instructor directs you to submit your files electronically, go to step 3.

2 Press [Ctrl] + [End] to move to the end of the document. From **Backstage** view, click the **Print** tab. Under **Settings**, click the **Print All Pages** button, and then click **Print Current Page**. Click the **Print** button.

> Only the last letter of the 29 letters is printed.

3 Save 🖫 and then **Close** [✕] the **Lastname_Firstname_3B_Supplier_Letters** document.

4 In the **Lastname_Firstname_3B_New_Tools** document, display **Backstage** view, and then click the **Info** tab. Click **Properties**, and then click **Show Document Panel**. In the **Author** box, type your firstname and lastname, in the **Subject** box, type your course name and section number, and then in the **Keywords** box, type **letter, merge fields** **Close** [✕] the Document Information Panel.

5 Save 🖫 the **Lastname_Firstname_3B_New_Tools** document, and then from **Backstage** view, click the **Close** tab to close the document but leave Word open.

Objective 6 | Use Mail Merge in Word to Create Envelopes Using Access Data

Another feature of mail merge is the ability to create customized envelopes. Using the same data source that you used for the letters, you can enter or edit the delivery and return addresses, specify the formatting of text, and choose the envelope size. You can either save the completed envelopes for later editing and printing, or you can print the envelopes without saving the document.

Activity 3.15 | Starting Mail Merge for Envelopes and Inserting a Return Address

1 In Word, press [Ctrl] + [N] to display a new document. **Save** the document to your **Integrated Projects Chapter 3** folder with the file name Lastname_Firstname_3B_Envelopes

2 Click the **Mailings tab**, in the **Start Mail Merge group**, click the **Start Mail Merge** button, and then click **Envelopes**.

3 In the **Envelopes Options** dialog box, under **Envelope size**, verify that **Size 10** is selected, and then click **OK**. Compare your screen with Figure 3.26.

> A standard business size envelope displays. A return address may display in the top left corner of the envelope, depending on your computer settings.

Figure 3.26

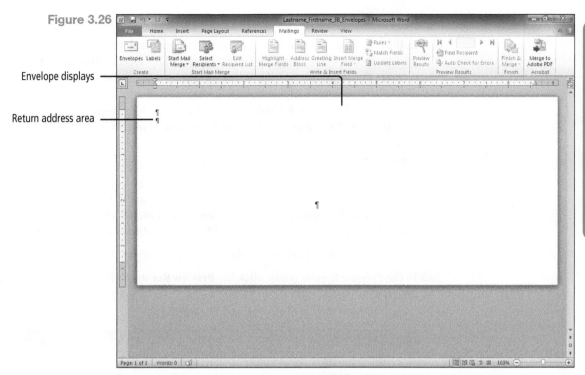

Envelope displays

Return address area

4 On the **Mailings tab**, in the **Start Mail Merge group**, click the **Select Recipients** button. On the displayed list, click **Use Existing List**. Navigate to your **Integrated Projects Chapter 3** folder, select your **Lastname_Firstname_3B_Tool_Suppliers** file, and then click **Open**. In the **Select Table** dialog box, verify that **Supplier Contacts** is selected, and then click **OK**.

5 In the **Start Mail Merge group**, click the **Edit Recipient List** button. In the **Mail Merge Recipients** dialog box, scroll to the right, and then click the field column heading **Contact Last Name** to sort the records by last name in ascending order. Click **OK**.

6 If necessary, click to position the insertion point at the top left corner of the envelope. Using your own name, type **Firstname Lastname** and then press Enter. Type **4715 E. Hamblin Dr.** press Enter, and then type **Phoenix, AZ 85017** Compare your screen with Figure 3.27.

Figure 3.27

Return address

7 **Save** 💾 your changes.

Activity 3.16 | Completing and Printing Envelopes

1 In the middle of the envelope, a paragraph mark displays. Click one time on the paragraph mark to display the address placeholder. On the **Mailings tab**, in the **Write & Insert Fields group**, click the **Address Block** button. In the **Insert Address Block** dialog box, under **Specify address elements**, verify that the **Joshua Randall Jr.** format is selected. Click the **Match Fields** button, and then under **Required for Address Block**, click the **First Name arrow**, and then click **Contact First Name**. Click the **Last Name arrow**, and then click **Contact Last Name**. Click the **Company arrow**, and then click **Supplier**.

2 In the **Match Fields** dialog box, click **OK**. If a dialog box displays telling you data may be read by others, click **Yes**. In the **Insert Address Block** dialog box, under **Preview**, confirm that the **Contact First Name**, **Contact Last Name**, and **Supplier** name display in the address, and then at the bottom of the **Insert Address Block** dialog box, click **OK**.

> The address block mail merge field is inserted in your envelope.

3 In the **Preview Results group**, click the **Preview Results** button, and then compare your screen with Figure 3.28.

Figure 3.28

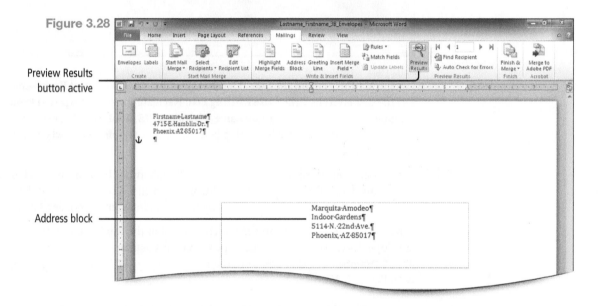

Preview Results button active

Address block

4 In the **Finish group**, click the **Finish & Merge** button, and then on the displayed list, click **Edit Individual Documents**. In the **Merge to New Document** dialog box, verify that the **All** option button is selected, and then click **OK**.

5 From **Backstage** view, display the **Save As** dialog box, and then navigate to the **Integrated Projects Chapter 3** folder. In the **File name** box, delete the existing text, type **Lastname_Firstname_3B_Supplier_Envelopes** and then click **Save**.

6 Near the bottom of the envelope, double-click to open the footer area. Using **Quick Parts**, insert the **FileName** field, and then double-click in the document to close the footer area.

> You are inserting a footer only for purposes of this instruction. Normally, an envelope does not include a footer.

7 If your instructor directs you to submit your files electronically, go to step 8.

8 Press Ctrl + End to move to the end of the document. From **Backstage** view, click the **Print** tab. Under **Settings**, click the **Print All Pages** button, and then click **Print Current Page**. Click the **Print** button.

Only the last envelope of the 29 envelopes is printed.

9 Display **Backstage** view, and then click the **Info tab**. Click **Properties**, and then click **Show Document Panel**. In the **Author** box, type your firstname and lastname, in the **Subject** box, type your course name and section number, and then in the **Keywords** box, type **supplier envelopes, merged Close** ☒ the Document Information Panel.

10 Save 🖫, and then **Close** ☒ the **Lastname_Firstname_3B_Supplier_Envelopes** document.

11 In your **Lastname_Firstname_3B_Envelopes** document, display **Backstage** view, and then click the **Info** tab. Click **Properties**, and then click **Show Document Panel**. In the **Author** box, type your firstname and lastname, in the **Subject** box, type your course name and section number, and then in the **Keywords** box, type **envelopes, merge fields Close** ☒ the Document Information Panel.

12 Save 🖫 the **Lastname_Firstname_3B_Envelopes** document, and then **Close** ☒ Word.

Objective 7 | Create and Modify a Query in Access

Recall that a query is a database object that requests data from a database. A query answers a question such as *Which tool suppliers live within a specific ZIP code?* Database users rarely need to see all of the records in all of the tables. That is why a query is useful; it creates a *subset* of records—a portion of the total records—according to your specifications and then displays only those records.

Activity 3.17 | Creating a Query using the Query Wizard

In this activity, you will create a *select query*. A select query is a type of query that retrieves specific data from one or more tables or queries, displaying the selected data in a datasheet. You can create a select query in Design view or by using a wizard.

1 **Start** Access. Click the **Recent tab**, and then under **Recent Databases**, click your database **Lastname_Firstname_3B_Tool_Suppliers**. If a Security Warning displays on the **Message Bar**, click the **Enable Content** button.

The database window opens, and the database name displays in the title bar.

2 In the **Navigation Pane**, click the **Supplier Contacts: Table**. Click the **Create tab**, and in the **Queries group**, click the **Query Wizard** button. In the **New Query** dialog box, verify that **Simple Query Wizard** is selected, and then click **OK**. Compare your screen with Figure 3.29.

The name of the table is selected as the data source, and the fields in the table are displayed.

Figure 3.29

Simple Query Wizard dialog box

Selected table

Available Fields

Another Way

Double-click the field name to move it to the Selected Field list.

> ➌ Under **Available Fields**, click **Supplier**, and then click the **Add Field** button ▸ to move the field to the **Selected Fields** list on the right.
>
> The Available Fields list includes all the fields in the selected table or query. The Selected Fields list contains the fields you want to include in your new query.

➍ Using the technique you just practiced, add the following fields to the **Selected Fields** list: **Address, City, State, ZIP, Contact First Name**, and **Contact Last Name**. Compare your screen with Figure 3.30.

Figure 3.30

Add Field button

Selected Fields

➎ At the bottom of the **Simple Query Wizard** dialog box, click the **Next** button. Under **Would you like a detail or summary query?**, verify that the **Detail** option button is selected, and then click **Next**. On the next screen, under **What title do you want for your query?**, type Lastname Firstname 3B Supplier Query and then click **Finish**.

Access saves and *runs* the query. To run a query is the process in which Access searches the records in the table(s) included in a query design, finds the records that match the specified criteria, and then displays those records in a datasheet. Only the fields that have been included in the query design display.

The new query name displays in the Navigation Pane. When you save a query, only the design of the query is saved; the records still reside in the table object. Each time you open a query, Access will run the query and display results based on the updated data stored in the table.

Integrated Projects | Integrating Word and Access

144

Activity 3.18 | Sorting and Filtering Data in a Query

Henry Cavazos, the Southwest Gardens Marketing Manager, has created an invitation for the upcoming open house. He has asked you to customize the invitations for the suppliers in the 85016 and 85017 ZIP Code areas.

1 Click the **Home tab**, and then in the **Views group**, click the **View** button to switch to Design view. In the design grid, in the **Sort row**, click in the **ZIP** field (below Supplier Contacts) to position the insertion point and to display an arrow. Click the **Sort arrow**, and then in the displayed list, click **Ascending**. Compare your screen with Figure 3.31.

Figure 3.31

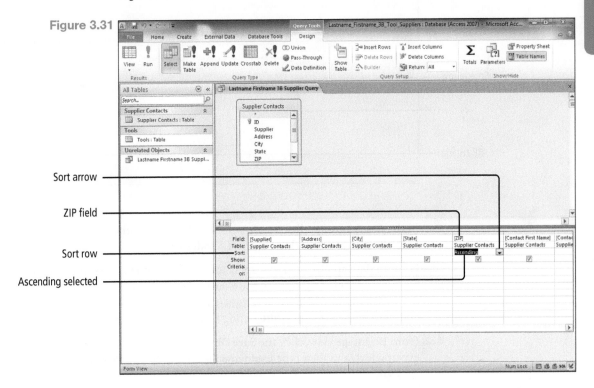

Sort arrow

ZIP field

Sort row

Ascending selected

2 On the **Design tab**, in the **Results group**, click the **Run** button.

Records are sorted in ZIP code order with the lowest number displayed first.

3 On the **Home tab**, in the **Views group**, click the **View** button to switch to Design view. In the design grid, in the **Criteria row**, click in the **ZIP** field. Type **85016** and then press ⬇ to move to the next row—with the row heading **or**. Type **85017** and then compare your screen with Figure 3.32.

By typing particular ZIP codes as the *criteria*, the data will be *filtered*. Criteria are the conditions in a query that identify the specific records for which you are looking. Filtering is the process of displaying only a portion of the data based on matching a specific value to show only the data that meets the criteria you specify. In this case, when the query is run, only records containing the 85016 and 85017 ZIP codes will display.

Figure 3.32

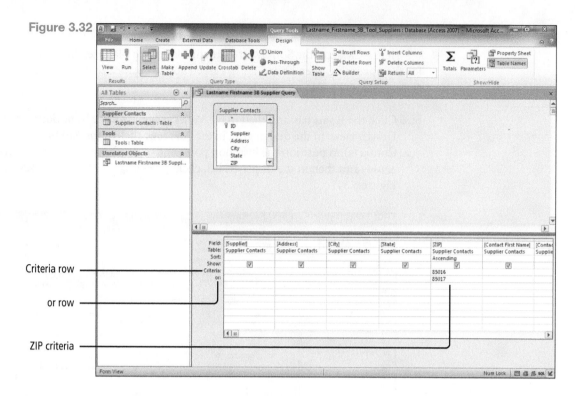

Criteria row ———

or row ———

ZIP criteria ———

4 In the **Results group**, click the **Run** button. Notice that the data has been filtered to hide all records except those with ZIP codes 85016 or 85017.

5 Point to the **Supplier** field to display the ⬇ pointer. Hold down the left mouse button, and then drag right to the **Contact Last Name** field to select all the fields. Point to the field name **ZIP**, and then right-click. On the shortcut menu, click **Field Width**, and then in the **Column Width** dialog box, click **Best Fit**.

6 From **Backstage** view, click the **Save Object As** tab. In the **Save As** dialog box, delete the existing text, and then type **Lastname Firstname 3B Suppliers by Zip Query** and then click **OK**.

Access creates a new query based on a copy of your query Lastname Firstname 3B Tool Supplier Query. It is not necessary to save all queries, but you should save a query if you think you will need the same information again.

7 In **Backstage** view, click the **Print tab**, and then click **Print Preview**. On the **Print Preview tab**, in the **Page Layout group**, click **Landscape**.

8 If you are submitting your files electronically, go to Step 9. If you are printing your files, in the **Print group**, click the **Print** button, and then in the **Print** dialog box, click **Print**.

9 In the **Close Preview group**, click the **Close Print Preview** button. Right-click the **Lastname Firstname 3B Suppliers by ZIP Query tab**, and then on the shortcut menu, click **Close**.

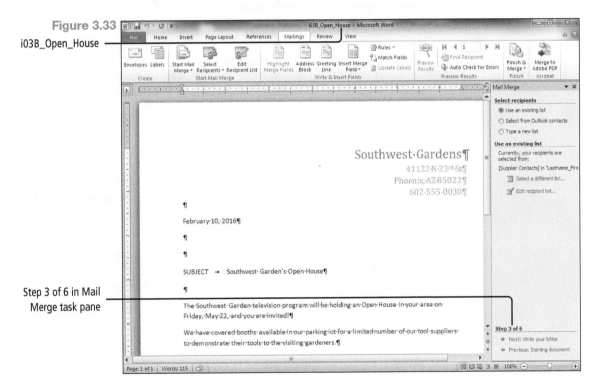

Objective 8 | Use Mail Merge in Access

The Word Mail Merge Wizard is available in Access. It permits you to set up the mail merge process that uses a table or query in an Access database as the data source for letters, envelopes, and labels. When you are in Access with the source database open, the Export group has a link to the Mail Merge Wizard. You can choose to link the source data to an existing document, or you can choose to create a new document.

Activity 3.19 | Starting Mail Merge in Access

1 Click the **External Data tab**. In the **Export group**, click the **Word Merge** button. In the **Microsoft Word Mail Merge Wizard** dialog box, under **What do you want the wizard to do?**, confirm that the **Link your data to an existing Microsoft Word document** option button is selected, and then click **OK**.

2 In the **Select Microsoft Word Document** dialog box, navigate to the student data files, select the document **i03B_Open_House**, and then click **Open**. On the taskbar, click the **Word** button, and then **Maximize** the Word window. On the horizontal scroll bar, scroll to display the left edge of the document, and then compare your screen with Figure 3.33.

The document i03B_Open_House opens in Word, and the Mail Merge task pane opens to Step 3 of 6.

Figure 3.33
i03B_Open_House ——

Step 3 of 6 in Mail
Merge task pane ——

3 From **Backstage** view, display the **Save As** dialog box, and then save the document to your **Integrated Projects Chapter 3** folder with the file name Lastname_Firstname_3B_Invitations Be sure formatting marks display.

Activity 3.20 | Completing the Mail Merge

1 In the **Mail Merge** task pane, under **Select recipients**, confirm that the **Use an existing list** option button is selected. Under **Use an existing list**, click **Select a different list**. Navigate to your **Integrated Projects Chapter 3** folder, select **your Lastname_Firstname_3B_Tool_Suppliers** file, and then click **Open** to display the **Select Table** dialog box. Compare your screen with Figure 3.34.

> In the Select Table dialog box, both tables and queries are listed. You may use either object as a data source for a mail merge.

Figure 3.34

Select Table dialog box ——

Tables and queries listed ——

2 In the **Select Table** dialog box, verify that **Lastname Firstname 3B Suppliers by ZIP Query** is selected, and then click **OK**. In the **Mail Merge Recipients** dialog box, click **OK**.

3 At the bottom of the **Mail Merge** task pane, click **Next: Write your letter**. In the first blank line below the date, click to position the insertion point. In the **Mail Merge** task pane, under **Write your letter**, click **Address block**. In the **Insert Address Block** dialog box, under **Specify address elements**, verify that the **Joshua Randall Jr.** format is selected. Click **Match Fields**. Under **Required for Address Block**, click the **First Name arrow**, and then click **Contact First Name**. Click the **Last Name arrow**, and then click **Contact Last Name**. Click the **Company arrow**, click **Supplier**, and then click **OK**. At the bottom of the **Insert Address Block** dialog box, click **OK**.

4 In your document, select the **<<AddressBlock>>** field, being sure to include the paragraph mark. Click the **Page Layout tab**, and then in the **Paragraph group**, under **Spacing**, use the **down spin box arrow** to set the **After** box to **0 pt**.

5 At the bottom of the **Mail Merge** task pane, click **Next: Preview your letters** to display **Step 5 of 6**.

6 At the bottom of the **Mail Merge** task pane, click **Next: Complete the merge**. Under **Merge**, click **Edit individual letters**. In the **Merge to New Document** dialog box, verify that the **All** option button is selected, and then click **OK**.

> A new document with 16 letters is created.

7 Save 💾 the document to the **Integrated Projects Chapter 3** folder with the file name Lastname_Firstname_3B_Supplier_Invitations Press Ctrl + Home to move to the beginning of the document. If your instructor directs you to submit your files electronically, go to step 9.

8 From **Backstage** view, click the **Print tab**. Under **Settings**, click the **Print All Pages** button, and then click **Print Current Page**. Click the **Print** button.

Only the first letter is printed.

9 Near the bottom of the document, double-click to open the footer area. Using **Quick Parts**, insert the **FileName** field, and then double-click in the document to close the footer area.

10 Display **Backstage** view, and then click the **Info tab**. Click **Properties**, and then click **Show Document Panel**. In the **Author** box, type your firstname and lastname, in the **Subject** box, type your course name and section number, and then in the **Keywords** box, type **supplier invitations, merged Close** ⊠ the Document Information Panel.

11 **Save** 🖫, and then **Close** ⊠ the **Lastname_Firstname_3B_Supplier_Invitations** document.

12 In your **Lastname_Firstname_3B_Invitations** document, display **Backstage** view, and then click the **Info** tab. Click **Properties**, and then click **Show Document Panel**. In the **Author** box, type your firstname and lastname, in the **Subject** box, type your course name and section number, and then in the **Keywords** box, type **invitations, merge fields Close** ⊠ the Document Information Panel, and then **Save** 🖫 your document.

13 **Close** ⊠ Word. If a message box displays asking you to save changes, click **Yes**. **Close** ⊠ Access.

14 Submit your printed or electronic files as directed by your instructor.

End **You have completed Project 3B** ————————————————

Contents-Based Assessments

Summary

An Access database is one way for a business to manage its data and be able to quickly retrieve data when it is requested. You can use tables, forms, or queries to modify—update, delete, sort, or filter—data. The data in tables can be exported to a Word document, and it can be formatted as a table or used with the Mail Merge Wizard to complete letters, envelopes, and labels in Word.

Key Terms

Bound	Field	Navigation Pane	Sorting
Cell	Filtering	Object	Subset
Criteria	Form	Populate	Table
Data source	Form view	Primary key	Template
Data type	Layout view	Query	Text box
Database	Mail Merge	Record	Wizard
Datasheet view	Main document	Run	
Design view	Message Bar	Select query	

Matching

Match each term in the second column with its correct definition in the first column by writing the letter of the term on the blank line in front of the correct definition.

_____ 1. An organized collection of facts about people, events, things, or ideas related to a particular topic or purpose.

_____ 2. The basic parts of a database that you create to store your data and to work with your data.

_____ 3. All of the categories pertaining to one person, place, thing, event, or idea, and which is formatted as a row in a database table.

_____ 4. A single piece of information that is stored in every record and formatted as a column in a database table.

_____ 5. An Access view that displays the detailed structure of a table, query, form, or report, and the view in which some tasks must be performed.

_____ 6. A field that uniquely identifies a record in a table.

_____ 7. The characteristic that defines the kind of data that can be entered into a field, such as numbers, text, or dates.

_____ 8. The action of filling a database table with records.

_____ 9. A database object used to enter data, edit data, or display data from a table or query.

_____ 10. A database object that retrieves specific data from one or more database objects and then, in a single datasheet, displays only the data you specify.

_____ 11. The Access view in which you can make changes to a form or to a report while the object is running—the data from the underlying data source displays.

A Criteria

B Data type

C Database

D Design view

E Field

F Form

G Layout view

H Objects

I Primary key

J Populate

K Query

L Record

M Sorting

N Text box

O Wizard

_____ 12. A feature in Microsoft Office that walks you step by step through a process.

_____ 13. A movable, resizable container for text or graphics.

_____ 14. The process of arranging data in a specific order based on the value in each field.

_____ 15. The conditions in a query that identify the specific records for which you are looking.

Multiple Choice

Circle the correct answer.

1. A preformatted database designed for a specific purpose is called a:
   A. built-in object
   B. read only file
   C. template

2. The Access object that stores data organized in an arrangement of columns and rows, and which is the foundation of an Access dataset is a:
   A. form
   B. query
   C. table

3. The area directly below the Ribbon that displays information such as security alerts when there is potentially unsafe, active content in an Office file that you open is:
   A. Message Bar
   B. Message pane
   C. Status bar

4. The area of the Access window that displays and organizes the names of the objects in a database and where you can open objects for use is the:
   A. Object Pane
   B. Navigation Pane
   C. Task bar

5. The Access view that displays data organized in columns and rows similar to an Excel worksheet is:
   A. Datasheet view
   B. Design view
   C. Print Preview

6. A term that describes objects and controls that are based on data stored in one or more tables or queries in the database is:
   A. bound
   B. restricted
   C. unbound

7. The Access view in which you can view the records in a form, but you cannot change the layout or design of the form:
   A. Datasheet view
   B. Form view
   C. Draft view:

8. A list of variable information, such as names and addresses, that is merged with a main document to create customized form letters, envelopes, or labels is called the:
   A. address block
   B. data source
   C. merge fields

9. A portion of the total records available in a table is called a:
   A. subgroup
   B. subordinate group
   C. subset

10. The process of displaying only a portion of the data based on matching a specific value to show only the data that meets the criteria you specify is called:
    A. filtering
    B. merging
    C. sorting

Apply 3A skills from these Objectives:
1. Create an Access Database Using a Template
2. Use an Access Form to Enter and Edit Records
3. Export an Access Table to a Word Document
4. Format a Word Document

Skills Review | Project **3C Community Gardens**

In the following Skills Review, you will use an Access template to create a new database listing the names of local community gardens. You will include this information in a memo to the President of Southwest Gardens. Your completed files will look similar to Figure 3.35.

Project Files

For Project 3C, you will need the following files:

New blank Access database
i03C_Garden_Parade

You will save your files as:

Lastname_Firstname_3C_Community_Gardens
Lastname_Firstname_3C_Garden_Parade

Project Results

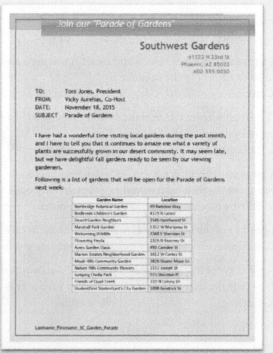

Figure 3.35

Integrating Word and Access

152

1. **Start** Access. Under **Available Templates**, click **Sample templates**, and then click **Events**. In the lower right portion of the screen, to the right of the **File Name** box, click the **Browse** button. In the **File New Database** dialog box, navigate to the **Integrated Projects Chapter 3** folder. In the **File name** box, delete the existing text, type **Lastname_Firstname_3C_Community_Gardens** and then click **OK**. Under the **File Name** box, click **Create**.

   a. On the **Message Bar**, if a security warning displays, click the **Enable Content** button.

   b. Right-click the **Event List form tab**, and then click **Close**. If necessary **Open** the **Navigation Pane**. In the **Navigation Pane**, click the **Events Navigation arrow**, and then click **Object Type**. Under **Tables**, right click **Events**, and then on the shortcut menu, click **Rename**. Type the new table name **Lastname Firstname 3C Community Gardens** and then press Enter. Double-click the renamed table to open the table.

   c. On the **Home tab**, in the **Views group**, click the **View button arrow**, and then click **Design View**.

   d. To the left of the **Description** field name, click the row selector box. On the **Design tab**, in the **Tools group**, click the **Delete Rows** button.

   e. To the left of the **Location** field, click the row selector box. Point to the row selector box, hold down the left mouse button, and then drag the **Location** field below the **Title** field.

2. Click the **Title** field, delete the contents of the cell, and then type **Garden Name** On the Quick Access Toolbar, click **Save**. On the **Design tab**, in the **Views group**, click the **View** button to display Datasheet view.

   a. Click the **Start Time** field name, and then drag right to select the field names **End Time** and **Attachments**—the paper clip symbol. Right-click the **Start Time** field name, and then on the shortcut menu, click **Hide Fields**. Click **Save.**

   b. In the first cell, below **Garden Name**, click in the cell, and then type **Northridge Botanical Garden** Press Tab, in the **Location** cell, type **49 Bamboo Way** and then press Tab three times. Enter the following gardens in the table:

Garden Name	Location
Bridlemile Children's Garden	4129 N Lanier
Desert Garden Neighbors	1546 Hazelwood St
Marshall Park Garden	1352 W Mariposa St
Welcoming Wildlife	3348 E Sheridan St
Flowering Fiesta	34 Lacey Tr
Ayers Garden Oasis	493 Camden St

   c. Right click the **Lastname Firstname 3C Community Gardens table tab**, and then on the shortcut menu, click **Close**. When asked if you want to save the table layout, click **Yes**.

Integrating Word and Access

3. In the navigation pane, with **Lastname Firstname 3C Community Gardens** table selected, on the **Create tab**, in the **Forms group**, click the **Form** button. Click **Save**. In the **Save As** dialog box, type **Lastname Firstname 3C Community Gardens Form**, and then click **OK**.

    a. On the **Design tab**, in the **Views group**, click the **View** button. At the bottom of the form, in the navigation area, click the **New (blank) record** button.

    b. Press Ⓣab. In the **Garden Name** field, type **Marion Estates Neighborhood Garden** and then press Ⓣab. Type **3612 W Cortez St** and then press Ⓣab. Using the same technique, enter the following information:

Garden Name	Location
Moab Hills Community Garden	3826 Sloane Muse Ln
Nature Hills Community Flowers	1152 Joseph St
Jumping Cholla Park	923 Sheridan Pl
Friends of Quali Creek	310 N Colony Dr
Saddle Brooke	9012 S Charles St

    c. Enter the following data using your own **First Name** and **Last Name**, and then press Ⓣab to display a new blank record.

Garden Name	Location
Firstname Lastname's City Garden	1808 Kendrick St

    d. In the **Navigation Pane**, double-click the **Lastname Firstname 3C Community Gardens** table, and then verify that your record displays in the table.

    e. At the top of the object widow, click the **Lastname Firstname 3C Community Gardens Form tab** to display the form. In the navigation area, click the **First record** button.

4. Click in the **Garden Name** field. On the **Home tab**, in the **Find group**, click the **Find** button. In the **Find and Replace** dialog box, in the **Find What** box, type **Flowering Fiesta** and then click **Find Next**. In the **Location** field, select the text **34 Lacey Tr**, and then type **2326 N Kearney Dr** Press Ⓣab.

    a. Click in the **Garden Name** field, and then click the **Find and Replace** dialog box to make it active. In the **Find What** box, type **Saddle Brooke**, and then click **Find Next**. **Close** the **Find and Replace** dialog box. On the **Home tab**, in the **Records group**, click the **Delete button arrow**, and then click **Delete Record**. In the message box, click **Yes** to confirm the deletion.

    b. Right-click the **Lastname Firstname 3C Community Gardens Form tab**, and then on the shortcut menu, click **Close**.

5. In the **Lastname Firstname 3C Community Gardens** table, drag to select the field names **Garden Name** and **Location**, right-click, and then on the shortcut menu, click **Field Width**. In the **Column Width** dialog box, click **Best Fit**, and then click **Save**.

    a. Right-click the **Lastname_Firstname 3C Community Gardens tab**, and then click **Close**.

    b. In the **Navigation Pane**, verify that the **Lastname Firstname 3C Community Gardens** table is selected.

Integrating Word and Access

c. On the **External Data tab**, in the **Export group**, click the **More** button, and then click **Word**. In the **Export – RTF File** dialog box, click the **Browse** button, and then navigate to your **Integrated Projects Chapter 3** folder. In the **File Save** dialog box, in the **File name** box, select the existing text, type **Lastname_Firstname_3C_Community_Gardens** and then click **Save**. In the **Export – RTF File** dialog box, click the **OK** button. In the next dialog box, if necessary clear the **Save export steps** check box, and then click the **Close** button.

d. Display **Backstage** view, and then click **View and edit database properties**. In the **Properties** dialog box, on the **Summary tab**, in the **Subject** box, type your course name and section number, in the **Author** box, type your firstname and lastname, and then in the **Keywords** box, type **garden form** Click **OK** to close the dialog box, click the **Home tab**, and then **Close** Access.

6. **Start** Word. **Open** the file **i03C_Garden_Parade**. **Save** the document in the **Integrated Projects Chapter 3** folder as **Lastname_Firstname_3C_Garden_Parade** Insert the file name in the footer, and then display formatting marks.

a. Press `Ctrl` + `End` to move to the end of the document. On the **Insert tab**, in the **Text group**, click the **Object button arrow**, and then click **Text from File**. In the **Insert File** dialog box, navigate to the **Integrated Projects Chapter 3** folder, click the RTF file name **Lastname_Firstname_3C_Community_Gardens**, and then click **Insert**.

b. In the inserted table, click in the first cell—**ID**—to make it the active cell. On the **Layout tab**, in the **Row & Columns group**, click the **Delete** button, and then click **Delete Columns**. If necessary, select the middle columns, **Start Time** and **End Time**, and then delete both columns. In the **Cell Size group**, click the **AutoFit** button, and then click **AutoFit Contents**.

c. On the **Design tab**, in the **Table Styles group**, click the **More** button, and then under **Built-In**, in the third row, click the fourth style—**Light Grid Accent 3**. On the **Layout tab**, in the **Table group**, click the **Properties** button. In the **Table Properties** dialog box, on the **Table tab**, under **Alignment**, click **Center**, and then click **OK**.

7. Press `Ctrl` + `Home`. Select the first paragraph of the document—*Southwest Gardens*. On the **Home tab**, in the **Styles group**, click **Heading 1**. In the **Font group**, click the **Font Size button arrow**, and then click **24**. Select the second, third, and fourth paragraphs. In the **Styles group**, click **Heading 2**. Select the first four paragraphs, and then in the **Paragraph group**, click the **Align Text Right** button. Click the **Line Spacing** button, and then click **Remove Space Before Paragraph**.

a. Click anywhere in the document to deselect the paragraphs. On the **Insert tab**, in the **Text group**, click the **Text Box** button, and then click **Tiles Sidebar**. With the text box still selected, type **Join our "Parade of Gardens"** Select all the text in the text box, and then from the Mini toolbar, click the **Grow Font** button two times.

b. On the **Page Layout tab**, in the **Page Background group**, click the **Page Borders** button. In the **Borders and Shading** dialog box, on the **Page Border tab**, under **Setting**, click **3-D**. Click the **Color button arrow**, and then in the seventh column, click the fifth color—**Olive Green, Accent 3, Darker 25%**. Click the **Width button arrow**, click 2 ¼ **pt**. Under **Apply to**, be sure **Whole Document** displays, and then click **OK**.

Integrating Word and Access

c. In the **Page Background group**, click the **Page Color** button. Under **Theme Colors**, in the seventh column, click the third color—**Olive Green, Accent 3, Lighter 60%**. In the **Themes group**, click the **Themes** button, and then click **Opulent**.

d. Display **Backstage** view, click **Properties**, and then click **Show Document Panel**. In the **Author** box, type your firstname and lastname, in the **Subject** box, type your course name and section number, and then in the **Keywords** box, type **garden table** **Close** the Document Information Panel, **Save** your document, and then **Close** Word.

e. Submit your printed or electronic files as directed by your instructor.

You have completed Project 3C

Integrating Word and Access

3B skills from these Objectives:

5. Use Mail Merge in Word to Complete Letters Using Access Data
6. Use Mail Merge in Word to Create Envelopes Using Access Data
7. Create and Modify a Query in Access
8. Use Mail Merge in Access

In the following Skills Review, you will use mail merge to create individualized letters and envelopes to be sent to children interested in gardening. You will create additional letters using a filtered list. Your completed files will look similar to Figure 3.36.

Project Files

For Project 3D, you will need the following files:

New blank Word document
i03D_Child_Gardeners
i03D_Gardening_Letter
i03D_Ayers_Academy

You will save your files as:

Lastname_Firstname_3D_Child_Gardeners
Lastname_Firstname_3D_Gardening_Letter
Lastname_Firstname_3D_Child_Letters
Lastname_Firstname_3D_Gardening_Envelopes
Lastname_Firstname_3D_Child_Envelopes
Lastname_Firstname_3D_Ayers_Academy
Lastname_Firstname_3D_Ayers_Letters

Project Results

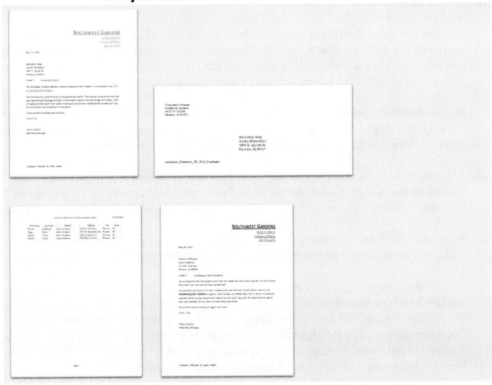

Figure 3.36

Integrating Word and Access

1. From the **Start** menu, navigate to your student data files, and then click one time to select the Access file **i03D_Child_Gardeners**. Right-click the file, and then on the shortcut menu, click **Copy**.

    a. Navigate to your **Integrated Projects Chapter 3** folder, right-click, and then click **Paste**. Right- click the selected file, and then on the shortcut menu, click **Rename**. Type **Lastname_Firstname_3D_Child_Gardeners** and then press Enter **Close** the window.

    b. Word. Open the document **i03D_Gardening_Letter**. **Save** the file in your **Integrated Projects Chapter 3** folder as **Lastname_Firstname_3D_Gardening_Letter**

    c. On the **Mailings tab**, in the **Start Mail Merge group**, click the **Start Mail Merge** button, and then click **Step by Step Mail Merge Wizard** to display the **Mail Merge** task pane.

    d. Under **Select document type**, verify that the **Letters** option button is selected. Click **Next: Starting document**, and then under **Select starting document**, verify that the **Use the current document** option button is selected, and then click **Next: Select recipients**.

    e. Under **Select recipients**, verify that the **Use an existing list** option button is selected. Under **Use an existing list**, click **Browse**. Navigate to your **Integrated Projects Chapter 3** folder, select the **Lastname_Firstname_3D_Child_Gardeners** file, and then click **Open** to display the **Select Table** dialog box. If necessary, in the **Select Table** dialog box, click **Child Gardeners**, and then click **OK** to display the **Mail Merge Recipients** dialog box. Scroll to the right, and then click the field column heading **School**. At the bottom of the Mail Merge Recipients dialog box, click **OK**.

2. At the bottom of the task pane, click **Next: Write your letter**. In your letter, move the insertion point to the second blank line below the date, in the **Mail Merge** task pane, under **Write your letter**, click **Address block**. In the **Insert Address Block** dialog box, under **Specify address elements**, verify that the **Joshua Randall Jr.** format is selected.

    a. Near the bottom of the **Insert Address Block** dialog box, click **Match Fields**. Under **Required for Address Block**, click the **Company arrow**, and then click **School**. At the bottom of the **Match Fields** dialog box, click **OK**. If a message box displays, click **Yes**, and then at the bottom of the **Insert Address Block** dialog box, click **OK**.

    b. In your document, select the **<<AddressBlock>>** field, being sure to include the paragraph mark. On the **Page Layout tab**, in the **Paragraph group**, use the **spin box down arrow** to set the **Before** and **After** boxes to **0 pt**. Click **OK** to close the dialog box.

    c. At the bottom of the task pane, click **Next: Preview your letter**, and then click **Next: Complete the merge**. Under **Merge**, click **Edit individual letters**. In the **Merge to New Document** dialog box, verify that the **All** option button is selected, and then click **OK**.

    d. Press Ctrl + Home, and then **Save** the new document in **your Integrated Projects Chapter 3** folder as **Lastname_Firstname_3D_Child_Letters** Insert the file name in the footer.

    e. Display **Backstage** view, click **Properties**, and then click **Show Document Panel**. In the **Author** box, type your firstname and lastname, in the **Subject** box, type your course name and section number, and then in the **Keywords** box, type **letters, merged Close** the Document Information Panel, **Save** your changes, and then **Close** the document. In the document **Lastname_Firstname_3D_Gardening_Letter**, insert the file name in the footer, **Save** your changes, and then from **Backstage** view, click the **Close** tab.

3. Press [Ctrl] + [N] to display a new document. Save the document in your **Integrated Projects Chapter 3** folder as **Lastname_Firstname_3D_Gardening_Envelopes**

  a. On the **Mailings tab**, in the **Start Mail Merge group**, click the **Start Mail Merge** button, and then click **Envelopes**. In the **Envelope Options** dialog box, under **Envelope size**, verify that **Size 10** is selected, and then click **OK**. In the **Mail Merge group**, click the **Select Recipients** button, and then click **Use Existing List**. Navigate to your **Integrated Projects Chapter 3** folder, select the file **Lastname_Firstname_3D_ Child_Gardeners**, and then click **Open**. If necessary, in the **Select Table** dialog box, click **Child Gardeners**, and then click **OK**.

  b. In the **Mail Merge group**, click the **Edit Recipient List** button. In the **Mail Merge Recipients** dialog box, scroll to the right, and then click the field column heading **School**. At the bottom of the **Mail Merge Recipients** dialog box, click **OK**.

4. With the insertion point at the top left corner of the envelope, using your own name, type **Firstname Lastname** and then press [Enter]. Type **Southwest Gardens** and then press [Enter]. Type **41122 N 23rd St** press [Enter], and then type **Phoenix, AZ 85022**

  a. In the middle of the envelope, click one time on the paragraph mark to display the address placeholder. On the **Mailings tab**, in the **Write & Insert Fields group**, click the **Address Block** button.

  b. In the **Insert Address Block** dialog box, click the **Match Fields** button, and then under **Required for Address Block**, click the **Company arrow**, and then click **School**. In the **Match Fields** dialog box, click **OK**. If a dialog box displays telling you data may be read by others, click **Yes**.

  c. In the **Insert Address Block** dialog box, under **Preview**, verify that the **School** displays in the address, and then at the bottom of the **Insert Address Block** dialog box, click **OK**.

  d. In the **Finish group**, click the **Finish & Merge** button, and then click **Edit Individual Documents**. In the **Merge to New Document** dialog box, verify that the **All** option button is selected, and then click **OK**. **Save** the new document in your **Integrated Projects Chapter 3** folder with the file name **Lastname_Firstname_3D_Child_Envelopes** Insert the file name in the footer.

  e. Display **Backstage** view, click **Properties**, and then click **Show Document Panel**. In the **Author** box, type your firstname and lastname, in the **Subject** box, type your course name and section number, and then in the **Keywords** box, type **envelopes, merged** Close the Document Information Panel, **Save** your changes, and then **Close** the document. In the document **Lastname_Firstname_3D_Gardening_Envelopes**, insert the file name in the footer, **Save** your changes, and then **Close** Word.

5. **Start** Access. Click the **Recent tab**, and then under **Recent Databases**, click your database **Lastname_Firstname_3D_Child_Gardeners**. If a Security Warning displays on the **Message Bar**, click the **Enable Content** button.

a. In the **Navigation Pane**, if necessary, select the **Child Gardeners** table. On the **Create tab**, in the **Queries group**, click the **Query Wizard** button. In the **New Query** dialog box, verify that **Simple Query Wizard** is selected, and then click **OK**.

b. Under **Available Fields**, click **First Name**, and then click the **Add Field** button. Using the same technique, add the following fields to the **Selected Fields** list: **Last Name**, **School**, **Address**, **City**, **State**, and **ZIP**.

c. At the bottom of the **Simple Query Wizard** dialog box, click the **Next** button. Under **Would you like a detail or summary query?**, verify that the **Detail** option button is selected, and then click **Next**. On the next screen, under **What title do you want for your query?**, type **Lastname Firstname 3D Child Gardeners Query** and then click **Finish**.

d. On the **Home tab**, in the **Views group**, click the **View** button to switch to Design view. In the design grid, in the **Sort row**, click in the **School** field, click the **Sort arrow**, and then click **Ascending**. On the **Design tab**, in the **Results group**, click the **Run** button.

e. On the **Home tab**, in the **Views group**, click the **View** button to switch to Design view. In the design grid, in the **Criteria row**, click in the **School** field. Type **Ayers Academy** and then in the **Results group**, click the **Run** button. In **Backstage** view, click the **Save Object As** tab. In the **Save As** dialog box, delete the existing text, and then type **Lastname Firstname 3D Ayers Academy Query** and then click **OK**.

f. In **Backstage** view, click the **Print tab**, and then click **Print Preview**. On the **Print Preview tab**, in the **Page Layout group**, click **Landscape**. In the **Close Preview group**, click the **Close Print Preview** button. **Save** your changes, right-click the **Lastname Firstname 3D Ayers Academy Query tab**, and then on the shortcut menu, click **Close**.

6. On the **External Data tab**, in the **Export group**, click the **Word Merge** button. In the **Microsoft Word Mail Merge Wizard** dialog box, under **What do you want the wizard to do?**, confirm that the **Link your data to an existing Microsoft Word document** option button is selected, and then click **OK**.

a. In the **Select Microsoft Word Document** dialog box, navigate to the data file **i03D_Ayers_Academy**, and then click **Open**. **Maximize** the Word window. **Save** the document in your **Integrated Projects Chapter 3** folder as **Lastname_Firstname_3D_Ayers_Academy**

b. In the **Mail Merge** task pane, under **Select recipients**, verify that the **Use an existing list** option button is selected. Under **Use an existing list**, click **Select a different list**. Navigate to your **Integrated Projects Chapter 3** folder, select the Access file **Lastname_Firstname_3D_Child_Gardeners**, and then click **Open**. In the **Select Table** dialog box, click **Lastname Firstname 3D Ayers Academy Query**, and then click **OK** In the **Mail Merge Recipients** dialog box, click **OK**.

c. At the bottom of the task pane, click **Next: Write your letter**. Move the insertion point to the second blank line below the date. In the **Mail Merge** task pane, under **Write your letter**, click **Address block**. Click **Match Fields**, under **Required for Address Block**, click the **Company arrow**, and then click **School**. Click **OK**. At the bottom of the **Insert Address Block** dialog box, click **OK**.

Integrating Word and Access

d. In your document, select the **<<AddressBlock>>** field. Be sure to include the paragraph mark. On the **Page Layout tab**, in the **Paragraph group**, under **Spacing**, use the **spin box down arrow** to set the **Before** and **After** boxes to **0 pt**. At the bottom of the task pane, click **Next: Preview your letters**. At the bottom of the task pane, click **Next: Complete the merge**. Under **Merge**, click **Edit individual letters**. In the **Merge to New Document** dialog box, verify that the **All** option button is selected, and then click **OK**.

e. **Save** the document to the **Integrated Projects Chapter 3** folder as **Lastname_Firstname_3D_Ayers_Letters** Insert the file name in the footer.

f. Display **Backstage** view, click **Properties**, and then click **Show Document Panel**. In the **Author** box, type your firstname and lastname, in the **Subject** box, type your course name and section number, and then in the **Keywords** box, type **Ayers, merged Close** the Document Information Panel, **Save** your changes, and then **Close** the document. In the document **Lastname_Firstname_3D_Ayers_Academy**, insert the file name in the footer, and then **Save** your changes. **Close** Word, and then Close Access.

g. Submit your printed or electronic files as directed by your instructor.

You have completed Project 3D

**Apply 3A skills
from these
Objectives:**

1. Create an
    Access
    Database Using
    a Template
2. Use an Access
    Form to Enter
    and Edit
    Records
3. Export an
    Access Table to
    a Word
    Document
4. Format a Word
    Document

In the following Mastering Integration project, you will create a list of local
garden shows for Southwest Gardens. Your completed files will look similar to
Figure 3.37.

Project Files

For Project 3E, you will need the following files:

New blank Access database
i03E_Shows_Memo

You will save your files as:

Lastname_Firstname_3E_Garden_Shows
Lastname_Firstnmae_3E_Shows_Memo

Project Results

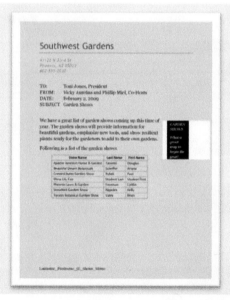

Figure 3.37

1. **Start** Access. Locate the **Sample Template** named **Students. Save** the database in your **Integrated Projects Chapter 3** folder with the file name **Lastname_Firstname_3E_Garden_Shows** If necessary, on the **Message Bar**, click **Enable Content**. **Close** any open objects. If necessary, click the **Open** button to expand the **Navigation Pane**.

2. In the **Navigation Pane**, click the **Students Navigation arrow**, and then click **Object Type**. **Delete** all **Reports**, all **Queries**, and all **Forms. Delete** the **Guardians** table. If any message boxes display, click **Yes. Rename** the **Students** table as **Lastname Firstname 3E Garden Shows** Drag down to select all fields beginning with **E-mail Address** and ending with **Business Phone**. With all eight rows selected, click **Delete Rows**. In a similar manner, delete the fields **Mobile Phone** and **Fax Number**, and then beginning with **Country/Region**, delete the last 12 fields in the table.

3. In the **State/Province** field, delete the text **/Province**. In the **ZIP/Postal Code** field, delete **/Postal Code**. Move the **Home Phone** field below the **First Name** field. Rename the **Company** field as **Show Name** Assign the **Primary Key** to the **Show Name** field, and then delete the **ID** field. Click **Save**, and then display the table in datasheet view. Enter the following garden shows in the table:

Show Name	Last Name	First Name	Home Phone	Address	City	State	ZIP
Phoenix Lawn & Garden	Freeman	Caitlin	480-555-5356	1123 W Apache St	Phoenix	AZ	85009
Apache Junction Home & Garden	Taranto	Douglas	480-555-3999	4918 E Holly St	Phoenix	AZ	85029
Beautiful Desert Botanicals	Scheffer	Briana	480-555-0481	12003 S 35th Ct	Phoenix	AZ	85009
Gilbert Flower Festival	Hevey	Miranda	480-555-6111	7981 Krisdale Dr	Phoenix	AZ	85016

4. **Create** a **Form** based on the **Lastname Firstname 3E Garden Shows** table. **Save** the form with the name **Lastname Firstname 3E Shows Form** and then using the form, enter the following information. In the last record, use your name in the **Last Name** and **First Name** fields.

Show Name	Last Name	First Name	Home Phone	Address	City	State	ZIP
Crested Butte Garden Show	Rybak	Paul	480-555-0488	6430 Stroebel Rd	Phoenix	AZ	85016
Tucson Botanical Garden Show	Vales	Brian	480-555-3021	1707 Erie St	Phoenix	AZ	85016
Snowbird Garden Show	Napoles	Kelly	480-555-0195	599 Krystall Ave	Phoenix	AZ	85017
Mesa Lily Fair	Last Name	First Name	480-555-5032	289 Michigan Ave	Phoenix	AZ	85009

5. Find the record for **Beautiful Desert Botanicals**, change the **Address** to **4687 Colonial Dr** and then change the **ZIP** to **85029** Find the record for **Gilbert Flower Festival**, and then **Delete** the record. In the **Lastname Firstname 3E Shows** table, in Datasheet view, adjust the **Column Width** of all columns to display all data. Change the **Page Layout** to **Landscape**.

6. **Export** the **Lastname Firstname 3E Garden Shows** table to your **Integrated Projects Chapter 3** folder as an **RTF File**. Save the file with the same name as the table. Do not save the export steps. Close any open objects.

Integrating Word and Access

7. Display **Backstage** view, and then click **View and edit database properties**. In the **Properties** dialog box, on the **Summary tab**, in the **Subject** box, type your course name and section number, in the **Author** box, type your firstname and lastname, and then in the **Keywords** box, type **shows form** Click **OK** to close the dialog box, click the **Home tab**, and then **Close** Access.

8. **Start** Word. Open the file **i03E_Shows_Memo**, and then **Save** the document in your **Integrated Projects Chapter 3** folder as **Lastname_Firstname_3E_Shows_Memo** Insert the file name in the footer. Move to the end of the document, and **Insert** the **Lastname Firstname 3E Garden Shows** RTF file. In the new table, display the columns **Show Name**, **Last Name**, and **First Name**, and then delete any other columns. Adjust the **Cell Size** to **AutoFit to Contents**, change the **Table Style** to the fourth style in the second row—**Light List – Accent 3**, and then **Center** align the table.

9. Select the first paragraph—*Southwest Gardens*, and then change the **Style** to **Title**. Select the second, third, and fourth paragraphs, and then change the **Style** to **Subtitle**. With the paragraphs still selected, click the **Line Spacing** button, and then click the **Remove Space After Paragraph** button. Deselect the text, and then **Insert** a **Text Box** with the style **Contrast Quote**. In the text box, type **GARDEN SHOWS** Press Enter, and then type **What a great way to begin the year!** Change the text box **Height** to **1.6"** and the **Width** to **2"**, and then move the text box to the right of the paragraph beginning *We have a great list*. Change the **Page Color** to **Blue, Accent 1, Lighter 60%**, and then apply the theme—**Urban**.

10. Display **Backstage** view, click **Properties**, and then click **Show Document Panel**. In the **Author** box, type your firstname and lastname, in the **Subject** box, type your course name and section number, and then in the **Keywords** box, type **shows table** **Close** the Document Information Panel, **Save** your document., and then **Close** Word.

11. Submit your printed or electronic files as directed by your instructor.

You have completed Project 3

<table>
<tr><td>

Apply 3B skills from these Objectives:

5. Use Mail Merge in Word to Complete Letters Using Access Data
6. Use Mail Merge in Word to Create Envelopes Using Access Data
7. Create and Modify a Query in Access
8. Use Mail Merge in Access

</td><td>

In the following Mastering Integration project, you will use the Mail Merge Wizard to create letters and envelopes for local gardening experts. Using a filtered list, you will create additional letters. Your completed files will look similar to Figure 3.38.

Project Files

For Project 3F, you will need the following files:

New blank Word document
i03F_Gardening_Basics
i03F_Gardening_Experts
i03F_Gardening_Fun

You will save your files as:

New blank Word document
Lastname_Firstname_3F_Gardening_Basics
Lastname_Firstname_3F_Gardening_Experts
Lastname_Firstname_3F_Expert_Letters
Lastname_Firstname_3F_Experts_Envelopes
Lastname_Firstname_3F_Merged_Envelopes
Lastname_Firstname_3F_Gardening_Fun
Lastname_Firstname_3F_Fun_Letters

</td></tr>
</table>

Project Results

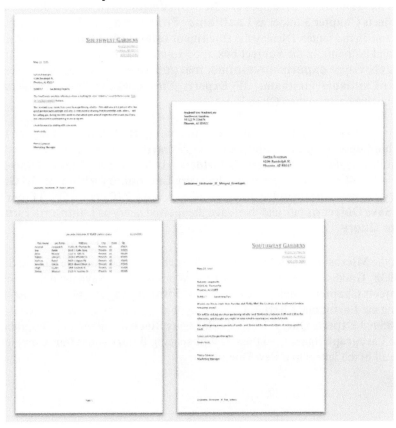

Figure 3.38

Integrating Word and Access

1. Navigate to the student data file, **i03F_Gardening_Basics**. **Copy** the file, and then **Paste** the file in your **Integrated Projects Chapter 3** folder. **Rename** the file with the file name **Lastname_Firstname_3F_Gardening_Basics**

2. **Start** Word, open the file **i03F_Gardening_Experts**. **Save** the file in your **Integrated Projects Chapter 3** folder as **Lastname_Firstname_3F_Gardening_Experts** Start the **Step by Step Mail Merge Wizard**. Confirm that you will create letters. **Select Recipients** using the **Lastname_Firstname_3F_Gardening_Basics** file and the **Gardening Experts** table. Insert the **Address Block** in the second blank paragraph below the date. Adjust the **Paragraph Spacing** so there is **0 pt** spacing **Before** and **After**.

3. **Complete the merge**, and merge all letters to a **New Document**. **Save** the new document in your **Integrated Projects Chapter 3** folder as **Lastname_Firstname_3F_Expert_Letters** Insert the file name in the footer. Display the **Document Information Panel**. In the **Author** box, type your firstname and lastname, in the **Subject** box, type your course name and section number, and then in the **Keywords** box, type **expert letters, merged Close** the Document Information Panel. **Close** the document. With the file **Lastname_Firstname_3F_Gardening_Experts** displayed, insert the file name in the footer, **Save** your changes, and then from **Backstage** view, click the **Close** tab.

4. Open a new, blank Word document. **Save** the document in your **Integrated Projects Chapter 3** folder as **Lastname_Firstname_3F_Experts_Envelopes** Start **Mail Merge**, and click **Envelopes**. Verify that the **Envelope Options** is set as a **Size 10** envelope. **Select Recipients** using the **Lastname_Firstname_3F_Gardening_Basics** file and the **Gardening Experts** table. As a return address, type your **Firstname Lastname** and then press [Enter]. Type **Southwest Gardens** and then press [Enter]. Type **41122 N 23rd St** press [Enter], and then type **Phoenix, AZ 85022** Insert the **Address Block**, and then merge all of the envelopes to a **New Document**. **Save** the new document in your **Integrated Projects Chapter 3** folder as **Lastname_Firstname_3F_Merged_Envelopes** Insert the file name in the footer. Display the **Document Information Panel**. In the **Author** box, type your firstname and lastname, in the **Subject** box, type your course name and section number, and then in the **Keywords** box, type **experts envelopes, merged Save** your changes, and then **Close** the document. In the **Lastname_Firstname_3F_Experts_Envelopes** file, insert the file name in the footer, **Save** your changes, and then **Close** Word.

5. Open the Access file **Lastname_Firstname_3F_Gardening_Basics**. If necessary, on the **Message Bar**, click **Enable Content**. Open the **Simple Query Wizard**, and then select the **Gardening Experts** table. Add the following fields to the **Selected Fields: First Name, Last Name, Address, City, State**, and **ZIP**. Show a **Detail** query, and then name the query **Lastname Firstname 3F Gardening Experts Query** Set the **Criteria** of the query to only show the **ZIP** code **85009** From **Backstage** view, click the **Save Object As** tab, and then save the revised query as **Lastname Firstname 3F 85009 Experts Query**

6. In Access, start the **Microsoft Word Mail Merge Wizard**, and then from the student data files, select the document **i03F_Gardening_Fun**. **Maximize** the Word window. **Save** the document in the **Integrated Projects Chapter 3** folder as **Lastname_Firstname_3F_Gardening_Fun Select Recipients** using the **Lastname_Firstname_3F_Gardening_Basics** file and the **Lastname Firstname 3F 85009 Experts Query**. Insert the **Address Block** in the second paragraph below the date. Adjust the **Paragraph Spacing** so there is **0 pt** spacing **Before** and **After**. Complete the merge, and then merge all of the letters to a **New Document**.

Integrating Word and Access

7. **Save** the new document in your **Integrated Projects Chapter 3** folder as **Lastname_Firstname_3F_Fun_Letters** Insert the file name in the footer. Display the **Document Information Panel**. In the **Author** box, type your firstname and lastname, in the **Subject** box, type your course name and section number, and then in the **Keywords** box, type **fun letters, merged Save** your changes, and **Close** the document. In the **Lastname_Firstname_3F_Gardening_Fun** file, insert the file name in the footer. **Save** your changes, and then **Close** Word. **Close** Access.

8. Submit your printed or electronic files as directed by your instructor.

You have completed Project 3F

Rubric

The following outcomes-based assessments are open-ended assessments. That is, there is no specific correct result; your result will depend on your approach to the information provided. Make Professional Quality your goal. Use the following scoring rubric to guide you in how to approach the problem and then to evaluate how well your approach solves the problem.

The *criteria*—Software Mastery, Content, Format and Layout, and Process—represent the knowledge and skills you have gained that you can apply to solving the problem. The *levels of performance*—Professional Quality, Approaching Professional Quality, or Needs Quality Improvements—help you and your instructor evaluate your result.

	Your completed project is of **Professional Quality**	Your completed project is of **Approaching Professional Quality**	Your completed project **Needs Quality Improvements**
1-Software Mastery	Chooses and applies the most appropriate skills, tools, and features and identifies efficient methods to solve the problem.	Chooses and applies some appropriate skills, tools, and features, but not in the most efficient manner.	Chooses inappropriate skills, tools, or features, or is inefficient in solving the problem.
2-Content	Constructs a solution that is clear and well organized, containing content that is accurate, appropriate to the audience and purpose, and complete. The solution contains no errors of spelling, grammar, or style.	Constructs a solution in which some components are unclear, poorly organized, inconsistent, or incomplete. May misjudge the needs of the audience. May contain some errors in spelling, grammar, or style, but the errors do not detract from comprehension.	Constructs a solution that is unclear, incomplete, or poorly organized, containing some inaccurate or inappropriate content. May contain many errors of spelling, grammar, or style. May fail to solve the problem.
3-Format and nLayout	Formats and arranges all elements to communicate information and ideas, clarify function, illustrate relationships, and indicate relative importance.	Applies appropriate format and layout features to some elements, but not others. Or, overuses features, causing minor distraction.	Applies format and layout that fails to communicate information or ideas or clearly. May fail to use format and layout features to clarify function, illustrate relationships, or indicate relative importance. Or, may use available features excessively, causing distraction.
4-Process	Uses an organized approach that integrates planning, development, self-assessment, revision, and reflection.	Demonstrates an organized approach in some areas, but not others. Or, uses an insufficient process of organization throughout.	Does not use an organized approach to solve the problem.

Integrating Word and Access

Apply a combination of the 3A and 3B skills.

Project Files

For Project 3G, you will need the following files:

New blank Word document
New blank Access database
i03G_Gardeners_Flyer
i03G_Gardeners_Letter

You will save your files as:

Lastname_Firstname_3G_Xeriscape_Gardeners
Lastname_Firstname_3G_Gardeners_Flyer
Lastname_Firstname_3G_Gardeners_Letter
Lastname_Firstname_3G_Xeriscape_Letters
Lastname_Firstname_3G_Xeriscape_Envelopes

Southwest Gardens is going to begin a new feature on xeriscaping—landscaping with slow-growing, drought tolerant plants to conserve water and reduce yard trimmings. The show wants to contact local designers who have created xeriscaped garden areas to see how much water they save. You have been asked to enter the contact information for the gardeners in a database, modify a flyer including the contact information, and then create individualized letters and envelopes using mail merge.

Save a new blank Access database as **Lastname_Firstname_3G_Xeriscape_Gardeners** In Access, save a new table as **Lastname Firstname 3G Gardeners Table** Create a new form based on the table, and then save it as **Lastname Firstname 3G Gardeners Form** Enter the contact information listed below. Open the i03G_Gardeners_Flyer. Insert an exported Access table in the flyer, and then delete the Phone column. Format the flyer to display as a one-page document and include a page color, page border, and theme. Save the flyer as **Lastname_Firstname_3G_Gardeners_Flyer**

Open the i03G_Gardeners_Letter, and save it as **Lastname_Firstname_3G_Gardeners_Letter** Using mail merge, include appropriate merge fields from the database in the letter. Complete the merge, and then save the merged letters as **Lastname_Firstname_3G_Xeriscape_Letters** Create envelopes to be used with the letters, using Southwest Gardens' address as the return address. Save the merged envelopes as **Lastname_Firstname_3G_Xeriscape_Envelopes** Insert the file name in the footer for each of the four Word documents. Insert appropriate document properties in all five files. Submit your printed or electronic files as directed by your instructor.

First Name	Last Name	Address	City	State	ZIP	Phone
Isaiah	Manzke	4106 Randolph St	Phoenix	AZ	85017	480-555-6111
Andrea	Bramley	7100 N 19th St	Phoenix	AZ	85029	480-555-0488
Vanessa	Mangrove	3622 E. Agave Rd	Phoenix	AZ	85016	480-555-3999
Trevor	Josephson	40716 N Citrus Trl	Phoenix	AZ	85016	480-555-4721
Ariel	Rios	6038 E Calle Rosa	Phoenix	AZ	85029	480-555-4774
Anton	Vega	3239 E Weldon Ave	Phoenix	AZ	85029	480-555-3031

You have completed Project 3G

| Apply a combination of the 3A and 3B skills. |

GO! Think | Project 3H Garden Clubs

Project Files
For Project 3H, you will need the following files:

New blank Word document
i03H_Garden_Clubs
i03H_Club_Information
i03H_Contacts_Letter

You will save your files as:

Lastname_Firstname_3H_Garden_Clubs
Lastname_Firstname_3H_Club_Information
Lastname_Firstname_3H_Contacts_Letter
Lastname_Firstname_3H_Club_Letters
Lastname_Firstname_3H_Club_Envelopes

Southwest Gardens is planning to feature a garden club each week in their show and wants to invite garden clubs to apply. You have been asked to update the contact information for the clubs in a database, modify an information sheet including the contact information, and then create individualized letters and envelopes using mail merge.

Copy the file i03H_Garden_Clubs. Paste the file where you are saving your files, and then rename it as **Lastname_Firstname_3H_Garden_Clubs** In Access, rename the Garden Clubs table as **Lastname Firstname 3H Garden Clubs** Create a new form based on the table with the form name **Lastname Firstname 3H Clubs Form** Enter the information below, using your First Name and Last Name for the last record. Update the Address Field for the Backyard Gardeners to **9847 Fairmount Ave** and delete the record for Bridlemile Garden Gloves. Export the table as an RTF file. Open the i03H_Club_Information file. Insert the RTF file and delete one or more columns. Format the information sheet to display as a one-page document and include a page color, page border, and theme. Save the document as **Lastname_Firstname_3H_Club_Information**

Open the i03H_Contacts_Letter, and save it as **Lastname_Firstname_3H_Contacts_Letter** Using mail merge, include appropriate merge fields from the database in the letter. Complete the merge, and then save the merged letters as **Lastname_Firstname_3H_Club_Letters** Create envelopes to be used with the letters, using Southwest Gardens' address as the return address. Save the merged envelopes as **Lastname_Firstname_3H_Club_Envelopes** Insert the file name in the footer for each of the four Word documents. Insert appropriate document properties in all five files. Submit your printed or electronic files as directed by your instructor.

Club Name	First Name	Last Name	Address	City	State	ZIP	Phone	E-mail Address
Garden Groupies	Penny	Rudder	6550 Windslow Ave	Phoenix	AZ	85009	480-555-3031	Penny@phoenixmail.com
Ocotillo Club	Greta	Myers	14820 S 25th Way	Phoenix	AZ	85029	480-555-0902	Greta@phoenixmail.com
Pots and Planters	First Name	Last Name	4126 W Mercer Ln	Phoenix	AZ	85009	480-555-5032	Firstname@phoenixmail.com

You have completed Project 3H

Integrating Word and Access

<table>
<tr><td>Apply a combination of the 3A and 3B skills.</td></tr>
</table>

Project Files

For Project 3I, you will need the following files:

New blank Access database
i03I_Designers_Newsletter

You will save your files as:

Lastname_Firstname_3I_Designers_Information
Lastname_Firstname_3I_Desingers_Newsletter

The owners of Southwest Gardens want to become more involved with the local businesses that design gardens. You have been asked to create a database that includes the contact information for the garden design companies. The owners also want to create a newsletter that includes the design company information.

Create a new blank Access database and save it as **Lastname_Firstname_3I_Designers_Information** In the database create a table with the name **Lastname Firstname 3I Designers Table** and create a form with the name **Lastname Firstname Designers Form** Use the information below to enter the information in the database.

Open the file i03I_Designers_Newsletter. Insert an exported Access table in the newsletter. Format the newsletter to display as a one-page document and include a page color, page border, and theme. Save the newsletter as **Lastname_Firstname_3I_Designers_Newsletter** Insert the file name in the footer of the document and add appropriate document properties to both files. Submit your printed or electronic files as directed by your instructor.

Garden Designer Company	First Name	Last Name	Address	City	State	ZIP	Phone
Clay's Nurseries & Design	Clay	Jones	4334 N 24th St	Phoenix	AZ	85016	480-555-3031
Tucson Landscapers	Karren	Kostka	4222 E Ray Rd	Phoenix	AZ	85017	480-555-0902
Desert Environments	Tanisha	Xie	222 E Helena Dr	Phoenix	AZ	85029	480-555-5032
Southwest Water Design	Lonnie	Kroon	21060 E Tonto Rd	Phoenix	AZ	85017	480-555-5356
Green Thumb Design	Cody	Benesh	18418 N 30th St	Phoenix	AZ	85029	480-555-3999
Phoenix Landscapes	Elinor	Riter	583 S 19th Way	Phoenix	AZ	85009	480-555-0488
Arizona Water Gardens	Jamison	Prada	2517 E Beryl Ave	Phoenix	AZ	85009	480-555-3021
Las Pilitas Design	Ava	Timpson	3610 W Belmont St	Phoenix	AZ	85029	480-555-0195
Southwest Cactus Nursery	Max	Vossen	620 E Briles Rd	Phoenix	AZ	85016	480-555-4721

You have completed Project 3I

Integrating Word and Access

Integrating Excel and Access

OUTCOMES
At the end of this chapter you will be able to:

OBJECTIVES
Mastering these objectives will enable you to:

PROJECT 4A
Import Excel data into an Access database and sort or filter in either Excel or Access.

1. Modify an Excel Table
2. Import Excel Data into Access Using the Import Spreadsheet Wizard
3. Sort and Filter Data in an Access Table
4. Create, Modify, and Print an Access Report

PROJECT 4B
Create an Access table and query and export Access data into an Excel workbook.

5. Create an Access Table
6. Create an Access Query
7. Export Access Data to Excel

Lisa F. Young/Shutterstock

In This Chapter

In this chapter, you will use the powerful tools of Excel and Access to work with large amounts of data. In Excel, you can analyze and manage your data. In Access, you can track and report your data. Use the import and export features to take advantage of a particular application's features. If you enter a large amount of data into either an Excel workbook or an Access table, it can be difficult to find the results you are seeking. Sorting and filtering data in Excel and Access allows you to view only the desired results.

The projects in this chapter relate to **Midwest HVAC Manufacturer**, one of the country's largest suppliers of heating, ventilation, and air conditioning (HVAC) equipment. The company delivers high-performance climate control parts and systems primarily to wholesale customers. Because of the growing popularity of do-it-yourself projects, they also have two local retail stores. Two times each year, Midwest HVAC Manufacturer updates its parts catalog, which includes supplies such as fans, motors, heating and cooling coils, filter units, and dehumidification and humidification units. They design and manufacture all of their own products and have won several engineering and product awards.

From Chapter 4 of *GO! with Microsoft® Office 2010 Integrated Projects Comprehensive*, First Edition, Shelley Gaskin, Carol L. Martin.
Copyright © 2012 by Pearson Education, Inc. Published by Pearson Prentice Hall. All rights reserved.

Project 4A HVAC Report

Project Activities

In Activities 4.01 through 4.10, you will sort and filter data in an Excel table provided by the retail store to Ray and Noreen Leven, who own a 25-year-old house in Lincoln, Nebraska that needs a new heating, ventilation, and air conditioning (HVAC) unit. You will then import the Excel data into Access, and then sort and filter the data in an Access table. You will create an Access report that lists the HVAC options for the Levens. Your completed files will look similar to Figure 4.1.

Project Files

For Project 4A, you will need the following files:

New blank Access database
i04A_HVAC_Units
i04A_Midwest_Logo

You will save your files as:

Lastname_Firstname_4A_HVAC_Units
Lastname_Firstname_4A_Levens_HVAC

Project Results

Figure 4.1
Project 4A HVAC Report

Objective 1 | Modify an Excel Table

Looking at a large group of data in an Excel workbook can be confusing and time-consuming. By using the sort feature, you can organize the data to understand the results more easily. An *Excel table* helps you manage and analyze data. An Excel table is a series of rows and columns that contains related data that is managed independently from the data in other rows and columns in the worksheet.

Activity 4.01 | Sorting Data in an Excel Table

In this activity, you will sort the manufacturer data in an HVAC Units workbook to determine which units provide the highest cooling capacity, and then you will sort the data to determine which units provide the highest heating capacity. Recall that sorting is the process of arranging data in a specific order based on the value in each field.

1 **Start** Excel. From your student files, locate and open the file **i04A_HVAC_Units**. In the location where you are saving your files for this chapter, create a new folder named **Integrated Projects Chapter 4** and then save the file in the folder as **Lastname_Firstname_4A_HVAC_Units**

2 Click the **Insert tab**, and then in the **Text group**, click the **Header & Footer** button. On the **Design tab**, in the **Navigation group**, click the **Go to Footer** button. In the **Footer** area, click in the box just above the word **Footer**, and then in the **Header & Footer Elements group**, click the **File Name** button. Click any cell in the workbook to exit the footer.

3 On the right side of the status bar, click the **Normal** button, and then press Ctrl + Home to make cell **A1** the active cell.

4 On the **Insert tab**, in the **Tables group**, click the **Table** button. In the **Create Table** dialog box, under **Where is the data for your table?**, verify that the range =$A$1:$I$28 displays, verify that the **My table has headers** check box is selected, and then click **OK**. Compare your screen with Figure 4.2.

The column titles in row 1 form the table headers. Sorting and filtering arrows display in the table's header row.

Figure 4.2

Sorting and filtering arrow

Header row

Range converted to table

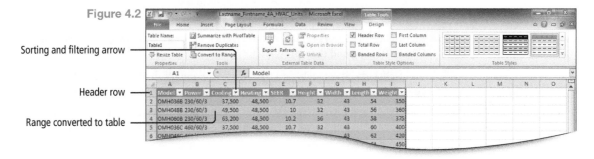

5 In the header row of the table, click the **Cooling arrow**, and then on the menu, click **Sort Largest to Smallest**. Compare your screen with Figure 4.3.

The rows in column C, the Cooling column, are sorted in *descending order*—text is arranged in reverse alphabetical order (Z to A) or numbers from the highest to the lowest value. *Ascending order* arranges text in alphabetical order (A to Z) or numbers from the lowest to the highest value. In cell C1, to the right of the Sort and Filter arrow, notice the small arrow pointing downward indicating that the column is sorted in descending order.

Figure 4.3

Descending sort arrow

Column C sorted in descending order

6 Right-click the **Sheet1 tab**, and then on the list, click **Move or Copy**. In the **Move or Copy** dialog box, click **(move to end)**, select the **Create a copy** check box, and then click **OK**.

A copy of Sheet1 is created and automatically named Sheet1 (2) to indicate it is a copy. Sheet1 (2) displays and is the active worksheet.

7 On **Sheet1 (2)**, at the top of the **Heating column**—column D—click the **Heating arrow**, and then click **Sort Largest to Smallest**.

To the right of the Heating arrow, notice that the small arrow points downward, indicating the column is sorted in descending order. When you use the Sort and Filter arrow to sort on a different column, the previous sort is turned off. In this case, the arrow pointing downward to the right of the Cooling arrow no longer displays.

8 Right-click the **Sheet1 (2) tab**, and then click **Rename**. With **Sheet1 (2)** selected, type **4A Levens Heating** and then press Enter.

9 Right-click the **Sheet1 tab**, and then click **Rename**. With **Sheet1** selected, type **4A Levens Cooling** and then press Enter. Compare your screen with Figure 4.4.

Notice that the data in the 4A Levens Cooling worksheet remains sorted by the Cooling column. Creating a copy of a worksheet is one way to keep various sort orders available to view at a later time.

Figure 4.4

Descending sort arrow

Sheets renamed

10 Save 🔲 the workbook.

Activity 4.02 | Setting a Custom AutoFilter

Similar to Access tables, when data is sorted, all of the data still displays in the workbook. When you use the *AutoFilter* feature, only a portion of the data (a subset) that meets the criteria you specify is displayed; data that does not meet the criteria is hidden—not deleted. In this case, the Levens want to see a list of units with gross cooling capacity greater than or equal to 45,000 BTUs (British Thermal Units), and, because they are concerned about shipping costs, they want to see a list of units that weigh less than 500 pounds.

1 Click the **4A Levens Heating sheet tab** to make it the active sheet. At the top of the **Cooling column**—column C, click the **Cooling arrow**, point to **Number Filters**, and then click **Greater Than Or Equal To**. In the **Custom AutoFilter** dialog box, under **Show rows where**, verify that **is greater than or equal to** is selected. In the box to the right, type **45000** and then compare your screen with Figure 4.5.

Figure 4.5

Custom Filter dialog box

Cooling column criteria

2 In the **Custom AutoFilter** dialog box, click **OK**. At the top of the **Weight column**—column I, click the **Weight arrow**, point to **Number Filters**, and then click **Less Than**. In the **Custom AutoFilter** dialog box, under **Show rows where**, verify **is less than** is selected. In the box to the right, type **500** and then click **OK**. Compare your screen with Figure 4.6.

Only the rows containing Cooling values greater than or equal to 45000 and Weight values less than 500 display; the remaining rows are hidden from view. A small funnel—the filter icon—indicates that a filter is applied to the data in the table. Additionally, the row numbers display in blue to indicate that some rows are hidden from view. A filter hides entire rows in the worksheet.

Figure 4.6

Filter icon
Row numbers display in blue
Hidden rows
Column C cells greater than or equal to 45,000
Column D sorted in descending order
Column I cells less than 500

3 At the top of the **Weight column**—column I—click the **Weight arrow**, and then click **Sort Smallest to Largest**.

To the right of the Weight arrow, a small arrow points upward, indicating the column is sorted in ascending order. The descending arrow in the Heating column no longer displays.

4 Save the workbook.

Activity 4.03 | Inserting a Calculated Column

One of the advantages of using Excel instead of a calculator is having the application calculate numeric results for you. The cost of shipping the HVAC units to the Levens' region is $1.75 per pound. In this activity, you will use a calculated column to find out how much it costs to ship each unit.

1 Click cell **J1**, type **Shipping Cost** and then press Enter.

AutoExpansion is an Excel table feature in which a new column is automatically included as part of the existing table. In this case, the Shipping Cost column automatically becomes part of the table.

2 Verify cell **J2** is the active cell. Type the formula **=I2*1.75** and then on the **Formula Bar**, click the **Enter** button to accept the entry and keep cell J2 as the active cell. Compare your screen with Figure 4.7.

A *calculated column* displays in column J. The calculated column uses a single formula that adjusts for each row of a column. The values from the formula display in the cells; and the *underlying formula* displays on the Formula Bar. An underlying formula is the formula entered in a cell and visible only on the Formula Bar. Recall the Formula Bar is an element in the Excel window that displays the value or formula contained in the active cell; you can also enter or edit values or formulas.

Figure 4.7

Underlying formula displays on Formula Bar

Calculated column

3 Click the **Formulas tab**, and then in the **Formula Auditing group**, click the **Show Formulas** button. If necessary, scroll right to view the formulas in column J.

> Recall that the relative cell reference feature will change the cell reference to the correct row, but the number 1.75 remains constant form one row to the next.

4 In the **Formula Auditing group**, click the **Show Formulas** button to turn off the feature.

5 Select the range **J2:J24**. Click the **Home tab**, and then in the **Number group**, click the **Accounting Number Format** button $ ▾. In the **Number group**, click the **Decrease Decimal** button two times.

6 Save the workbook.

Activity 4.04 | Applying Conditional Formatting

Analyzing data is simplified by using conditional formatting to highlight cells that meet certain conditions.

1 Verify the cells in **column J** are still selected. On the **Home tab**, in the **Styles group**, click the **Conditional Formatting** button. In the list, point to **Highlight Cells Rules**, and then click **Less Than**. In the **Less Than** dialog box, type **750** Click the **with arrow**, and then click **Yellow Fill with Dark Yellow Text**. Click **OK**, and then click anywhere in the table to deselect the cells in column J.

> A *conditional format* is a format that changes the appearance of a cell—for example, by adding cell shading or changing font color—based on a condition; if the condition is true, the cell is formatted based on that condition, if the condition is false, the cell is *not* formatted. In this case, the cells in column J that contain a number less than 750 are formatted with yellow fill and dark yellow text.

2 Select **columns A:J**. Point to the line between the column headings A and B until the ⊞ pointer displays, and then double-click.

> The widths of columns A through J automatically adjust to the best fit for each column so that all data can be read. Columns will vary in width.

3 At the top of the **Shipping Cost column**—column J—click the **Shipping Cost arrow**, click **Sort Largest to Smallest**. Click in an empty cell, and then compare your screen with Figure 4.8.

> The table is no longer sorted by Weight in ascending order; the data is sorted by Shipping Cost in descending order.

Project 4A: HVAC Report | **Integrated Projects**

Figure 4.8

Shipping Cost column in
descending order

Conditional format applied

---

4 On the **Quick Access Toolbar**, click the **Undo** button .

The Excel table is once again sorted by Weight in ascending order.

Another Way

On the Home tab, in
the Cells group, click
the Delete button
arrow, and then click
Delete Sheet.

5 Click the **Sheet2 tab**, hold down Ctrl, and then click the **Sheet3 tab**. Release Ctrl, and then with both sheets selected (the tab background is white), point to either of the selected sheet tabs, right-click, and then on the shortcut menu, click **Delete**.

The blank worksheets are deleted from the workbook.

6 Click the **4A Levens Cooling sheet tab** to make it the active sheet. Select cells **A1:A3**. On the **Home tab**, in the **Cells group**, click the **Insert button arrow**, and then click **Insert Sheet Rows**.

Blank rows are inserted above the selected rows. Because you selected cells in three rows, three new blank rows are inserted.

7 In cell **A1**, type **Models by Cooling Capacity – Levens** and then on the **Formula Bar**, click the **Enter** button ✓ to accept the entry and keep cell A1 the active cell.

8 Select cells **A1:I1**, and then on the **Home tab**, in the **Alignment group**, click the **Merge & Center** button . In the **Font group**, click the **Increase Font Size** button A˙ two times, and then click the **Bold** button B. Click the **Font Color button arrow** A˙ , and then in the fifth column, click the first color—**Blue, Accent 1**. Click the **Fill Color button arrow** , and then in the fifth column, select the second color—**Blue, Accent 1, Lighter 80%**.

9 Select **columns A:I**. Point to the line between the column headings A and B until the ↔ pointer displays, and then double-click to adjust the column widths to the best fit. Compare your screen with Figure 4.9.

Figure 4.9

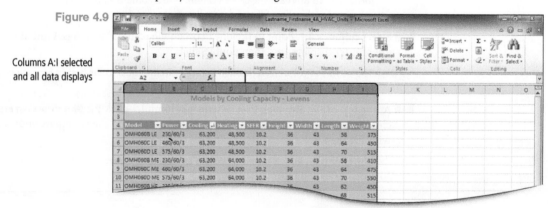

Columns A:I selected
and all data displays

Integrated Projects | Integrating Excel and Access

10 Select **columns E:H**. Right-click the **Column E** heading, and then on the shortcut menu, click **Hide**. Press Ctrl + Home.

11 Hold down Shift, and then click the **4A Levens Heating sheet tab**.

> Both Excel worksheets are selected.

12 Click the **Page Layout tab**. In **the Page Setup group**, click the **Orientation** button, and then click **Landscape**.

> Because two worksheets are selected, page formatting is applied to both worksheets at the same time.

13 In the **Page Setup group**, click the **Margins** button, and then click **Custom Margins**. In the **Page Setup** dialog box, verify that the **Margins tab** is selected. Under **Center on page**, click the check box for **Horizontally**, and then click the **Print Preview** button. Use the navigation area to view your work and to verify that two pages will print. If your instructor directs you to submit your files electronically, click the **Home tab**, and then go to Step 15.

14 From **Backstage** view, with the **Print Preview** displayed on the right, under **Settings**, verify that **Print Active Sheets** displays, and then click the **Print** button to print both worksheets.

15 Display **Backstage** view, and then click the **Info tab**. On the right, click **Properties**, and then click **Show Document Panel**. In the **Author** box, type your firstname and lastname, in the **Subject** box, type your course name and section number, and then in the **Keywords** box, type **HVAC units, Levens Close** ✖ the Document Information Panel.

16 Save 🔲 your workbook, and then **Close** ✖ Excel.

Objective 2 | Import Excel Data into Access Using the Import Spreadsheet Wizard

Access enables you to import data from an Excel workbook, which places a copy of the data in an Access table. Importing data is faster and more accurate than retyping the data. You can import the data from Excel to an Access table by copying and pasting the data, importing an entire worksheet or range of cells, or linking to an Excel worksheet from an Access database.

The Import Spreadsheet Wizard takes you through the import process step by step. If the Excel data is being imported into a new Access table, the wizard will give you the option of using your Excel column headings as the field names in the Access table. The wizard also allows you to set the data type of each new field and to create a primary key field. If you plan to import Excel data again, you can save the import settings to be used at a later time.

Activity 4.05 | Using the Import Spreadsheet Wizard

When you import data from Excel into Access, a copy of the data is placed in an Access table without altering the Excel data. Even if you have filters applied to the Excel data, where some rows are hidden in your Excel worksheet, all the data will be copied from Excel to Access.

1 **Start** Access. Under **Available Templates**, be certain **Blank database** is selected. On the right side of your screen, to the right of the **File Name** box, click the **Browse** button ⬚. In the **File New Database** dialog box, navigate to the **Integrated Projects Chapter 4** folder. In the **File name** box, delete the existing text. Using your own name, type **Lastname_Firstname_4A_Levens_HVAC** and then press [Enter]. In the lower right corner of your screen, click the **Create** button.

Access creates a new database and opens a table named Table1.

2 Click the **External Data tab**, and then in the **Import & Link group**, click the **Excel** button. In the **Get External Data - Excel Spreadsheet** dialog box, click the **Browse** button, and then navigate to your **Integrated Projects Chapter 4** folder. Click the file **Lastname_Firstname_4A_HVAC_Units**, and then click **Open**.

3 Verify that the **Import the source data into a new table in the current database** option button is selected, and then click **OK**. In the **Import Spreadsheet Wizard** dialog box, click the **4A Levens Heating** sheet name, and then compare your screen with Figure 4.10.

You can use the Import Spreadsheet Wizard to import the data from a worksheet or a named range in an Excel workbook.

Figure 4.10

Excel sheet names

Columns to be imported

4 Click **Next**. Verify that the **First Row Contains Column Headings** check box is selected, and then click **Next**.

The Import Spreadsheet Wizard enables you to select the data type for each column. Notice that all hidden rows and columns are imported from the Excel worksheet.

5 Click in the **Shipping Cost column**. Near the top of the dialog box, under **Field Options**, click the **Data Type arrow**, and then click **Currency**. Compare your screen with Figure 4.11.

Integrated Projects | Integrating Excel and Access

Figure 4.11

Data Type field option

Shipping Cost heading

6 Click **Next**. Verify that the **Let Access add primary key** option button is selected, and then click **Next**. Under **Import to Table**, with the existing text selected, type **Lastname Firstname 4A Levens Unit** and then click **Finish**. Verify that the **Save import steps** check box is not selected, and then click **Close**.

7 In the **Navigation Pane**, double-click the **Lastname Firstname 4A Levens Unit** table name to open the table. Right-click the **Table1 tab**, and then on the shortcut menu, click **Close**.

8 **Close** ⟪ the Navigation Pane.

Objective 3 | Sort and Filter Data in an Access Table

Sorting and filtering data in Access is similar to sorting and filtering data in Excel. You can use a filter to find one or more specific Access records. Access filters are easy to apply and remove. There are various types of filters, such as Filter by Form, Filter by Selection, and Advanced Filter/Sort. Filters are commonly used to provide a quick answer, and the result is not generally saved for future use; however, if a filter is applied frequently, you can save it as a query.

Activity 4.06 | Sorting Data in an Access Table

Sorting data in Access provides an easy-to-read list. You can sort on one or more fields in an Access table. In this activity, you will sort the HVAC models in descending order by cooling capacity.

1 In the **Lastname Firstname 4A Levens Unit** table, in the **Cooling** field, click the **Cooling arrow**, and then click **Sort Largest to Smallest**.

2 Point to the field name **Height** to display the ⬇ pointer. Hold down the left mouse button, and then drag right to the field name **Length**.

The fields Height through Length are selected.

3 Point to the field name **Height**, right-click, and then on the shortcut menu, click **Hide Fields**.

The fields Height, Width, and Length no longer display.

4 Point to the field name **ID** to display the ⬇ pointer. Hold down the left mouse button, and then drag right to the field name **Shipping Cost**. With all fields selected, right-click the selection, and then on the shortcut menu, click **Field Width**. In the **Column Width** dialog box, click **Best Fit**. Compare your screen with Figure 4.12.

The column widths of all the selected columns are adjusted to fit the existing data.

Project 4A: HVAC Report | **Integrated Projects**

Figure 4.12

Column widths adjusted

5 On the **Quick Access Toolbar**, click **Save** 💾 to save the changes you have made to the table's design.

Activity 4.07 | Filtering by Selection

By clicking the value that you want to use as the basis for filtering, you can use the filter to find one or more specific Access records. In this activity, you will find the HVAC units that use 460/60/3 power—the type of units requested by the Levens.

1 In the **Power** field, click any cell that contains **460/60/3**. Click the **Home tab**. In the **Sort & Filter group**, click the **Selection** button, and then click **Equals "460/60/3"**. Compare your screen with Figure 4.13.

The Access table is filtered, and the nine records that match the selection are displayed. Notice that the Toggle Filter button is active, and the word *Filtered* displays in the navigation area indicating that the table is filtered.

Figure 4.13

Toggle Filter button
Filter icon on
Power heading

Filtered displays in
navigation area

2 Right-click the field name **Heating**, and then on the shortcut menu, click **Unhide Fields**. In the **Unhide Columns** dialog box, select the **Height** check box, and then click **Close**.

The Height field displays in the table.

3 In the **Height** field, click any cell that contains **32**. On the **Home tab**, in the **Sort & Filter group**, click the **Selection** button, and then click **Less Than or Equal To 32**.

The Levens realize that the height of the unit must be restricted to a maximum of 32 inches, so they are only interested in units that meet that requirement. The table is filtered on both the Power and Height fields—six records display.

4 Save 🖫 your changes to the table's design.

Activity 4.08 | Filtering by Advanced Filter/Sort

The Advanced Filter/Sort feature helps you apply a filter that is not a common filter and allows you to save the filter settings as a new query. This type of filtering uses *comparison operators*—symbols that evaluate each field value to determine if it is the same (=), greater than (>), less than (<), or in between a range of values as specified by the criteria. In this activity, you will provide the Levens with a list of HVAC units with the highest heating capacity and then the highest cooling capacity.

1 On the **Home tab**, in the **Sort & Filter group**, click the **Toggle Filter** button.

No filters are applied, and all 27 records display in the table. The Width and Length columns remain hidden. The word *Unfiltered* displays in the navigation area, indicating that filters have been created but are not currently applied.

Note | Toggle Filter Button

On the Home tab, the Toggle Filter button is used to apply or remove a filter. If no filter has been created, the button is not active—it is not highlighted. After a filter is created, this button becomes active. Because it is a toggle button used to apply and remove filters, the ScreenTip that displays for this button alternates between Apply Filter—when a filter is created but not currently applied—and Remove Filter—when a filter is applied.

---

2 Click any cell in the **Cooling** field. On the **Home tab**, in the **Sort & Filter group**, click the **Advanced** button, and then click **Advanced Filter/Sort**. Compare your screen with Figure 4.14.

The Advanced Filter window and a *field list*—a list of the field names in a table—for the Levens Unit table displays. The Advanced Filter window is similar to the Query window—the *table area* (upper pane) displays the field lists for tables that are used in the filter and the *design grid* (lower pane) displays the design of the filter.

When you started the advanced filter, because your insertion point was in the Cooling field, which was sorted in descending order, this field displays in the design grid and *Descending* displays in the Sort row. The criteria for the filters in the Power and Height fields also display in the design grid.

Figure 4.14

Filter tab

Field list

Table area

Fields added to design grid

Design grid

3 Point to the lower right corner of the **Lastname Firstname 4A Levens Unit** field list to display the pointer, and then drag down and to the right to expand the height and width of the field list until all of the field names are visible. Compare your screen with Figure 4.15.

Figure 4.15

Field list expanded

4 In the **Lastname Firstname 4A Levens Unit** field list, double-click the field name **Heating**.

The Heating field is added to the design grid.

5 In the design grid, in the **Sort** row, click the cell in the **Heating** field, click the **Sort arrow**, and then click **Descending**.

6 On the **Home tab**, in the **Sort & Filter group**, click the **Toggle Filter** button to apply the filter, and then compare your screen with Figure 4.16.

The table displays with the filter applied. Fields that have a Sort designation are sorted from left to right—that is, the sorted field on the left (Cooling) becomes the outermost sort field and the sorted field on the right (Heating) becomes the innermost sort field.

Integrated Projects | Integrating Excel and Access

Figure 4.16

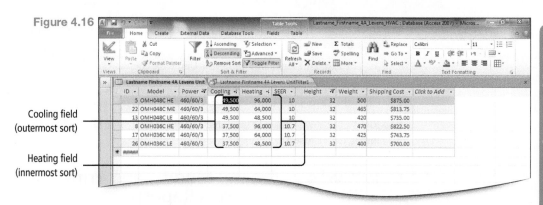

Cooling field (outermost sort)

Heating field (innermost sort)

7 Click the **Lastname Firstname 4A Levens UnitFilter1 tab**. In the **Lastname Firstname 4A Levens Unit** field list, scroll as necessary, and then double-click the field name **Shipping Cost**.

Because the Levens are concerned about shipping costs, the Shipping Cost field is added to the design grid.

8 In the **Criteria** row, click in the **Shipping Cost** field, type **<650** and then press Enter. Compare your screen with Figure 4.17.

Figure 4.17

Shipping Cost field

Criteria for Shipping Cost <650

9 In the **Sort & Filter group**, click the **Toggle Filter** button.

The table displays with the filters applied, but no data displays because no data meets all the criteria.

10 Click the **Lastname Firstname 4A Levens UnitFilter1 tab**. In the **Criteria** row, click in the **Shipping Cost** field. Select **<650**, type **<800** and then click the **Toggle Filter** button.

The three records that meet the Power criteria of 460/60/3, the Height criteria of 32 or less, and the Shipping Cost criteria of less than $800 display.

11 Click the **Lastname Firstname 4A Levens UnitFilter1 tab**, and then click **Save**. In the **Save As Query** dialog box, type **Lastname Firstname 4A Levens Query** and then click **OK**.

The Advanced filter is saved as a query.

Project 4A: HVAC Report | **Integrated Projects**

187

12 **Open** ⟫ the Navigation Pane. If necessary, click the **Access Objects arrow**, and then click **Object Type**.

> The Lastname Firstname 4A Levens Unit table and the Lastname Firstname 4A Levens Query display in the Navigation Pane.

13 Click the **Lastname Firstname 4A Levens Unit table tab**, and then click **Save** 🖫.

14 Right-click the **Lastname Firstname 4A Levens Unit table tab**, and then on the shortcut menu, click **Close All**.

Objective 4 | Create, Modify, and Print an Access Report

An Access *report* is a database object that summarizes the fields and records from a table (or tables) or from a query in an easy-to-read format suitable for printing. A variety of reports ranging from simple to complex can be created. By thinking about your *record source*—the tables or queries that provide the underlying data for a report—you can create a simple listing of records, or you can group, summarize, or sort the data in a report. To display data in a professional-looking format, consider creating and printing a report, rather than printing a table or query.

Activity 4.09 | Creating and Modifying an Access Report

The *Report tool* is an Access feature that creates a report with one mouse click, which displays all of the fields and records from the record source that you select—a quick way to look at the underlying data. You can modify a rough draft of a report in Layout view or Design view. In Layout view, you can see the data while making changes to the report design.

1 In the **Navigation Pane**, double-click **Lastname Firstname 4A Levens Query**, and then **Close** ⟪ the Navigation Pane.

2 Click the **Create tab**, and then in the **Reports group**, click the **Report** button.

> A report based on the query results displays in Layout view. Recall that in Layout view the report margins and page breaks are visible and you can make changes to a form or to a report.

3 Click the **Page Setup tab**, and then in the **Page Layout group**, click the **Landscape** button. Scroll to the right, and then compare your screen with Figure 4.18.

> Notice the total of the Shipping Cost field displays. This was inserted by default when Access created the report.

Figure 4.18

Page Break

Shipping Cost total

4 Press [Ctrl] + [Home]. Click the field name **ID** to surround it with an orange border and to select the entire column. Right-click the selected field name, and then on the shortcut menu, click **Delete Column**.

> The ID field is deleted from the report.

5 Click the field name **SEER**, press and hold [Ctrl], and then click the field names **Width** and **Length**. With all three fields selected, right-click any of the selected field names, and then on the shortcut menu, click **Delete Column**.

> The three columns are deleted, and the report is now a one-page document.

6 Click the field name **Shipping Cost**. Click the **Design tab**, and then in the **Grouping & Totals group**, click the **Totals** button.

> A check mark displays to the left of the Sum option, which means it is selected and the column total displays. In this report, a sum for the Shipping Cost field is meaningless because the Levens would never purchase three HVAC models.

7 In the displayed list, click **Sum** to toggle off the column total.

> The Shipping Cost column total no longer displays; however, a horizontal line still displays below the Shipping Cost column.

8 Below the **Shipping Cost** column, click on the horizontal line to display an orange border, and then press [Del].

9 Double-click in the **Title** box, double-click the word **Query**, and then press [Backspace] two times.

> The word Query and a space are deleted from the title of the report.

10 At the top right corner of the report, click the **time** to surround it with an orange border, and then press [Del] to delete the time from the report.

11 At the top right corner, click the **date** to select it. Point to the lower right corner of the date border until the [⬚] pointer displays, and then drag the date to the right until it is right-aligned with the **Shipping Cost** field. Compare your screen with Figure 4.19.

Figure 4.19

Date displays above Shipping Cost

Report title

12 Click **Save** [💾]. In the **Save As** dialog box, type **Lastname Firstname 4A Levens Report** and then click **OK**. Right-click the **Lastname Firstname 4A Levens Report tab**, and then on the shortcut menu, click **Close All**.

Project 4A: HVAC Report | **Integrated Projects**

Activity 4.10 | Grouping Data and Printing an Access Report

Information in an Access report is often easier to read and comprehend when it is separated into groups. You can print a report while it is closed or while you have it open in any view. In this activity, you will use the Report Wizard to group your data by the Heating field.

1 Open » the Navigation Pane, and then in the **Navigation Pane**, click the **Lastname Firstname 4A Levens Unit** table to select it. Click the **Create tab**, and then in the **Reports group**, click **the Report Wizard** button.

> The *Report Wizard* is an Access feature with which you can create a report by answering a series of questions; Access designs the report based on your answers.

2 In the **Report Wizard** dialog box, under **Tables/Queries**, verify that **Table: Lastname Firstname 4A Levens Unit** is selected.

Another Way
Double-click a field name to move it to the Selected Fields list.

3 Use the **One Field** button > to move the following fields to the **Selected Fields** list in this order: **Model, Cooling, Heating,** and **Shipping Cost**. Click **Next**.

4 In the **Report Wizard** dialog box, under **Do you want to add any grouping levels?**, double-click the **Heating** field, and then compare your screen with Figure 4.20.

Figure 4.20

Heating field grouping level

5 Click **Next**. Click the **Sort arrow**, and then click **Shipping Cost**. To the right of the **Sort arrow**, click the **Ascending** button to toggle it to the **Descending** button, and then click **Next**.

6 Under **Layout**, click the **Block** option button. Under **Orientation**, verify that the **Portrait** option button is selected, and then at the bottom of the dialog box, verify that the **Adjust the field width so all fields fit on a page** check box is selected. Click **Next**.

7 Under **What title do you want for your report?**, type **Lastname Firstname 4A Heating** and then click **Finish**.

> The Lastname Firstname 4A Heating report displays in Print Preview. Notice the units are grouped by the Heating field.

8 In the **Close Preview group**, click the **Close Print Preview** button. **Close** « the Navigation Pane.

9 On the **Design tab**, in the **Header/Footer group**, click the **Logo** button. In the **Insert Picture** dialog box, navigate to the location of your student files, locate the file **i04A_Midwest_Logo**, and then double-click the file name.

> The logo is inserted in the *report header* where information such as logos, titles, and dates is printed at the beginning of a report.

Integrated Projects | Integrating Excel and Access

10 With the logo selected, in the **Tools group**, click the **Property Sheet** button to open the **Property Sheet** pane. On the **Property Sheet** pane, on the **All tab**, to the right of **Size Mode**, click the **Size Mode** box. Click the **Size Mode arrow**, and then click **Stretch**. To the right of **Width**, click the **Width** box, select the number, and then type **1.8** In the **Tools group**, click the **Property Sheet** button. Display the ⬚ pointer, and then drag the logo to the right so the left border is at approximately **6 inches on the horizontal ruler.**

11 On the **Design tab**, in the **Views group**, click the **Views button arrow**, and then click **Print Preview**. Compare your screen with Figure 4.21.

The report displays with the logo in the top right corner.

Figure 4.21

Logo resized and moved

Shipping Cost sorted in descending order

Report grouped by Heating

12 **Save** 🖫 the report. In the **Close Preview group**, click the **Close Print Preview** button.

13 Display **Backstage** view, and then click **View and edit database properties**. In the **Properties** dialog box, on the **Summary** tab, in the **Subject** box, type your course name and section number, in the **Author** box, type your firstname and lastname, in the **Keywords** box type **Levens reports, cooling, heating** and then click **OK**.

14 Click the **Home tab**. If your instructor directs you to submit your files electronically, go to Step 16.

15 With the **Lastname Firstname 4A Heating** report displayed, from **Backstage** view, click the **Print tab**, and then click the **Print** button to print the report. **Open** 》 the **Navigation Pane**, double-click the **Lastname Firstname 4A Levens** report. Using the technique you just practiced, print the **Lastname Firstname 4A Levens** report.

16 Right-click the **Lastname Firstname 4A Heating report tab**, and then click **Close All**. **Close** ⬛ Access.

17 Submit your printed or electronic files as directed by your instructor.

End **You have completed Project 4A**

Project 4B HVAC Table

In Activities 4.11 through 4.18, you will create a new table in an existing Access database and insert records in the table. You will create a one-to-many relationship between tables and create a relationship report. After creating an Access query, you will export the data to Excel. In Excel, you will create a new table style, and then apply the table style and insert subtotals in the table. Your completed files will look similar to Figure 4.22.

Project Files

For Project 4B, you will need the following files:

New blank Excel workbook
i04B_HVAC_Parts

You will save your files as:

Lastname_Firstname_4B_HVAC_Parts
Lastname_Firstname_4B_HVAC_Models

Project Results

Figure 4.22
Project 4B HVAC Table

Integrated Projects | Integrating Excel and Access

192

Objective 5 | Create an Access Table

Recall that a table is an Access object that stores your data and is organized in an arrangement of columns and rows. A database may have many tables, with each table containing data about a particular subject. The data in a table can contain many fields with different data types. You can create tables by typing the data in a new blank table or by importing or linking to information stored in a different location.

Activity 4.11 | Creating an Access Table and Entering Data

In this activity, you will add a table to an existing database.

1 **Start** Access. Click **Open**, navigate to the location of your student files, and then open the database **i04B_HVAC_Parts**.

2 Click the **File tab**, and then click the **Save Database As tab**. In the **Save As** dialog box, navigate to your **Integrated Projects Chapter 4** folder. Using your own name, save the database as **Lastname_Firstname_4B_HVAC_Parts** If necessary, on the **Message Bar**, click the **Enable Content** button.

3 If necessary, **Open** [»] the Navigation Pane. Double-click each of the three table names to open and view the tables.

4 Click the **Create tab**, and then in the **Tables group**, click the **Table Design** button. Compare your screen with Figure 4.23.

Table1 displays in Design view. Notice there are no entries in the Field Name and Data Type columns.

Figure 4.23

Field Name column

Data Type column

Design view

5 In the **Field Name column**, type **Cartridge Filter ID** and then press [Tab] to move to the **Data Type column.**

In the Data Type column, notice that *Text* is the *default value*—the value that is automatically entered in a new record.

6 Press [Tab] two times to move to the next row. In the **Field Name** column, type **Area (sq ft)** and then press [Tab] to move to the **Data Type** column. Click the **Data Type arrow**, and then click **Number**. Press [Tab] two times to move to the next row. Type **CF Cost** and then press [Tab]. In the **Data Type** column, click the **Data Type arrow**, and then click **Currency**.

Project 4B: HVAC Table | **Integrated Projects**

7 Click the field name **Cartridge Filter ID**. On the **Design tab**, in the **Tools group**, click the **Primary Key** button, and then compare your screen with Figure 4.24.

> A small key displays in the record selector box of the Cartridge Filter ID field, indicating that this field is the primary key. Recall that a primary key is the field that uniquely identifies a record in a table.

Figure 4.24

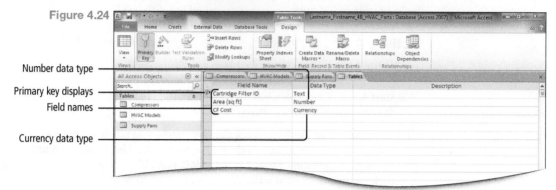

Number data type

Primary key displays

Field names

Currency data type

8 On the **Design tab**, in the **Views group**, click the **View** button to switch to **Datasheet** view. In the message box, click **Yes** to save the table. In the **Save As** dialog box, type **4B Cartridge Filters** and then click **OK**.

> The table design is saved, the table displays in Datasheet view, and the table name displays in the Navigation Pane.

9 Enter the following information in the table:

Cartridge Filter ID	Area (sq ft)	CF Cost
CF1090	20	25
CF2180	24	32
CF3700	40	35
CF4520	50	50

10 Right-click the **4B Cartridge Filters table tab**, and then on the shortcut menu, click **Close All**.

More Knowledge | Good Table Design

When you create a database, you do not want redundant—duplicate—data because it will increase the possibility of errors and it will take additional time to enter the data multiple times. Because you can use relationships to join—connect—tables, you only need to type data such as a customer name, address, or telephone number one time.

When designing your database tables, divide the information into subject-based tables and consider separating data into its smallest elements. For example, instead of having City, State, and ZIP Code as one field, create three separate fields, one for each element. This enables you to sort or filter by any of the three fields.

Activity 4.12 | Creating a One-to-Many Relationship

Access is a *relational database*—a sophisticated type of database that has multiple collections of data within the file that are related to one another. A high-quality database design attempts to remove redundant data. By adding data in one table and creating a *relationship*—an association that you establish between two tables based on common fields—the data only needs to be entered one time but can be referenced by any other related table. In this activity, you will create relationships between the four Access tables.

Another Way
Double-click a table name to add it to the Relationships window.

1 Click the **Database Tools tab**, and then in the **Relationships group**, click the **Relationships** button. In the **Show Table** dialog box, on the **Tables tab**, verify the **4B Cartridge Filters** table name is selected, and then click **Add** to display the table in the Relationships window. Using this technique, add the tables **Compressors**, **HVAC Models**, and **Supply Fans**. **Close** the **Show Table** dialog box, and then compare your screen with Figure 4.25.

Figure 4.25

Relationships window

Added tables

Note | Extra Tables in the Relationships Window

In the Relationships window, if you have accidentally added an extra table, right-click the table name, and then on the shortcut menu, click Hide Table.

2 Point to the **HVAC Models** title, hold down the left mouse button and drag the field list down and to the right side of the Relationships window. Using the same technique, drag the **Supply Fans** field list below the **Compressors** field list, and then drag the **4B Cartridge Filters** field list below the **Supply Fans** field list. Compare your screen with Figure 4.26.

Figure 4.26

HVAC Models field list

Compressors field list

Supply Fans field list

4B Cartridge Filters field list

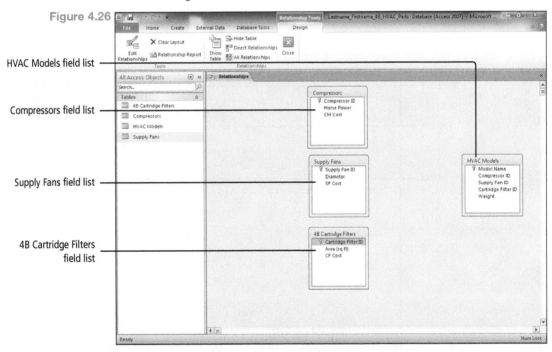

Project 4B: HVAC Table | **Integrated Projects**

3 In the **Compressors** field list, point to **Compressor ID**, hold down the left mouse button, and then drag to the right to the **HVAC Models** field list until the ⬚ pointer is on top of the **Compressor ID** field name. Release the mouse button.

The Edit Relationships dialog box displays.

4 In the **Edit Relationships** dialog box, verify that **Compressor ID** displays under both **Table/Query** and **Related Table/Query**. If not, click **Cancel**, and then repeat Step 3. In the **Edit Relationships** dialog box, select the **Enforce Referential Integrity** check box, and then click **Create**.

A *one-to-many relationship* is created. A one-to-many relationship is a relationship between two tables where one record in the first table corresponds to many records in the second table—the most common type of relationship in Access. In this case, the one-to-many relationship is between one compressor and many HVAC models. A *foreign key* is the field that is included in the related table so that it can be joined to the primary key in another table for the purpose of creating a relationship.

Referential integrity is a set of rules that Access uses to ensure that the data between related tables is valid. In this project, it means that records must be added to the Compressor table before matching records can be added to the HVAC Models table.

5 Using the same technique, create a one-to-many relationship between the **Supply Fan ID** field in the **Supply Fans** field list and the **Supply Fan ID** field in the **HVAC Models** field list. Create a one-to-many relationship between the **Cartridge Filter ID** field in the **4B Cartridge Filters** field list and the **Cartridge Filter ID** field in the **HVAC Models** field list. Compare your screen with Figure 4.27.

A *join line*, in the Relationships window, is the line joining two tables that visually indicates the related field and the type of relationship. The infinity symbol ∞ at the right end of the join lines, next to the HVAC Models field, indicates that the data may occur more than once in the HVAC Models table. The number 1 at the left end of the join lines, next to each of the other tables, indicates that a data item can only be listed one time in each of those tables.

Figure 4.27

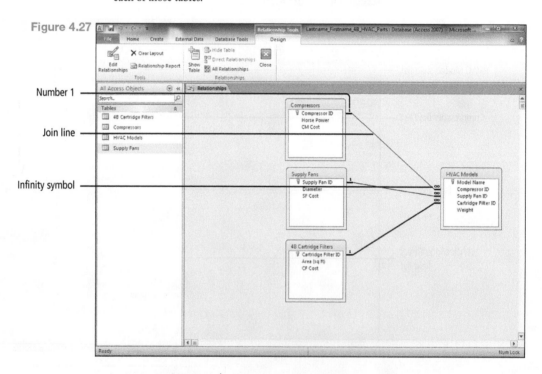

6 On the **Design tab**, in the **Tools group**, click the **Relationship Report** button.

A report showing the relationship between the two tables displays.

Alert! | **Do you have a two-page report?**

Close the report without saving it. In the Relationships window, drag the HVAC Models field list to the left, closer to the other field lists. Click the Relationship Report button again, and then verify that you have a one-page report.

---

7 Click the **Save** button 🖫. In the **Save As** dialog box, type **Lastname Firstname 4B HVAC Relationships**, and then click **OK**. If your instructor directs you to submit your files electronically, go to Step 9.

8 To print the report, in the **Print group**, click the **Print** button, and then in the **Print** dialog box, click **OK**.

9 Right-click the **Lastname Firstname 4B HVAC Relationships report tab**, and then click **Close All**.

Activity 4.13 | Adding a Totals Row in an Access Table

A Totals row can be inserted in an Access table. The Totals row uses the functions SUM, AVERAGE, COUNT, MIN, or MAX to quickly summarize the numbers in the column. Gerardo Sanjurjo, the Director of Sales for Midwest HVAC Manufacturer, has asked you to give him the average weight of the HVAC Models.

1 In the **Navigation Pane**, double-click the **HVAC Models** table name to display the table, and then **Close** ⟪ the Navigation Pane.

2 On the **Home tab**, in the **Records group**, click the **Totals** button.

A Total row is added at the bottom of the table.

3 If necessary, scroll down, and then in the **Total row**, click in the **Weight** field to position the insertion point and display an arrow. Click the **arrow**, and then click **Average**. Compare your screen with Figure 4.28.

The average weight of the HVAC units displays.

Figure 4.28

Average value in Weight column

Total row

4 In the **Total row**, click in the **Compressor ID** field, click the **arrow**, and then click **Count**.

The number of HVAC units (27) displays.

5 **Save** 🖫 the table's design. Right-click the **HVAC Models table tab**, and then click **Close**.

Project 4B: HVAC Table | **Integrated Projects**

Objective 6 | Create an Access Query

There are several different types of Access queries. You should choose a specific query based on the desired outcome. An *action query* changes the data in the data source or creates a new table. Examples of action queries are an *append query* that adds a set of records from one or more source tables to one or more destination tables and an *update query* that adds or changes data in one or more existing records. Another type of query—a *parameter query*—prompts you to supply the criteria when the query is run. In this project, as you have done previously, you will create a select query—a database object that retrieves specific data from one or more tables and then displays the specified data in Datasheet view.

Activity 4.14 | Creating a Select Query

In a relational database, tables are joined by associating common fields. This relationship allows you to include data from more than one table in a query. In this activity, you will create a query that retrieves cost information from three tables.

1 Click the **Create tab**, and then in the **Queries group**, click the **Query Design** button. In the **Show Table** dialog box, double-click each of the four table names to add them to the table area of the Query window, and then **Close** the **Show Table** dialog box.

The four field lists with the relationship join lines display.

2 Point to the lower right corner of the **Compressor** field list until the ⬉ pointer displays, and then drag upward to make the field list smaller. In a similar manner, make the **Supply Fans** and **4B Cartridge Filters** field lists smaller.

3 Move the **Supply Fans** field list below the **Compressors** field list, and then move the **4B Cartridge Filters** field list below **Supply Fans**. Compare your screen with Figure 4.29.

Figure 4.29

Join line

Resized and repositioned field lists

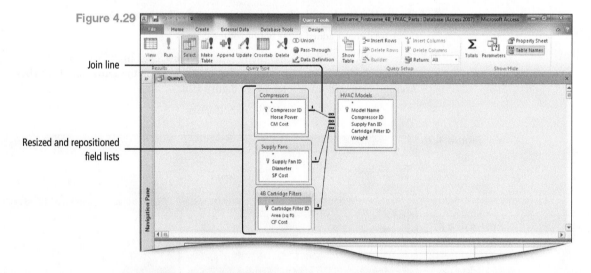

4 In the **HVAC Models** field list, double-click **Model Name** to add the field to the grid. In the **Compressors** field list, double-click the **CM Cost** field name. In the **Supply Fans** field list, double-click the **SF Cost** field name, and then in the **4B Cartridge Filters** field list, double-click the **CF Cost** field name.

The fields Model Name, CM Cost, SF Cost, and CF Cost display in the design grid.

Integrated Projects | Integrating Excel and Access

5 On the **Design tab**, in the **Results group**, click the **Run** button to display the results of the query.

6 Click **Save** 📄. In the **Save As** dialog box, type **Lastname Firstname 4B Cost Query** and then click **OK**.

Activity 4.15 | Adding a Calculated Field to a Query

After you run a query, you might return to Design view to make modifications. In this activity, you will modify the query by adding a *calculated field* to sum the cost of the different parts to determine the total HVAC unit cost. A calculated field is a field that stores the value of a mathematical operation.

1 Click the **View** button to switch to **Design** view. In the **Field** row, right-click in the fifth column—a blank column, and then on the shortcut menu, click **Zoom**.

Although you can type a calculation in the empty Field box in the design grid, the Zoom dialog box gives you more space.

2 In the **Zoom** dialog box, type **HVAC Cost:[CM Cost]+[SF Cost]+[CF Cost]** and then compare your screen with Figure 4.30.

The first element, HVAC Cost, is the new field name. Following the new field name is a colon (:), which separates the new field name from the expression. CM Cost, SF Cost, and CF Cost are each in square brackets, indicating they are existing field names. The plus sign will sum the field contents.

Figure 4.30
Zoom dialog box
New field name
Calculated value

3 In the **Zoom** dialog box, click **OK**, and then in the **Results group**, click the **Run** button. Compare your screen with Figure 4.31.

Figure 4.31
HVAC Cost calculated field
Row totals

Alert! | Does your screen differ?

If your calculations in a query do not work, switch to Design view, and then in the Zoom dialog box, correct the expression you typed. Spelling or syntax errors prevent calculated fields from working properly.

Project 4B: HVAC Table | **Integrated Projects**

4 Click the **View** button to switch to **Design** view. In the **Show** row, in the **CM Cost** field, click the check box to clear it. Using the same technique, clear the check box in the **SF Cost** field and the **CF Cost** field. **Run** the query.

> Only the fields Model Name and HVAC Cost display. You do not want to show the individual cost fields in this query.

5 Click the **File tab** to display **Backstage** view, and then click **Save Object As**. In the **Save As** dialog box, type **Lastname Firstname 4B Total Unit Cost** and then click **OK**.

6 Click the **Create tab**, and then in the **Reports group**, click the **Report** button.

> A basic report based on the data from the Lastname Firstname 4B Total Unit Cost query displays.

7 Double-click the report title, and then select the text **Lastname Firstname 4B Total Unit Cost**. Click the **Home tab**, and then in the **Text Formatting group**, click the **Font Size arrow** [11 ▾] and then click **16**.

8 **Save** 🔲 the report. In the **Save As** dialog box, type **Lastname Firstname 4B Total Unit Cost Report** and then click **OK**. If your instructor directs you to submit your files electronically, go to Step 9.

9 If you are printing your files, display **Backstage** view, click the **Print tab**, and then click the **Print** button. In the **Print** dialog box, click **OK**.

10 Right-click the **Lastname Firstname 4B Total Unit Cost Report tab**, and then on the shortcut menu, click **Close All**.

11 Display **Backstage** view, and then click **View and edit database properties**. In the **Properties** dialog box, on the **Summary tab**, in the **Subject** box, type your course name and section number, in the **Author** box, type your firstname and lastname, in the **Keyword**s box, type **HVAC Costs** and then click **OK**. Click the **External Data tab**.

Objective 7 | Export Access Data to Excel

You can export data stored in an Access database to an Excel workbook. When you export the Access data or a database object, a copy of the data is created in the Excel workbook.

Activity 4.16 | Exporting Access Data

1 **Open** 〉〉 the Navigation Pane. In the **Navigation Pane**, click one time on the **HVAC Models** table name to select the table. On the **External Data tab**, in the **Export group**, click the **Excel** button. In the **Export – Excel Spreadsheet** dialog box, click the **Browse** button. Navigate to your **Integrated Projects Chapter 4** folder, type the file name **Lastname_Firstname_4B_HVAC_Models** and then click **Save**.

2 In the **Export – Excel Spreadsheet** dialog box, verify that the **File format** is **Excel Workbook (*.xlsx)** and then click **OK**. Do not save the export steps. Click **Close**, and then **Close** ⊠ Access.

3 **Start** Excel. Navigate to your **Integrated Projects Chapter 4** folder, and then open the file **Lastname_Firstname_4B_HVAC_Models**.

4 Click the **Insert tab**, and then in the **Text group**, click the **Header & Footer** button. On the **Design tab**, in the **Navigation group**, click the **Go to Footer** button. In the **Footer** area, click just above the word **Footer**, and then in the **Header & Footer Elements group**, click the **File Name** button. Click any cell in the workbook to exit the footer.

5 Near the right side of the status bar, click the **Normal** button 🖽, and then press Ctrl + Home to make cell **A1** the active cell. Compare your screen with Figure 4.32.

Figure 4.32

Imported Access data

6 Right-click the column header **A**, and then on the shortcut menu, click **Column Width**. In the **Column Width** dialog box, type **15** and then click **OK**. Select columns **B:D**, and then using the same technique, change the column width to **20**

7 Right-click the **HVAC_Models sheet tab**, and then on the shortcut menu, click **Move or Copy**. In the **Move or Copy** dialog box, click **(move to end)**, select the **Create a copy** check box, and then click **OK**.

A copy of the HVAC_Models sheet is created.

8 Right-click the **HVAC_Models (2) sheet tab**, and then on the shortcut menu, click **Rename**. With **HVAC_Models (2)** selected, type **4B Parts** and then press Enter. Using the same technique, rename the **HVAC_Models sheet tab** as **4B Subtotals**

9 Click the **4B Parts sheet tab**. Right-click the column header **E**, and then on the shortcut menu, click **Delete**.

Column E—Weight—is deleted from the 4B Parts worksheet.

10 Save 🖫 the workbook.

Activity 4.17 | Using Table Styles in Excel

Recall that a table style is a predefined set of formatting characteristics, including font, alignment, and cell shading. In this activity, you will create a custom table style.

1 With the 4B Parts worksheet displayed, press Ctrl + Home. On the **Home tab**, in the **Styles group**, click the **Format as Table** button. At the bottom of the **Table Styles** gallery, click **New Table Style**.

2 In the **New Table Quick Style** dialog box, in the **Name** box, type **Parts Table Style**

3 Under **Table Element**, click **Header Row**, and then click **Format**. On the **Font tab**, under **Font style**, click **Bold**. Click the **Color arrow**, and then in the third column, click the sixth color—**Tan, Background 2, Darker 90%**. Click the **Fill tab**, and then in the eighth column, click the third color (light purple). Click **OK** two times to close the dialog boxes.

4 In the **Styles group**, click the **Format as Table** button. At the top of the **Table Styles** gallery, under **Custom**, point to the first style, and then compare your screen with Figure 4.33.

Figure 4.33

Parts Table Style

Table Styles gallery

5 In the **Table Styles** gallery, click the **Parts Table Style**. In the **Format As Table** dialog box, under **Where is the data for your table?**, verify that the range is =**$A$1:$D$28**, verify that the **My table has headers** check box is selected, and then click **OK**.

The range is converted to an Excel table, and the Parts Table Style is applied to the table.

6 On the **Design tab**, in the **Table Styles group**, right-click the **Parts Table Style**—the first style—and then on the shortcut menu, click **Modify**. In the **Modify Table Quick Style** dialog box, under **Table Element**, click **Second Row Stripe**. Click the **Stripe Size arrow**, and then click **2**. Click the **Format** button.

7 In the **Format Cells** dialog box, on the **Fill tab**, in the eighth column, click the second color, and then click **OK** two times to close the dialog boxes. Click in a blank cell to deselect the table and then compare your screen with Figure 4.34.

Figure 4.34

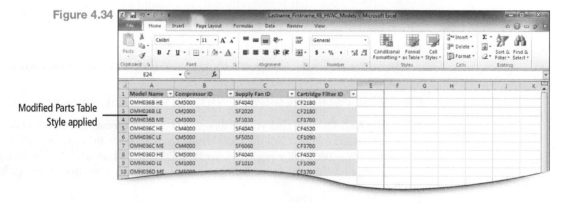

Modified Parts Table Style applied

8 Press Ctrl + Home, and then **Save** the workbook.

Activity 4.18 | Inserting Subtotals in Excel

In Excel, a list of data can be grouped and summarized in an outline, and then the outline details can be expanded or collapsed. You should sort a column before inserting subtotals. In the following activity, you will count how many Compressor IDs are used by the various HVAC models, and then hide the detail of all Compressor IDs except the CM3000.

1 Click the **4B Subtotals sheet tab**. Select the range **A1:A28**, and then point to the right border of the selected range until the 🔣 pointer displays. Compare your screen with Figure 4.35.

Figure 4.35

Cells A1:A28 selected

Pointer at right border of selection

2 Hold down the left mouse button, drag the selected range to the right to column **F**, and then release the mouse button.

The range A1:A28 is moved to cells F1:F28, and the title Model Name displays in cell F1.

3 Right-click column heading **A**, and then on the shortcut menu, click **Delete**.

The blank column A is deleted, and the other columns move to the left.

4 Click cell **A1**. On the **Home tab**, in the **Editing group**, click the **Sort & Filter** button, and then click **Sort A to Z**.

5 Click the **Data tab**, and then in the **Outline group**, click the **Subtotal** button. In the **Subtotal** dialog box, verify that under **At each change in**, Compressor ID displays, and under **Use function**, Count displays. Under **Add subtotal to**, select the **Compressor ID** check box to display a check mark, and then clear the **Model Name** check box. Compare your screen with Figure 4.36.

Figure 4.36

Subtotal dialog box

Compressor ID

Count function

Compressor ID check box selected

Model Name check box not selected

Project 4B: HVAC Table | **Integrated Projects**

6 In the **Subtotal** dialog box, click **OK**. Select columns **A:F**. Between the column headings **A** and **B**, point to the column separator until the ⊞ pointer displays, and then double-click to resize all the columns. Click cell **A1**, and then compare your screen with Figure 4.37.

> The widths of columns A through F are adjusted to best fit the data in each column. Data is grouped by Compressor ID and, for each group, a row displays the Count heading and total count. When you use the Subtotal feature in Excel, outline symbols display that allow you to show specific row levels and show or hide details in a group.

Figure 4.37

Row level buttons

Hide details button
Count headings

7 At the top left corner of your screen, click the **level** button **2**.

> Only the subtotal rows—level 2 rows—display.

8 To the left of row **15**, click the **Show details** button ⊞.

> The details of the CM3000 Compressor ID group are displayed in rows 8 through 14.

9 If your instructor directs you to submit your files electronically, go to Step 10. To print your workbook, display **Backstage** view, and then click the **Print** tab. Under **Settings**, click the **Print Active Sheets arrow**, and then click **Print Entire Workbook**. Click the **Print** button to print both worksheets.

10 Display **Backstage** view, verify the **Info tab** is selected, click **Properties**, and then click **Show Document Panel**. In the **Author** box, type your firstname and lastname, in the **Subject** box, type your course name and section number, and then in the **Keywords** box, type **HVAC Compressors, subtotals Close** ☒ the Document Information Panel.

11 **Save** 🔛 the workbook, and then **Close** ☒ Excel.

12 Submit your printed or electronic files as directed by your instructor.

End **You have completed Project 4B** ———————————————

Contents Based Assessments

Summary

The Excel and Access applications each have advantages when working with large amounts of data. You should work with data in the application that best meets your needs. If you require different results, use the import and export features of Excel and Access to change to a different application. Use the sort and filter features of Excel and Access to display specific data that meets particular criteria.

Key Terms

Action query	Conditional format	One-to-many relationship	Report header
Append query	Default value	Parameter query	Report tool
Ascending order	Descending order	Record source	Report Wizard
AutoExpansion	Design grid	Referential Integrity	Table area
AutoFilter	Excel table	Relational database	Underlying formula
Calculated column	Field list	Relationship	Update query
Calculated field	Foreign key	Report	
Comparison operators	Join line		

Matching

Match each term in the second column with its correct definition in the first column by writing the letter of the term on the blank line in front of the correct definition.

_____ 1. Text is arranged in reverse alphabetical order (Z to A) or numbers from the highest to the lowest value.

_____ 2. Text is arranged in alphabetical order (A to Z) or numbers from the lowest to the highest value.

_____ 3. An Excel table feature in which a new column is automatically included as part of the existing table.

_____ 4. An Excel feature that uses a single formula that adjusts for each row of a column in a data table.

_____ 5. The upper pane of the Advanced Filter window that displays the field lists for tables that are used in the filter.

_____ 6. The lower pane of the Advanced Filter window that displays the design of the filter.

_____ 7. The tables or queries that provide the underlying data for a report.

_____ 8. An Access feature that creates a report with one mouse click, which displays all the fields and records from the record source that you select.

_____ 9. An Access feature with which you can create a report by answering a series of questions; Access designs the report based on your answers.

_____ 10. Information—such as logos, titles, and dates—printed once at the beginning of a report.

A Action query

B Ascending order

C AutoExpansion

D Calculated column

E Default value

F Descending order

G Design grid

H Foreign key

I Parameter query

J Record source

K Relationship

L Report header

M Report tool

N Report Wizard

O Table area

Content-Based Assessments

_____ 11. The value that is automatically entered in a new record.

_____ 12. An association that you establish between two tables based on common fields.

_____ 13. The field that is included in the related table so the field can be joined with the primary key in another table for the purpose of creating a relationship.

_____ 14. A query that changes the data in the data source or creates a new table.

_____ 15. A query that prompts you to supply the criteria when the query is run.

Multiple Choice

Circle the correct answer.

1. The Excel feature where only a portion of the data (a subset) that meets the criteria you specify is displayed is:
   A. AutoExpansion   **B.** AutoFill   **C.** AutoFilter

2. The formula that is entered in a cell and visible only on the Formula Bar is called an:
   A. underlying cell reference   **B.** underlying formula   **C.** underlying function

3. A format that changes the appearance of a cell based on a condition; if the condition is true, the cell is formatted based on that condition, if the condition is false, the cell is not formatted is called a:
   A. conditional format   **B.** contextual format   **C.** filtered format

4. Symbols that evaluate each field value to determine if it is the same (=), greater than (>), less than (<), or in between a range of values as specified by the criteria are called:
   A. comparison operators   **B.** logic operators   **C.** mathematical operators

5. A database object that summarizes the fields and records from a table (or tables) in an easy-to-read format suitable for printing is a:
   A. form   **B.** query   **C.** report

6. A relationship between two tables where one record in the first table corresponds to many records in the second table—the most common type of relationship in Access—is:
   A. many-to-one   **B.** one-to-many   **C.** one-to-one

7. A set of rules that Access uses to ensure that the data between related tables is valid is called:
   A. conditional integrity   **B.** referential integrity   **C.** referential validity

8. In the Relationships window, the line joining two tables that visually indicates the related field and the type of relationship is called a:
   A. join line   **B.** relationship connector   **C.** relationship line

9. The name of a query that adds or changes data in one or more existing records is:
   A. append query   **B.** parameter query   **C.** update query

10. A field that stores the value of a mathematical expression is called a:
    A. calculated field   **B.** numeric data type   **C.** numeric field

Apply 4A skills from these Objectives:

1. Modify an Excel Table
2. Import Excel Data into Access Using the Import Spreadsheet Wizard
3. Sort and Filter Data in an Access Table
4. Create, Modify, and Print an Access Report

Skills Review | Project **4C Heating Costs**

In the following Skills Review, you will create a calculated column in Excel to calculate the heating cost for each of the HVAC units based on an expected cost of $0.0015 per BTU. You will import the worksheet into Access, and then filter the data to create a report. Your completed files will look similar to Figure 4.38.

Project Files

For Project 4C, you will need the following files:

New blank Access database
i04C_Heating_Costs

You will save your files as:

Lastname_Firstname_4C_Heating_Costs
Lastname_Firstname_4C_Heating_Data

Project Results

Figure 4.38

Integrating Excel and Access

1. **Start** Excel. Open the file **i04C_Heating_Costs**. Navigate to the **Integrated Projects Chapter 4** folder, and then save the file as **Lastname_Firstname_4C_Heating_Costs**

   a. On the **Insert tab**, in the **Text group**, click the **Header & Footer** button. On the **Design tab**, in the **Navigation group**, click the **Go to Footer** button. In the **Footer** area, click just above the word *Footer*, and then in the **Header & Footer Elements group**, click the **File Name** button. Click any cell in the workbook to exit the footer. Near the right side of the status bar, click the **Normal** button, and then press Ctrl + Home.

   b. On the **Insert tab**, in the **Tables group**, click the **Table** button. In the **Create Table** dialog box, under **Where is the data for your table?**, verify that the range is =$A$1:$H$28, verify that the **My table has headers** check box is selected, and then click **OK**.

   c. At the top of the **Heating column**, click the **Heating AutoFilter arrow**, and then click **Sort Largest to Smallest**.

2. Click the **Heating AutoFilter arrow**, point to **Number Filters**, and then click **Greater Than or Equal To**. In the **Custom AutoFilter** dialog box, under **Show rows where**, verify **is greater than or equal to** is selected. In the box to the right, type **70000** and then click **OK**.

   a. Click cell **I1**, type **Heating Cost** and then press Enter. In cell **I2**, type the formula **=D2*0.0015** and then on the **Formula Bar**, click the **Enter** button.

   b. Select the range **I2:I16**. On the **Home tab**, in the **Number group**, click the **Accounting Number Format** button, and then click the **Decrease Decimal** button two times. With the cells still selected, on the **Home tab**, in the **Styles group**, click **Conditional Formatting**, point to **Highlight Cells Rules**, and then click **Less Than**. In the **Less Than** dialog box, type **125** in the **with** box, verify **Light Red Fill with Dark Red Text** displays, and then click **OK**.

   c. Right-click the **Sheet1 tab**, and then on the shortcut menu, click **Rename**. With **Sheet1** selected, type **4C Heating** and then press Enter.

   d. Click the **Sheet2 tab**, hold down Ctrl, and then click the **Sheet3 tab**. Point to either of the selected sheet tabs, right-click, and then on the shortcut menu, click **Delete**.

   e. Select **columns E:G**. Right-click the **Column F** heading, and then on the shortcut menu, click **Hide**.

   f. Display **Backstage** view. On the right, click **Properties**, and then click **Show Document Panel**. In the **Author** box, type your firstname and lastname, in the **Subject** box, type your course name and section number and then in the **Keywords** box, type **costs,filtered** Save your workbook, and then **Close** Excel.

3. **Start** Access. Under **Available Templates**, be certain **Blank database** is selected. On the right side of your screen, to the right of the **File Name** box, click the **Browse** button. In the **File New Database** dialog box, navigate to the **Integrated Projects Chapter 4** folder. In the **File name** box, delete the existing text, type **Lastname_Firstname_4C_Heating_Data** and then press Enter. Click the **Create** button.

a. On the **External Data tab**, in the **Import group**, click the **Excel** button. In the **Get External Data– Excel Spreadsheet** dialog box, click the **Browse** button. Navigate to your **Integrated Projects Chapter 4** folder, click the file **Lastname_Firstname_4C_Heating_Costs**, and then click **Open**.

b. Verify that the **Import the source data into a new table in the current database** option button is selected, and then click **OK**. Verify that the **First Row Contains Column Headings** check box is selected, and then click **Next** two times. Verify that the **Let Access add primary key** option button is selected, and then click **Next**. Under **Import to Table**, select the name, type **LastnameFirstname 4CHeatingTable** and then click **Finish**. Verify that the **Save import steps** check box is not selected, and then click **Close**.

c. In the **Navigation Pane**, double-click the table name **Lastname Firstname 4C Heating Table** to open the table. Right-click the **Table1 tab**, and then on the shortcut menu, click **Close**.

4. Point to the field name **Height**. Hold down the left mouse button, and then drag to the right to the **Weight** field name to select four fields. Point to the field name **Height**, right-click, and then on the shortcut menu, click **Hide Fields**.

a. Point to the field name **ID**. Hold down the left mouse button, and then drag right to the field name **Heating Cost** to select six fields. Point to the field name **ID**, and then right click. On the shortcut menu, click **Field Width**, and then in the **Column Width** dialog box, click **Best Fit**.

b. In the **Heating Cost** field, click a cell that contains **$108**. On the **Home tab**, in the **Sort & Filter group**, click the **Selection** button, and then click **Less Than or Equal to $108**.

c. On the **Home tab**, in the **Sort & Filter group**, click the **Advanced Filter Options** button, and then click **Advanced Filter/Sort**. Point to the lower right corner of the field list, and then drag down to the right to expand the height and width of the field list until all of the field names are visible.

d. In the **Lastname Firstname 4C Heating Table** field list, double-click the field name **Cooling**. In the design grid, on the **Sort** row, click the cell in the **Cooling** field, click the **Sort arrow**, and then click **Descending**. On the **Home tab**, in the **Sort & Filter group**, click the **Toggle Filter** button.

e. Click **the Lastname Firstname 4C Heating TableFilter1 tab**, and then click **Save**. In the **Save As Query** dialog box, type **LastnameFirstname4CHeatingQuery** and then click **OK**. Right-click the **Lastname Firstname 4C Heating TableFilter1 tab,** and then click **Close**.

f. On the **Home tab**, in the **Sort & Filter group**, click the **Toggle Filter** button. Right-click the **Lastname_Firstname4C Heating Table tab**, and then click **Close**. In the message box asking if you want to save the table layout, click **Yes**.

5. In the **Navigation Pane**, click **Lastname Firstname 4C Heating Query**. On the **Create tab**, in the **Reports group**, click the **Report** button. On the **Page Setup tab**, in the **Page Layout group**, click the **Landscape** button.

Integrating Excel and Access

a. Click the field name **ID** to surround it with an orange border and to select the entire column. Right- click the selected name, and then on the shortcut menu, click **Delete**. Using the same technique, delete the columns **Power**, **Height**, **Width**, and **Length**.

b. Double-click the **Title**. In the title, double-click the word **Query**, and then type **Cost**

c. Click **Save**. In the **Save As** dialog box, type **Lastname Firstname 4C Heating Report** and then click **OK**. Right-click the **Lastname Firstname 4C Heating Report tab**, and then on the shortcut menu, click **Close**.

6. In the **Navigation Pane**, click **Lastname Firstname 4C Heating Table**, and then on the **Create tab**, in the **Reports group**, click the **Report Wizard** button.

a. In the **Report Wizard** dialog box, use the **One Field** button to move the following fields to the **Selected Fields** list in this order: **Model**, **Height**, and **Heating Cost**. Click **Next**. In the **Report Wizard** dialog box, under **Do you want to add any grouping levels?**, double-click the **Height** field, and then click **Next**.

b. Click the **Sort arrow**, and then click **Heating Cost**. Click **Next** two times. Under **What title do you want for your report?**, type **LastnameFirstname4CHeight** and then click **Finish**.

c. Display **Backstage** view, and then click **View and edit database properties**. In the **Properties** dialog box, on the **Summary tab**, in the **Subject** box, type your course name and section number, in the **Author** box, type your firstname and lastname, in the **Keywords** box, type **cooling,filtered** and then click **OK**.

d. Right-click the **Lastname Firstname 4C Height tab**, and then click **Close**. **Close** Access. e. Submit your printed or electronic files as directed by your instructor.

You have completed Project 4C

Integrating Excel and Access

Apply 4B
skills from
these
Objectives:

5. Create an
    Access Table
6. Create an
    Access Query
7. Export
    Access Data
    to Excel

In the following Skills Review, you will add a table to an existing Access database, create relationship between tables, and create a query. Using exported Access data, you will apply a custom table style and add subtotals. Your completed files will look similar to Figure 4.39.

Project Files

For Project 4D, you will need the following files:

New blank Excel workbook
i04D_Cooling_Coils_Schedule

You will save your files as:

Lastname_Firstname_4D_Cooling_Coils
Lastname_Firstname_4D_Coil_Parts

Project Results

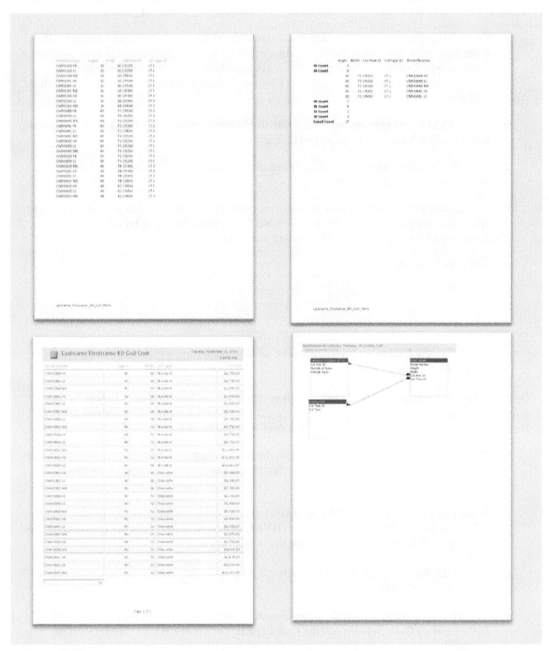

Figure 4.39

Integrating Excel and Access

1. **Start** Access. Locate and open the database **i04D_Cooling_Coils**. Display **Backstage** view, and then click **Save Database As**. In the **Save As** dialog box, navigate to your **Integrated Projects Chapter 4** folder, and then save the database as **Lastname_Firstname_4D_Cooling_Coils**

    a. On the **Message Bar**, click the **Enable Content** button, and then **Open** the Navigation Pane. b On the **Create tab**, in the **Tables group**, click the **Table Design** button. In the **Field Name column**, type **CoilRowID** and press Enter. Click anywhere in the text you just typed—*Coil Row ID*—and then click the **Primary Key** button. Press the down arrow key to move to the next row.

    b. In the **Field Name column**, type **Number of Rows** press Tab, click the **Data Type arrow**, and then click **Number**. Press Tab two times.

    c. In the **Field Name column**, type **CostperSqIn** and then press Tab. Click the **Data Type arrow**, and then click **Currency**.

    d. On the **Design tab**, in the **Views group**, click the **View** button to switch to **Datasheet** view. In the message box, click **Yes** to save the table. In the **Save As** dialog box, type **LastnameFirstname4D CoilRows** and then click **OK**.

    e. Enter the following data:

CR10	1	.75
CR20	2	1.5
CR30	3	2.25
CR40	4	3.1

    f. Right-click the **Lastname Firstname 4D Coil Rows** table tab, and then on the shortcut menu, click **Close**.

2. On the **Database Tools tab**, in the **Relationships group**, click the **Relationships** button. In the **Show Table** dialog box, on the **Tables tab**, double-click the tables **Lastname Firstname 4D Coil Rows, Cooling Coils**, and **HVAC Model**. **Close** the **Show Table** dialog box.

    a. Point to the **Cooling Coils** title, hold down the left mouse button and drag the field list to the left side of the Relationships window, under the **Lastname Firstname 4D Coil Rows** field list.

    b. In the **Lastname Firstname 4D Coil Rows** field list, point to **Coil Row ID**, hold down the left mouse button, drag to the right to the **HVAC Model** field list until your mouse pointer is on top of **Coil Row ID**, and then release the mouse button.

    c. In the **Edit Relationships** dialog box, select the **Enforce Referential Integrity** check box, and then click **Create**.

    d. Using the same technique, create a one-to-many relationship between the **Coil Type ID** field in the **Cooling Coils** field list and the **Coil Type ID** field in the **HVAC Model** field list. e. On the **Design tab**, in the **Tools group**, click the **Relationship Report** button.

    e. Click the **Save** button. In the **Save As** dialog box, type **LastnameFirstname4DCoilRelationships** and then click **OK**.

    f. Right-click the **Lastname Firstname 4D Coil Relationships tab**, and then click **Close All**.

Integrating Excel and Access

3. On the **Create tab**, in the **Queries group**, click the **Query Design** button. In the **Show Table** dialog box, double-click each of the tables to add them to the table area of the Query window, and then **Close** the **Show Table** dialog box.

   a. If necessary, move the field lists to display the join lines.

   b. In the **HVAC Model** field list, double-click the field names **Model Number, Height,** and **Width** to add the fields to the design grid. In the **Lastname Firstname 4D Coil Rows** field list, double-click the **Cost per Sq In** field name. In the **Cooling Coils** field list, double-click the **Coil Type** field name.

   c. On the **Design tab**, in the **Results group**, click the **Run** button. Click **Save**. In the **Save As** dialog box, type **LastnameFirstname4DCoilCost** and then click **OK**.

   d. Click the **View** button to return to **Design** view. In the **Field** row, right-click in the sixth column—a blank column, and then on the shortcut menu, click **Zoom**.

   e. In the **Zoom** dialog box, type **CoilCost:[Height]*[Width]*[CostperSqIn]** and then click **OK**.

   f. On the **Show** row, in the **Cost per Sq In** column, select the check box to clear the check mark. In the **Results group**, click the **Run** button.

   g. Click the **Save** button. Right-click the **Lastname Firstname 4D Coil Cost query tab**, and then on the shortcut list, click **Close**.

4. In the **Navigation Pane**, click the **Lastname Firstname 4D Coil Cost** query, and then on the **Create tab**, in the **Reports group**, click the **Report** button. Click **Save**. In the **Save As** dialog box, type **LastnameFirstname4DCoilCostReport** and then click **OK**.

   a. Right-click the **Lastname Firstname 4D Coil Cost Report tab**, and then click **Close**. Display **Backstage** view, and then click **View and edit database properties**. In the **Properties** dialog box, on the **Summary** tab, in the **Subject** box, type your course name and section number, in the **Author** box, type your firstname and lastname, in the **Keywords** box, type costs,calculated and then click **OK**. Click the **Home tab**.

   b. In the **Navigation Pane**, click one time on the **HVAC Model** table name to select the table. On the **External Data tab**, in the **Export group**, click the **Excel** button. Navigate to the **Integrated Projects Chapter 4** folder, type the file name **Lastname_Firstnmae_4D_Coil_Parts** and then click **Save**.

   c. In the **Export – Excel Spreadsheet** dialog box, verify the **File format** is **Excel Workbook (*.xlsx)**, and then click **OK**. Do not save the export steps. Click **Close**, and then **Close** Access. d. **Start** Excel. Navigate to the **Integrated Projects Chapter 4** folder, and then open the file **Lastname_Firstname_4D_Coil_Parts**.

   d. On the **Insert tab**, in the **Text group**, click the **Header & Footer** button. On the **Design tab**, in the **Navigation group**, click the **Go to Footer** button. In the **Footer** area, click just above the word **Footer**, and then in the **Header & Footer Elements group**, click the **File Name** button. Click any cell in the worksheet to exit the footer.

Integrating Excel and Access

e. Right-click the **HVAC_Model sheet tab**, and then click **Move or Copy**. In the **Move or Copy** dialog box, click **(move to end)**, select the **Create a copy** check box, and then click **OK**.

f. Right-click the **HVAC_Model (2) sheet tab**, and then click **Rename**. With **HVAC_Model (2)** selected, type **4DSubtotals** and then press Enter. Using the same technique, rename the **HVAC_Model sheet tab** as **4DPartsTable** and then **Save** your changes.

5. On the **Home tab**, in the **Styles group**, click the **Format as Table** button. At the bottom of the **Table Styles** gallery, click **New Table Style**.

a. In the **New Table Style** dialog box, in the **Name** box, type **CoilTableStyle**

b. Under **Table Element**, click **Header Row**, and then click **Format**. On the **Font tab**, under **Font style**, click **Bold**. Click the **Color arrow**, and then in the tenth column, click the first color— **Orange, Accent 6**. Click **OK** two times to close the dialog boxes.

c. In the **Styles group**, click the **Format as Table** button. At the top of the **Table Styles** gallery, under **Custom**, click the **Coil Table Style**. In the **Format as Table** dialog box, under **Where is the data for your table?**, verify that the range is =$A$1:$E$28, verify that the **My table has headers** check box is selected, and then click **OK**.

6. Click the **4D Subtotals sheet tab**. Select the range **A1:A28**, hold down the left mouse button, and then drag the selected range to the right of column **E**. Right-click column heading **A**, and then on the shortcut menu, click **Delete**. Click cell **A1**. On the **Home tab**, in the **Editing group**, click the **Sort & Filter** button, and then click **Sort Z to A**.

a. On the **Data tab**, in the **Outline group**, click the **Subtotal** button. In the **Subtotal** dialog box, verify that under **At each change in**, **Height** is displayed, and under **Use function**, **Count** is displayed. Under **Add subtotal to**, select the **Height** check box, and then clear the **Model Number** check box. Click **OK**.

b. Select columns **A:F**. Point to the column separator between the column headings **A** and **B**, and then double-click to adjust the column widths.

c. At the top left corner of your screen, click the **level** button **2**. To the left of row **22**, click the **Show details** button.

d. Click cell AI. Display Backstage view, click Properties, and then click Show Document Panel. In the Author box, type your firstname and lastname, in the Subject box, type your course name and section number, and then in the Keywords box, type coil parts, subtotals Close the Document Information Panel.

e. Save your workbook, and then Close Excel.

f. Submit your printed or electronic files as directed by your instructor.

You have completed Project 4D

Integrating Excel and Access

Apply 4A skills from these Objectives:

1. Modify an Excel Table
2. Import Excel Data into Access Using the Import Spreadsheet Wizard
3. Sort and Filter Data in an Access Table
4. Create, Modify, and Print an Access Report

In the following Mastering Integration project, you will create a calculated column in Excel to determine the installation cost of HVAC units. In Access you will use the imported worksheet to filter the data and create two reports. Your completed files will look similar to Figure 4.40.

Project Files

For Project 4E, you will need the following files:

> New blank Access database
> i04E_HVAC_Installation

You will save your files as:

> Lastname_Firstname_4E_HVAC_Installation
> Lastname_Firstname_4E_Installation_Cost

Project Results

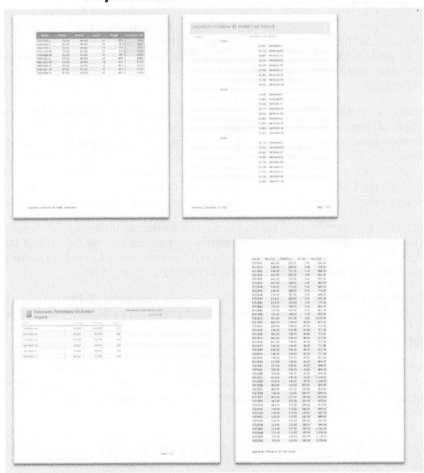

Figure 4.40

Integrating Excel and Access

217

1. **Start** Excel. Open the file **i04E_HVAC_Installlation**. Navigate to your **Integrated Projects Chapter 4** folder, and then save the file with the name **Lastname_Firstname_4E_HVAC_Installation** Insert the file name as a field in the footer. In **Normal** view, make cell **A1** the active cell.

2. Create a table using the Excel data range **A1:H28**. Change the column width of columns **A:H** to 12.00 (89 pixels). Sort the **Weight column** in **Ascending** order. **Rename** *Sheet1* as **4EInstallationCost**

3. Click the **Length AutoFilter arrow**, and then filter the column to show rows **Less Than Or Equal To 60** Click cell **I1**, type **InstallationCost** and then press [Enter]. In cell **I2**, type the formula **=H2*10** and then on the **Formula Bar**, click the **Enter** button. Format the numbers in column **I** with the **Accounting Number Format**, and then click the **Decrease Decimal** button two times. Adjust the width of column **I** to automatically widen to **Best Fit**. In column **I**, apply **Conditional Formatting to the numbers less than 40,000** to display with **Light Red Fill**.

4. Hide the **Power**, **Height**, and **Width** columns. In the **Page Setup** dialog box, center the page **Horizontally**, and then **Delete** worksheets **Sheet2** and **Sheet3**.

5. Display the Document Information Panel. In the **Author** box, type your firstname and lastname, in the **Subject** box, type your course name and section number, and then in the **Keywords** box, type **calculatedcosts Save** your workbook, and then **Close** Excel.

6. **Start** Access, and then create a new blank database in your **Integrated Projects Chapter 4** folder with the file name **Lastname_Firstname_4E_Installation_Cost** Import the Excel file **Lastname_Firstname_4E_HVAC_Installation** Let Access add a primary key, name the new Access table **LastnameFirstname4EInstallCost** and then open the table in **Datasheet view**. **Close** the **Table1 tab**

7. Hide the columns **ID**, **Height**, **Width**, and **Length**, and then adjust the **Field Width** of the remaining columns to **Best Fit**. Sort the **Heating** field in **Descending** order, and then filter the **Cooling column** to display numbers **greater than or equal to 40,000**. Click the **Advanced filter** button, and then add the field **Power** to the design grid. On the **Criteria row** of the **Power** field, type **=575/60/3** and then click the **Toggle Filter** button. **Save** the query with the name **LastnameFirstname4EPower Query** Right-click **the Lastname Firstname 4E Install Cost Filter1 tab**, and then click **Close**. Click the **Toggle Filter** button, and then click **Save**. **Close** the **Lastname Firstname 4E Install Cost** table.

8. Click the **Report** button to create a new report based on the **Lastname Firstname 4E Power Query**. Change the title to **LastnameFirstname4EPowerReport** and then **Delete** the columns **ID**, **Power**, **Height**, **Width**, **Length**, and **Installation Cost**. Change the **Page Layout** to **Landscape**. **Save** the report as **LastnameFirstname4EPowerReport** and then **Close All** objects.

9. Click the **Report Wizard** button, and then from the **Lastname Firstname 4E Install Cost** table, add the fields **Model**, **Cooling**, and **Installation Cost**. Group by the **Cooling** field, and then sort by the **Installation Cost** field in **Ascending** order, and then type the report name **LastnameFirstname4E Install CostReport**

10. Display **Backstage** view, and then click **View and edit database properties**. On the **Summary** tab, in the Subject box, type your course name and section number, in the **Author** box, type your firstname and lastname, in the **Keywords** box, type **costquery,reports** and then click **OK**. **Close** Access. Submit your printed or electronic files as directed by your instructor.

You have completed Project 4E

<table>
<tr><td>

Apply 4B skills from these Objectives:

5. Create an Access Table
6. Create an Access Query
7. Export Access Data to Excel

</td></tr>
</table>

In the following Mastering Integration project, you will add a table to an existing Access database, create a relationship between tables, and add a calculated field to a query. In Excel, using the exported Access data, you will apply a custom table style. Your completed files will look similar to Figure 4.41.

Project Files

For Project 4F, you will need the following files:

New blank Excel workbook
i04F_Fan_Types

You will save your files as:

Lastname_Firstname_4F_Fan_Types
Lastname_Firstname_4F_Fan_Costs

Integrating Excel and Access

Project Results

Figure 4.41

Integrating Excel and Access

1. **Start** Access. Open the database **i04F_Fan_Types**. Save the database in your **Integrated Projects Chapter 4** folder as **Lastname_Firstname_4F_Fan_Types** Enable the file content. Create a new table, and then in **Design** view, add the following field names and data types:

Field Name	Data Type
RPMID	Text
RPM	Text
RPMCost	Currency

2. Set the field **RPM ID** as the **Primary Key**. **Save** the table as **RPM** display the table in **Datasheet** view, and then add the following data:

RPM ID	RPM	RPM Cost
RPM70100	900	$123
RPM70200	1200	$136
RPM70300	1800	$152
RPM70400	3600	$171
RPM70500	1800/900	$230
RPM70600	1800/1200	$240

3. **Close All** open objects. In the **Relationships** window, add the four tables, and then move the **Fan** field list to the right and the **Horse Power ID**, **RPM**, and **Voltage** field lists to the left. Create a **Relationship** and **Enforce Referential Integrity** between the following fields: **Horse Power ID** in the **Horse Power** field list and the **Horse Power ID** in the **Fan** field list; **RPM ID** in the **RPM** field list and **RPM ID** in the **Fan** field list; and **Voltage ID** in the **Voltage** field list and **Voltage ID** in the **Fan** field list. Click the **Relationship Report** button, save a copy of the report as **Lastname Firstname 4F Fan Relationship** and then **Close All** open objects.

4. Open the **Fan** table, and then insert a **Totals row**. In the **Voltage ID** field, in the **Totals row**, **Count** the number of records. **Save** the **Fan** table, and then **Close** the table. Create a new **Query**, and then add the four tables to the table area of the **Query** window. Adjust the location and size of the four field lists to display all fields and join lines. In the **design grid**, add the fields **Fan ID**, **HP Cost**, **RPM Cost**, and **V Cost**. Insert a calculated column with the field name **FanCost** that adds the three cost fields. **Run** the query. **Save** the query as **Lastname_Firstname_4F_Fan_Costs** and then **Close** the query.

5. Use the **Report** tool to create a report based on the **Lastname_Firstname_4F_Fan_Costs** query. Save the report as **LastnameFirstname4FFanCostReport** and then **Close** the report object. Use the **Report Wizard** to create a report based on the **Fan** table. Add **Fan ID**, **Horse Power ID**, **RPM ID**, and **Voltage ID** to the report. Group by **Voltage ID**, and then sort by **Horse Power ID** in **Descending** order. Name the report **LastnameFirstname4FFanParts** and then **Close** the report object.

6. Export the **Lastname_Firstname_4F_Fan_Costs** query to Excel. In Access, display the **Properties** dialog box. In the **Subject** box, type your course name and section number, in the **Author** box, type your firstname lastname, in the **Keywords** box, type **fancosts,calculated** and then click **OK**. **Close** Access.

Integrating Excel and Access

7. In the Excel file **Lastname_Firstname_4F_Fan_Costs**, insert the file name as a field in the footer. Create a new Table Style named **Fan Table Style**. Format the **Header row** with **Bold**; Font Color **Red, Accent 2**; and Fill Color **Red, Accent 2, Lighter 80%**. Apply the **Fan Table Style** to your data.

8. Modify the **Fan Table Style**. Format the **Second Row Stripe**, with Stripe Size **3** and Fill Color **Red, Accent 2, Lighter 80%**. Adjust the column width of columns **A:E** to display all data. **Rename** the sheet tab as **4FFanStyle**

9. Display **Backstage** view. Click **Properties**, and then click **Show Document Panel**. In the **Author** box, type your firstname and lastname, in the **Subject** box, type your course name and section number, and then in the **Keywords** box, type **customtablestyle** **Close** the Document Information Panel. **Save** the workbook, and then **Close** Excel.

10. Submit your printed or electronic files as directed by your instructor.

You have completed Project 4F

Rubric

The following outcomes-based assessments are open-ended assessments. That is, there is no specific correct result; your result will depend on your approach to the information provided. Make Professional Quality your goal. Use the following scoring rubric to guide you in how to approach the problem and then to evaluate how well your approach solves the problem.

The *criteria*—Software Mastery, Content, Format and Layout, and Process—represent the knowledge and skills you have gained that you can apply to solving the problem. The *levels of performance*—Professional Quality, Approaching Professional Quality, or Needs Quality Improvements—help you and your instructor evaluate your result.

	Your completed project is of Professional Quality	Your completed project is of Approaching Professional Quality	Your completed project Needs Quality Improvements
1-Software Mastery	Chooses and applies the most appropriate skills, tools, and features and identifies efficient methods to solve the problem.	Chooses and applies some appropriate skills, tools, and features, but not in the most efficient manner.	Chooses inappropriate skills, tools, or features, or is inefficient in solving the problem.
2-Content	Constructs a solution that is clear and well organized, containing content that is accurate, appropriate to the audience and purpose, and complete. The solution contains no errors of spelling, grammar, or style.	Constructs a solution in which some components are unclear, poorly organized, inconsistent, or incomplete. May misjudge the needs of the audience. May contain some errors in spelling, grammar, or style, but the errors do not detract from comprehension.	Constructs a solution that is unclear, incomplete, or poorly organized, containing some inaccurate or inappropriate content. May contain many errors of spelling, grammar, or style. May fail to solve the problem.
3-Format and Layout	Formats and arranges all elements to communicate information and ideas, clarify function, illustrate relationships, and indicate relative importance.	Applies appropriate format and layout features to some elements, but not others. Or, overuses features, causing minor distraction.	Applies format and layout that fails to communicate information or ideas or clearly. May fail to use format and layout features to clarify function, illustrate relationships, or indicate relative importance. Or, may use available features excessively, causing distraction.
4-Process	Uses an organized approach that integrates planning, development, self-assessment, revision, and reflection.	Demonstrates an organized approach in some areas, but not others. Or, uses an insufficient process of organization throughout.	Does not use an organized approach to solve the problem.

Integrating Excel and Access

<table>
<tr><td>

Apply a combination of the 4A and 4B skills.

</td><td>

GO! Think | **Project 4G Filter Efficiency**

Project Files

For Project 4G, you will need the following files:

New blank Access database
i04G_Filter_Efficiency

You will save your files as:

Lastname_Firstname_4G_Filter_Efficiency
Lastname_Firstname_4G_Filter_Costs

</td></tr>
</table>

Midwest HVAC Manufacturer offers a number of different filters for their heating and cooling units. Information about the HVAC filters is located in file i04G_Filter_Efficiency. You have been asked to prepare an efficiency report. Open the Excel file and save it as
Lastname_Firstname_4G_Filter_Efficiency Create an Excel table from the existing data, and then sort the Efficiency column in descending order. Select any size in the Width column, and then create an AutoFilter for that size. Insert a calculated column that calculates the filter cost using $0.10 per square inch (Length*Width*.10). Create a conditional format for the Cost column. Apply a table style to the table. Insert the file name in the footer. Create a new database with the file name
Lastname_Firstname_4G_Filter_Costs. Import the Excel file, and then sort the Width column in ascending order. Create a query that displays the filters with an Efficiency of 65% or higher, and then create a report based on the query. Add appropriate document properties to both files. Submit your printed or electronic files as directed by your instructor.

You have completed Project 4G

GO! Think | **Project 4H Shipping Costs**

Project Files

For Project 4H, you will need the following files:

New blank Excel workbook
i04H_Shipping_Weights

You will save your files as:

Lastname_Firstname_4H_Shipping_Weights
Lastname_Firstname_4H_Shipping_Costs

Midwest HVAC manufacturer ships merchandise by air. You have been asked to calculate shipping costs based on a cost of $0.65 per pound. Open the file i04H_Shipping_Weights. Save the file as **Lastname_Firstname_4H_Shipping_Weights** Create a new table named **Lastname_Fistname_4H_Mixing_Box** Assign a Number data type to the MB Weight field. Use the data below to enter records in the table. Create relationships between the five tables and enforce referential integrity, and then create and save a Relationship Report. Create a query that includes the CFM ID and the weight from each of the tables. Create a calculated column to calculate the total weight. Save your query as **Lastname_Firstname_4H_Shipping_Costs** Create a report based on your query. Export the query to Excel.

Open the Excel file Lastname_Firstname_4H_Shipping_Costs. Convert the Excel range to a table and sort the Total column in descending order. Add a calculated column to determine the shipping costs. Insert the file name in the footer of the Excel workbook and add appropriate document properties to both files. Submit your printed or electronic files as directed by your instructor.

Mixing Box ID	MB Weight
MB5900	275
MB6000	350
MB6010	425
MB6020	500
MB6030	575

You have completed Project 4H

Integrating Excel and Access

GO! Think | Project 4I Cooling Costs

Project Files

For Project 4I, you will need the following files:

New blank Access database
i04I_HVAC_Cooling

You will save your files as:

Lastname_Firstname_4I_HVAC_Cooling
Lastname_Firstname_4I_Cooling_Costs

Karen Laroque, Associate Director of Sales as Midwest HVAC Manufacturer, has asked you to calculate the cost of running HVAC units in summer and provide a report. In the file i04I_HVAC_Cooling, create an Excel table. Insert a calculated column that calculates the cost of cooling using $0.00124 per Cooling BTU. Filter the data to display only one Heating BTU number of your choice. Insert the file name in the footer, and save the file as **Lastname_Firstname_4I_HVAC_Cooling** In Access, create a new database and save it as **Lastname_Firstname_4I_Cooling_Costs** Import the Excel file, and then filter the data to show only data for the Cooling BTU greater than 50,000 and the Power unit of your choice. Create a report based on your results. Add appropriate document properties to the Access and Excel files. Submit your printed or electronic files as directed by your instructor.

You have completed Project 4I

Integrating Excel and PowerPoint

OUTCOMES
At the end of this chapter you will be able to:

OBJECTIVES
Mastering these objectives will enable you to:

PROJECT 5A
Create Excel charts and link them to a PowerPoint presentation.

1. Create and Format Excel Charts
2. Link Excel Charts and Data to a PowerPoint Presentation
3. Apply Slide Transitions, Use the Document Inspector, and Mark as Final

PROJECT 5B
Create illustrations and paste PowerPoint objects and slides into an Excel worksheet.

4. Create and Modify Illustrations in PowerPoint
5. Copy a PowerPoint Slide and Object into an Excel Workbook
6. Create Hyperlinks
7. Freeze Rows, Repeat Headings, and Insert Comments in Excel

Sportstock/Shutterstock

In This Chapter

In this chapter, you will create charts—graphical representations of numeric data—in an Excel worksheet. Excel provides various types of charts to display the data in a professional and meaningful way. You can modify a chart by formatting a chart title, moving or hiding the legend, or displaying additional chart elements, such as axis titles and data labels. You will also create presentations using PowerPoint's wide range of formatting options, including themes, layouts, and styles. You can create designer-quality graphics using the SmartArt feature. Finally, you will use the copy and paste and hyperlink features to share date between Excel and PowerPoint

The projects in this chapter relate to **Board Anywhere Surf and Snowboard Shop**, a retail store founded by college classmates Dana Connolly and J. R. Kass. The men grew up in the sunshine of Orange County, California, but they also spent time in the mountain snow. After graduating with business degrees, they combined their business expertise and their favorite sports to open their shop. The store carries top brands of men's and women's apparel, goggles and sunglasses, and boards and gear. The surfboard selection includes both classic boards and the latest high-tech boards. Snowboarding gear can be purchased in packages or customized for the most experienced boarders. Connolly and Kass are proud to count many of Southern California's extreme sports games participants among their customers.

From Chapter 5 of *GO! with Microsoft® Office 2010 Integrated Projects Comprehensive*, First Edition, Shelley Gaskin, Carol L. Martin. Copyright © 2012 by Pearson Education, Inc. Published by Pearson Prentice Hall. All rights reserved.

Project 5A Sales Charts

Project Activities

In Activities 5.01 through 5.08, you will use Excel to create a column chart to display the sales data of individual items. Also, you will create a pie chart to compare the monthly sales figures from one year to the next. You will modify a picture in PowerPoint and link the Excel charts to the presentation. Finally, you will change the Excel data and view those changes in PowerPoint. Your completed files will look similar to Figure 5.1.

Project Files

For Project 5A, you will need the following files:

i05A_Snowboarding_Sales
i05A_Sales_Presentation

You will save your files as:

Lastname_Firstname_5A_Snowboarding_Sales
Lastname_Firstname_5A_Sales_Presentation

Project Results

Figure 5.1
Project 5A Sales Charts

Integrated Projects | Integrating Excel and PowerPoint

Objective 1 | Create and Format Excel Charts

You can quickly create professional-looking charts in Excel. Various chart types already exist; however, you must determine which chart type will illustrate your data in the best manner. A *column chart* is a chart in which the data is arranged in columns. It is useful for showing data changes over a period of time or for illustrating comparisons among items. A *pie chart* is a chart that shows the relationship of each part to a whole. Consider using a pie chart when you have only one column or row to plot and each category of data represents part of a total value.

Activity 5.01 | Inserting and Modifying a Column Chart

Excel data that is arranged in columns or rows can be plotted in a column chart. The *category axis* is the area along the bottom of a chart that identifies the categories of data; it is also referred to as the *x-axis*. The *value axis* is a numerical scale on the left side of a chart that shows the range of numbers for the data points; it is also referred to as the *y-axis*.

1 **Start** Excel. From your student files, locate and open the file **i05A_Snowboarding_Sales**. In the location where you are saving your files for this chapter, create a new folder named **Integrated Projects Chapter 5** and then **Save** the file in the folder as **Lastname_Firstname_5A_Snowboarding_Sales**

2 Click the **Insert tab**, and then in the **Text group**, click the **Header & Footer** button. On the **Design tab**, in the **Navigation group**, click the **Go to Footer** button. In the **Footer area**, click in the box just above the word **Footer**, and then in the **Header & Footer Elements group**, click the **File Name** button. Click in any cell in the workbook to exist the footer.

3 Near the right side of the status bar, click the **Normal** button 🔲, and then press Ctrl + Home to make cell **A1** the active cell.

4 Click cell **D2**, type **Sales Increase** and then press Enter. In cell **D3**, type the formula **=C3-B3** and then on the **Formula Bar**, click the **Enter** button ✓ to accept the entry. Point to the fill handle to display the ➕ pointer. Drag down to cell **D23**, and then release the mouse button. Select cells **B3:D3**. On the **Home tab**, in the **Number group**, click the **Accounting Number Format** button $ ▾. Click cell **A1**, and then compare your screen with Figure 5.2.

Excel copies the formula into cell D3 to cells D4:D23 and displays the values in the cells.

Figure 5.2

Values in column D

Accounting Number Format applied

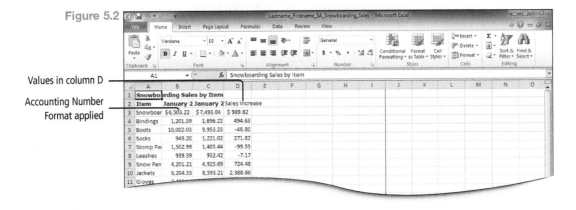

5 Select cells **A1:D1**. On the **Home tab**, in the **Alignment group**, click the **Merge & Center** button ▦. In the **Styles group**, click the **Cell Styles** button. In the **Cell Styles** gallery, under **Themed Cell Styles**, click **Accent6**.

6 Select cells **A2:D2**. In the **Alignment group**, click the **Center** button ▤. In the **Styles group**, click the **Cell Styles** button. In the **Cell Styles** gallery, under **Themed Cell Styles**, click **20% - Accent6**.

7 Select **columns A:D**. Point to the column A header, right-click to display a shortcut menu, and then click **Column Width**. In the **Column Width** dialog box, type **15** and then click **OK**.

8 Select cells **B23:C23**. On the **Home tab**, in the **Editing group**, click the **Sum** button Σ. Click cell **B3**. In the **Clipboard group**, click the **Format Painter** button ✦. Select cells **B23:D23**.

The column totals display in cells B23 and C23, and the Sales Increase displays in cell D23. Recall that you copied a formula from cell D3 to cell D23. After inserting data in cells B23 and C23, the formula in cell D23 provides the Sales Increase result.

9 Select cells **A2:C22**. Click the **Insert tab**. In the **Charts group**, click the **Column** button, and then under **Cylinder**, click the first style—**Clustered Cylinder**. On the **Design tab**, in the **Location group**, click the **Move Chart** button. In the **Move Chart** dialog box, click the **New sheet** option button, in the **New sheet** box, type **January Sales** and then click **OK**.

A chart is created and moved to a new sheet named January Sales.

10 On the **Design tab**, in the **Data group**, click the **Switch Row/Column** button. In the **Chart Styles group**, click the **More** button ▾. In the **Chart Styles** gallery, in the fifth row, click the eighth style—**Style 40**. In the **Chart Layouts group**, click the **More** button ▾, and then in the **Chart Layouts** gallery, in the third row, click the second layout—**Layout 8**.

The *Chart Styles gallery* is a group of predesigned *chart styles*—the overall visual look of a chart in terms of its graphic effects, colors, and backgrounds; for example, you can have flat or beveled columns, colors that are solid or transparent, and backgrounds that are dark or light. In the *Chart Layout gallery*, you can select a predesigned *chart layout*—a combination of chart elements, which can include a title, legend labels for the columns, and the table of charted cells.

11 Click the **Layout tab**, and then in the **Axes group**, click the **Gridlines** button. In the displayed list, point to **Primary Horizontal Gridlines**, and then click **Major Gridlines**. In the **Labels group**, click the **Legend** button, and then click **Show Legend at Right**. Compare your screen with Figure 5.3

The *legend* is a chart element that identifies the patterns or colors that are assigned to the categories in the chart.

Figure 5.3

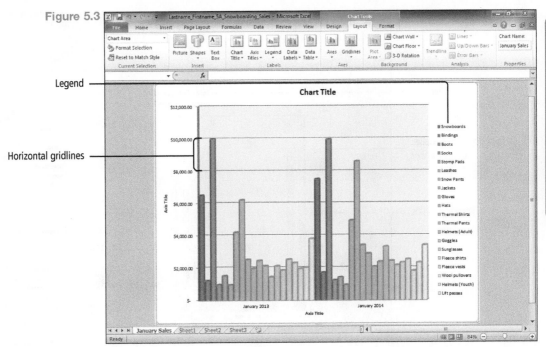

Legend

Horizontal gridlines

12 On the **Layout tab**, at the top of the **Current Selection group**, click the **Chart Elements arrow**, and then click **Vertical (Value) Axis**. In the **Current Selection group**, click the **Format Selection** button. In the **Format Axis** dialog box, click **Number**, and then under **Category**, click **Currency**. In the **Decimal places** box, delete the number **2**, type **0** and then click **Close**.

The values on the vertical axis are formatted as Currency with no decimal places.

13 In the **Current Selection group**, click the **Chart Elements arrow**, and then click **Vertical (Value) Axis Title**. On the **Formula Bar**, type **Sales** and then press Enter. On the **Home tab**, in the **Font group**, click the **Font Size button arrow** `11  ▾`, and then click **14**.

The title Sales displays on the vertical axis.

14 Click the **Layout tab**. In the **Current Selection group**, click the **Chart Elements arrow**, and then click **Horizontal (Category) Axis Title**. With the horizontal axis title selected at the bottom of the chart, press Del to delete the title.

15 Click the **Chart Title**. In the **Formula Bar**, type **Sales Comparison** press Alt + Enter, and then type **January 2013 and 2014** Press Enter to accept the new chart title.

The title displays on two lines at the top of the chart. Pressing Alt + Enter allows you to display multiple lines of text in a single cell.

16 Click the **Legend**. Click the **Home tab**. In the **Font group**, click the **Increase Font Size** button A⁺ two times, and then click the **Bold** button B. Compare your screen with Figure 5.4.

Figure 5.4

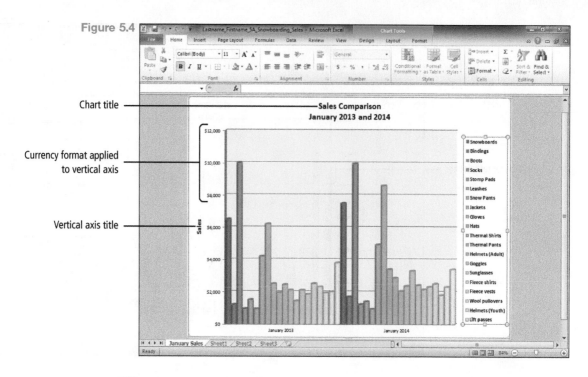

Chart title

Currency format applied to vertical axis

Vertical axis title

17 Right-click the **January Sales sheet tab**, and then on the shortcut menu, click **Move or Copy**. In the **Move or Copy** dialog box, click (**move to end**), select the **Create a copy** check box, and then click **OK**. Right-click the **January Sales (2) sheet tab**, and then on the shortcut menu, click **Rename**. With **January Sales (2)** selected, type **5A Sales by Item** and then press Enter.

18 Click in a blank area of the chart. Click the **Design tab**, and then in the **Data group**, click the **Switch Row/Column** button. In the **Chart Layouts group**, in the first row, click the third layout—**Layout 3**.

The Switch Row/Column button exchanges the row and column data in a chart and changes the legend accordingly. This allows you to display a chart that presents your data in the best manner.

19 Click the **Chart Title**, in the Formula Bar, type **Sales by Item** and then press Enter. Compare your screen with Figure 5.5.

Integrated Projects | Integrating Excel and PowerPoint

232

Figure 5.5

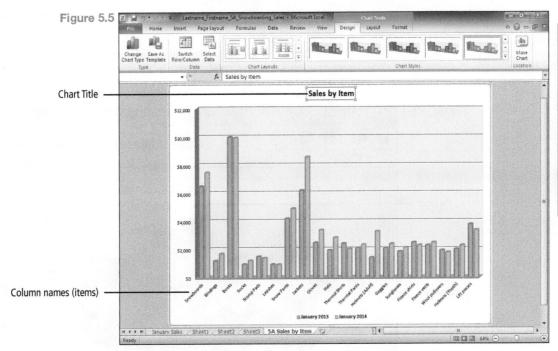

Chart Title

Sales by Item

Column names (items)

20 Right-click the **Sheet1 tab**, and then on the shortcut menu, click **Rename**. With **Sheet1** selected, type **5A Sales Data** and then press Enter. Click the **Sheet2 tab**, hold down Shift and then click the **Sheet3 tab**. Right-click the **Sheet 3 tab**, and then on the shortcut menu, click **Delete** to delete the two sheets.

21 Save the workbook.

Activity 5.02 | Inserting and Modifying a Pie Chart

Data that is in one column or one row of an Excel worksheet can be displayed in a pie chart. In a pie chart, the size of each pie slice is equal to its ***data point***—the value that originates in a worksheet cell—compared to the total value of all the slices. The data points display as a percentage of the whole pie. Each pie slice is referred to as a ***data marker***. A data marker is a column, bar, area, dot, pie slice, or other symbol in a chart that represents a single data point.

1 Click the **5A Sales Data sheet tab**. Select cells **A3:A22**, hold down Ctrl, and then select cells **C3:C22**.

Cells A3:A22 and C3:C22 are selected. Recall that you can hold down Ctrl to select nonadjacent columns or rows.

2 On the **Insert tab**, in the **Charts group**, click the **Pie** button, and then under **3-D Pie**, click the first chart type—**Pie in 3-D**. On the **Design tab**, in the **Location group**, click the **Move Chart** button. In the **Move Chart** dialog box, click the **New sheet** option button, in the **New sheet** box, type **January 2014 Sales** and then click **OK**. Compare your screen with Figure 5.6.

The January 2014 *data series*—the related data points represented by data markers—displays in a pie chart. The data points determine the size of each slice and the legend identifies the pie slices.

Figure 5.6

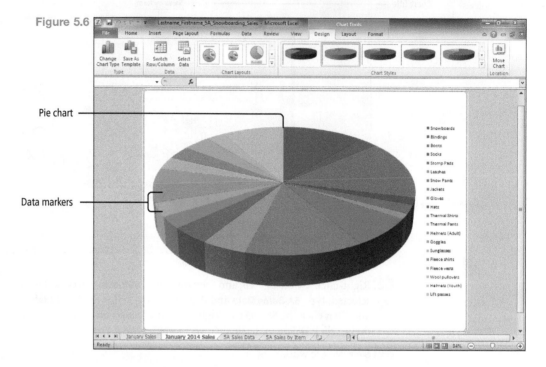

Pie chart

Data markers

▣ On the **Design tab**, in the **Chart Layouts group**, click the first layout—**Layout 1**.

▣ Click the **Chart Title**, type **January 2014 Sales** and then press Enter.

▣ Click the **Layout tab**. In the **Current Selection group**, click the **Chart Elements arrow**, and then click **Series 1 Data Labels**. Click the **Home tab**, and then in the **Font group**, click the **Bold** button [B].

▣ Click the **Layout tab**. In the **Current Selection group**, click the **Chart Elements arrow**, and then click **Chart Area**. In the **Current Selection group**, click the **Format Selection** button. In the **Format Chart Area** dialog box, click the **Gradient fill** option button. Click the **Color arrow**, and then in the tenth column, click the fourth color—**Orange, Accent 6, Lighter 40%**. Click **Close**, and then compare your screen with Figure 5.7.

Integrated Projects | Integrating Excel and PowerPoint

234

Figure 5.7

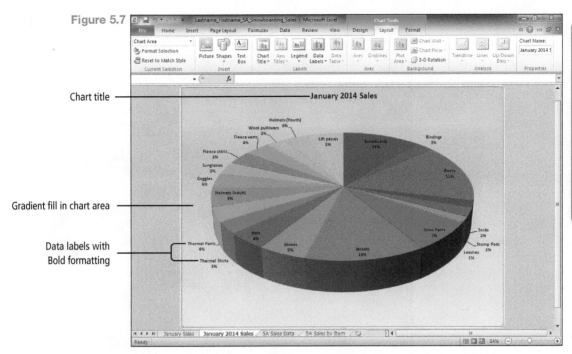

Chart title —

Gradient fill in chart area —

Data labels with Bold formatting —

7 On the **Layout tab**, in the **Background group**, click the **3-D Rotation** button. In the **Format Chart Area** dialog box, under **Rotation**, in the **X** text box, select **0**, type **145** and then click **Close**.

The Snowboards data marker is rotated to the bottom right of the pie chart.

8 Click on the chart to select all the data markers, and then click the **Snowboards** data marker.

Only the Snowboards data marker—pie slice—is selected.

9 Point to the **Snowboards** data marker to display the pointer. Drag down approximately 0.5 inches, and then release the mouse button. Compare your screen with Figure 5.8.

The Snowboards data marker is pulled out—*exploded*. You can explode one or more slices of a pie chart for emphasis. The entire pie automatically adjusts to a smaller size to fit all the data markers on the chart sheet.

Project 5A: Sales Charts | **Integrated Projects**

235

Figure 5.8

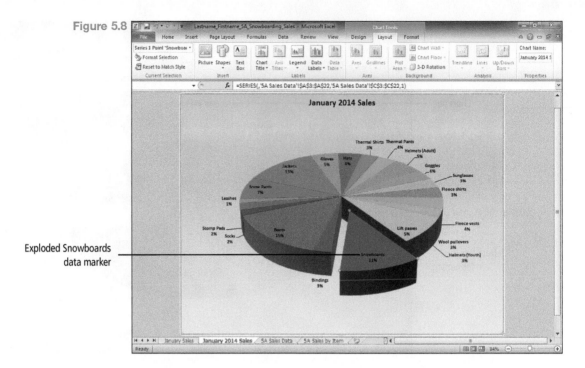

Exploded Snowboards data marker

10 Save the workbook.

Activity 5.03 | Inserting an Absolute Cell Reference

In an Excel worksheet, the intersecting column letter and row number form the *cell reference*—also called the *cell address*. An Excel formula that includes a cell reference—that may be in a different part of the same worksheet, or in a different worksheet or workbook—uses the data in the cell reference to calculate the value of the formula.

1 Click the **5A Sales Data sheet tab**, and then click cell **F1**. Type **Sales Commission** and then press Tab. In cell **G1**, type **3%** and then on the **Formula Bar**, click the **Enter** button ✓ to accept the entry. Point to the line between the headings F and G until the ⊞ pointer displays, and then double-click.

> The width of column F automatically adjusts to the best fit—all of the text in cell F1 displays.

2 Click cell **A25**, type **Commissions** and then press Tab. In cell **B25**, type **=B23*G1** and then press F4. On the **Formula Bar**, click the **Enter** button ✓.

> On the Formula Bar, the formula *=B23*$G$1* displays a dollar sign to the left of G and to the left of 1, making it an *absolute cell reference*. An absolute cell reference refers to cells by their fixed position in a worksheet; an absolute cell reference remains the same when a formula is copied to other cells.

3 In cell **B25**, point to the fill handle to display the ⊞ pointer. Drag right to cell **C25**. Click the **Formulas tab**, and then in the **Formula Auditing group**, click the **Show Formulas** button. Compare your screen with Figure 5.9.

> The formula is copied from cell B25 to cell C25. The reference to cell G1 does not change because it is an absolute cell reference. The reference to cell B23 changes to cell C23 because it is a relative cell reference. Recall that a relative cell reference is the address of a cell based on the relative position of the cell that contains the formula and the cell referred to.

Integrated Projects | Integrating Excel and PowerPoint

Figure 5.9

$G$1 absolute cell
references in cells B25:C25

4 In the **Formula Auditing group**, click the **Show Formulas** button to turn off the display of formulas.

5 Click the **Page Layout tab**. In the **Page Setup group**, click the **Orientation** button, and then click **Landscape**. Right-click the **January Sales sheet tab**, and then on the shortcut menu, click **Select All Sheets**. Click the **Insert tab**, and then in the **Text group**, click the **Header & Footer** button. In the **Page Setup** dialog box, on the **Header/Footer tab**, click the **Footer arrow**, and then click the file name **Lastname_Firstname_5A_Snowboarding_Sales**. Click **OK**. Right-click the **5A Sales Data sheet tab**, and then on the shortcut menu, click **Ungroup Sheets**.

6 Display **Backstage** view, and then click the **Info tab**. On the right, click **Properties**, and then click **Show Document Panel**. In the **Author** box, type your firstname and lastname, in the **Subject** box, type your course name and section number, and then in the **Keywords** box, type **sales data, charts Close** ☒ the Document Information Panel.

7 **Save** 🖫 the workbook.

Objective 2 | Link Excel Charts and Data to a PowerPoint Presentation

When you want to paste Excel data or a chart in a PowerPoint presentation, the Paste Special feature allows you to create a link—an external reference—from PowerPoint back to the Excel file. This allows you to update the chart or data in Excel and have those changes reflected in the presentation.

Activity 5.04 | Linking Excel Charts to a PowerPoint Presentation

Ali Cardona, the Purchasing Manager at Board Anywhere Surf and Snowboard Shop, is presenting the sales data to the employees. He would like to determine if the sales of jackets, gloves, hats, and thermal shirts have been sufficient to keep carrying the lines in the retail store. In this activity, you will finish the PowerPoint presentation Mr. Cardona created by linking Excel charts to specific slides.

1 **Start** PowerPoint. From your student files, locate and open the file **i05A_Sales_Presentation**. **Save** the file in your **Integrated Projects Chapter 5** folder with the file name **Lastname_Firstname_5A_Sales_Presentation** If necessary, maximize the window.

2 Click the **Insert tab**, and then in the **Text group**, click the **Header & Footer** button. In the **Header and Footer** dialog box, click the **Notes and Handouts tab**. Under **Include on page**, click the **Date and time** check box, select the Footer check box, and then in the **Footer** box, type **Lastname Firstname 5A Sales Presentation** Click **Apply to All**.

3 On **Slide 1**, click the subtitle placeholder, type **Comparing Snowboarding Sales** and then press Enter. Type **January 2013 to January 2014** and then in the **Slides/Outline pane**, click **Slide 2**.

Another Way

To decrease the list level, hold down Shift and press Tab.

4 On **Slide 2**, in the bulleted list, click to the right of the last bullet point *Purchasing Manager*, and then press Enter. Click the **Home tab**, and then in the **Paragraph group**, click the **Decrease List Level** button. Type **Shinpei Kawano** and then press Enter. Press Tab to decrease the list level—indent it, and then type **Sales Associate** Compare your screen with Figure 5.10.

> The text on the slide is organized according to *list levels*. A list level is an outline level in a presentation represented by a bullet symbol and identified in a slide by the indentation and the size of the text.

Figure 5.10

Main bullet point

List level of bullet point decreased

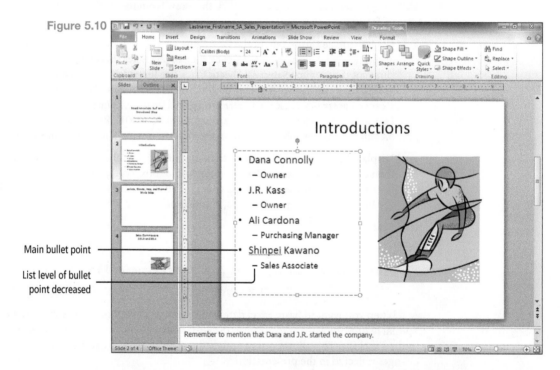

5 On the taskbar, click the **Excel** button to make the **Lastname_Firstname_5A_Snowboarding_Sales** window active. Click the **January Sales sheet tab**, and then click a blank section of the Chart Area to select the chart. Click the **Home tab**, and then in the **Clipboard group**, click the **Copy** button.

6 On the taskbar, click the **PowerPoint** button to make the **Lastname_Firstname_ 5A_Sales_Presentation** window active. If necessary, click Slide 2 to make it the active slide. On the **Home tab**, in the **Slides group**, click the **New Slide button arrow**, and then click **Blank**.

A new blank slide 3 is inserted in the presentation.

7 On the **Home tab**, in the **Clipboard group**, click the **Paste** button, and then compare your screen with Figure 5.11.

The clustered column chart is pasted and is linked to the Excel workbook.

Figure 5.11

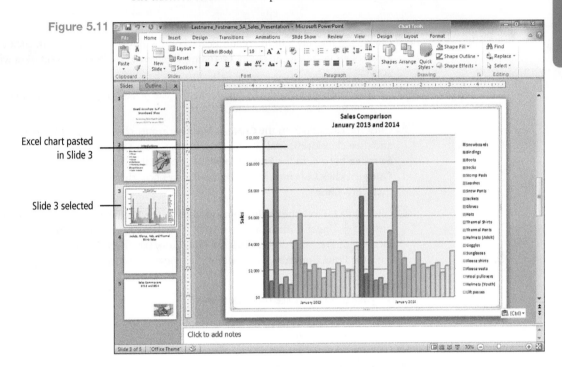

Excel chart pasted in Slide 3

Slide 3 selected

8 Click **Slide 4**. In the lower placeholder, click the **Insert Chart** button. In the **Insert Chart** dialog box, click **Bar**. Under **Bar**, in the first row, click the seventh chart—**Clustered Horizontal Cylinder**. Click **OK**.

A split window named Chart in Microsoft PowerPoint opens and displays the sample data.

9 On the taskbar, click the Excel button, and then click the **Lastname_Firstname_5A_ Snowboarding_Sales** thumbnail to make the window active. If necessary, maximize the Excel window. Click the **5A Sales Data sheet tab**. Select cells **A10:C13**. Right-click cell **A10**, and then on the shortcut menu, click **Copy**. On the taskbar, click the **Chart in Microsoft PowerPoint** button, and then click cell **A2**. On the **Home tab**, in the **Clipboard group**, click the **Paste** button.

The data copied from Excel replaces the sample data.

10 Select cells **B1:C1**. On the **Home tab**, in the **Number group**, click the **Number Format button arrow** General, in the list, scroll as necessary, and then click **Text**. Click cell **B1**, type **January 2013** and then press `Tab`. Type **January 2014** and then press `Enter`.

11 Point to the bottom right corner of cell **D5** to display the pointer. Drag left to deselect **column D** from the chart data range. Compare your screen with Figure 5.12.

Project 5A: Sales Charts | **Integrated Projects**

239

Integrated Projects

Figure 5.12

Column D deselected

Chart data range is A1:C5

12 **Close** [×] the Chart in Microsoft PowerPoint window. On the taskbar, click the **PowerPoint** button to make the **Lastname_Firstname_5A_Sales_Presentation** window active.

> Slide 4 displays the bar chart comparing the sales of jackets, gloves, hats, and thermal shirts for January 2013 and January 2014.

13 Click the **Layout tab**. In the **Current Selection group**, click the **Chart Elements arrow**, and then click **Horizontal (Value) Axis**. In the **Current Selection group**, click the **Format Selection** button. In the **Format Axis** dialog box, click **Number**, and then under **Category**, click **Currency**. In the **Decimal places** box, delete the number **2**, type **0** and then click **Close**.

14 Click **Slide 1**. Click the **Design tab**, and then in the **Themes group**, click the **More** button ⬇. Under **Built-In**, in the fifth row, click the fifth theme—**Trek**. Note: The location of *Trek* may differ. Click the **Slide Show tab**, in the **Start Slide Show group**, click the **From Beginning** button, and then view your entire presentation.

Alert! | **What if I don't see the Trek theme?**

Themes are arranged alphabetically. Use the ScreenTips to locate the correct theme.

---

15 **Save** 💾 your presentation.

More Knowledge | **Opening a Linked File**

When you open a file that has a link to an external file, a security notice will automatically display. The notice will inform you that the file contains links and you have the option to update the links. If you trust the source of the file, it is safe to update the links. If you do not know where a file originated, you should cancel the update and investigate where the file was initiated before updating a link.

Activity 5.05 | Linking Excel Cells to a PowerPoint Presentation

You can link individual cells in Excel to a PowerPoint presentation. Dana Connolly, one of the owners of Boards Anywhere Surf and Snowboard Shop, wants to increase the sales commission that all of the sales associates earn. In this activity, you will update the Excel file and verify that the presentation displays the current commission rate.

1 On the taskbar, click the **Excel** button to make the **Lastname_Firstname_5A_Snowboarding_Sales** window active. On the **5A Sales Data sheet**, select cells **F1:G1**. Right-click cell **F1**, and then on the shortcut menu, click **Copy**. On the taskbar, click the **PowerPoint** button to make the **Lastname_Firstname_5A_Sales_Presentation** window active. Click **Slide 5**. On the **Home tab**, in the **Clipboard group**, click the **Paste button arrow**, and then click **Paste Special**. In the **Paste Special** dialog box, click the **Paste link** option button, and then under **As**, verify that **Microsoft Excel Worksheet Object** is selected. Click **OK**.

The Excel cells are pasted in Slide 5.

2 With the linked object selected, Click the **Format tab**, and then in the **Size group**, in the **Shape Height** box, use the spin box up arrow to change the height to **.5**. Drag the linked object so that it is left aligned with the slide title and approximately 0.5 inches below the slide title. Compare your screen with Figure 5.13.

Figure 5.13

Linked object moved below slide title

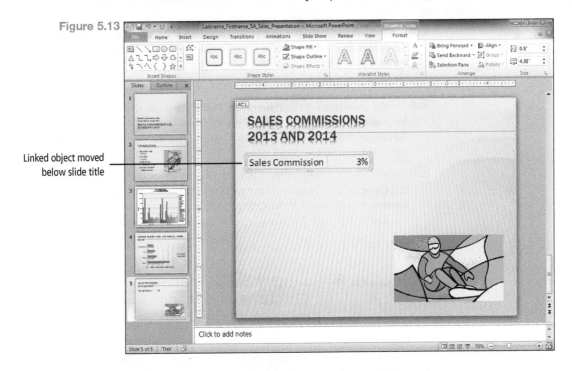

3 On the taskbar, click the **Excel** button to make the **Lastname_Firstname_5A_Snowboarding_Sales** window active. Press Esc to deselect cells **F1:G1**. Select cells **A25:C25**, right-click cell **A25**, and then on the shortcut menu, click **Copy**.

4 On the taskbar, click the **PowerPoint** button to make the **Lastname_Firstname_5A_Sales_Presentation** window active. Click the **Home tab**, in the **Clipboard group**, click the **Paste button arrow**, and then click **Paste Special**. In the **Paste Special** dialog box, click the **Paste link** option button. Under **As**, verify that **Microsoft Excel Worksheet Object** is selected, and then click **OK**.

5 With the linked object selected, Click the **Format tab**, and then in the **Size group**, in the **Shape Height** box, use the spin box up arrow to change the height to **.5**. Drag the linked object under the first linked object so that it displays as shown in Figure 5.14.

Project 5A: Sales Charts | **Integrated Projects**

Figure 5.14

Second linked object

On the taskbar, click the **Excel** button to make the **Lastname_Firstname_5A_ Snowboarding_Sales** window active. Press Esc to deselect cells **A25:C25**. Click cell **G1**, type **5** and then press Enter. **Save** 🖫 the workbook.

The commissions in both cells B25 and C25 are updated.

On the taskbar, click the **PowerPoint** button to make the **Lastname_Firstname_5A_Sales_Presentation** window active, and then verify that the Sales Commission has been updated to 5% and the Commissions have been updated to $2,918.46 and $3,350.78.

On **Slide 5**, click the picture. Click the **Format tab**, and then in the **Adjust group**, click the **Color** button. In the **Recolor** gallery, in the third row, click the second color— **Orange, Accent color 1 Light**. Using the technique you just practiced, select the picture on **Slide 2**, and then **Recolor** the picture using **Orange, Accent color 1 Light**.

Save 🖫 the presentation.

Objective 3 | Apply Slide Transitions, Use the Document Inspector, and Mark as Final

PowerPoint provides a number of features to ensure that your presentation is completed in a professional manner. During a presentation, when you move from one slide to the next, the first slide disappears, and the next slide displays. To indicate that the presentation is changing to a new slide, you can add *slide transitions*—the motion effects that occur in Slide Show view when you move from one slide to the next during a presentation.

If you plan to provide an electronic copy of your file to others, you should use the *Document Inspector* feature before you share the copy. The Document Inspector enables you to find and remove hidden data and personal information in a file. Finally, to avoid making inadvertent changes to a finished presentation, you can use the *Mark as Final* feature. The Mark as Final feature changes the file to a read-only file—typing and editing commands are turned off.

Activity 5.06 | Inserting Slide Transitions

You can control the speed and type of slide transitions in a presentation.

Integrated Projects | Integrating Excel and PowerPoint

1 Click **Slide 1**. Click the **Transitions tab**, and then in the **Transition to This Slide group**, click the **More** button ⏷. In the **Transitions** gallery, under **Exciting**, in the first row, point to the fifth transition—**Ripple**. Compare your screen with Figure 5.15.

Figure 5.15

Transitions gallery ———

Ripple transition ———

2 In the **Transitions** gallery, under **Exciting**, click **Ripple**. In the **Timing group**, click the **Duration spin box up arrow** to change the time to **01.75**. In the **Timing group**, click **Apply to All** button.

> The transition is applied to all slides in the presentation. Although you can vary the transitions applied to different slides in a presentation, the result can be distracting to your audience.

3 Click the **Slide Show tab**, in the **Start Slide Show group**, click the **From Beginning** button, and then view your presentation.

> The presentation is shown with the Ripple transition applied to all slides.

4 Click the **Transitions tab**. In the **Transition to This Slide group**, click the **More** ⏷ button, and then in the first row, click the third transition—**Fade**. In the **Transition to This Slide group**, click the **Effect Options** button, and then click **Through Black**. In the **Timing group**, click the **Duration spin box up arrow** to change the time to **03.00**, and then click the **Apply to All** button.

5 Click the **Slide Show tab**, in the **Start Slide Show group**, click the **From Beginning** button, and then view your presentation.

> The presentation is shown with the Fade - Through Black transition applied to all slides.

6 Display **Backstage** view, and then click the **Info tab**. On the right, click **Properties**, and then click **Show Document Panel**. In the **Author** box, type your firstname and lastname, in the **Subject** box, type your course name and section number, and then in the **Keywords** box, type **sales chart, commission linked Close** ✖ the Document Information Panel.

7 **Save** 💾 the presentation.

Activity 5.07 | Running the Document Inspector

Any file you create may contain hidden data and personal information that you may not want to share with others. Hidden data could include comments, revision marks, versions, document properties, or personal information. In this activity, you will use the Document Inspector to check your file for hidden data.

1 With **Slide 1** the active slide, click the **File tab**, and verify the **Info tab** is selected. Click the **Check for Issues** button, and then click **Inspect Document**. In the **Document Inspector** dialog box, verify that all check boxes are selected. If a check box is not selected, click to select it. Click the **Inspect** button, and then compare your screen with Figure 5.16.

> The Document Inspector dialog box displays the inspection results, indicating specific data that was found—including comments and presentation notes.

Figure 5.16
Document Inspector
dialog box

Inspection results

2 In the **Document Inspector** dialog box, click **Close**, and then click the **Home tab**.

3 Click **Slide 2**, the *Introductions* slide. Notice the note in the Notes Pane. Click **Slide 5**, the *Sales Commissions* slide. In the top left corner, click the comment **AC1** to display a comment from Ali Carbona.

> A *comment* is a note that can be added from the Review tab and is not generally printed. When you provide an electronic copy of your file to others, you may not want to share the presentation notes and comments.

4 Click the **File tab**, click the **Check for Issues** button, and then click **Inspect Document**. In the **Document Inspector** dialog box, verify that all check boxes are selected. If a check box is not selected, click to select it. Click the **Inspect** button. To the right of **Comments and Annotations**, click the **Remove All** button. To the right of **Presentation Notes**, click the **Remove All** button.

> Although you might want to remove Document Properties and Personal Information, for purposes of this instruction, you will not remove them.

5 Click the **Reinspect** button. Click the **Inspect** button, and then verify that no hidden comments or presentation notes were found. **Close** the Document Inspector dialog box.

6 Click the **Home tab**, click **Slide 2**, and then verify that the note has been deleted. Click **Slide 5**, and then verify that the comment has been deleted.

7 **Save** the presentation.

Activity 5.08 | Using Mark as Final

1 Click the **File tab**, and verify that the **Info** tab is selected. Click the **Protect Presentation** button, and then click **Mark as Final**. In the message box, click **OK**. In the second message box, read the message, and then click **OK**. Click the **Home tab**, and then compare your screen with Figure 5.17.

> The file becomes a read-only file. A Message Bar displays below the Ribbon indicating that the presentation is marked as final—thereby preventing the user from making inadvertent changes. The Marked as Final icon displays on the status bar.

Figure 5.17

Message bar

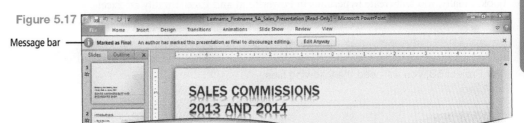

> **Note** | Marking a Presentation as Final
>
> The Mark as Final feature is not a security feature. Anyone who receives an electronic copy of a file that has been marked as final can remove the Mark as Final status by clicking the Edit Anyway button on the Message Bar. The user can now make changes to the file.

2 If your instructor directs you to submit your files electronically, go to Step 3. To print your presentation, click the **File tab**, and then click the **Print tab**. Under **Settings**, click the **Full Page Slides arrow**, and then under **Handouts**, click **6 Slides Horizontal**. Click the **Print** button. On the taskbar, click the Excel button. Click the **File tab**, and then click the **Print tab**. Under **Settings**, click the **Print Active Sheets arrow**, and then click **Print Entire Workbook**. Click the **Print** button. **Close** ⊠ Excel without saving changes, and then **Close** ⊠ PowerPoint without saving changes. Go to Step 4.

3 **Close** ⊠ PowerPoint without saving changes, and then **Close** ⊠ Excel without saving changes.

4 Submit your printed or electronic files as directed by your instructor.

End **You have completed Project 5A**

Project 5B Sessions Presentation

Project Activities

In Activities 5.09 through 5.19, you will insert and modify graphics in a PowerPoint presentation. The Board Anywhere Surf and Snowboard Shop sends its most popular surf instructors to the world's best surfing beaches for two, three, and four day training sessions. You have been asked to finish the presentation. You will insert and modify SmartArt graphics and Clip Art, and then copy some of the presentation objects to an Excel workbook. Finally, you will create hyperlinks in PowerPoint and Excel, modify an Excel workbook, and insert comments. Your completed files will look similar to Figure 5.18.

Project Files

For Project 5B, you will need the following files:

> i05B_Surf_Sessions
> i05B_Sessions_Presentation
> i05B_Wave

You will save your files as:

> Lastname_Firstname_5B_Surf_Sessions
> Lastname_Firstname_5B_Sessions_Presentation

Project Results

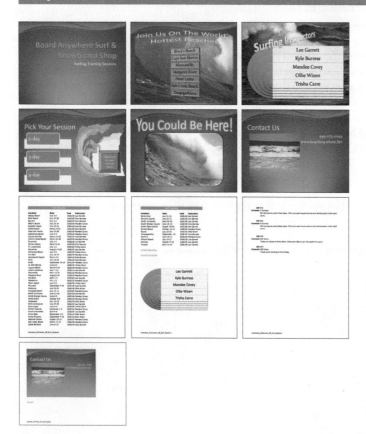

Figure 5.18
Project 5B Sessions Presentation

Integrated Projects | Integrating Excel and PowerPoint

Objective 4 | Create and Modify Illustrations in PowerPoint

Illustrations and graphics can enhance the text in your presentation and help your audience better understand and recall the information. A bulleted list on a slide can quickly be converted into a SmartArt graphic. Adding animation to a PowerPoint object provides additional emphasis. You can change the order of the slides to provide a better presentation.

Activity 5.09 | Inserting and Animating SmartArt Graphics

Recall that a SmartArt graphic is a designer-quality visual representation of your information that you can create by choosing from among many different layouts to communicate your message or ideas effectively. In this activity, you will modify a PowerPoint presentation started by Shinpei Kawano, a Sales Associate.

1 **Start** PowerPoint. From your student files, locate and open the file **i05B_Sessions_Presentation**. **Save** the file in your **Integrated Projects Chapter 5** folder with the file name **Lastname_Firstname_5B_Sessions_Presentation**

2 Click the **Insert tab**, and then in the **Text group**, click the **Header & Footer** button. In the **Header and Footer** dialog box, click the **Notes and Handouts tab**. Under **Include on page**, select the **Date and time** check box, and then click the **Fixed** option button. Select the **Footer** check box, and then in the **Footer** box, type **Lastname Firstname 5B Sessions Presentation** Click **Apply to All**.

3 Click the **Design tab**, and then in the **Themes group**, click the **More** button ⊞. Locate and then click the **Flow** theme. In the **Themes group**, click the **Effects** button, and then click **Foundry**. In the **Background group**, click the **Dialog Box Launcher** ⊡. In the **Format Background** dialog box, verify that the **Gradient fill** option button is selected, click the **Color** button, and then in the fifth column, click the fifth color—**Blue, Accent 1, Darker 25%**. Click **Apply to All**, and then click **Close**. In the **Background group**, click the **Background Styles** button, and then in the second row, click the third style—**Style 7**. Compare your screen with Figure 5.19.

Figure 5.19

Flow theme

Formatted slides

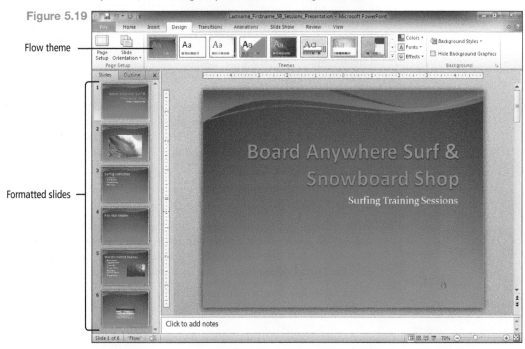

Project 5B: Sessions Presentation | **Integrated Projects**

4 Click **Slide 3**—*Surfing Instructors*. Click the **Home tab**. In the **Slides group**, click the **Layout** button, and then click **Title and Content**.

5 In **Slide 3**, click the placeholder containing the names. On the **Home tab**, in the **Paragraph group**, click the **Convert to SmartArt Graphic** button. In the **SmartArt** gallery, in the first row, click the fourth graphic—**Target List**. On the **SmartArt Tools Design contextual tab**, in the **SmartArt Styles group**, click the **More** button, and then under **Best Match for Document**, click the fifth style—**Intense Effect**. Click in a blank area of the slide to deselect the SmartArt, and then compare your screen with Figure 5.20.

> When you create a SmartArt graphic, the SmartArt Text Pane displays by default; this feature may be toggled off. When you deselect the SmartArt graphic, the SmartArt Text Pane no longer displays.

Figure 5.20

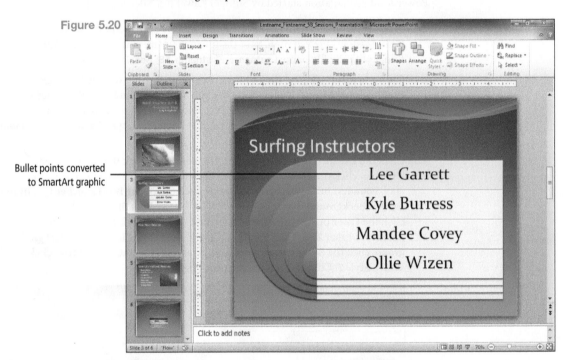

6 Click the SmartArt graphic. If the SmartArt Text Pane does not display, click the **SmartArt Tools Design contextual tab**, and then in the **Create Graphic group**, click the **Text Pane** button. In the Text Pane, click to the right of the name *Ollie Wizen*, and then press Enter. Type **Trisha Carre** and then in the **Create Graphic group**, click the **Text Pane** button to close the Text Pane.

> Recall that in the SmartArt Text Pane you can enter and edit text that displays in the SmartArt graphic.

7 With the SmartArt graphic selected, click the **Animations tab**, and then in the **Animations group**, click the **More** button. In the **Animation Effects** gallery, under **Entrance**, in the second row, click the first effect—**Wipe**. In the **Animations group**, click the **Effect Options** button, and then under **Sequence**, click **One by One**.

> An *animation* effect is added to the graphic. Animation is a visual or sound effect added to an object or text on a slide.

Integrated Projects | Integrating Excel and PowerPoint

8 Click the **Design tab**—not the SmartArt Tools Design tab—and then in the **Background group**, click the **Dialog Box Launcher** 🔲. In the **Format Background** dialog box, click the **Picture or texture fill** option button, and then under **Insert from,** click **File**. Navigate to the location of your student data files, click the file **i05B_Wave**, and then click **Insert**. In the **Format Background** dialog box, click **Close**, and then compare your screen with Figure 5.21.

Figure 5.21

Background graphic

Wave picture in slide background

Trisha Carre added to SmartArt graphic

9 On the **Design tab**, in the **Background group**, select the **Hide Background Graphics** check box.

The graphic that was part of the original theme no longer displays at the top of the slide.

Note | Formatting Slide Titles

Generally, when designing a presentation, you want to maintain consistency in formats. For example, you should create one slide title format and apply that format to all slide titles in the presentation. Having a variety of slide titles can be distracting to your audience. In this project, however, because you are learning how to apply formatting, you will apply different formats to the various slide titles.

---

10 Select the slide title text—*Surfing Instructors*. On the Mini toolbar, click the **Font Size button arrow** ⬚, and then click **72**. With the title selected, click the **Format tab**, and then in the **WordArt Styles group**, click the **More** button ⬚. In the **WordArt Styles** gallery, under **Applies to Selected Text**, in the third row, click the fifth style—**Fill – Turquoise, Accent 2, Double Outline – Accent 2**. In the **WordArt Styles group**, click the **Text Outline button arrow** ⬚, and then in the fourth column, click the first color— **Light Turquoise, Text 2**. Click the **Text Outline button arrow** ⬚, point to **Weight**, and then click **2¼ pt**.

WordArt is a gallery of text styles with which you can create decorative effects, such as shadowed or 3-D text.

Project 5B: Sessions Presentation | **Integrated Projects**

11 With the title still selected, on the **Format tab**, in the **Shape Styles group**, click the **Shape Effects** button. Point to **3-D Rotation**, and then under **Perspective**, in the third row, click the first effect—**Perspective Contrasting Right**. On **the Format tab**, in the **Arrange group**, click the **Bring Forward button arrow**, and then click **Bring to Front**. Deselect the title and then compare your screen with Figure 5.22.

> The title displays in front of the Smart Art graphic.

Figure 5.22

WordArt applied to selected text

12 Click **Slide 5**, and then click the left placeholder. On the **Home tab**, in the **Paragraph group**, click the **Convert to SmartArt Graphic** button. In the **SmartArt** gallery, in the first row, click the second graphic—**Vertical Block List**. On the **SmartArt Tools Design contextual tab**, in the **SmartArt Styles group**, click the **More** button, and then under **3-D**, in the third row, click the first style—**Metallic Scene**.

13 Click the **Animations tab**, and then in the **Animations group**, click the **More** button. In the **Animation Effects** gallery, under **Entrance**, in the second row, click the first effect—**Wipe**. In the **Animations group**, click the **Effects Option** button, and then under **Sequence**, click **All At Once**.

14 If necessary, click the SmartArt graphic to select it. Click the **Format tab**, and then in the **Size group**, click the **Size** button. Click the **Width** box, type **9** and then press Enter.

> The width of the SmartArt graphic is increased to 9 inches.

15 Click the picture. Click the **Format tab**, and then in the **Size group**, click in the **Shape Width** box. Type **9.5** and then press Enter. On the **Format tab**, in the **Arrange group**, click the **Align** button, and then click **Align Center**. In the **Arrange group**, click the **Align** button, and then click **Align Bottom**.

> The picture is in the centered in the middle of the slide but covers the title and the SmartArt graphic.

16 On the **Format tab**, in the **Arrange group**, click the **Send Backward button arrow**, and then click **Send to Back**. Compare your screen with Figure 5.23.

> The picture displays in back of the title and SmartArt graphic.

Integrated Projects | Integrating Excel and PowerPoint

Figure 5.23

Picture aligned center and bottom

SmartArt graphic

17 Save 💾 the presentation.

Activity 5.10 | Inserting Clip Art

Clip art—predefined graphics included with Microsoft Office or downloaded from the Internet—can make your presentation more interesting and visually appealing.

1 Click **Slide 4**, and then in the right placeholder, click the **Clip Art** button 🖼 to open the Clip Art task pane on the right side of the window. In the **Clip Art** task pane, in the **Results should be** box, verify that **All media file types** displays. If necessary, to the left of **Include Office.com content**, click the check box to select it. In the **Search for** box, type **breakers** and then click **Go**. Scroll, if necessary, to locate the image as shown in Figure 5.24.

Figure 5.24

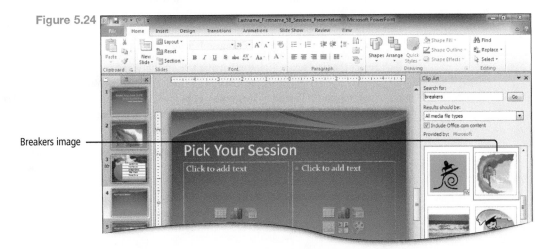

Breakers image

Alert! | Is the image missing from your task pane?

If the image is not found in the Clip Art task pane, select another appropriate picture or consult your instructor.

2 Click the image to insert it in the slide. With the clip art selected, on the **Format tab**, in the **Size group**, click the **Shape Height** box ⊞. Type **5** and then press [Enter]. In the **Arrange group**, click the **Align** button ⊞, and then click **Align Right**. In the **Arrange group**, click the **Align** button ⊞, and then click **Align Middle**. **Close** ⊠ the Clip Art task pane.

3 In the left placeholder, click the **Insert SmartArt Graphic** button ⊞. In the **Choose a SmartArt Graphic** dialog box, under **List**, in the second row, click the second graphic—**Vertical Box List**, and then click **OK**. In the SmartArt graphic, click the top box containing the word *Text*, type **2-day** and then click in the middle box. Type **3-day** click in the bottom box, and then type **4-day**

4 Click the border of the SmartArt graphic to select the entire graphic. Click the **Animations tab**, and then in the **Animations group**, click the **More** button ⊞. In the **Animation Effects** gallery, under **Entrance**, in the second row, click the first effect—**Wipe**. In the **Animations group**, click the **Effects Options**, and then under **Sequence**, click **All at Once**.

5 Click the **Transitions tab**, and then in the **Transition to This Slide group**, click **Fade**. In the **Transition to This Slide group**, click the **Effect Options** button, and then click **Through Black**. In the **Timing group**, click in the **Duration** box, type **1.5** and then press [Enter]. In the **Timing group**, click the **Apply To All** button.

The Fade - Through Black transition is applied to all slides in the presentation; the transition time between two slides is 1.5 seconds.

6 Click the **Slide Show tab**, and then in the **Start Slide Show group**, click the **From Beginning** button. View your presentation.

You must click to display the SmartArt graphics because you added animation effects.

7 **Save** ⊞ your presentation.

Activity 5.11 | Modifying Objects with Effects

You can change the look of an object by adding an effect, such as a reflection or glow.

1 Click **Slide 2**. Click the title placeholder, and then type **You Could Be Here!** Click the **Home tab**, and then in the **Paragraph group**, click the **Center** button ⊞.

2 Select the title text. Click the **Format tab**. In the **WordArt Styles group**, click the **Text Effects** button ⊞, point to **Glow**, and then under **Glow Variations**, in the third row, click the second effect—**Turquoise, 11 pt glow, Accent color 2**. In the **WordArt Styles group**, click the **Text Effects** button ⊞, point to **Transform**, and then under **Warp**, in the sixth row, click the second effect—**Deflate**.

3 In **Slide 2**, click the picture. Click the **Format tab**, and then in the **Picture Styles group**, click the **More** button ⊞. In the **Picture Styles** gallery, in the fourth row, click the third style—**Bevel Rectangle**. Note: The location of *Bevel Rectangle* may differ. In the **Picture Styles group**, click the **Picture Effects** button, point to **Shadow**, and then under **Outer**, in the second row, click the second effect—**Offset Center**. Deselect the picture, and then compare your screen with Figure 5.25.

Figure 5.25

WordArt applied
to selected text

Picture formatted
with Shadow effect

4 Click **Slide 5**, and then select the picture. Click the **Format tab**. In the **Picture Styles group**, click the **Picture Effects** button, point to **Soft Edges**, and then click **10 Point**.

5 In the title placeholder, click to the left of *World's Hottest Beaches*, type **Join Us On The** and then press Spacebar. Select the entire title. On the Mini toolbar, click the **Font Size button arrow** 44, click **60**, and then click the **Center** button. Click the **Format tab**. In the **WordArt Styles group**, click the **Text Effects** button, point to **Transform**, and then under **Warp**, in the second row, click the first effect—**Chevron Up**. Click the **Text Effects** button, point to **Glow**, and then under **Glow Variations**, in the first row, click the first effect—**Blue, 5 pt glow, Accent color 1**. Click on the slide to deselect the title, and then compare your screen with Figure 5.26.

Figure 5.26

WordArt applied to title

Picture formatted
with soft edges

Project 5B: Sessions Presentation | **Integrated Projects**

6 Click **Slide 6**. Click in the title placeholder, and then type **Contact Us** On the **Home tab**, in the **Slides group**, click the **Layout** button, and then click **Two Content**. In the right placeholder, type **949-555-0049** and then press [Enter]. Type **www.boardanywhere. biz** Select all the text in the right placeholder. On the **Home tab**, in the **Paragraph group**, click the **Bullets button arrow** [≔▾], and then click **None**. In the **Paragraph group**, click the **Align Text Right** button [≡].

7 Click the picture in the left placeholder. Click the **Format tab**. In the **Picture Styles group**, click the **Picture Effects** button, point to **Reflection**, and then under **Reflection Variations**, click the first effect—**Tight Reflection, touching**. In the **Size group**, click the **Shape Width** box [⬛], type **4.75** and then press [Enter]. In the **Arrange group**, click the **Align** button [⬛], and then click **Align Middle**.

8 **Save** [💾] your presentation.

Activity 5.12 | Using Slide Sorter View

When you are editing a presentation, you may realize that the presentation would be better if the slides were in a different order. *Slide Sorter View*, useful for rearranging slides, is a presentation view that displays *thumbnails* of all of the slides in a presentation. Thumbnails are miniature images of presentation slides.

1 Click the **View tab**, and then in the **Presentation Views group**, click the **Slide Sorter** button. Click **Slide 2**, and then drag down and to the right until you see the vertical move bar to the left of **Slide 6**. Compare your screen with Figure 5.27.

The vertical move bar indicates where the slide will be moved.

Figure 5.27

Selected slide

Vertical move bar to left of Slide 6

2 Release the mouse button to move **Slide 2** between **Slide 5** (*Join Us*) and **Slide 6** (*Contact Us*).

When you rearrange slides, all slides are renumbered based on their new positions.

3 Click **Slide 4**, and then in the same manner, move **Slide 4** to the right of **Slide 1**.

The moved slide becomes the second slide in the presentation.

Integrated Projects | Integrating Excel and PowerPoint

4 Click the **Slide Show tab**, and then in the **Start Slide Show group**, click the **From Beginning** button, and then view your presentation.

5 Click the **View tab**, and then in the **Presentation Views group**, click the **Normal** button.

6 **Save** 🖫 your presentation.

Objective 5 | Copy a PowerPoint Slide and Object into an Excel Workbook

If you create a SmartArt graphic or shape in PowerPoint, you can copy it and then paste it into an Excel workbook. This saves you the time of recreating the object. Additionally, you can copy an entire PowerPoint slide and paste it into an Excel workbook.

Activity 5.13 | Copying and Pasting a PowerPoint Slide

In the following activity, you will copy the Contact Information slide and paste it into an Excel workbook.

1 **Start** Excel. From your student files, open the file **i05B_Surf_Sessions**. **Save** the file in your **Integrated Projects Chapter 5** folder with the file name **Lastname_Firstname_5B_ Surf_Sessions**

2 Select **columns A:D**. Point to the line between the headings A and B until the ⊞ pointer displays, and then double-click.

> The widths of columns A:D automatically adjust to the best fit for each column so that all data can be read. The columns vary in width.

3 Select cells **A1:D1**, and then on the **Home tab**, in the **Alignment group**, click the **Merge & Center** button 🔳. In the **Styles group**, click the **Cell Styles** button. In the **Cell Styles** gallery, under **Themed Cell Styles**, click **Accent1**. In the **Font group**, click the **Increase Font Size** button 𝖠ᐟ two times.

4 On the taskbar, click the **PowerPoint** button to make the **Lastname_Firstname_5B_ Sessions_Presentation** window active. Click **Slide 6**. On the **Home tab**, in the **Clipboard group**, click the **Copy** button 🖹.

5 On the taskbar, click the **Excel** button to make the **Lastname_Firstname_5B_ Surf_Sessions** window active. Click the **Sheet2 sheet tab**. Verify that cell **A1** is the active cell.

6 On the **Home tab**, in the **Clipboard group**, click the **Paste** button. With the pasted slide selected, point to the bottom right sizing handle until the ↘ pointer displays, and then drag down and to the right to resize the slide to cover cells **A1:J24**. Compare your screen with Figure 5.28.

Figure 5.28

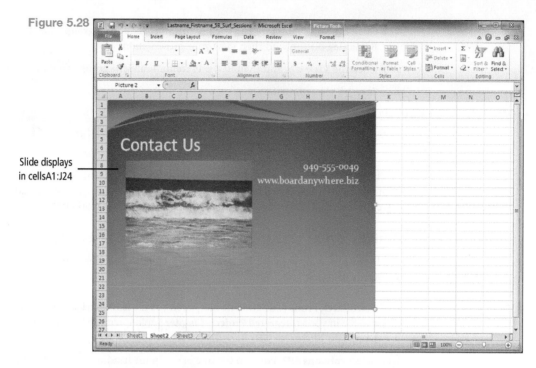

Slide displays in cells A1:J24

7 Click the **Page Layout tab**. In the **Page Setup group**, click the **Orientation** button, and then click **Landscape**.

8 **Save** 🖫 your workbook.

Activity 5.14 | Copying and Pasting an Object

Once you create an object in one Microsoft Office application, you can copy and paste that object into a different application. In this activity, you will copy a SmartArt graphic in PowerPoint and paste it into an Excel workbook.

1 On the taskbar, click the **PowerPoint** button to make the **Lastname_Firstname_5B_Sessions_Presentation** window active. Click **Slide 3**—*Surfing Instructors*. Click the SmartArt graphic, and then click the border of the SmartArt graphic.

> By clicking the border of an object, you select the entire object, not just a part of the object.

2 On the **Home tab**, in the **Clipboard group**, click the **Copy** button 🗐.

3 On the taskbar, click the **Excel** button to make the **Lastname_Firstname_5B_Surf_Sessions** window active. Click the **Sheet1 sheet tab**, and then click cell **A66** to make it the active cell. Click the **Home tab**, and then in the **Clipboard group**, click the **Paste** button.

> The SmartArt graphic is pasted in Sheet1. The top left corner of the graphic is in cell A66.

4 Click the **Format tab**, and then in the **Size group**, click the **Size** button. In the **Shape Height** box, type **4** in the **Shape Width** box, type **5** and then press Enter. Compare your screen with Figure 5.29.

> The graphic is resized.

Integrated Projects | Integrating Excel and PowerPoint

Figure 5.29

SmartArt graphic – beginning in A66

5 Right-click the **Sheet1 sheet tab**, and then on the shortcut menu, click **Rename**. Type **Session Instructors** and then press Enter. Right-click the **Sheet2 sheet tab**, and then on the shortcut menu, click **Rename**. Type **Contact Info** and then press Enter. Right-click the **Sheet3 sheet tab**, and then on the shortcut menu, click **Delete**.

6 **Save** the workbook.

7 On the taskbar, click the **PowerPoint** button to make the **Lastname_Firstname_5B_ Sessions_Presentation** window active. **Save** the presentation, and then **Close** PowerPoint.

Objective 6 | Create Hyperlinks

Hyperlinks are text, buttons, pictures, or other objects that when clicked access other sections of the current file, or another file, or a Web page. A hyperlink gives you immediate access to associated information in another location. The most common type of hyperlink is a *text link*—a link applied to a selected word or phrase. Text links usually display as blue underlined text.

Activity 5.15 | Inserting Hyperlinks in Excel

1 In the **Lastname_Firstname_5B_Surf_Sessions** workbook, click the **Session Instructors sheet tab**, click cell **A60**, type **Contact Information** and then on the **Formula Bar**, click the **Enter** button to accept the entry.

2 Click the **Insert tab**, and then in the **Links group**, click the **Hyperlink** button. In the **Insert Hyperlink** dialog box, under **Link to**, click **Place in This Document**, and then compare your screen with Figure 5.30.

Figure 5.30

Insert Hyperlink dialog box

Place in This Document selected

Excel worksheet names

---

3 Under **Or select a place in this document**, click **'Contact Info'**—the Contact Info worksheet name.

4 Click the **ScreenTip** button. In the **Set Hyperlink ScreenTip** dialog box, under **ScreenTip text**, type **Go to the Contact Information sheet** and then click **OK** two times to close the dialog boxes. Point to cell **A60** to view the ScreenTip, and then compare your screen with Figure 5.31.

The 🖑 pointer—the **Link Select** pointer—displays when you point to a hyperlink.

Figure 5.31

ScreenTip

Link Select pointer

---

5 In cell **A60**, click the hyperlink to make the Contact Info sheet the active worksheet.

6 On the **Contact Info** sheet, click cell **A27**. Type **Instructors** and then on the **Formula Bar**, click the **Enter** button ✓ to accept the entry. On the **Insert tab**, in the **Links group**, click the **Hyperlink** button. In the **Insert Hyperlink** dialog box, under **Link to**, verify that **Place in This Document** is selected, and then under **Or select a place in this document**, click **'Session Instructors'**. Click the **ScreenTip** button. In the **Set Hyperlink ScreenTip** dialog box, under **ScreenTip text**, type **Go to the Session Instructors sheet** and then click **OK** two times to close the dialog boxes.

7 Point to cell **A27** to display the ScreenTip, and then click the hyperlink.

The Session Instructors sheet becomes the active worksheet.

8 On the **Session Instructors** sheet, click cell **A62**. Type **Sessions Presentation** and then on the **Formula Bar**, click the **Enter** button ✓ to accept the entry.

9 On the **Insert tab**, in the **Links group**, click the **Hyperlink** button. In the **Insert Hyperlink** dialog box, under **Link to**, click **Existing File or Web Page**. If necessary, navigate to your **Integrated Projects Chapter 5 folder**. Click the PowerPoint file name **Lastname_Firstname_5B_Sessions_Presentation**.

Integrated Projects | Integrating Excel and PowerPoint

10 In the **Insert Hyperlink** dialog box, click the **ScreenTip** button. In the **Set Hyperlink ScreenTip** dialog box, under **ScreenTip text**, type **Go to our Sessions Presentation** and then click **OK** two times to close the dialog boxes. In cell **A62**, click the hyperlink to view the PowerPoint presentation.

> **Alert!** | **What if my PowerPoint presentation does not display?**
>
> If your presentation does not display, click in cell A62, and then press Del. Repeat Steps 8 through 10, being careful to follow all instructions exactly.

11 With your presentation displayed, click the **Slide Show tab**, and then in the **Start Slide Show group**, click the **From Beginning** button. View the presentation.

Activity 5.16 | Inserting a Hyperlink from a PowerPoint Slide to an Excel Worksheet

1 If necessary, to display the rulers, click the **View tab**, and then in the **Show group**, select the **Ruler** check box. Click **Slide 4**—*Pick your session*. Click the **Insert tab**, and then in the **Illustrations group**, click the **Shapes** button. In the **Shapes** gallery, under **Basic Shapes**, in the third row, click the first shape—**Bevel**.

2 Position the ⊞ pointer at **0 on the vertical ruler** and at **2 1/2 inches to the right of 0 on the horizontal ruler**. Hold down Shift and drag down and to the right to draw a square that measures approximately 2 inches. Compare your screen with Figure 5.32.

Figure 5.32

Bevel shape

3 Type **Click here to view session dates**

4 Click on the shape border to select the shape. On the **Insert tab**, in the **Links group**, click the **Hyperlink** button. In the **Insert Hyperlink** dialog box, under **Link to**, verify that **Existing File or Web Page** is selected. Navigate to your **Integrated Projects Chapter 5** folder, and then click the Excel file name **Lastname_Firstname_5B_Surf_Sessions**.

5 In the **Insert Hyperlink** dialog box, click the **ScreenTip** button. In the **Set Hyperlink ScreenTip** dialog box, under **ScreenTip text**, type **Go to a list of our Surf Sessions** and then click **OK** two times to close the dialog boxes.

6 Click the **Slide Show tab**, and then in the **Start Slide Show group**, click the **From Current Slide** button. In the slide, point to the shape to view the ScreenTip, and then click the shape to view the Excel workbook.

7 On the taskbar, point to the **PowerPoint** button to display two thumbnails of your presentation window—one in Normal view and the other in Slide Show view. In the **PowerPoint Slide Show** thumbnail, click the **Close** [icon] button, and then on the taskbar, click the **PowerPoint** button to display your presentation in Normal view.

8 With **Slide 4** displayed, click the picture to select it. Click the **Format tab**, and then in the **Adjust group**, click the **Color** button. In the **Color** gallery, under **Recolor**, in the third row, click the second color—**Blue, Accent color 1 Light**.

> After viewing a presentation in Slide Show view, one often makes minor adjustments to the slides.

9 Display **Backstage** view, and then click the **Info tab**. On the right, click **Properties**, and then click **Show Document Panel**. In the **Author** box, type your firstname and lastname, in the **Subject** box, type your course name and section number, and then in the **Keywords** box, type **sessions, hyperlink, Excel Close** [X] the Document Information Panel.

10 **Save** [icon] the presentation.

Objective 7 | Freeze Rows, Repeat Headings, and Insert Comments in Excel

A *pane* is a portion of a worksheet bounded by and separated from other portions by vertical and horizontal bars. You can *freeze panes*—a command that enables you to select one or more rows and columns and freeze (lock) them into place; the locked rows and columns become separate panes.

If you are printing a multiple page worksheet, you can display row or column descriptive headings on every page by specifying the rows or columns that you wish to repeat. This makes it easier for the reader to identify the information.

Activity 5.17 | Freezing Excel Rows

1 On the taskbar, click the **Excel** button to make the **Lastname_Firstname_5B_ Surf_Sessions** window active.

2 Press [Ctrl] + [Home] to make cell **A1** the active cell. Scroll down until **row 40** displays at the top of your Excel window, and notice that all the identifying information in the column headings is out of view.

3 Press [Ctrl] + [Home], and then in the **row heading area**, click to select **row 4**. Click the **View tab**. In the **Windows group**, click the **Freeze Panes** button, and then click **Freeze Panes**. Click any cell to deselect the row, and then notice that a line displays along the upper border of **row 4**.

> By selecting row 4, the rows above—rows 1 through 3—are frozen in place and will not move as you scroll down.

4 Scroll down to bring **row 40** into view again. Notice that rows 1 through 3 continue to display—they are frozen in place. Compare your screen with Figure 5.33.

> Use the Freeze Panes feature when you have long or wide worksheets.

Integrated Projects | Integrating Excel and PowerPoint

Figure 5.33

Freeze Panes button

Rows 1–3

Row 40

5 In the **Windows group**, click the **Freeze Panes** button, and then click **Unfreeze Panes** to unlock all rows and columns.

6 Press Ctrl + Home. **Save** 🖫 your workbook.

More Knowledge | Freeze Columns or Freeze both Rows and Columns

You can freeze columns that you want to remain in view on the left of the worksheet. Select the column to the right of the column(s) that you want to remain in view while scrolling to the right, and then click the Freeze Panes command. You can also use the command to freeze both rows and columns; click a *cell* to freeze the rows *above* the cell and the columns to the *left* of the cell.

Activity 5.18 | Repeating Headings on Multiple Pages

Freezing rows and columns makes it easier to work with a large worksheet on the screen; however, it does not affect the printed pages. To create a professional appearance, print the row or column headings on every page of a multiple page worksheet.

1 Display **Backstage** view, and then click the **Print** tab to display the Print Preview. Below the **Print Preview**, in the navigation bar, click the **Next Page** button ▶ to display Page 2.

Notice that no column headings display at the top of Page 2.

2 Click the **Page Layout tab**, and then in the **Page Setup group**, click the **Dialog Box Launcher** 🖾. In the **Page Setup** dialog box, on the **Sheet tab**, under **Print titles**, click the **Rows to repeat at top** box.

3 In your worksheet, point to the **row 1** header, and then drag down to select **row 1** through **row 3**. Compare your screen with Figure 5.34.

Notice $1:$3 displays in the Rows to repeat at top box. This will allow the header rows to display on all pages of the worksheet.

Figure 5.34
Page Setup dialog box

Rows to repeat at top

Rows 1 through 3 selected

4 In the **Page Setup** dialog box, click **Print Preview**, and then in the navigation bar, click the **Next Page** button ▶ to display Page 2. Compare your screen with Figure 5.35.

Rows 1 through 3 display at the top of Page 2.

Figure 5.35

Rows 1 through 3 display at the top of page 2

5 Click the **Home tab**, and then **Save** 🖫 your workbook.

Activity 5.19 │ Inserting and Editing Comments

If more than one person is working on a file, you can insert comments to communicate with each other. Recall a comment is a note that can be inserted from the Review tab. Comments can be edited or deleted when no longer needed.

1 On the **Session Instructors** sheet, press Ctrl + Home. To the left of the **Formula Bar**, in the **Name Box**, verify that **A1** displays. Click the **Name box**, type **A15** and then press Enter.

> The *Name Box* is an element of the Excel window that displays the name of the selected cell, table, chart, or object. In this case, A15 is the selected cell. In addition to displaying the active cell or range of cells, the Name Box can be used to assign a specific name to a cell or range of cells.

2 With cell **A15** selected, point to cell **B15** to display a comment text box. Compare your screen with Figure 5.36.

> In addition to the comment, the name of the person who wrote the comment displays in the comment text box. A red triangle displays in the top right corner of cell B15 to indicate that the cell has a comment attached to it. Notice that cell B24 also has a comment inserted. When you point to a cell containing a red triangle, the attached comment displays.

Figure 5.36

Name Box

Comment attached to cell B15 displays

Red triangles indicate comments

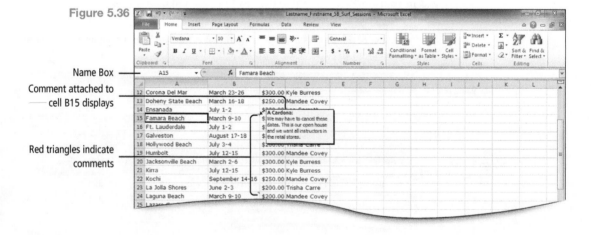

Integrated Projects │ Integrating Excel and PowerPoint

3 Click the **Name Box**, type **B39** and then press Enter. Click the **Review tab**, and then in the **Comments group**, click the **New Comment** button. In the comment text box, type **Trisha can't attend on these dates. Check with Kyle to see if he wants this session.**

Note | Displaying a Name in the Comment Text Box

The User Name automatically displays at the top of the comment text box. The name in your comment text box will vary. If you are using your own computer, your name may display.

---

4 Click in an empty cell to deselect the comment. Click the **Name Box**, type **D57** and then press Enter. On the **Review tab**, in the **Comments group**, click the **New Comment** button. In the comment text box, type **Thank Lee for working on his birthday.**

5 Click cell **B39**, and then in the **Comments group**, click the **Edit Comment** button. In the comment text box, select *Kyle* type **Ollie** and then deselect the cell to hide the comment. Point to cell **B39** to verify the change.

6 In the **Comments group**, click the **Show All Comments** button.

Notice that the comments attached to cells in column B cover the data in columns C and D.

7 Click the comment attached to cell **B39**. Point to the comment text box border—not a sizing handle—until the pointer displays. Drag the comment text box to the right of **column D**, and then release the mouse button. Compare your screen with Figure 5.37.

Figure 5.37

Comment moved to columns E and F

8 Using the same technique, move the comments in cells **B15**, **B24**, and **D57** to the right of **column D**.

All four comments display in columns E and F.

9 Click the **Page Layout tab**, and then in the **Page Setup group**, click the **Dialog Box Launcher**. In the **Page Setup** dialog box, on the **Sheet tab**, click the **Comments arrow**, and then click **At end of sheet**. Click **Print Preview**, and then below the **Print Preview**, in the navigation bar, click the **Next Page** button ► two times.

The comments display on a separate page—Page 3.

10 Click the **Home tab**. With the **Session Instructors** sheet displayed, hold down Ctrl, and then click the **Contact Info sheet tab**. Click the **Insert tab**, and then in the **Text group**, click the **Header & Footer** button. On the **Design tab**, in the **Navigation group**, click the **Go to Footer** button. In the **Footer** area, click just above the word **Footer**, and then in the **Header & Footer Elements group**, click the **File Name** button. Click in any cell in the workbook to exit the footer. On the right side of the status bar, click the **Normal** button ▦, and then press Ctrl + Home.

11 Right-click the **Contact Info sheet tab**, and then on the shortcut menu, click **Ungroup Sheets**.

12 Display **Backstage** view, and then click the **Info tab**. On the right, click **Properties**, and then click **Show Document Panel**. In the **Author** box, type your firstname and lastname, in the **Subject** box, type your course name and section number, and then in the **Keywords** box, type **sessions, hyperlinks Close** ☒ the Document Information Panel.

13 **Save** 🔲 your workbook. If your instructor directs you to submit your files electronically, **Close** ☒ Excel, **Close** ☒ PowerPoint, and then go to Step 16.

14 To print your workbook, click the **File tab**, and then click the **Print tab**. Under **Settings**, click the **Print Active Sheets arrow**, and then click **Print Entire Workbook**. Click the **Print** button, and then **Close** ☒ Excel.

15 To print your presentation, click the **File tab**, and then click the **Print tab**. Under **Settings**, click the **Full Page Slides arrow**, and then under **Handouts**, click **6 Slides Horizontal**. Click the **Print** button, and then **Close** ☒ PowerPoint.

16 Submit your printed or electronic files as directed by your instructor.

End **You have completed Project 5B** ———————————————————

Content-Based Assessments

Summary

In Excel, you can insert and modify charts that are more visually appealing than reviewing large data-filled worksheets. In a worksheet, you can freeze rows and columns, repeat headings on multiple printed pages, and insert comments. The copy and paste commands allow you to insert an object in another location or file. In PowerPoint, create a professional-looking presentation by adding slide transitions, inserting and formatting SmartArt graphics, clip art, and shapes. You can create hyperlinks to access related information within the current file or in another file. Features such as the Document Inspector and Mark as Final help you polish your file before sharing it with others.

Key Terms

Absolute cell reference	Chart Styles galley	Explode	Slide Sorter view
Animation	Clip art	Freeze Panes	Slide transitions
Category axis	Column chart	Hyperlinks	Text link
Cell address	Comment	Legend	Thumbnails
Cell reference	Data marker	Mark as Final	Value axis
Chart layout	Data point	Name Box	WordArt
Chart Layouts gallery	Data series	Pane	x-axis
Chart style	Document Inspector	Pie chart	y-axis

Matching

Match each term in the second column with its correct definition in the first column by writing the letter of the term on the blank line in front of the correct definition.

_____ 1. A chart that is useful for showing data changes over a period of time or for illustrating comparisons among items.

_____ 2. A chart that shows the relationship of each part to a whole.

_____ 3. The area along the bottom of a chart that identifies the categories of data.

_____ 4. The numerical scale on the left side of a chart that shows the range of numbers for the data points.

_____ 5. The overall visual look of a chart in terms of its graphic effects, colors, and backgrounds.

_____ 6. The combination of chart elements that can be displayed in a chart such as a title, legend, labels for the columns, and the table of charted cells.

_____ 7. A chart element that identifies patterns or colors that are assigned to the categories in the chart.

_____ 8. The identification of a specific cell by its intersecting column letter and row number.

_____ 9. The motion effect that occurs in Slide Show view when you move from one slide to the next during a presentation.

_____ 10. A Microsoft Office feature that enables you to find and remove hidden data and personal information in a file.

A Animation

B Cell reference

C Chart layout

D Chart style

E Column chart

F Document Inspector

G Hyperlinks

H Legend

I Mark as Final

J Name Box

K Pie chart

L Slide transition

M Thumbnails

N x-axis

O y-axis

Integrated Projects | Integrating Excel and PowerPoint

_____ 11. A Microsoft Office feature that changes the file to a read-only file—typing and editing commands are turned off.

_____ 12. A visual or sound effect that is added to an object or text on a slide.

_____ 13. In PowerPoint, miniature images of presentation slides.

_____ 14. Text, buttons, pictures, or other objects that, when clicked, access other sections of the current file, another file, or a Web page.

_____ 15. An element of the Excel window that displays the name of the selected cell, table, chart, or object.

Multiple Choice

Circle the correct answer.

1. A numerical scale on the left side of a chart that shows the range of numbers is called the:
   A. category axis   **B.** value range   **C.** value axis

2. The value that originates in a worksheet cell and that is represented in a chart by a data marker is called a:
   A. data point   **B.** data value   **C.** data series

3. The action of pulling out one or more pie slices from a pie chart for emphasis is called:
   A. expanding   **B.** exploding   **C.** extracting

4. The identification of a specific cell by its intersecting column letter and row number is a:
   A. cell address   **B.** data address   **C.** data reference

5. A cell reference that refers to cells by their fixed position in a worksheet is:
   A. a relative cell reference   **B.** a relative data reference   **C.** an absolute cell reference

6. In Excel, a note that can be added from the Review tab and is generally not printed is called a:
   A. comment   **B.** message   **C.** note

7. Predefined graphics included with Microsoft Office or downloaded from the Internet are called:
   A. SmartArt   **B.** clip art   **C.** WordArt

8. A presentation view that displays thumbnails of all of the slides in a presentation is:
   A. Print Preview   **B.** Slide view   **C.** Slide Sorter view

9. In Excel, a portion of a worksheet bounded by and separated from other portions by vertical and horizontal bars is called a:
   A. panel   **B.** pane   **C.** window

10. The command that enables you to select one or more rows and columns and lock them into place is:
    A. Freeze Panes   **B.** Lock Panes   **C.** Split Panes

Apply 5A skills from these Objectives:

1. Create and Format Excel Charts
2. Link Excel Charts and Data to a PowerPoint Presentation
3. Apply Slide Transitions, Use the Document Inspector, and Mark as Final

In the following Skills Review, you will create and format Excel charts, and link the charts to a PowerPoint presentation that summarizes events sponsored by Board Anywhere Surf and Snowboard Shop. Your completed files will look similar to Figure 5.38.

Project Files

For Project 5C, you will need the following files:

i05C_Events_Charts
i05C_Events_Presentation

You will save your files as:

Lastname_Firstname_5C_Events_Charts
Lastname_Firstname_5C_Events_Presentation

Project Results

Figure 5.38

Integrating Excel and PowerPoint

1. **Start** Excel. Open the Excel file **i05C_Event_Charts**. **Save** the file in the **Integrated Projects Chapter 5** folder with the file name **Lastname_Firstname_5C_Events_Charts**

   a. Click cell **D2**, type **ExpectedFees** and then press Enter. In cell **D3**, type the formula **=B3*C3** and then on the **Formula Bar**, click the **Enter** button. Copy the formula down through cell **D18**.

   b. Select cells **B3:D18**. On the **Home tab**, in the **Number group**, click the **Comma Style** button. In the **Number group**, click the **Decrease Decimal** button two times.

   c. Select cells **A1:D1**. On the **Home tab**, in the **Alignment group**, click the **Merge & Center** button. In the **Styles group**, click the **Cell Styles** button. In the **Cell Styles** gallery, under **Themed Cell Styles**, click **Accent2**. In the **Font group**, click the **Font Size button arrow**, and then click **18**.

   d. Select cells **A2:D2**. In the **Alignment group**, click the **Dialog Box Launcher**. In the **Format Cells** dialog box, on the **Alignment tab**, under **Text control**, select the **Wrap text** check box, and then click **OK**. In the **Styles group**, click the **Cell Styles** button. In the **Cell Styles** gallery, under **Themed Cell Styles**, click **40% - Accent2**. In the **Alignment group**, click the **Center** button.

2. Select **columns A:D**. Point to the column separator between the column headings **A** and **B**, and then double-click to adjust the column widths.

   a. Click cell **A19**, and then type **Totals** Select cells **B19:D19**. On the **Home tab**, in the **Editing group**, click the **Sum** button. Select cells **C3:C19**. In the **Number group**, click the **Comma Style** button, and then click the **Decrease Decimal** button two times.

   b. Click cell **B3**. Hold down Ctrl, and then click cells **B19, D3**, and **D19**. In the **Number group**, click the **Accounting Number Format** button, and then click the **Decrease Decimal** button two times.

   c. Select cells **A2:A18**. Hold down Ctrl, and then select cells **D2:D18**. On the **Insert tab**, in the **Charts group**, click the **Column** button, and then under **3-D Column**, click **3-D Clustered Column**. On the **Design tab**, in the **Location group**, click the **Move Chart** button. In the **Move Chart** dialog box, click the New **sheet** option button, type **Registration Fees** and then click **OK**.

   d. On the **Design tab**, in the **Location group**, click the **Move Chart** button. In the **Move Chart** dialog box, click the New **sheet** option button, type **Registration_Fees** and then click **OK**.

   e. On the **Design tab**, in the **Chart Styles group**, click the **More** button. In the **Chart Styles** gallery, in the fifth row, click the fourth style—**Style 36**. In the **Chart Layouts group**, click **Layout 3**.

3. Click the **Sheet1 sheet tab**. Select cells **A3:A18**, hold down Ctrl, and then select cells **C3:C18**. On the **Insert tab**, in the **Charts group**, click the **Pie** button, and then under **3-D Pie**, click **Pie in 3-D**.

   a. On the **Design tab**, in the **Location group**, click the **Move Chart** button. In the **Move Chart** dialog box, click the **New Sheet** option button, type **Number of Participants** and then click **OK**.

b. On the **Design tab**, in the **Chart Layouts group**, click the **More** button, and then click **Layout 5**. Click the **Chart Title**, type **Extreme Events – Expected Participants** and then click in a blank area of the chart.

c. On the **Layout tab**, in the **Current Selection group**, click the **Chart Elements arrow**, and then click **Series 1 Data Labels**. On the **Home tab**, in the **Font group**, click the **Bold** button. On the **Layout tab**, in the **Current Selection group**, click the **Format Selection** button. In the **Format Data Labels** dialog box, under **Label Contains**, select the **Value** check box, and then click **Close**.

d. On the **Layout tab**, in the **Current Selection group**, click the **Chart Elements arrow**, and then click **Chart Area**. In the **Current Selection group**, click the **Format Selection** button. In the **Format Chart Area** dialog box, click the **Gradient fill** option button. Click the **Color arrow**, and then in the **Color** gallery, in the sixth column, click the fifth color—**Red, Accent2, Darker 25%**. Click **Close**.

e. Right-click the **Sheet1 sheet tab**, and then on the shortcut menu, click **Rename**. Type **Event Details** and then press ⌷Enter⌷. Click the **Sheet2 sheet tab**, hold down ⌷Ctrl⌷, and then click the **Sheet3 sheet tab**. On the **Home tab**, in the **Cells group**, click the **Delete button arrow**, and then click **Delete Sheet**.

4. In the **Event Details sheet**, click cell **F1**. Type **Expense** and then press ⌷Tab⌷. In cell **G1**, type **70%** and then press ⌷Enter⌷ Click cell **A21**, type **Expenses** and then press ⌷Tab⌷.

   a. In cell **B21**, type **=B19*G1** and then press ⌷F4⌷ to make cell G1 an absolute reference. On the **Formula Bar**, click the **Enter** button.

   b. On the **Home tab**, in the **Clipboard group**, click the **Copy** button. Click cell **D21**, and then in the **Clipboard group**, click the **Paste** button. Press ⌷Esc⌷. Hold down ⌷Ctrl⌷ and then click cell **B21**. In the **Number group**, click the **Accounting Number Format** button, and then click the **Decrease Decimal** button two times.

   c. On the **Page Layout tab**, in the **Page Setup group**, click the **Orientation** button, and then click **Landscape**.

   d. Right-click the **Event Details sheet tab**, and then on the shortcut menu, click **Select All Sheets**. On the **Insert tab**, in the **Text group**, click the **Header & Footer** button. In the **Navigation group**, click the **Go to Footer** button. In the **Footer** area, click just above the word **Footer**, and then in the **Header & Footer Elements group**, click the **File Name** button. Click in any cell to exit the footer, and then click the **Normal** button. Right click the **Event Details sheet tab**, and then on the shortcut menu, click **Ungroup Sheets**. Press ⌷Ctrl⌷ + ⌷Home⌷.

   e. Display **Backstage** view. Click **Properties**, and then click **Show Document Panel**. In the **Author** box, type your firstname and lastname, in the **Subject** box, type your course name and section number, and then in the **Keywords** box, type **expenses,charts** Close the Document Information Panel, and then **Save** the workbook.

5. **Start** PowerPoint. Open the file **i05C_Events_Presentation**. **Save** the file in the **Integrated Projects Chapter 5** folder with the file name **Lastname_Firstname_5C_Events_Presentation**

Integrating Excel and PowerPoint

a. On the **Insert tab**, in the **Text group**, click the **Header & Footer** button. In the **Header and Footer** dialog box, click the **Notes and Handouts tab**. Under **Include on page**, select the **Date and time** check box, and then select the **Footer** check box. In the **Footer** box, type **LastnameFirstname 5CEventsPresentation** and then click **Apply to All**.

b. On **Slide 1**, click the subtitle placeholder, type **An Extreme Event Sponsored By** and then press Enter. Type **Board Anywhere Surf and Snowboard Shop** and then click **Slide 2**.

c. On **Slide 2**, click the picture. On the **Format tab**, in the **Size group**, in the **Shape Height** box, type **4** and then press Enter. Drag the picture so that it displays in the middle of the slide. In the title placeholder, click to the right of *Burgess*, press Enter, press Tab, and then type **At Last Year's Extreme Fest**

d. On the **Home tab**, in the **Slides group**, click the **New Slide button arrow**, and then click **Blank**. On the taskbar, click the **Lastname_Firstname_5C_Events_Charts** button. Click the **Number of Participants sheet tab**, and then on the **Home tab**, in the **Clipboard group**, click the **Copy** button.

e. On the taskbar, click the **Lastname_Firstname_5C_Events_Presentation** button. On the **Home tab**, in the **Clipboard group**, click the **Paste** button.

6. Click **Slide 4**. In the placeholder, click the **Insert Chart** button. In the **Insert Chart** dialog box, click **Column**. Under **Column**, click the first chart—**Clustered Column**.

a. On the taskbar, click the **Lastname_Firstname_5C_Events_Charts** button. Click the **Event Details sheet tab**, select cells **A2:B18**. Right-click **A2**, and then on the shortcut menu, click **Copy**. On the taskbar, click the **Chart in Microsoft PowerPoint** button, and then click cell **A1**. On the **Home tab**, in the **Clipboard group**, click **Paste**. In the Message box, click OK.

b. Point to the bottom right corner of cell **D18**, drag left to deselect **column C** and **column D**. **Close** the Chart in Microsoft PowerPoint window.

c. On the taskbar, click the **PowerPoint** button to make the **Lastname_Firstname_5C_Events_Presentation** active. On the right side of the chart, right-click the **Legend**, and then on the shortcut menu, click **Delete**.

d. Click **Slide 1**. On the **Design tab**, in the **Themes group**, click the **More** button. Under **Built-In**, in the first row, click the sixth theme—**Aspect**.

e. Click **Slide 6**. Click the lower placeholder, and then type **Join Us!** On the **Home tab**, in the **Paragraph group**, click the **Center** button.

7. On the **Transitions tab**, in the **Transition to This Slide group**, click the **More** button. In the **Transitions** gallery, under **Exciting**, in the second row, click the first transition—**Flip**. In the **Timing group**, click the **Duration spin box up arrow**, to change the time to **2.00**. In the **Timing group**, click the **Apply To All** button.

Integrating Excel and PowerPoint

a. Display **Backstage** view. Click **Properties**, and then click **Show Document Panel**. In the **Author** box, type your firstname and lastname, in the **Subject** box, type your course name and section number, and then in the **Keywords** box, type **Excelcharts Close** the Document Information Panel, and then **Save** your changes.

b. Click the **File tab**, click the **Check for Issues** button, and then click **Inspect Document**. In the Document **Inspector** dialog box, verify that all check boxes are selected. Click the **Inspect** button. To the right of **Presentation Notes**, click the **Remove All** button.

c. Verify all presentation notes were removed, and then click **Close**.

d. Click the **Home tab**, and then **Save** your presentation. **Close** PowerPoint. With your Excel workbook displayed, press Ctrl + Home. **Save** your changes, and then **Close** Excel.

e. Submit your printed or electronic files as directed by your instructor.

You have completed Project 5C

Integrating Excel and PowerPoint

Apply 5B skills from these Objectives:

4. Create and Modify Illustrations in PowerPoint
5. Copy a PowerPoint Slide and Object into an Excel Workbook
6. Create Hyperlinks
7. Freeze Rows, Repeat Headings, and Insert Comments in Excel

In the following Skills Review, you will edit a PowerPoint presentation by applying a theme, inserting SmartArt, modifying graphics, and creating a hyperlink to an Excel workbook. In the workbook, you will paste a PowerPoint object, create titles on multiple pages, and insert comments. Your completed files will look similar to Figure 5.39.

Project Files

For Project 5D, you will need the following files:

i05D_Outerwear_Presentation
i05D_Outerwear_Costs

You will save your files as:

Lastname_Firstname_5D_Outerwear_Presentation
Lastname_Firstnmae_5D_Outerwear_Costs

Project Results

Figure 5.39

Integrating Excel and PowerPoint

1. **Start** PowerPoint. Locate and open the file **i05D_Outerwear_Presentation**. **Save** the file in the **Integrated Projects Chapter 5** folder with the filename **Lastname_Firstname_5D_Outerwear_Presentation**

   a. On the **Insert tab**, in the **Text group**, click the **Header & Footer** button. In the **Header and Footer** dialog box, click the **Notes and Handouts tab**. Under **Include on page**, select the **Date and time** check box. In the **Header and Footer** dialog box, select the **Footer** check box, and then in the **Footer** text box, type **LastnameFirstname5DOuterwearPresentation** Click **Apply to All**

   b. On the **Design tab**, in the **Themes group**, click the **More** button, and then in the third row, click the fourth theme—**Oriel**. In the **Themes group**, click the **Colors** button, and then click **Flow**. In the **Background group**, click the **Background Styles** button, and then click **Style 6**.

   c. Click **Slide 3**. Click the title placeholder, and then type **Outerwear Lines** On the **Home tab**, in the **Slides group**, click the **Layout** button, and then click **Title and Content**. Click the placeholder containing the bulleted list. On the **Home tab**, in the **Paragraph group**, click the **Convert to SmartArt Graphic** button. In the **SmartArt** gallery, click the first list—**Vertical Bullet List**. On the **SmartArt Design tab**, in the **SmartArt Styles group**, click the **More** button, and then under **3-D**, click **Polished**.

   d. On **Slide 3**, with the SmartArt graphic selected, on the **Animations tab**, in the **Animation group**, click the **More** button. In the **Animation** gallery, under **Entrance**, click **Fly In**. In the **Animations group**, click the **Effect Options** button, and then under **Sequence**, click **One by One**.

   e. Click **Slide 2**. Click the title placeholder, and then type **Our Hats and Gloves Coming At You In Style** and then select the title. On the **Format tab**, in the **WordArt Styles group**, click the **More** button, and then in the third row, click the fourth style—click **Gradient Fill – Blue, Accent 1**. In the **WordArt Styles group**, click the **Text Effects** button, point to **3-D Rotation**, and then under **Perspective**, click **Perspective Contrasting Left**. On the **Home tab**, in the **Font group**, click the **Font Size button arrow**, and then click **48**. In the **Paragraph group**, click the **Center** button.

2. On **Slide 2**, click the picture. On the **Format tab**, in the **Size group**, click the **Shape Width** box, type **3.5** and then press Enter. Drag the picture to the left side of the slide. The top left corner of the picture should be approximately at **1 1/2 inches above the 0 on the vertical ruler** and at **4 inches to the left of 0 on the horizontal ruler**. In the **Arrange group**, click the **Send Backward button arrow**, and then click the **Send to Back** button.

   a. With the picture selected, on the **Format tab**, in the **Picture Styles group**, click the **Picture Effects** button. In the **Picture Effects** gallery, point to **Soft Edges**, and then click **10 Point**. Click the title placeholder, and then click the border of the placeholder. Drag the placeholder down and to the right. The top right corner of the placeholder should be approximately at **2 1/2 inches above the 0 on the vertical ruler** and at **4 inches to the right of 0 on the horizontal ruler**.

   b. Click **Slide 4**. Click the title placeholder and then type **We Carry The Hottest Youth Clothing Lines** On the **Home tab**, in the **Slides group**, click the **Layout** button, and then click **Title and Content**. c. Click the picture. On the **Format tab**, in the **Size group**, click in the **Shape Width** box, type **6** and then press Enter. On the **Format tab**, in the **Arrange group**, click the **Align** button, and then click **Align Middle**. Click the **Send to Back** button. In the **Picture Styles group**, click the **Picture Effects** button, point to **Soft Edges**, and then click **25 Point**.

3. Click **Slide 5**. Click the title placeholder, and then type **Competitive Pricing**

    a. Click the right placeholder, and then click the **ClipArt** button. In the **Clip Art** task pane, in the **Results should be** box, verify that **All media file types** displays. If necessary, to the left of **Include Office.com content**, click the check box to select it. In the **Search for** box, type **snowboarders, men,wmf** and then click **Go**.

    b. Locate the picture as shown in Figure 5.39, and then click the picture to insert it in the slide. **Close** the Clip Art task pane. **Save** the presentation.

4. **Start** Excel. Open the file **i05D_Outerwear_Costs**. **Save** the file in the **Integrated Projects Chapter 5** folder with the file name **Lastname_Firstname_5D_Outerware_Costs**

    a. Select **columns A:B**. Point to the line between the headings **A** and **B**, and then double-click. Select cells **A1:B1**, and then on the **Home tab**, in the **Alignment group**, click the **Merge & Center** button. In the **Styles group**, click the **Cell Styles** button, and then click **Accent5**. In the **Font group**, click the **Increase Font Size** button two times.

    b. On the taskbar, click the **Lastname_Firstname_5D_Outerwear_Presentation** button. Click **Slide 3**—*Outerwear Lines*. Click the SmartArt graphic, and then click the border of the SmartArt graphic. On the **Home tab**, in the **Clipboard group**, click the **Copy** button.

    c. On the taskbar, click the **Lastname_Firstname_5D_Outerwear_Costs** button. On **Sheet 1**, click cell **A46**, and then on the **Home tab**, in the **Clipboard group**, click the **Paste** button. On the **Format tab**, in the **Size group**, click the **Size** button. Click the **Shape Width** box, type **5.5** and then press ⏎

    d. Right-click the **Sheet1 tab**, and then on the shortcut menu, click **Rename**. Type **Outerwear Cost** and then press ⏎. Click the **Sheet2 tab**, hold down ⇧, and then click the **Sheet3 tab**. Right-click the **Sheet3 tab**, and then on the shortcut menu, click **Delete**.

5. Click cell **D3**, type **Outerwear Presentation** and then on the **Formula Bar**, click the **Enter** button. On the **Insert tab**, in the **Links group**, click the **Hyperlink** button.

    a. In the **Insert Hyperlink** dialog box, under **Link to**, click **Existing File or Web Page**. Navigate to the **Integrated Projects Chapter 5** folder, and then click the PowerPoint file **Lastname_Firstname_5D_Outerwear_Presentation**.

    b. In the **Insert Hyperlink** dialog box, click the **ScreenTip** button. In the **Set Hyperlink ScreenTip** dialog box, under **ScreenTip text**, type **Go to our presentation** and then click **OK**. In the **Insert Hyperlink** dialog box, click **OK**.

    c. On the taskbar, click the **Lastname_Firstname_5D_Outerwear_Presentation** button. Click **Slide 5**, click the arrow shape, and then type **Click here to see our prices.**

    d. Click the shape border. On the **Insert tab**, in the **Links group**, click the **Hyperlink** button. In the **Insert Hyperlink** dialog box, under **Link to**, verify that **Existing File or Web Page** is selected. Navigate to the **Integrated Projects Chapter 5** folder, and then click the Excel file **Lastname_Firstname_5D_Outerwear_Costs**.

Integrating Excel and PowerPoint

e. In the **Insert Hyperlink** dialog box, click the **ScreenTip** button. In the **Set Hyperlink ScreenTip** dialog box, under **ScreenTip text**, type **View the outerwear prices** and then click **OK**. In the **Insert Hyperlink** dialog box, click **OK**.

f. In your presentation, display **Backstage** view. Click **Properties**, and then click **Show Document Panel**. In the **Author** box, type your firstname and lastname, in the **Subject** box, type your course name and section number, and then in the **Keywords** box, type **Excel hyperlink** Close the Document Information Panel. **Save** the presentation, and then **Close** PowerPoint.

6. With the **Lastname_Firstname_5D_Outerwear_Costs** file displayed, on the **Page Layout tab**, in the **Page Setup group**, click the **Print Titles** button. In the **Page Setup** dialog box, on the **Sheet tab**, under **Print titles**, click the **Rows to repeat at top** box. Click the **row 1** header. In the **Page Setup** dialog box, click **Print Preview**, and then in the navigation bar, click the **Next Page** button. Verify that the title displays on Page 2. Click the **Home tab**.

a. Click cell **B6**. On the **Review tab**, in the **Comments group**, click the New Comment button. In the comment text box, type **This is a high price because 20mm waterproofing fabric is used.**

b. Click cell **B34**. On the **Review tab**, in the **Comments group**, click the **New Comment** button. In the comment text box, type **This is a good price. Let's purchase more before the winter season.** Deselect the comment. In the **Comments group**, click the **Show All Comments** button.

c. On the **Page Layout tab**, in the **Page Setup group**, click the **Dialog Box Launcher**. In the **Page Setup** dialog box, on the **Sheet tab**, click the **Comments arrow**, and then click **At end of sheet**. Click **OK**.

d. On the **Insert tab**, in the **Text group**, click the **Header & Footer** button. On the **Design tab**, in the **Navigation group**, click the **Go to Footer** button. In the **Footer** area, click just above the word **Footer**, and then in the **Header & Footer Elements group**, click the **File Name** button. Click any cell in the workbook to exit the footer. On the status bar, click the **Normal** button, and then press Ctrl + Home.

e. Display **Backstage** view. Click **Properties**, and then click **Show Document Panel**. In the **Author** box, type your firstname and lastname, in the **Subject** box, type your course name and section number, and then in the **Keywords** box, type **presentation hyperlink** Close the Document Information Panel. **Save** the workbook, and then **Close** Excel.

f. Submit your printed or electronic files as directed by your instructor.

You have completed Project 5D

Apply 5A skills from these Objectives:

1. Create and Format Excel Charts
2. Link Excel Charts and Data to a PowerPoint Presentation
3. Apply Slide Transitions, Use the Document Inspector, and Mark as Final

Mastering Integration | Project 5E Snowboarding Bags

In the following Mastering Integration project, you will create charts in an Excel workbook and copy charts and data from Excel into a PowerPoint presentation. Your completed files will look similar to Figure 5.40.

Project Files

For Project 5E, you will need the following files:

i05E_Snowboarding_Bags
i05E_Bags_Presentation

You will save your files as:

Lastname_Firstname_5E_Snowboarding_Bags
Lastname_Firstname_5E_Bags_Presentation

Project Results

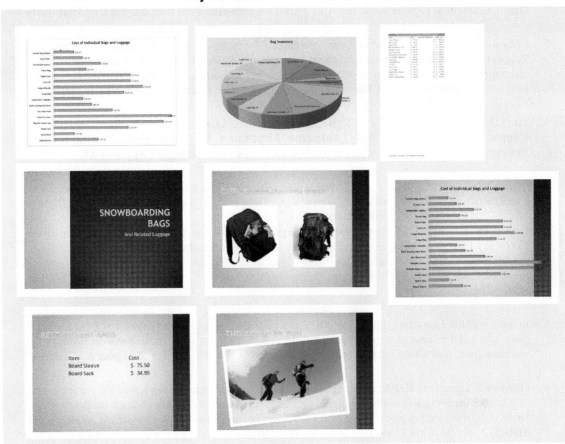

Figure 5.40

Integrating Excel and PowerPoint

1. **Start** Excel. Open the Excel file **i05E_Snowboarding_Bags**. **Save** the file in the **Integrated Projects Chapter 5** folder with the file name **Lastname_Firstname_5E_SnowboardingBags** In cell **D2**, type **TotalCost** In cell **D3**, type the formula **=B3*C3** and then copy the formula down through cell **D18**.

2. Select cells **A1:D1**. Apply the cell style **Accent4**, and then **Merge & Center** the selected cells. Select cells **A2:D2**, and then apply the cell style **20% - Accent4**. Select columns **A:D**, and then adjust the column width automatically to accommodate the widest item in each column.

3. Select cells **A2:B18**. Insert a **Clustered Bar in 3-D** chart, and then move the chart to a chart sheet, with the sheet name **Cost Chart** Apply the **Chart Layout 2**, right-click the **Legend**, and then click **Delete**. Format the **Vertical (Category) Axis** as **Bold**. Change the **Chart Title** to **Cost of Individual Bags and Luggage** Rename the **Sheet1** tab as **Inventory Cost** and then delete **Sheet2** and **Sheet3**. Insert the file name as a field in the footer of all worksheets. Return to **Normal** view.

4. Select cells **A3:A18** and **C3:C18**, and then insert a **Pie in 3-D** chart. Move the chart to a chart sheet, with the sheet name **Available Bags** Apply the **Chart Style 14** and the **Chart Layout 4**. Format the **Series 1 Data Labels** as **Bold**. Format the **Chart Area** with **Gradient fill** and the **Color** as **Orange, Accent 6, Lighter 40%**. Insert a **Chart Title** above the chart with the text **Bag Inventory**

5. Click the **Inventory Cost sheet tab**, and then press Ctrl + Home.. Display **Backstage** view. Click **Properties**, and then click **Show Document Panel**. In the **Author** box, type your firstname and lastname, in the **Subject** box, type your course name and section number, and then in the **Keywords** box, type **inventory,charts** Close the Document Information Panel, and then **Save** the workbook.

6. **Start** PowerPoint. Open the file **i05E_Bags_Presentation**. Save the file in the **Integrated Projects Chapter 5** folder with the file name **Lastname_Firstname_5E_Bags_Presentation** Insert the filename as a footer in the **Notes and Handouts tab**, add a **Fixed Date**, and **Apply to All**.

7. Click **Slide 2**, and then insert a new *Slide 3* with the **Blank** layout. **Copy** the **Cost Chart** form the Excel workbook, and then **Paste** it in the new blank **Slide 3**. Insert a new *Slide 4* with the **Title Only** layout. Add the title **Best Selling Bags** In the Excel file **Lastname_Firstname_5E_Snowboarding_Bags**, be sure you are in Normal View, and then on the **Inventory Cost** sheet, copy cells **A2:B4**. **Paste Link** the cells into the new **Slide 4** of the presentation. Change the **Height** of the linked object to **1.5**, and then move the object to the center of the slide. Click **Slide 1**. Apply the design theme **Opulent**, and then change the **Background Style** to **Style 6**.

8. In the Excel file **Lastname_Firtname_5E_Snowboarding_Bags**, on the **Inventory Cost** sheet, press Esc, and then change the number in cell **B3** to **$75.50** Press Ctrl + Home., **Save** the Excel workbook, and then **Close** Excel. Verify the change has been made on Slide 4 of your presentation.

9. On **Slide 5**, change the **Height** of the picture to **5** Drag the picture to the top left so the top left corner is at the **0.5 inches to left of the 0 on the horizontal ruler and at 2 inches above 0 on the vertical ruler**. Adjust the picture placement if necessary. Change the **Picture Style** to **Rotated, White**. Click **Slide 1**. Apply the **Slide Transition** using the **Wipe** transition, change the **Duration** to **1.50**, and then **Apply to All** slides.

Integrating Excel and PowerPoint

10. Display **Backstage** view. Click **Properties**, and then click **Show Document Panel**. In the **Author** box, type your firstname and lastname, in the **Subject** box, type your course name and section number, and then in the **Keywords** box, type **Excelcharts** Close the Document Information Panel. From **Backstage** view, **Mark as Final**, and then click **OK** two times. **Save** the presentation, and then **Close** PowerPoint.

11. Submit your printed or electronic files as directed by your instructor.

You have completed Project 5E

Integrating Excel and PowerPoint

4. Create and Modify Illustrations in PowerPoint
5. Copy a PowerPoint Slide and Object into an Excel Workbook
6. Create Hyperlinks
7. Freeze Rows, Repeat Headings, and Insert Comments in Excel

Mastering Integration | Project 5F Tee Shirts

In the following Mastering Integration project, you will edit a PowerPoint presentation by applying a theme, inserting SmartArt, modifying graphics, and creating a hyperlink to an Excel workbook. In the workbook, you will paste a PowerPoint object, create titles on multiple pages, and insert comments. Your completed files will look similar to Figure 5.41.

Project Files

For Project 5F, you will need the following files:

i05F_Tee_Shirts
i05F_Shirt_Presentation

You will save your files as:

Lastname_Firstname_5F_Tee_Shirts
Lastname_Firstname_5F_Shirt_Presentation

Project Results

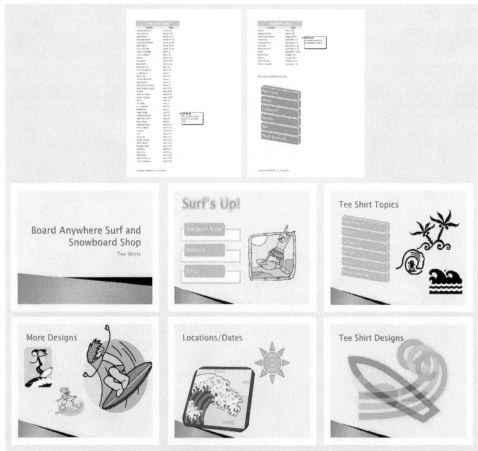

Figure 5.41

Integrating Excel and PowerPoint

1. **Start** PowerPoint. Open the file **i05F_Shirt_Presentation**. **Save** the file in the **Integrated Projects Chapter 5** folder with the file name **Lastname_Firstname_5F_Shirt_Presentation** Add the name of the file on the Handouts footer, and then **Apply to All**. Apply the theme **Concourse**. Change the theme **Color** to **Oriel**, and the **Background Style** to **Style 10**.

2. On **Slide 3**, in the left placeholder, use the **Convert to SmartArt Graphic** button to insert the graphic **Vertical Bullet List**. Format the object **Width** to **4** and the **Height** to **4.5** Change the **SmartArt Style** to **Brick Scene**. Animate the graphic with the **Fade** animation, **As One Object**.

3. Insert a new **Slide 4** with the **Title and Content** layout. In the title placeholder, type **TeeShirt Designs** In the lower placeholder, click the **Clip Art** button. Search for **surfboard,waves,wmf** and **Include Office.com content**. Insert the second image in the first row, as show in Figure 5.41, or select another appropriate picture. Change the picture **Height** to <u>6</u> and then **Align Center** and **Align Middle**. On **Slide 5**, select the picture on the right. Change the **Height** to **6** and then **Align Right**, **Align Top**, and **Send to Back**.

4. On **Slide 2**, add the title **Surf's Up!** Select the title, and then apply the **WordArt Style—Gradient Fill – Accent 1**. Click the **Text Effects** button, and then under **Bevel**, apply the **Slope** effect. Change the **Font Size** to **66**. In the left placeholder, insert the SmartArt graphic **Vertical Box List**. In the graphic, type the names of the beaches **Margaret River Ventura** and **Kirra** Add the **Slide Transition— Uncover Right**. Change the **Duration** to **1.5** and then **Apply to All**.

5. **Start** Excel. Open the file **i05F_Tee_Shirts**. **Save** the file in the **Integrated Projects Chapter 5** folder with the file name **Lastname_Firstname_5F_Tee_Shirts** Insert the file name as a field in the footer. Return to **Normal** view. **Rename** the **Sheet1 tab** as **ShirtLocations** and then **Delete** *Sheet2* and *Sheet3*.

6. Adjust the column width of **columns A:B** to display all data. Select cells **A1:B1**, and then apply the **Cell Style—Accent 6**. **Merge & Center** the cells, apply **Bold** format, and then change the **Font Size** to **20**. Select cells **A2:B2**, apply the **Cell Style—40% - Accent6**, apply **Bold** format, and then **Center** the cells.

7. In cell **A62**, type **Watch our TeeShirt Presentation** and then **Insert** a **Hyperlink** to your file **Lastname_Firstname_5F_Shirt_Presentation**. Add a **ScreenTip** with the text **See our great teeshirt designs.**

8. Make the PowerPoint presentation the active window. On **Slide 6**, click the **Sun** shape, and then **Insert** a **Hyperlink** to the Excel file **Lastname_Firstname_5F_Tee_Shirts**. In the left placeholder, select the picture. Change the picture **Width** to <u>5</u> and apply the **Picture Style—Bevel Perspective**.

9. On **Slide 3**, **Copy** the SmartArt graphic. Make the Excel window active, and then in cell **A66**, **Paste** the SmartArt object. Change the **Height** of the graphic to <u>4</u> and the **Width** to <u>3</u> Click cell **B31**, and then **Insert** the **Comment This has been our best location for selling tee shirts.** Click cell **B50**, and then **Insert** the **Comment We should move this to Thanksgiving weekend.**

10. Set the comments to print **As displayed on sheet**. Format the **Print Titles** so the **Rows to repeat at top** include row 1 and row 2. Press Ctrl + Home.. Display **Backstage** view. Click **Properties**, and then click **Show Document Panel**. In the **Author** box, type your firstname and lastname, in the **Subject** box, type your course name and section number, and then in the **Keywords** box, type **hyperlink,comments Close** the Document Information Panel. **Save** the workbook, and then **Close** Excel.

Integrating Excel and PowerPoint

11. In your presentation, click **Slide 1**. Display **Backstage** view. Click **Properties**, and then click **Show Document Panel**. In the **Author** box, type your firstname and lastname, in the **Subject** box, type your course name and section number, and then in the **Keywords** box, type **Excelhyperlink** Close the Document Information Panel. **Save** your presentation, and then **Close** PowerPoint.

12. Submit your printed or electronic files as directed by your instructor.

You have completed Project 5F

Integrating Excel and PowerPoint

Rubric

The following outcomes-based assessments are open-ended assessments. That is, there is no specific correct result; your result will depend on your approach to the information provided. Make Professional Quality your goal. Use the following scoring rubric to guide you in how to approach the problem and then to evaluate how well your approach solves the problem.

The *criteria*—Software Mastery, Content, Format and Layout, and Process—represent the knowledge and skills you have gained that you can apply to solving the problem. The *levels of performance*—Professional Quality, Approaching Professional Quality, or Needs Quality Improvements—help you and your instructor evaluate your result.

	Your completed project is of Professional Quality	Your completed project is of Approaching Professional Quality	Your completed project Needs Quality Improvements
1-Software Mastery	Chooses and applies the most appropriate skills, tools, and features and identifies efficient methods to solve the problem.	Chooses and applies some appropriate skills, tools, and features, but not in the most efficient manner.	Chooses inappropriate skills, tools, or features, or is inefficient in solving the problem.
2-Content	Constructs a solution that is clear and well organized, containing content that is accurate, appropriate to the audience and purpose, and complete. The solution contains no errors of spelling, grammar, or style.	Constructs a solution in which some components are unclear, poorly organized, inconsistent, or incomplete. May misjudge the needs of the audience. May contain some errors in spelling, grammar, or style, but the errors do not detract from comprehension.	Constructs a solution that is unclear, incomplete, or poorly organized, containing some inaccurate or inappropriate content. May contain many errors of spelling, grammar, or style. May fail to solve the problem.
3-Format and Layout	Formats and arranges all elements to communicate information and ideas, clarify function, illustrate relationships, and indicate relative importance.	Applies appropriate format and layout features to some elements, but not others. Or, overuses features, causing minor distraction.	Applies format and layout that fails to communicate information or ideas or clearly. May fail to use format and layout features to clarify function, illustrate relationships, or indicate relative importance. Or, may use available features excessively, causing distraction.
4-Process	Uses an organized approach that integrates planning, development, self-assessment, revision, and reflection.	Demonstrates an organized approach in some areas, but not others. Or, uses an insufficient process of organization throughout.	Does not use an organized approach to solve the problem.

Integrating Excel and PowerPoint

GO! Think | **Project 5G Protective Gear**

Project Files

For Project 5G, you will need the following files:

i05G_Protective_Gear
i05G_Protective_Presentation

You will save your files as:

Lastname_Firstname_5G_Protective_Gear
Lastname_Firstname_5G_Protective_Presentation

Dana Connolly, one of the owners of Board Anywhere Surf and Snowboard Shop, believes it is important to stress snowboarder safety. He wants his sales associates to emphasize snowboarding protective gear—such as helmets, goggles, and shin guards—that is available in the retail store.

Modify the i05G_Protective_Gear file by adjusting column widths so that all data displays. Apply a style to the titles and set the titles to repeat on all printed pages. Create a chart on a new sheet. Format the chart, using a chart layout and chart style. Rename the sheets containing data and delete any blank worksheets. Insert the file name in the footer of all worksheets. Save the file as **Lastname_Firstname_5G_Protective_Gear** Open the file i05G_Protective_Presentation. Add appropriate titles to the slides and adjust the size, color, or effects of the pictures. On a new blank slide, paste the Excel chart as a link. Insert a shape on one of the slides and modify the shape with at least two effects. Insert appropriate text in the shape and create a hyperlink to the Excel workbook. Save the presentation as **Lastname_Firstname_5G_Protective_Presentation** In both files, add appropriate information to the Document Panel. Submit your printed or electronic files as directed by your instructor.

You have completed Project 5G

GO! Think | **Project 5H Surfing Footwear**

Project Files

For Project 5H, you will need the following files:

> i05H_Surfing_Footwear
> i05H_Footwear_Presentation

You will save your files as:

> Lastname_Firstname_5H_Surfing_Footwear
> Lastname_Firstname_5H_Footwear_Presentation

Ali Cardona, Purchasing Manager of Board Anywhere Surf and Snowboarding Shop, has asked to prepare a PowerPoint presentation and a related Excel workbook that contains information regarding the surfing footwear available in the store.

Open the file i05H_Surfing_Footwear. Adjust the column widths so that all data displays, and then add a style to the titles. Insert a minimum of two comments. Rename the sheets containing data and delete any blank worksheets. Save the file as **Lastname_Firstname_5H_Surfing_Footwear** Insert the file name in the footer on the worksheet. Open the file i05H_Footwear_Presentation. Create at least one SmartArt graphic, insert one shape two appropriate clip art images. Modify a minimum of three objects by changing their size and applying effects. Insert a shape, add appropriate text, and create a hyperlink to the Excel workbook. Add appropriate titles to the slides, add a design theme, and rearrange the slide order. Save the presentation as **Lastname_Firstname_5H_Footwear_Presentation** Insert the file name in the handouts footer. In both files, add appropriate information to the Document Panel. Submit your printed or electronic files as directed by your instructor.

You have completed Project 5H

Integrating Excel and PowerPoint

Apply a combination of the 5A and 5B skills.

Project Files

For Project 5I, you will need the following files:

i05I_Board_Logos
i05I_Logos_Presentation

You will save your files as:

Lastname_Firstname_5I_Board_Logos
Lastname_Firstname_5I_Logos_Presentation

J. R. Kass, one of the owners of Board Anywhere Surf and Snowboard Shop, wants to commission an artist to create a new board logo for the company. Mr. Kass has created an Excel workbook that lists the artists and their commission prices. He has also narrowed the field down to four logos and placed them in a PowerPoint presentation. He has asked you to complete both files.

Open the file i05I_Board_Logos. Adjust the column widths so that all data displays and add a style to the title. Create a chart on a new sheet. Format the chart using a chart layout and a chart style. Insert at least two comments. Rename the sheets containing data and delete any blank worksheets. Insert the file name in the footer of all worksheets. Save the file as **Lastname_Firstname_5I_Board_Logos** Open the file i05I_Logos_Presentation. In the presentation, apply a design theme. Add titles containing the names of artists to the slides; select any names from the Excel workbook. For each logo, adjust the size or add an effect. Insert a new slide, and then Past link the Excel chart. Save the presentation as **Lastname_Firstname_5I_Logos_Presentation** Insert the file name in the handouts footer. In both files, add appropriate information to the Document Panel. Submit your printed or electronic files as directed by your instructor.

You have completed Project 5I

Integrating Publisher and Access

OUTCOMES
At the end of this chapter you will be able to:

OBJECTIVES
Mastering these objectives will enable you to:

PROJECT 6A
Build a newsletter in Publisher and insert recipients and data fields from Access.

1. Construct a Newsletter in Publisher
2. Format a Newsletter
3. Use Mail Merge to Insert Names from an Access Table into a Publication
4. Insert Access Data Fields into a Publication

PROJECT 6B
Set Access field properties and create a publication using a template.

5. Set Field Properties in an Access Table
6. Create a Publication Using a Publisher Template
7. Modify the Layout of a Publication

Monkey Business Images/Shutterstock

In This Chapter

In this chapter, you will create publications using Publisher. Publisher is the business publishing program that helps you create, design, and publish professional-looking promotional and communication materials to be used for print, e-mail, and the Internet. You can customize a publication by inserting names, addresses, or any field from an Access database. In Access tables, changing field settings allows you to enter the records quickly and more accurately. You can set default values and input masks for individual fields in a table. You should maintain database records on a regular basis to ensure that the data is current and accurate.

The projects in this chapter relate to **Florida Port Community College**, located in St. Petersburg, Florida—a coastal city near the Florida High Tech Corridor. With 60 percent of Florida's high-tech companies and a third of the state's manufacturing companies located in the St. Petersburg and Tampa Bay areas, the college partners with businesses to play a vital role in providing a skilled workforce. The curriculum covers many areas, including medical technology, computer science, electronics, aviation and aerospace, and simulation and modeling. The college also serves the community through cultural, athletic, and diversity programs and adult basic education.

From Chapter 6 of *GO! with Microsoft® Office 2010 Integrated Projects Comprehensive*, First Edition, Shelley Gaskin, Carol L. Martin. Copyright © 2012 by Pearson Education, Inc. Published by Pearson Prentice Hall. All rights reserved.

Project 6A Student Newsletter

Project Activities

In Activities 6.01 through 6.12, you will edit a newsletter for new students attending Florida Port Community College. You will modify the color, font, and text schemes. Additionally, you will insert and format clip art and other objects. After adding student records to an Access database, you will use Mail Merge to create a customized newsletter for each recipient. Your completed documents will look similar to Figure 6.1.

Project Files

For Project 6A, you will need the following files:

i06A_New_Students
i06A_Student_Data
i06A_Beach

You will save your files as:

Lastname_Firstname_6A_New_Students
Lastname_Firstname_6A_Merged_Students
Lastname_Firstname_6A_Student_Data

Project Results

Figure 6.1
Project 6A Student Newsletter

Objective 1 | Construct a Newsletter in Publisher

You can use Publisher templates to create various business publications including advertisements, awards, business cards, business forms, calendars, labels, newsletters, and resumes. When documents are used repeatedly, you can save the layout and then simply change the content as required for the new version. Aisha Leinen, the Admissions Director for Florida Port Community College, would like to send a newsletter to students who have been admitted to FPCC. Each week, she plans to send the newsletter to students who have been accepted that week.

Activity 6.01 | Constructing a Newsletter

Ms. Leinen has started the newsletter in Publisher and has asked you to complete it.

1 **Start** Publisher. From **Backstage** view, click the **Open** tab. In the **Open Publication** dialog box, navigate to the location of the student data files for this instruction, and then open the file **i06A_New_Students**. If necessary, to display the rulers, click the **View tab**, and then in the **Show group**, click the **Rulers** checkbox.

2 Click the **File tab**, and then click the **Save As tab**. In the **Save As** dialog box, navigate to the location where you are saving your files. Click the **New folder** button, type **Integrated Projects Chapter 6** and then press [Enter] two times. In the **File name** box, type **Lastname_Firstname_6A_New_Students** and then click **Save**. Take a moment to study the parts of the Publisher screen, as shown in Figure 6.2.

The Page Navigation pane, at the left of your screen, displays thumbnails of the pages in a publication. Page 1 of the publication displays.

Figure 6.2

Page Navigation pane
Rulers
Page 1

3 Click the **Insert tab**, and then in the **Header & Footer group**, click the **Footer** button.

A Footer text box displays on a *master page*. A master page contains the design and layout elements, including headers and footers, that you want to repeat on multiple pages of your publication. By default, every publication contains a master page.

4 In the **Footer** text box, type **Lastname_Firstname_6A_New_Students** and then on the **Master Page tab**, in the **Close group**, click the **Close Master Page** button.

The footer displays on all pages of the newsletter.

5 In the **Page Navigation** pane, click **Page 2**. Hold down [Shift], and then click **Page 3**. With both pages selected, right-click the selection, and then on the shortcut menu, click **Delete**. In the message box, click **Yes** to delete the pages.

Pages 2 and 3 are deleted. Page 4 is renumbered as Page 2.

6 In the **Page Navigation** pane, click **Page 1**. At the top of the page, select the text *Newsletter Title*, and then type **Welcome New FPCC Students**

7 At the top left corner of the page, in the text box, click **Newsletter Date**. Click the **Insert tab**, and then in the **Text group**, click the **Date & Time** button 🗓. In the **Date and Time** dialog box, under **Available formats**, click the format **May 11, 2015**—your date will differ—and then click **OK**.

> The date in the dialog box is determined by the date you complete this step of the activity.

8 To the right of the date, select the text **Your business name**, and then type **Florida Port Community College** Click in a blank area of the newsletter to deselect the text box.

9 Save 💾 the newsletter.

Activity 6.02 | Applying a Color Scheme and a Font Scheme

Publisher includes a number of color and font schemes to create a professional-looking document. You can select an existing scheme, or you can customize the colors and fonts in your publications.

1 Click the **Page Design tab**, and then in the **Schemes group**, click the **More** button ▾.

2 In the **Color Schemes** gallery, point to a few of the color schemes to view how the colors affect your publication. Scroll down, and then under **Built-In (classic)**, click the **Summer** color scheme.

> The Summer *color scheme* is applied to your newsletter. A color scheme is a predefined set of harmonized colors that can be applied to text and objects. In a publication, when you select a color scheme, the colors of various objects—such as text boxes, headings, and borders—are automatically changed.

3 On the **Page Design tab**, in the **Schemes group**, click the **Scheme Fonts** button. At the bottom of the **Font Scheme** gallery, click **Font Scheme Options**. In the **Font Scheme Options** dialog box, verify that all check boxes are selected, and then click **OK**.

> The selected check boxes allow you to update existing text styles, change text formatting, and adjust font sizes.

4 In the **Schemes group**, click the **Scheme Fonts** button. In the **Font Schemes** gallery, under **Built-In**, scroll down, and then click the **Median** font scheme. Compare your screen with Figure 6.3.

> The Median *font scheme* is applied to your newsletter. A font scheme is a predefined set of fonts that is associated with a publication. Within each font scheme, both a primary font and a secondary font are specified. Generally, a primary font is used for titles and headings, and a secondary font is used for body text. Font schemes make it easy to change all the fonts in a publication to give it a consistent appearance.

Figure 6.3

Median font scheme applied

Current date inserted – your date will differ

Summer color scheme applied

5 At the bottom of **Page 1**, select the title *Secondary Story Headline*, and then type **Student Activities and Organizations**

6 Click in the text box below the revised heading to select the text. Click the **Text Box Tools Format tab**. In the **Font group**, click the **Font Size button arrow** [10 ▾], and then click **11**. Type **Florida Port Community College offers its students a number of activities and events that are meant to enrich life on campus and to provide for a complete approach to your educational experience.** Press Enter.

7 Type **You have the opportunity to become a member of the FPCC Student Government or to join one of the many clubs and organizations that are active on campus. Some of the clubs include the BBQ Club, the Art Students Club, and the Medical Technology Club. Of course, given our location in sunny Florida, we have a number of athletic clubs, such as the Alligator Swim Club, the Tennis Club, the Ultimate Frisbee Club, and the Lacrosse Club.** Press Enter.

8 Type **FPCC is an active community member in the Tampa/St. Pete area, and we encourage our students to become energetic members in the various community organizations.** Press Enter, and then type **Stop by the Student Activities Office in the Student Union or look at the Student Activities Web page for more information.**

9 **Save** the newsletter.

Activity 6.03 | Inserting a Building Block

Building blocks are reusable pieces of content—for example, borders, text boxes, logos, and calendars—that are stored in galleries. In this activity, you will insert a Page Part—a text box—building block.

1 At the lower left corner of **Page 1**, click the object *Inside this issue*, and notice sizing handles display to indicate the entire object is selected. Right-click the object, and then on the shortcut menu, click **Delete Object**.

2 Click the **Insert tab**, and then in the **Building Blocks group**, click the **Page Parts** button. In the **Page Parts** ?gallery, scroll down if necessary, and then under **Pull Quotes**, click the first text box—**Brackets**. If necessary, on the **Status bar**, change the Zoom slider to **100%**.

3 With the **Brackets** text box selected, point to the border until the pointer displays, and then position the text box at the bottom left of **Page 1** so that the top left corner of the text box, not the sizing handle, is located at approximately **6.5 inches on the vertical ruler** and **0.75 inches on the horizontal ruler**.

As you move an object in a Publisher document, you will notice a black line displays on both the horizontal and vertical rulers, indicating where your cursor is located.

Project 6A: Student Newsletter | **Integrated Projects**

4 With the **Brackets** text box selected, point to the bottom right sizing handle until the ⬚ pointer displays, and then resize the text box so the bottom right corner is approximately at **10 inches on the vertical ruler** and **2.25 inches on the horizontal ruler**. If necessary, use the arrow keys to nudge the text box into the position shown in Figure 6.4.

Figure 6.4

Brackets text box insert and resized

5 Click in the text box to select the text. Click the **Text Box Tools Format contextual tab**, in the **Font group**, click the **Font Size button arrow** ⬚, click **12**. In the **Alignment group**, click the **Align Center** button ⬚.

6 With the text selected, type **Remember, education lasts a lifetime. Once you earn your certificate or degree, no one can ever take your education away from you.**

7 Deselect the text box, and then **Save** ⬚ the newsletter.

Activity 6.04 | Applying a Text Style

You can customize the styles of headings, bullets, or other text in your publication.

1 Scroll up to the top of **Page 1**, and then select the heading *Lead Story Headline*. On the **Text Box Tools Format tab**, in the **Font group**, click the **Font Size button arrow** ⬚, and then click **14**. Type **Steps to be a Successful Student at FPCC**

2 In the text box that displays a picture, click the picture to select it and the caption below it. Right-click the picture, and then on the shortcut menu, click **Cut**.

3 In the text box below the heading, click one time in the paragraph that begins *Congratulations on being admitted*. Press ⃞Ctrl⃞ + ⃞A⃞ to select all the text in the text box. On the **Text Box Tools Format tab**, in the **Font group**, click the **Font Size button arrow** ⬚, and then click **12**.

4 In the middle text box, click to the right of the text *6. Pay tuition and fees*, and then press ⃞Enter⃞.

This text is recognized by Publisher as a list; the number 7 automatically displays to continue the list.

5 Type **Obtain your student ID card** and then press ⏎. Type **Purchase textbooks** and then press ⏎. Type **Sign up for FPCC student e-mail** and then press ⏎. Type **Make parking arrangements** and then compare your screen with Figure 6.5.

A list of 10 items displays in the text box.

Figure 6.5

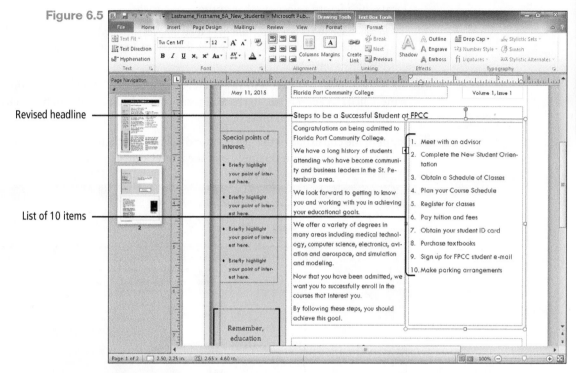

Revised headline

List of 10 items

6 In the lower text box, select the heading *Student Activities and Organizations*. On the **Home tab**, in the **Styles group**, click the **Styles** button. In the **Styles** gallery, scroll down, and then click **Heading 3**. On the **Home tab**, in the **Font group**, click the **Bold** button **B**.

7 Scroll up, and then at the top of the page, select the heading *Florida Port Community College*. In the **Styles group**, click the **Styles** button, scroll down, and then click **Organization Name 2**. In the **Font group**, click the **Font Size button arrow** [10 ▾], and then click **14**. Click the **Bold** button **B**. Click in a blank area of the page to deselect the text box.

8 **Save** 🖫 the newsletter.

Objective 2 | Format a Newsletter

You can format a publication in a number of ways. To control the flow of text, you can apply *text wrapping*—the manner in which text displays around an object, such as a picture or clip art. You can format the background of a document by adding a color, a texture, or an image.

Activity 6.05 | Changing Text Wrapping

In this activity, you will insert clip art and change the way the existing text wraps around the graphic.

1 Click the **Insert tab**. In the **Illustrations group**, click the **Clip Art** button. At the right of your screen, in the **Clip Art** task pane, click the **Results should be box arrow**, and then click **All media file types**. If necessary, to the left of **Include Office.com content**, click the check box to select it. In the **Search for** box, type **Australia, beaches** and then click **Go**. Scroll, if necessary, to locate the image as shown in Figure 6.6. If you cannot locate this picture, select another appropriate image.

Recall that clip art is a collection of graphic images included with Microsoft Office programs or downloaded from the Web that can make your publication more interesting and visually appealing.

2 Click the clip art to insert it in your newsletter, and then **Close** × the Clip Art task pane. Click the **Format tab**. In the **Size group**, click the **Shape Width** box, select the number, type **3** and then press Enter.

3 Point to the clip art until the ⬚ pointer displays, and then move the clip art to the center of the text box in the middle of the page. Compare your screen with Figure 6.6.

Figure 6.6
Format tab

Shape Width box

Clip art in center
of text box

4 On the **Format tab**, in the **Arrange group**, click the **Wrap Text** button, and then click **Top and Bottom**.

The text stops at the top of the picture's frame and continues below the bottom of the frame.

5 In the **Arrange group**, click the **Wrap Text** button, and then click **None**.

The clip art displays on top of the text.

6 In the **Arrange group**, click the **Send Backward button arrow**, and then click **Send to Back**.

The text displays on top of the clip art. The text will display as if the clip art isn't there. Use the commands in the Arrange group to indicate how images should display in relation to existing text.

7 In the **Adjust group**, click the **Brightness** button, and then click **+30%**. Click a blank area of your newsletter, and then compare your screen with Figure 6.7.

Increasing the brightness gives the clip art a washed out look.

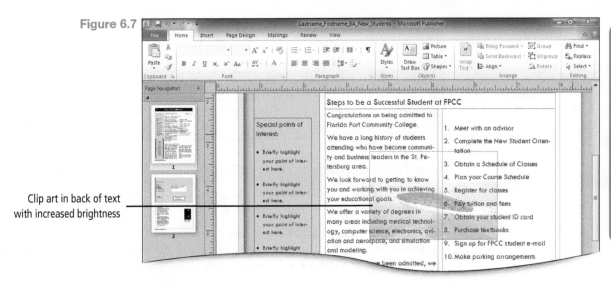

Figure 6.7

Clip art in back of text
with increased brightness

8 Save 🖫 the newsletter.

Activity 6.06 | Inserting a Design Accent

In this activity, you will add a design accent building block to your newsletter.

1 Click the **Insert tab**, and then in the **Building Blocks group**, click the **Borders & Accents** button. In the **Design Accent** gallery, under **Bars**, in the first row, point to the second accent—**Awning Stripes**. Compare your screen with Figure 6.8. Note: Your view may vary.

Figure 6.8

Borders & Accents button

Awning Stripes design
accent – your view
may vary

2 Click **Awning Stripes** to insert it in your newsletter.

3 With the **Awning Stripes** accent selected, point to the left border until the pointer displays, and then move the object so the top left corner is at approximately **7 inches on the vertical ruler** and **2.5 inches on the horizontal ruler**.

4 Point to the bottom right sizing handle until the pointer displays, and then resize the object so that the Awning Stripes accent is stretched and extends to the right margin. Use the arrow keys to position the Awning Stripes accent so the bottom border touches the top border of the lower text box. Click a blank section of your newsletter, and then compare your screen with Figure 6.9.

Figure 6.9

Awning Stripe positioned
between text boxes

> your point of inter-
> est here.

Now that you have be...
want you to successfully enroll in the
courses that interest you.

By following these steps, you should
achieve this goal.

Remember,
education
lasts a
lifetime.

Student Activities and Organizations

Florida Port Community College offers its | ber of athletic clubs, such as the Alligator

Page: 1 of 2   2.52, 6.97 in.   5.38 x 0.18 in.   100%

5 In the **Page Navigation** pane, click **Page 2**. Scroll up to display the top of **Page 2**.

6 On the **Insert tab**, in the **Building Blocks group**, click the **Borders & Accents** button. In the **Design Accent** gallery, under **Emphasis**, click **Stripes**.

7 With the object selected, click the **Format tab**, and then in the **Size group**, click the **Shape Height** box, type **2** and then press Enter. Click the **Shape Width** box, type **3** and then press Enter. In the **Arrange group**, click the **Send Backward** button.

8 Point to the border of the object to display the [⬚] pointer, and then move the object so the stripes display above and below the right text box that contains the text that begins *Type address here*. Compare your screen with Figure 6.10.

> The Stripes object surrounds the address text box.

Figure 6.10

Stripes design accent
surrounds text box

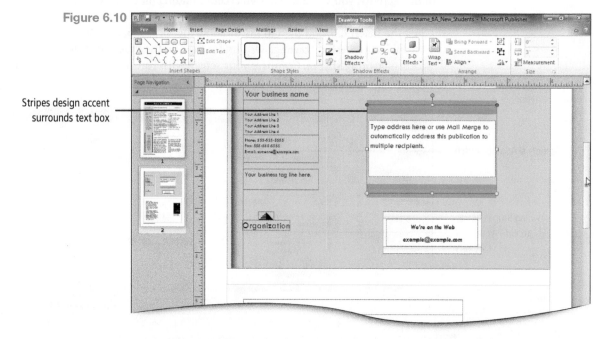

9 Below the address text box, in the text box beginning with the paragraph *We're on the Web*, select the text *example@example.com*, and then type **FloridaPortCC.edu** and then **Save** [💾] the newsletter.

Activity 6.07 | Formatting the Newsletter Background

1 On the **Page Navigation** pane, click **Page 1**. At the top left corner of the page, click the heading *Special points of interest* to select the heading, and then type **Remember:** Under the new heading, click the first bullet point.

> All of the bullet points are selected.

2 Type the following list, pressing Enter after each list item, except for the last item. Compare your screen with Figure 6.11.

Admission
Registration
Tuition and Fees
Financial Aid
Attend Classes
Graduate

Figure 6.11

Typed list

3 Click in a blank area of the newsletter to deselect the text box. Click the **Page Design tab**, and then in the **Page Background group**, click the **Background** button. In the **Background** gallery, under **Gradient Background**, in the first row, point to the third background—**Accent 3 Horizontal Gradient**, right-click the background, and then on the shortcut menu, click **Apply to All Pages**.

The selected background is applied to both pages of the newsletter.

4 Save the newsletter.

Activity 6.08 | Running the Design Checker

After you have created a publication, it is a good idea to review it. The *Design Checker* is a feature that automatically reviews your publication for a range of design and layout flaws and provides options to fix any identified problems.

1 In the **Page Navigation** pane, click **Page 2**. At the top left corner of the page, select the text *Your business name*, and then type **Florida Port Community College**

2 Below the active text box, in the next text box that begins with the text *Your Address*, select all four lines of text. Click the **Home tab**. In the **Font group**, click the **Font Size button arrow** 10 ▾, and then click **11**. Type **2745 Dartmouth Ave N** and then press Enter. Type **St. Petersburg, FL 33713** and then press Enter.

3 Below the active text box, in the next text box, select the phone number and then type **727-555-0030** Select the fax number, and then type **727-555-0031** Select the e-mail address, and then type **admissions @FloridaPortCC.edu**

Project 6A: Student Newsletter | **Integrated Projects**

4 In the next textbox, select the text *Your business tag line here.*, and then type **Learning for a lifetime**

5 Click the text box that contains the text *Organization* and the pyramid image. On the **Home tab**, in the **Clipboard group**, click the **Cut** button ✂ to delete the entire text box—the text and the image— from the publication. Compare your screen with Figure 6.12.

Figure 6.12

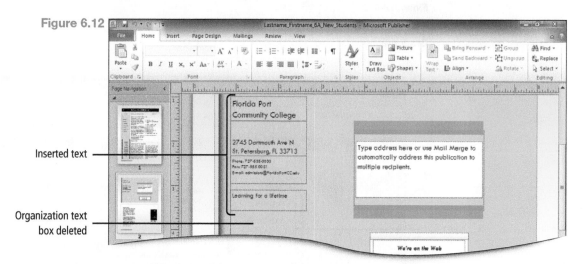

Inserted text

Organization text box deleted

6 Click the **File tab**, verify the **Info tab** is selected, and then click the **Run Design Checker** button.

The Design Checker automatically runs and displays the results in the Design Checker task pane.

7 At the bottom of the **Design Checker** task pane, click **Design Checker Options**. In the **Design Checker Options** dialog box, under **Page Range**, click the **Current page(s)** option button. Click the **Checks tab**. Under **Checks in this category**, scroll down to verify that all the check boxes are selected, and then click **OK**.

The Design Checker runs and displays the results in the Design Checker task pane.

8 On the **Design Checker** task pane, under **Select an item to fix**, locate the first item— **Text box is empty (Page 2)**.

This text box will be completed in a later activity.

9 On the **Design Checker** task pane, under **Select an item to fix**, click the **Low-resolution picture (Page 2) arrow**, and then click **Go to this Item**.

The picture on Page 2 is selected.

10 On the **Design Checker** task pane, under **Select an item to fix**, click the **Low-resolution picture (Page 2) arrow**, and then click **Explain**.

The Publisher Help window opens, and an explanation of a low-resolution picture displays. This picture will be modified in a later activity.

11 Read the explanation, and then **Close** ⬛ the Publisher Help window. Click in a blank area of the publication to deselect the picture.

12 **Close** ⬛ the Design Checker task pane.

13 Click the **Review tab**, and then in the **Proofing group**, click the **Spelling** button 🔤.

> Beginning at the current location, Publisher begins checking the spelling of text in your publication.

14 Check the spelling in your newsletter, making any necessary corrections. If a message box displays asking if you want to check the rest of your publication, click **Yes**. Continue making any necessary corrections, until a message box displays *The spelling check is complete.* Click **OK** to close the message box.

15 Save 🖫 the newsletter.

Objective 3 | Use Mail Merge to Insert Names from an Access Table into a Publication

Recall that in Word, Mail Merge is a feature that joins a main document and a data source to create customized letters or labels. In Publisher, you can use Mail Merge to insert the name and address of different individuals or businesses into a publication. Mail Merge also allows you to insert placeholders for other data fields to make each publication unique.

Activity 6.09 | Modifying an Existing Access Database

1 **Start** Access. From **Backstage** view, click the **Open tab**, navigate to the location where the student data files are located, and then open the file **i06A_Student_Data**. Click the **File tab**, and then click the **Save Database As tab**. In the **Save As** dialog box, navigate to your **Integrated Projects Chapter 6** folder, and then click **Open**. In the **File Name** box, delete the existing text, type **Lastname_Firstname_6A_Student_Data** and then click **Save**.

2 On the **Message Bar**, click the **Enable Content** button. In the **Navigation Pane**, under **Tables**, double-click the **Students** table.

> The Students table displays in Datasheet view.

3 Click the **Create tab**, and then in the **Forms group**, click the **Form** button. On the **Design tab**, in the **Views group**, click the **View** button to display the form in Form view.

4 On the Quick Access Toolbar, click the **Save** button 🖫. In the **Save As** dialog box, type **Students Form** and then click **OK**.

5 At the bottom of the form, click the **New (blank) record** button ▶️. Add the following records. When you type the last record, use your own name in the Firstname and Lastname fields. Compare your screen with Figure 6.13.

Student ID	Firstname	Lastname	Address	City	State	ZIP	Phone Number	Degree
20-8699944	Casey	Drees	908 Sydney Washer Rd	St. Petersburg	FL	33714	727-555-2187	Computer Information
20-7385522	Clifton	Durfey	8309 Dahlia Ave	Tampa	FL	33605	813-555-0185	Computer Information
20-6682011	Firstname	Lastname	3611 S Lois Ave	St. Petersburg	FL	33713	727-555-0286	Accounting

Figure 6.13

Students form

Record includes
student's name

New (blank) record button

Record 8 of 8

6 Press Enter to accept the record with your name.

7 At the bottom of the form, in the navigation area, click the **Previous Record** button ◀ to display record 8—the record containing your name. Carefully review the form to make sure you entered all data correctly. Using the same technique, review records 7 and 6.

It is important that your data is entered correctly because you will use the records in a later activity.

8 Click the **Create tab**, and then in the **Reports group**, click the **Report Wizard** button. In the **Report Wizard** dialog box, verify that the **Students** table is selected. Under **Available Fields**, double-click the fields **Firstname**, **Lastname**, **Address**, **City**, **State**, and **ZIP**, and then click **Next** two times.

9 Under **What sort order do you want for your records?**, click the **sort box arrow**, and then click **Lastname**. Click **Next**.

10 Under **Orientation**, click **Landscape**, and then click **Next**. Under **What title do you want for the report?**, select the existing text, type **Lastname Firstname Students Report** and then click **Finish**. Compare your screen with Figure 6.14.

The report displays in Print Preview.

Integrated Projects | Integrating Publisher and Access

Figure 6.14

Lastname Firstname Students Report

Sorted by Lastname in ascending order

11 Click the **File tab**, verify the **Info tab** is selected, and then at the right of your screen, click **View and edit database properties**. In the **Properties** dialog box, on the **Summary tab**, in the **Subject** box, type your course name and section number, in the **Author** box, type your firstname and lastname, and then in the **Keywords** box, type **students, contact info** Click **OK** to close the dialog box.

12 Click the **Print Preview tab**. If your instructor directs you to submit your files electronically, go to Step 13.

13 To print the report, on the **Print Preview tab**, in the **Print group**, click the **Print** button, and then click **OK**.

14 Right-click the **Lastname Firstname Students Report tab**, and then on the shortcut menu, click **Close All**. If a message box displays, click **Yes** to save the changes to the design of the report.

15 **Close** ![X] Access.

Activity 6.10 | Importing and Sorting a Recipient List from Access

You can import a recipient list to a new or existing publication. You can use an Outlook Contact list, an Excel workbook, a Word table, an Access database, or a text file as the data source for the recipient list. In this activity, you will import a recipient list from an Access database.

1 With your newsletter displayed, if necessary, in the **Page Navigation** pane, click **Page 2**. Click the **Mailings tab**. In the **Start group**, click the **Mail Merge button arrow**, and then click **Step by Step Mail Merge Wizard**.

The Mail Merge task pane displays.

2 In the **Mail Merge** task pane, under **Create recipient list**, verify that the **Use an existing list** option button is selected. At the bottom of the task pane, click **Next: Create or connect to a recipient list**.

3 In the **Select Data Source** dialog box, navigate to your **Integrated Projects Chapter 6** folder, select your Access file **Lastname_Firstname_6A_Student_Data**, and then click **Open** to display the **Mail Merge Recipients** dialog box. Compare your screen with Figure 6.15.

> The records from the Students table in your database display. The Mail Merge Recipients dialog box contains options for sorting and filtering the records.

Figure 6.15

Mail Merge
Recipients dialog box

4 In the **Mail Merge Recipients** dialog box, under **Refine recipient list**, click **Sort**. In the **Filter and Sort** dialog box, click the **Sort by arrow**, scroll down, and then click **Degree**. Verify that the **Ascending** option is selected, and then click **OK**. In the **Mail Merge Recipients** dialog box, scroll right to display the **Degree** field and then compare your screen with Figure 6.16.

Figure 6.16

Recipients in ascending
order by Degree

Sort link

5 In the **Mail Merge Recipients** dialog box, click **OK**. On **Page 2** of your publication, near the top right, click the text box containing the text that begins *Type address here*. Press Ctrl + A to select the entire paragraph, and then press Del.

6 In the **Mail Merge** task pane, under **More items**, click **Address block**. In the **Insert Address Block** dialog box, under **Specify address elements**, verify that the format **Joshua Randall Jr.** is selected, and then click **OK**.

> The Address Block merge field displays in the text box. Recall that when you insert a merge field, the field name is always surrounded by double angle brackets (<< >>).

Integrated Projects | Integrating Publisher and Access

304

7 On the **Mailings tab**, in the **Preview Results group**, click the **Preview Results** button to turn on the feature.

> Your name displays in the newsletter. Recall that you sorted the recipients by degree; because your degree program is Accounting, your name displays as the first record.

8 Save ⊟ the newsletter.

9 On the **Mailing tab**, in the **Preview Results group**, click the **Preview Results** button to turn off the feature.

Objective 4 | Insert Access Data Fields into a Publication

In addition to using the Mail Merge feature to insert the recipient's name and address, you can further personalize documents by inserting data fields. Most people appreciate mailings that include specific information related to their interests. These mailings help to build loyalty between an individual and the organization. In order to personalize a publication, you must have the information stored in a data source, such as Access.

Activity 6.11 | Inserting Data Fields

In your newsletter, you will insert the degree program in which each student is enrolled.

1 At the bottom right of your screen, on the Status bar, change the **Zoom level** to **80%**. Scroll to the bottom left of **Page 2**, and then click the paragraph that begins *We are pleased to inform you*. Press Ctrl + A to select all of the text in the text box. Click the **Home tab**, in the **Font group**, click the **Font Size button arrow** [10 ▾], and then click **12**.

> In the original publication, a link was created between the left text box and the right text box. When you increased the font size, the excess text that did not fit in the left text box was automatically inserted in the right text box.

2 In the text box, click at the end of the first paragraph, which ends *state of Florida*, and then press Enter. On the **Mail Merge** task pane, under **Prepare your publication**, click **Firstname**, type a comma, and then press Spacebar.

> The Firstname merge field is inserted in the newsletter.

3 Type **we see from your application that you are interested in the** and then press Spacebar.

4 In the **Mail Merge** task pane, under **Prepare your publication**, scroll down, click **Degree**, and then press Spacebar. Type **degree. This is an excellent program with superior instructors. Many of our instructors maintain business relationships with industry connections to stay current in their field. This is beneficial as it helps to provide contacts for student internships as well as future jobs.** Compare your screen with Figure 6.17.

> An *overflow* icon displays near the bottom right corner of the textbox. Overflow is text that does not fit within a text box. The text is hidden until it can be linked to flow into a new text box or until the existing text box is resized.

Figure 6.17

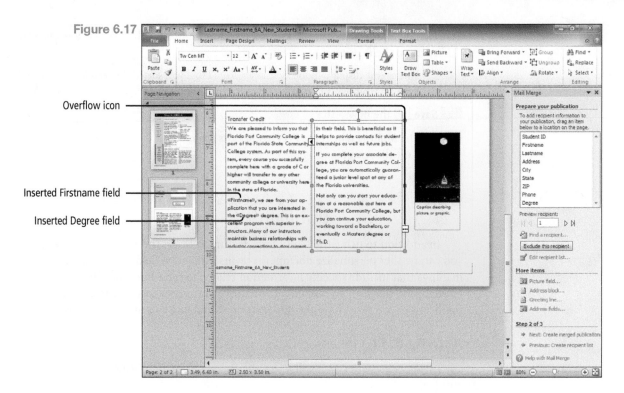

Overflow icon

Inserted Firstname field

Inserted Degree field

5 On **Page 2**, in the lower right corner, click the picture. Right-click the picture, and then on the shortcut menu, click **Delete Object**. Click in the text box with the paragraph that begins *We are pleased*. Click the **Text Box Tools Format tab**, and then in the **Linking group**, click the **Break** button. To the right of the existing text, right-click in the empty text box, and then on the shortcut menu, click **Cut**.

> Breaking the link causes the overflow text to be attached to the text box on the left. This action enabled you to cut the left text box without deleting any existing text.

6 Right-click the text box at the lower left corner of the page, and then on the shortcut menu, click **Format Text Box**. In the **Format Text Box** dialog box, click the **Size tab**. Under **Size and rotate**, delete the number in the **Width** box, type **6.5** and then click **OK**.

7 In the **Mail Merge** task pane, under **Step 2 of 3**, click **Next: Create merged publication**.

8 In the **Mail Merge** task pane, under **Create merged publications**, click **Print preview**. Below the **Print Preview**, in the navigation area, if necessary, click the **Next** button ▶ to display **Page 2**. At the bottom right corner of the window, change **the Zoom level** to **80%**. Compare your screen with Figure 6.18.

> Your name displays in the address block field. In the inserted paragraph, your first name displays in the Firstname field and Accounting displays in the Degree field

Figure 6.18

Address block displays
your name

Accounting degree displays

Your first name displays

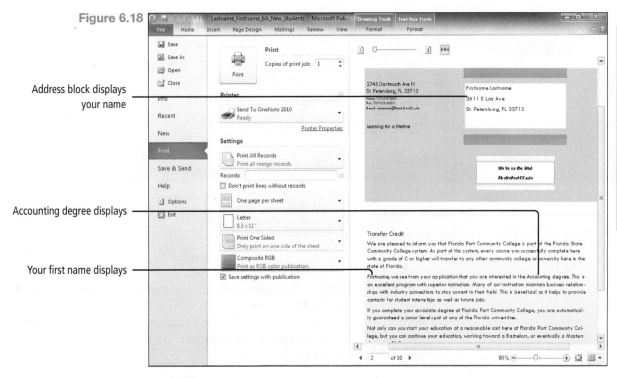

[9] Click the **Insert tab,** and then **Save** 💾 the newsletter.

Activity 6.12 | Completing and Printing the Merged Newsletter

When you complete the mail merge, a number of personalized documents are created within the file. You can print one or all of the documents.

[1] In the **Mail Merge** task pane, under **Create merged publications,** click **Merge to a new publication.**

> Eight newsletters—16 pages—are created. After completing the merge, the new publication is no longer connected to the data source.

[2] In the merged document, on the **Insert tab,** in the **Header & Footer group,** click the **Footer** button. In the footer, double-click the word **New,** and then type **Merged** On the **Master Page tab,** in the **Close group,** click the **Close Master Page** button.

> The footer *Lastname_Firstname_6A_Merged_Students* displays on all pages of the publication.

[3] In the **Mail Merge** task pane, under **Merged publication pages,** click **Save this publication.** In the **Save As** dialog box, navigate to your **Integrated Projects Chapter 6** folder. In the **File name** box, delete the existing text, type **Lastname_Firstname_6A_Merged_Students** and then click **Save.**

[4] **Close** ☒ the **Mail Merge** task pane. In the **Page Navigation** pane, click **Page 2** of the first newsletter. Scroll to display the top of the page, and then compare your screen with Figure 6.19.

> Your name displays in the address text box.

Figure 6.19

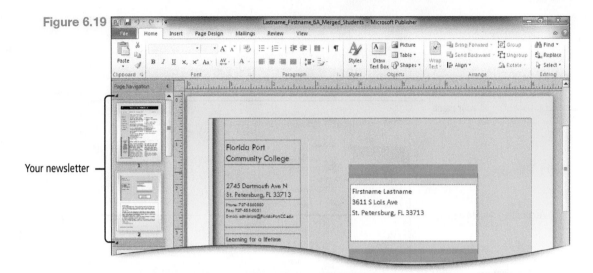

Your newsletter

5 Click the **File tab**, verify the **Info tab** is selected, click **Publication Properties**, and then click **Advanced Properties**. In the **Properties** dialog box, on the **Summary tab**, in the **Subject** box, type your course name and section number, in the **Author** box, type your firstname and lastname, and then in the **Keywords** box, type **student newsletter, merged** Click **OK** to close the dialog box.

6 Click the **Home tab**, and then **Save** 🖫 the newsletter. If your instructor directs you to submit your files electronically, go to Step 8.

7 To print your publication, click the **File tab** and then click the **Print tab**. Under **Settings**, click the **Print All Pages arrow**, and then click **Print Custom Pages**. In the **Pages** box, type **1-2** and then click **Print**.

8 **Close** ⊠ the **Lastname_Firstname_6A_Merged_Students** publication. With the **Lastname_Firstname_6A_New_Students** publication displayed, **Save** 🖫 the file, and then **Close** ⊠ Publisher.

9 Submit your printed or electronic files as direct by your instructor.

End You have completed Project 6A ————————————

Project 6B Internship Postcard

Project Activities

In Activities 6.13 through 6.22, you will add an input mask and a default value to Access data fields. After creating a lookup field and entering data, you will create a report. In Publisher, you will use a template to create a postcard. Finally, using Mail Merge, you will create postcards for specific recipients. Your completed files will look similar to Figure 6.20.

Project Files

For Project 6B, you will need the following files:

New blank Publisher publication
New blank Access database
i06B_FPCC_Logo

You will save your files as:

Lastname_Firstname_6B_FPCC_Students
Lastname_Firstname_6B_Technology_Postcard
Lastname_Firstname_6B_Internship_Postcard

Project Results

Figure 6.20
Project 6B Internship Postcard

Objective 5 | Set Field Properties in an Access Table

Recall that the structure of an Access table is the underlying design, including field names and data types. When you create an Access database, you can improve your data entry accuracy by setting *field properties*—characteristics of a field that control how the field displays and how data can be entered in the field.

Activity 6.13 | Inserting an Input Mask and a Default Value

You should set field properties before you enter any data in a table. If you change field properties after you have entered records in your table, you might lose some of the data. In this activity, you will set field properties for the ID, Phone, and State fields of a table.

1 **Start** Access. Under **Available Templates**, verify **Blank database** is selected. In the lower right portion of the screen, click the **Browse** button 📖. In the **File New Database** dialog box, navigate to your **Integrated Projects Chapter 6** folder. In the **File name** box, if necessary select the existing text, type **Lastname_Firstname_6B_FPCC_Students** and then click **OK**. In the lower right corner of the screen, click the **Create** button.

Access creates a new database and opens a table named Table1 in Datasheet view.

2 At the top of the second column, click the text *Click to Add* to display a list of data types.

Recall that a data type is the characteristic that defines the kind of data that can be entered in a field, such as numbers, text, or dates.

3 In the list of data types, click **Text**, and notice that in the second column, the text *Click to Add* changes to *Field1*, which is selected. Type **Firstname** and then press Enter.

The second column displays *Firstname* as the field name, and the data type list displays in the third column.

4 In the data type list, click **Text**, type **Lastname** and then press Enter. In a similar manner, add each of the following fields to the table, selecting the **Text** data type.

Address
City
State
ZIP
Phone
Birth Date
Degree

5 Click the **Birth Date** field. On the **Fields tab**, in the **Formatting group**, locate the **Data Type** box, and notice that the data type Text displays. Click the **Data Type box arrow**, and then click **Date/Time**.

When a table includes a field for entering dates, it is good practice to assign the Date/Time data type to the field. The data type determines the value that can be stored and the operations that can be performed.

6 Click the **ID** field. On the **Fields tab**, in the **Formatting group**, locate the **Data Type** box, and notice that the data type AutoNumber displays. Click the **Data Type box arrow**, and then click **Text**.

By default, when creating a new database, Access assigns the AutoNumber data type to the default ID field. It is necessary to change the data type because students are assigned IDs in a specific format.

Integrated Projects | Integrating Publisher and Access

310

7 On the **Fields tab**, in the **Views group**, click the **View** button to change to Design view. In the **Save As** dialog box, type **All FPCC Students** and then click **OK**.

8 Under **Field Name**, click **Phone**, and then in the lower portion of the screen, **Field Properties** area, click the **Input Mask** property box.

An *input mask* is a set of literal characters and placeholder characters that control what can and cannot be entered in an Access field. Use an input mask whenever you want users to enter data in a specific way.

9 On the right side of the **Input Mask** property box, click the **Build** button 🔲. In the **Input Mask Wizard** dialog box, under **Input Mask**, verify that **Phone Number** is selected, and then click **Finish**. **Save** 🔲 the table, and then compare your screen with Figure 6.21.

The input mask displays in the Field Properties area. A 0 placeholder indicates a required digit, and a 9 placeholder indicates an optional digit or space. The area code is enclosed in parentheses and a hyphen (-) separates the three-digit prefix from the four-digit number. The exclamation point (!) at the left of the input mask causes the field to be filled in from left to right. The field will display an underscore character (_) for each digit.

Figure 6.21

Phone field name selected

Field Properties area

Input mask

10 Under **Field Name**, click **ID**, and then in the **Field Properties** area, click the **Input Mask** property box. Type **12-0000000** and then press Enter. Compare your screen with Figure 6.22.

The input mask for the ID field displays. All student ID numbers begin with 12-. By typing 12- in the input mask, you will only need to type the unique seven-digit portion of each student's ID number. An input mask can be a *validation rule*—limiting or controlling what users can enter in a field. By using validation rules, data entry errors can be reduced.

Figure 6.22

ID field name selected

Birth Date data type

Input mask

---

11 Under **Field Name**, click **State**, and then in the **Field Properties** area, click the **Default Value** property box. Type **FL** and then press Enter.

Access automatically inserts quotes around the text you just typed, indicating that the default text FL will display in the State field. In an Access table, a ***default value*** is the data that is automatically entered in a field. If most of the records will have the same value for a particular field, creating a default value means you only need to enter data if it differs from the default value. In this case, because most of the students live in Florida, it makes sense to use the default value FL.

12 On the **Design tab**, in the **Views group**, click the **View** button to change to Datasheet view. In the message box, click **Yes** to save the table. Notice the State field displays FL as the default value.

Activity 6.14 | Modifying the Field Properties

When you assign data types to fields, specific field properties, such as format and ***field size*** are defined. A field size is the maximum number of characters you can enter in a field. You can modify these properties to suit your needs.

1 In the **Views group**, click the **View** button to change to Design view.

2 Under **Field Name**, click **Birth Date**. In the **Field Properties** area, click the **Format** property box, and then click the **Format arrow** to display various date and time formats. In the list, click the **Short Date** format, and then compare your screen with Figure 6.23.

The term Short Date displays in the Format property box. When a date is entered, it will display as mm/dd/yyyy. In the Field Property area, the last item—Show Date Picker— displays the property *For dates*. The ***date picker*** is a calendar control that is used to select a date. When entering a date in the Birth Date field, the Date Picker icon will display to the right of a cell. Clicking the Date Picker icon displays a calendar and allows the user to quickly select a date.

Integrated Projects | Integrating Publisher and Access

Figure 6.23

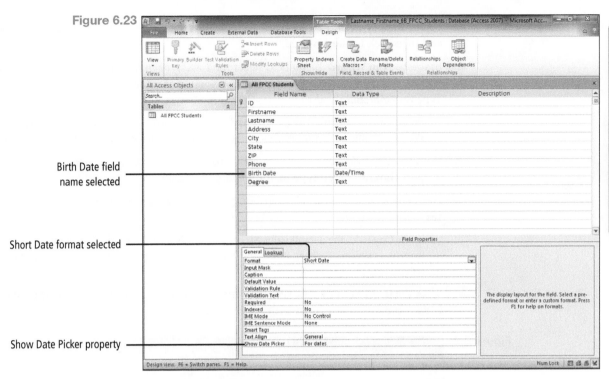

Birth Date field name selected

Short Date format selected

Show Date Picker property

3 Under **Field Name**, click **Firstname**, and then in the **Field Properties** area, click the **Field Size** property box. Select the number *255*, type **30** and then press Enter.

Recall that field size is the maximum number of characters you can enter in the field. You changed the Firstname field to 30 because you do not expect any student to have a first name longer than 30 characters.

4 Under **Field Name**, click **Lastname**, and then in the **Field Properties** area, click **Field Size**. Select the number *255*, type **30** and then press Enter.

5 Using the same technique, change the field size of the following fields.

Field Name	ID	Address	City	State	ZIP	Phone	Degree
Field Size	10	60	50	2	10	10	50

6 **Save** the table.

More Knowledge | Entering Data in a Table

If you have valid data in a field that contains more characters than allowed by the field size property, change to Design view, increase the Field Size for the field, change back to Datasheet view, and then continue entering your data.

Activity 6.15 | Inserting a Lookup Field

The ***Lookup Wizard*** creates a list box to look up a value in another table, a query, or a list of values. Most of the students at Florida Port Community College live in either Tampa or St. Petersburg. Using a list box for the City field will minimize the amount of typing when entering the student records.

1 Under **Data Type**, in the **City** field, click the **Text** data type, click the **Data Type arrow**, and then click **Lookup Wizard**.

2 In the **Lookup Wizard** dialog box, select the *I will type in the values that I want* option button, and then click **Next**. Verify that the **Number of columns** is **1**, and then press `Tab`. Type **St. Petersburg** and then press `Tab`. Type **Tampa** and then click **Finish**.

> Because many students live in St. Petersburg and Tampa, these cities are added to a list. When entering data, you can choose the city from a list instead of typing the entire name.

3 With the **City** field selected, in the **Field Properties** area, click the **Default Value** property box, and then type **St. Petersburg**

4 On the **Design tab**, in the **Views group**, click the **View** button. In the message box, click **Yes** to save the table.

> In the City field, the default value St. Petersburg displays. Since most of the students are from St. Petersburg, setting this as the default value will save time when entering student records.

5 Click the first cell under the **City** field, and then click the arrow to display the list of cities. Compare your screen with Figure 6.24.

Figure 6.24

List of cities

6 Right-click the **All FPCC Students table tab**, and then on the shortcut menu, click **Close**.

7 If necessary, in the Navigation Pane, click the All FPCC Students table to select it. Click the **Create tab**, and then in the **Forms group**, click the **Form** button.

8 In the **Views group**, click the **View** button to display the form in Form view. **Close** [«] the Navigation Pane.

Activity 6.16 | Inputting Data with a Lookup Field

1 In the **ID** field, type **5** and then press `Tab`. Compare your screen with Figure 6.25.

> A message box displays indicating that the value you entered is not appropriate for the input mask you created. Recall that you are required to enter seven digits in the ID field—one for each zero in the input mask. The input mask does automatically display *12-* to the left of any number you type, in this case 5.

Integrated Projects | Integrating Publisher and Access

Figure 6.25

5 entered in ID field

Message box indicates error

2 In the message box, click **OK**. In the **ID** field, with the insertion point to the right of 5, type **223461** and then press [Tab].

3 In the **Firstname** field, type **Frieda** and then press [Tab]. In the **Lastname** field, type **Ginsburg** and then press [Tab]. In the **Address** field, type **9506 N 13th St** and then press [Tab] three times.

> Because you used the Lookup Wizard to create a list and set St. Petersburg as the default value, you can skip the City field for St. Petersburg address when entering the student records by pressing [Tab] to move to the next field. Additionally, because you inserted FL as the default value for the State field, you can skip that field by pressing [Tab] to move to the next field.

4 In the **ZIP** field, type **33714** and then press [Tab]. In the **Phone** field, type **7275556632** and then press [Tab].

> Because you set up the phone input mask, you do not need to type the parentheses, the dash, or any spaces.

5 In the **Birth Date** field, type **5/9/93** and then compare your screen with Figure 6.26.

> You could click the Date Picker icon, which displays to the right of the Birth Date field, to select the date; however, you would be navigating through a large number of years. In this case, typing the date is a faster way to input the data.

Figure 6.26

ID entered

Date Picker icon

Birth Date entered

6 Press Tab, and then in the **Degree** field, type **Information Technology**

> The date is accepted, and Access automatically adjusts the date to 5/9/1993 to match the Short Date format property you set for the Birth Date field.

7 Press Tab to accept the student record and to move to the next new record.

8 In the **ID** field, type **4881127** and then press Tab. In the **Firstname** field, type **Michael** and then press Tab. In the **Lastname** field, type **Stober** and then press Tab. In the **Address** field type **828 Raysbrook Dr** and then press Tab

9 In the **City** field, type the letter **t** and then compare your screen with Figure 6.27.

> The city name tampa displays in the City field. A list item will display in the field when you type the first letter of an item in the list. You do not need to capitalize the letter—when you move to the next field, the first letter will be capitalized because that is the way the item was entered in your list. This feature makes data entry faster.

Figure 6.27

tampa displays —

10 Press Tab two times. In the **ZIP** field, type **33621** and then press Tab. In the **Phone** field, type **8135550031** and then press Tab. In the **Birth Date** field, type **11/26/89** and then press Tab.

11 In the **Degree** field, type **Accounting** and then press Tab to accept the record and move to the next new record.

12 Using the same technique, enter the following student records. For the last student, type your first name and last name. Press Tab after entering your Degree to accept the record. Note: Because all the students are from Florida, the State field is not listed in the following table; press Tab to skip the State field and accept FL.

Integrated Projects | Integrating Publisher and Access

ID	Firstname	Lastname	Address	City	ZIP	Phone	Birth Date	Degree
7820522	Jeff	Paolino	11008 Connacht Way	St. Petersburg	33713	7275550895	5/7/90	Radiation Therapy
4637811	Reva	Lanter	12825 Astonwood Dr	St. Petersburg	33709	7275555936	8/13/84	Accounting
6488259	Casey	Creeden	5502 Terrace Ct	St. Petersburg	33708	7275554926	9/12/91	Nursing
1184755	Ellen	Gula	10200 N Armenia Ave	St. Petersburg	33709	7275550137	4/28/86	Information Technology
1849915	Araceli	Saine	1326 New Bedford Dr	Tampa	33605	8135555832	12/27/80	Nursing
8335796	Sandy	Elzy	1910 S 47th St	St. Petersburg	33708	7275555637	3/28/92	Radiation Therapy
6184273	Firstname	Lastname	1003 Vista Cay Ct	St. Petersburg	33713	7275550361	10/12/84	Information Technology

13 At the bottom of your screen, in the navigation area, click the **Previous record** button ◀ to check all the data in each of the nine records and correct any data entry errors.

14 Right-click the **All FPCC Students form tab**, and then on the shortcut menu, click **Save**. In the **Save As** dialog box, under **Form Name**, type **All FPCC Students Form** and then click **OK**.

15 Right-click the **All FPCC Students Form tab**, and then on the shortcut menu, click **Close**.

Activity 6.17 | Grouping and Sorting in the Blank Report Tool

The *Blank Report tool* allows you to create a report from scratch by adding the fields you designate in the order you want them to display. This tool provides a quick way to build a report, especially if you are including only a few fields. In this activity, you will create a report listing the FPCC students—grouped by their degree program and sorted in ascending order by last name.

1 On the **Create tab**, in the **Reports group**, click the **Blank Report** button.

2 If necessary, on the **Design tab**, in the **Tools group**, click the **Add Existing Fields** button to display the Field List pane. In the **Field List** pane, click **Show all tables**, and then click the **plus sign** (+) next to **All FPCC Students**. In the **Field List** pane, double-click the field **Firstname**, and then compare your screen with Figure 6.28.

The Firstname field is added to the report.

Figure 6.28

Add Existing Fields button

Field List

Firstname field

3 In the **Field List** pane, double-click the fields **Lastname**, **Phone**, and **Degree** to add the fields to the report.

4 On the **Design tab**, in the **Grouping & Totals group**, click the **Group & Sort** button. Compare your screen with Figure 6.29.

The Group, Sort, and Total pane displays below the report. The pane contains an Add a group button and an Add a sort button.

Figure 6.29

Group & Sort button

Group, Sort, and Total pane

Add a group button

Add a sort button

5 Click the **Add a group** button, and then click **Degree**.

The Degree field moves to the left of the report; the students are grouped in ascending order by their degrees. *Grouping* enables you to separate groups of records visually and to display introductory and summary data for each group in a report.

6 Click the **Add a sort** button, and then click **Lastname**. Compare your screen with Figure 6.30.

The students are listed by the Degree field, and then within the Degree field, the students are sorted in ascending order by the Lastname field.

Figure 6.30

Grouped by Degree

Sorted by Lastname

7 On the **Design tab**, in the **Grouping & Totals group**, click the **Group & Sort** button to close the Group, Sort, and Total pane.

8 **Close** ☒ the Field List pane.

9 On the **Design tab**, in the **Tools group**, click the **Property Sheet** button to display the Property Sheet pane.

The *Property Sheet* is a list of characteristics—properties—for fields or controls on a form or report in which you can make precise changes to each property associated with the field or control.

10 In the report, click the **Degree** field name. In the **Property Sheet** pane, click the **Format tab**. In the **Width** box, select the number, type **2** and then press Enter. Compare your screen with Figure 6.31.

The width of the Degree column in the report is increased to 2 inches.

Figure 6.31

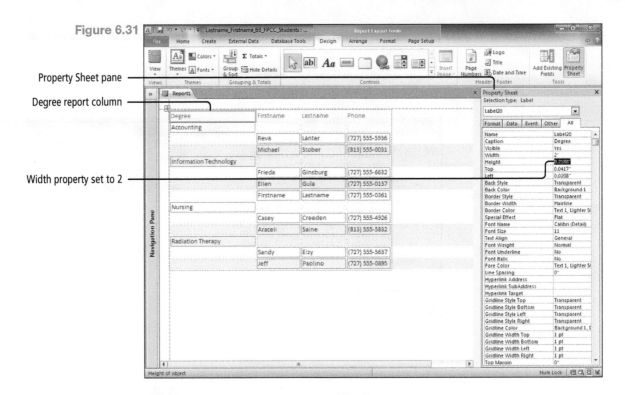

Property Sheet pane

Degree report column

Width property set to 2

11 In the report, click the field name **Firstname**, hold down Ctrl and then click the field names **Lastname** and **Phone**. In the **Property Sheet** pane, in the **Width** box, type **1.5** and then press Enter. **Close** ✕ the Property Sheet pane.

All three columns are widened to 1.5 inches.

12 On the Quick Access toolbar, click **Save** 🖫. In the **Save As** dialog box, type **Lastname Firstname Students by Degree** and then click **OK**.

13 On the **Design tab**, in the **Header/Footer group**, click the **Title** button.

The title displays at the top of the page in the *report header*. The report header is information printed once at the beginning of a report; it is used for logos, titles, and dates.

14 On the **Design tab**, and then in the **Themes group**, click the **Themes** button. In the **Themes** gallery, under **Built-In**, in the fourth row, click the third theme—**Equity**.

15 In the report, click the field name **Degree**, hold down Shift and then click the field name **Phone**. With all four field names selected, click the **Format tab**. In the **Font group**, click the **Background Color** button 🎨▾, and then under **Theme Colors**, in the eighth column, click the first color—**Brown, Accent 4**. Click the **Font Color button arrow** ▲▾, and then under **Theme Colors**, click the first color—**White, Background 1**.

16 In the report, click **Accounting**, hold down Shift, and then click **Radiation Therapy**. With all four fields selected, in the **Font group**, click the **Font Color button arrow** ▲▾, and then under **Theme Colors**, in the eighth column, click the first color—**Brown, Accent 4**.

17 Click the **Home tab**. In the **Views group**, click the **View button arrow**, and then click **Print Preview**. Compare your screen with Figure 6.32.

Figure 6.32

Report title

Field names formatted

Degree names formatted

18 From **Backstage** view, click **View and edit database properties**. In the **Properties** dialog box, on the **Summary** tab, in the **Subject** box, type your course name and section number, in the **Author** box, type your firstname and lastname, and then in the **Keywords** box, type **report, phone, degree** Click **OK** to close the dialog box, and then click the **Home tab**. If your instructor directs you to submit your files electronically, go to step 18.

19 To print the report, on the **Print Preview tab**, in the **Print group**, click the **Print** button, and then click **OK**.

20 Right-click the **Lastname Firstname Students by Degree report tab**, and then on the shortcut menu, click **Close**. In the message box, click **Yes** to save the changes to the design of the report. **Close** [X] Access.

Objective 6 | Create a Publication Using a Publisher Template

Creating a publication is easy when you use a template. Recall that a template is a preformatted publication designed for a specific purpose. There are templates to match almost any publication need. You can use a Publisher template installed on your computer, or you can download a template from Microsoft Office Online.

Activity 6.18 | Using a Publication Template

Brad Futral, the Director of the Student Job Placement Office, has arranged a job fair for technology students. He has asked you to create a postcard to remind them to attend the job fair.

1 **Start** Publisher. From **Backstage** view, under **Available Templates**, with **Installed and Online Templates** displayed, click the arrow, and then click **Installed Templates**. Under **Most Popular**, click **Postcards**, and then under **Marketing**, click **Arrows**. At the right, under **Customize**, click the **Color scheme box arrow**, and then click **Marine**. At the lower right corner of the dialog box, click **Create**.

A new publication based on the Arrows postcard template is created.

2 Click the **File tab**, and then click the **Save As tab**. In the **Save As** dialog box, navigate to your **Integrated Projects Chapter 6** folder, and then save the file as **Lastname_Firstname_6B_Internship_Postcard** Compare your screen with Figure 6.33.

Notice default text for contact information displays on the right side of Page 1.

Figure 6.33

Arrows postcard ——

Default contact information ——

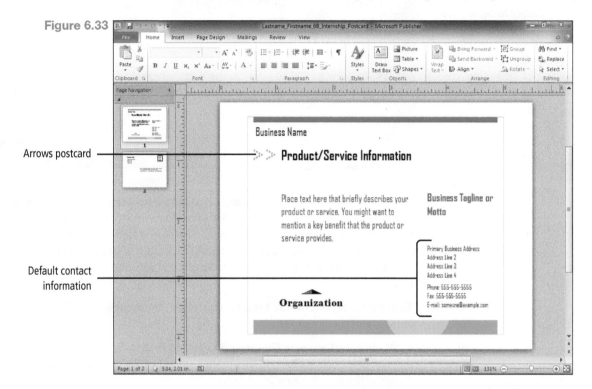

3 Click the **Insert tab**, and then in the **Header & Footer group**, click the **Footer** button. In the **Footer** text box, type **Lastname Firstname 6B Internship Postcard** and then on the **Master Page tab**, in the **Close group**, click the **Close Master Page** button.

Activity 6.19 | Inserting Business Information

A *business information set* is a customized group of information—including items such as a company name, address, phone number, e-mail address, and logo—that can be used to quickly fill in appropriate places in a publication.

Another Way

Click the Information SmartTag above the contact information text box, and then click Edit Business Information.

1 Click the **Insert tab**. In the **Text group**, click the **Business Information** button, and then near the bottom of the list, click **Edit Business Information**.

The Create New Business Information Set dialog box displays.

2 In the **Create New Business Information Set** dialog box, under **Individual name**, select the text, and then type **Brad Futral** Under **Job position or title**, select the text, and then type **Director, Student Job Placement**.

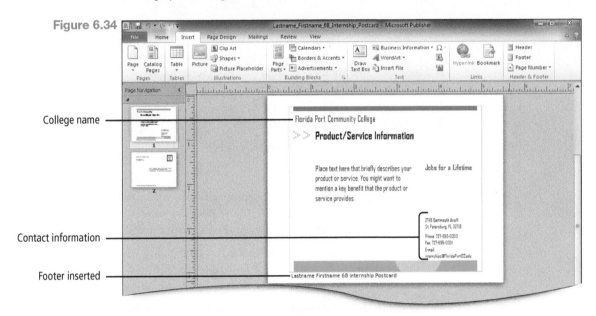

3 Under **Organization name**, select the text, and then type **Florida Port Community College** Under **Address**, select all the text, type **2745 Dartmouth Ave N** and then press Enter. Type **St. Petersburg, FL 33713** Under **Phone, fax and e-mail**, select the phone number, and then type **727-555-0030** Select the fax number, and then type **727-555-0031** Select the e-mail address, and then type **internships@FloridaPortCC.edu**

4 Under **Tagline or motto**, select the text *Business Tagline or Motto*, and then type **Jobs for a Lifetime** Under the default logo—Organization, click **Remove**, and then in the message box, click **Yes** to remove the logo.

5 In the **Business Information set name** box, select the text, type **Futral** and then click **Save**.

6 In the **Business Information** dialog box, click **Update Publication**, and then compare your screen with Figure 6.34.

> Notice the college name displays at the top of Page 1, and the new contact information displays at the right.

Figure 6.34

College name

Contact information

Footer inserted

7 On **Page 1**, click the heading **Product/Service Information**, and then type **Technology Internships**

8 With the text box selected, click the **Drawing Tools Format tab**, and in the **Size group**, click the **Shape Height** box, type **0.4** and then press Enter.

9 In the middle of the page, click the text box containing the paragraph that begins *Place text here*. Point to the border to display the pointer, and then drag the text box so the top left corner is located at approximately **0.75 inches on the horizontal ruler** and **1.25 inches on the vertical ruler**. Click the **Drawing Tools tab**, and in the **Size group**, click the **Shape Height** box, type **1.8** and then press Enter. Click in the text box, and then click the **Text Box Tools Format tab**. In the **Text group**, click the **Text Fit** button, and then click **Shrink Text on Overflow**.

> The Shrink Text on Overflow feature will automatically change the font size to accommodate the text that is typed in the text box.

10 With the entire paragraph that begins *Place text here* selected, type **We are pleased to announce the Summer Technology Internship Fair to be held at the Student Union in Ballroom C on Thursday, February 19th. This is an opportunity for all FPCC Technology students to meet potential employers for a summer internship and for possible full-time employment when you have graduated. Remember to stop by the Student Job Placement Office, or go to our Web page and sign up for a Resume Writing workshop.**

> Notice that as you type the font size is reduced to allow all the text to display in the text box.

11 Click the **Review tab**, and then in the **Proofing group**, click the **Spelling** button. Continue to check the spelling in your publication until a message box displays *The spelling check is complete*, and then click **OK**.

12 Save the publication.

Objective 7 | Modify the Layout of a Publication

Clip art, building blocks, and other images can add interest and focus to a publication. You can position these objects in an exact location in the publication when you use the *layout guides*. Layout guides are nonprinting lines that mark the margins, columns, rows, and baselines and are used to align the text, pictures, and other objects so that your publication has balance and uniformity.

Activity 6.20 | Inserting Images

In this activity, you will insert the college logo and clip art from the Publisher collection.

1 Click the **Insert tab**. In the **Text group**, click the **Business Information** button, and then click **Edit Business Information**. In the **Business Information** dialog box, under **Select a Business Information set**, verify that *Futral* displays, and then click **Edit**.

2 In the **Edit Business Information Set** dialog box, click the **Add logo** button. Navigate to the location of the student data files, select the file **i06B_FPCC_Logo**, and then click **Insert**. In the **Edit Business Information Set** dialog box, click **Save**.

3 In the **Business Information** dialog box, click **Update Publication**.

> The logo displays at the bottom left of Page 1.

4 Click the logo, and then click the **Picture Tools Format tab**. In the **Size group**, click the **Shape Height** box, type **0.5** and then press Enter. Click in the **Shape Width** box, type **1** and then press Enter. In the **Arrange group**, click the **Bring Forward button arrow**, and then click **Bring to Front**. Compare your screen with Figure 6.35.

Figure 6.35

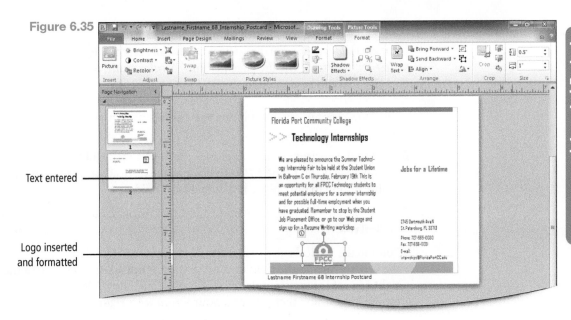

Text entered

Logo inserted
and formatted

5 In the **Page Navigation** pane, click **Page 2**. Click the **Insert tab**, and then in the **Illustrations group**, click the **Clip Art** button. In the **Clip Art** task pane, verify that *All media file types* displays. If necessary, to the left of **Include Office.com** content, click the check box to select it. In the **Search for** box, type **instructor** and then click **Go**. Scroll as necessary to locate the image as shown in Figure 6.36, and then click the image. If you cannot locate this image, select another appropriate image.

The selected clip art is inserted in the publication.

Figure 6.36

Instructor clip art selected

Instructor clip art inserted

6 Click in a blank area of the page. Click the **Page Design tab**, and then in the **Page Background group**, click the **Background** button. In the **Background** gallery, under **Solid Background**, in the second row, right-click the second background—**30% tint of Accent 2**, and then on the shortcut menu, click **Apply to All Pages**.

The background is applied to both pages of the publication.

7 **Close** ⊠ the task pane and **Save** 🖫 the publication.

Project 6B: Internship Postcard | **Integrated Projects**

Activity 6.21 | Using Layout Guides

Margin guides are nonprinting lines on the top, bottom, left, and right sides of the page that are used to define the page margins. A *ruler guide* is a nonprinting horizontal or vertical line that can be aligned to any position on the ruler.

1 Click the **View tab**, and then in the **Show group**, verify that the **Guides** check box is selected.

2 Point to the horizontal ruler to display the ⊞ pointer. Hold down the left mouse button, drag down to the **3.75 inch mark on the vertical rule**, and then release the mouse button to display the horizontal ruler guide.

3 Using the same technique, position another horizontal guide at the **3 inch mark on the vertical rule**.

4 Point to the vertical ruler to display the ⊞ pointer. Hold down Shift, and then drag the vertical ruler to the right of the 0 to the **0.5 inch mark on the horizontal ruler**. The right edge of the vertical ruler should be touching the 0.5 inch mark. Release the mouse button, and then compare your screen with Figure 6.37.

> The vertical ruler moves to the new location. You can be more precise when the ruler is closer to the objects in your publication.

Figure 6.37

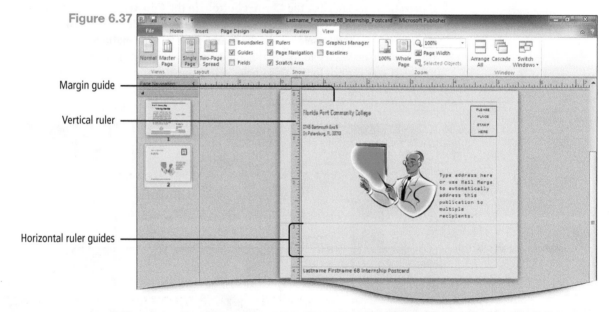

Margin guide

Vertical ruler

Horizontal ruler guides

5 Point to the clip art until the ⊞ pointer displays. Drag the clip art down and to the left until the bottom left corner is at **3.75 inches on the vertical ruler** and **0.5 inches on the horizontal ruler**.

> The clip art should be touching both the lower horizontal ruler guide and the vertical ruler.

6 With the clip art selected, point to the top right sizing handle until the ⊞ pointer displays, and then drag to decrease the size of the clip art so the top right corner is touching the horizontal ruler guide at **3 inches on the vertical ruler**. Compare your screen with Figure 6.40.

7 With the clip art selected, click the **Picture Tools Format tab**. In the **Picture Styles group**, click the **Picture Border button arrow** ⊞, and then under **Scheme Colors**, in the second column, click the first color—**Accent 1 (RGB (0,51.204))**.

Integrated Projects | Integrating Publisher and Access

326

8 In the **Arrange group**, click the **Rotate** button 🖼, and then click **Flip Horizontal**. Compare your screen with Figure 6.38.

The clip art has been flipped, and the instructor is facing the opposite direction.

Figure 6.38

Clip art flipped and border added
Clip art touching vertical ruler
Clip art touching both horizontal guides

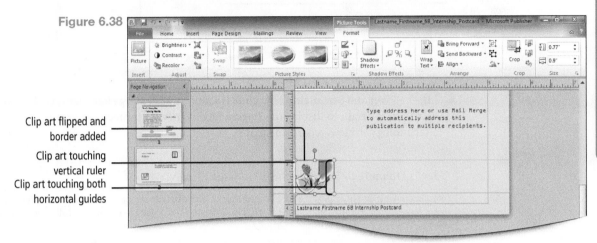

9 On **Page 2**, right-click the lower horizontal ruler guide, and then on the shortcut menu, click **Delete Guide**. Using the same technique, delete the other horizontal ruler guide. Point to vertical ruler to display the ⟨╫⟩ pointer, and then hold down ⟨Shift⟩ and drag to the left to position the ruler to the left of 0 at the **0.5 inch mark on the horizontal ruler**. The right edge of the ruler should be touching the 0.5 inch mark.

Because you are not finished with the publication, it is helpful to position the vertical ruler to the left of the page. When you exit Publisher, and then reopen the application, the ruler is automatically restored to its default position.

10 Save 🖫 the publication.

Activity 6.22 | Filtering Recipients with Mail Merge

In addition to inserting recipients' names and addresses into a publication, Mail Merge also enables you to filter the recipients. Recall that filtering is the process of displaying only a portion of the Access records based on matching a specific value. In this activity, you will use the Mail Merge feature to filter only the Information Technology students.

1 Verify that **Page 2** displays, and then click the **Mailings tab**. In the **Start group**, click the **Mail Merge button arrow**, and then click **Step by Step Mail Merge Wizard**.

2 In the **Mail Merge** task pane, under **Create recipient list**, verify that the **Use an existing list** option button is selected. At the bottom of the task pane, click **Next: Create or connect to a recipient list**. In the **Select Data Source** dialog box, navigate to your **Integrated Project Chapter 6** folder, select your Access file **Lastname_Firstname_6B_ FPCC_Students**, and then click **Open**.

3 In the **Mail Merge Recipients** dialog box, under **Refine recipient list**, click **Filter**. In the **Filter and Sort** dialog box, click the **Field arrow**, and then scroll down and click **Degree**. Verify that the **Comparison** box contains **Equal to**. Click in the **Compare to** box, type **Information Technology** and then compare your screen with Figure 6.39.

Figure 6.39

Degree in field box —

Equal to in
Comparison box

Information Technology in
Compare to box

4 In the **Filter and Sort** dialog box, click **OK**. In the **Mail Merge Recipients** dialog box, scroll to the right to display the **Degree** field. Verify that three Information Technology student records display.

> **Alert!** | Do more or less than three students display?
>
> If three students do not display, the data in your Access database is not accurate. Cancel the Mail Merge, open your Access database Lastname_Firstname_6B_FPCC_Students, and correct any incorrect data or misspelled words.

5 In the **Mail Merge Recipients** dialog box click **OK**. On **Page 2** of your publication, click the text box to select the paragraph that begins *Type address here*.

6 On the **Mail Merge** task pane, under **More items**, click **Address block**. In the **Insert Address Block** dialog box, under **Specify address elements**, verify that the format *Joshua Randall Jr.* is selected, and then click **OK**.

7 In the **Mail Merge** task pane, under **Step 2 of 3**, click **Next: Create merged publication**. In the **Mail Merge** task pane, under **Create merged publication**, click **Merge to a new publication**.

Three postcards are created.

8 Click the **Insert tab**, and then in the **Header & Footer group**, click the **Footer** button. In the footer, double-click the word **Internship**, and then type **Technology** On the **Master Page tab**, in the **Close group**, click the **Close Master Page** button.

9 In the **Mail Merge** task pane, under **Merged publication pages**, click **Save this publication**. Navigate to your **Integrated Projects Chapter 6** folder in the **File name** box, delete the existing text, type **Lastname_Firstname_6B_Technology_Postcard** and then click **Save. Close** ☒ the Mail Merge task pane.

10 Click the **File tab**, verify the **Info tab** is selected, click **Publication Properties**, and then click **Advanced Properties**. In the **Properties** dialog box, on the **Summary tab**, in the **Subject** box, type your course name and section number, in the **Author** box, type your firstname and lastname, and then in the **Keywords** box, type **technology postcards, merged** Click **OK** to close the dialog box.

11 Click the **Home tab**, and then **Save** 🖫 the publication. If your instructor directs you to submit your files electronically, go to Step 13.

12 To print your document, in the **Page Navigation** pane, click the **Page 2** that contains your name. Hold down ⇧Shift, and then click the **Page 1** directly above your Page 2. Click the **File tab**, and then click the **Print tab**. Under **Settings**, click the **Print All Pages arrow**, and then click **Print Selection**. Under **Settings**, in the **Copies of each page** box, type **1** Click the **Print** button.

13 **Close** 🗙 the **Lastname_Firstname_6B_Technology_Postcard** publication. **Close** 🗙 the **Mail Merge** task pane. **Save** 🖫 the **Lastname_Firstname_6B_ Internship_Postcard** publication, and then **Close** 🗙 Publisher.

14 Submit your printed or electronic files as directed by your instructor.

End **You have completed Project 6B** ─────────────────

Content-Based Assessments

Summary

In Microsoft Publisher, you can create many different types of publications. Use a template—located on your computer or downloaded from the Internet—to quickly begin a publication. You can insert pictures, clip art, or other images and then format the objects in Publisher. Publisher's Mail Merge Wizard allows you to personalize a publication by inserting a recipient list and other data fields located in an Access database. In Access, you can set field properties to make data entry faster and more accurate.

Key Terms

Blank Report tool	Default value	Input mask	Property Sheet
Building blocks	Design Checker	Layout guides	Ruler guide
Business information set	Field property	Lookup Wizard	Text wrapping
	Field size	Margin guides	Validation rule
Color scheme	Font scheme	Master page	
Date Picker	Grouping	Overflow	

Matching

Match each term in the second column with its correct definition in the first column by writing the letter of the term on the blank line in front of the correct definition.

_____ 1. The page that contains the design and layout elements, including headers and footers, that you want to repeat on multiple pages of your publication.

_____ 2. A predefined set of harmonized colors that can be applied to text and objects.

_____ 3. A predefined set of fonts that is associated with a publication, where a primary font and a secondary font are specified.

_____ 4. Reusable pieces of content—for example, borders, text boxes, logos, and calendars—that are stored in galleries.

_____ 5. The manner in which text displays around an object, such as a picture or clip art.

_____ 6. Characteristics of a field that control how the field displays and how data can be entered in the field.

_____ 7. A set of literal characters and placeholder characters that control what can and cannot be entered in the field.

_____ 8. Criteria that limit or control what users can enter in a field.

_____ 9. In Access, the data that is automatically entered in a field.

_____ 10. The maximum number of characters you can enter in a field.

_____ 11. A calendar control that is used to select a date.

_____ 12. An Access feature that creates a list box to look up a value in another table, query, or a list of values.

A Blank Report tool
B Building blocks
C Color scheme
D Date Picker
E Default value
F Field property
G Field size
H Font scheme
I Input mask
J Layout guide
K Lookup Wizard
L Margin guides
M Master page
N Text wrapping
O Validation rule

_____ 13. An Access tool with which you can create a report from scratch by adding the fields you designate in the order you want them to display.

_____ 14. Nonprinting lines that mark the margins, columns, rows, and baselines and are used to align the text, pictures, and other objects so that the publication has balance and uniformity.

_____ 15. Nonprinting lines on the top, bottom, left, and right sides of the page that are used to define the page margins.

Multiple Choice

Circle the correct answer.

1. A collection of graphic images included with Microsoft Office programs that can make your publication visually appealing is called:
   A. clip art   **B.** SmartArt   **C.** text effects

2. Predesigned graphic elements—for example, bars and emphasis images—display in the:
   A. Clip Art gallery   **B.** Design Accents gallery   **C.** Shapes gallery

3. A Publisher feature that automatically reviews a publication for a range of design and layout flaws and provides options to fix any identified problems is the:
   A. Design Checker   **B.** Design Troubleshooter   **C.** Design Wizard

4. Text that does not fit within a text box is called:
   A. excess   **B.** overflow   **C.** overspill

5. The characteristic that defines the kind of data that can be entered in a field, such as numbers, text, or dates, is the:
   A. field type   **B.** record type   **C.** data type

6. In a new blank database, Access creates a default ID field with the data type:
   A. AutoNumber   **B.** Number   **C.** Text

7. An Access report feature that allows you to separate groups of records visually and to display introductory and summary data for each group is a report is called:
   A. filtering   **B.** grouping   **C.** sorting

8. A list of characteristics for fields or controls on a form or report in which you can make precise changes to each property associated with a field or control is called a:
   A. Field List   **B.** Property List   **C.** Property Sheet

9. A customized group of information—including items such as a company name, address, phone number, e-mail address, and logo—that can be used to quickly fill in appropriate places in a publication is called a:
   A. business information set   **B.** personal building block   **C.** user information group

10. A nonprinting horizontal or vertical line that can be aligned to any position on the ruler is called a:
    A. column guide   **B.** row guide   **C.** ruler guide

Apply 6A skills from these Objectives:

1. Construct a Newsletter in Publisher
2. Format a Newsletter
3. Use Mail Merge to Insert Names from an Access Table into a Publication
4. Insert Access Data Fields into a Publication

Skills Review | Project **6C Award Certificates**

In the following Skills Review, you will use Publisher to create a certificate of achievement for students in each of the degree areas at Florida Port Community College. In Access, you will enter data listing students who will receive the degree, and use Mail Merge to personalize the certificates. Your completed files will look similar to Figure 6.40.

Project Files

For Project 6C, you will need the following files:

    i06C_Awards_Certificate
    i06C_Students_Information

You will save your files as:

    Lastname_Firstname_6C_Awards_Certificate
    Lastname_Firstname_6C_Students_Information
    Lastname_Firstname_6C_Merged_Certificates

Project Results

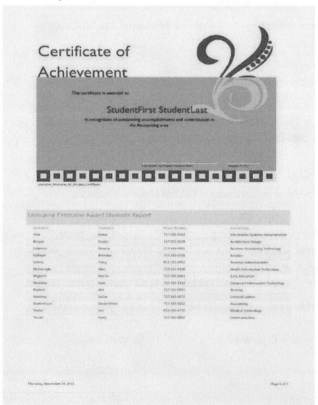

Figure 6.40

1. **Start** Publisher. Open the data file **i06C_Awards_Certificate**. If necessary, on the **View tab**, click the **Rulers** check box. Click the **File tab**, and then click the **Save As tab**. **Save** the file in your **Integrated Projects Chapter 6** folder, with the file name **Lastname_Firstname_6C_Awards_Certificate**

   a. Click the **Insert tab**, and then in the **Header & Footer group**, click the **Footer** button. In the **Footer** text box, type **Lastname_Firstname_6C_Awards_Certificate** and then on the **Master Page tab**, in the **Close group**, click the **Close Master Page** button.

   b. At the bottom of the page, select the text *Signature*, and then type **Leyla Barwari, Vice President, Academic Affairs** At the lower right corner, select the text *Date*. Click the **Insert tab**, and then in the **Text group**, click the **Date & Time** button. In the **Date and Time** dialog box, under **Available formats**, click the format **May 11, 2015**—your date will differ—and then click **OK**.

   c. Click the **Page Design tab**, and then in the **Schemes group**, click the **More** button. In the **Color Schemes** gallery, under **Built-In (classic)**, click the **Mulberry** color scheme.

   d. On the **Page Design tab**, in the **Schemes group**, click the **Scheme Fonts** button. In the **Font Scheme Options** dialog box, verify that all check boxes are selected, and then click **OK**.

   e. In the **Schemes group**, click the **Scheme Fonts** button. In the **Font Schemes** gallery, under **Built- In**, click the **Solstice** font scheme.

2. At the top of the page, select the heading *Certificate of Achievement*. On the **Home tab**, in the **Font group**, click the **Bold** button to turn off bold formatting. Click the **Font Color button arrow**, and then in the first row, click the second color—**Accent 1**.

   a. Click the **Insert tab**, and then in the **Building Block group**, click the **Borders & Accents** button. In the **Design Accent** gallery, under **Bars**, click **Double Square**.

   b. With the **Double Square** accent selected, move the object so the bottom left corner is at the left margin and at the top of the footer border. Resize the object so that the **Double Square** accent is stretched and extends to the right margin.

   c. Click the **File tab**, verify the **Info tab** is selected, and then click the **Run Design Checker** button. d. At the bottom of the **Design Checker** task pane, click **Design Checker Options**. In the **Design Checker Options** dialog box, under **Page Range**, click the **Current page(s)** option button, and then click **OK**. If necessary, fix any errors in your publication

   d. **Close** the **Design Checker** task pane, and then **Save** the publication.

3. **Start** Access. Navigate to your data files, and then open the Access file **i06C_Students_Information**. From **Backstage** view, click the **Save Database As tab**. **Save** the database in your **Integrated Projects Chapter 6** folder with the file name **Lastname_Firstname_6C_Students_Information**

   a. On the **Message Bar**, click the **Enable Content** button. In the **Navigation Pane**, under **Tables**, double-click the **Award Students** table.

   b. Click the **Create tab**, and then in the **Forms group**, click the **Form** button. On the **Design tab**, in the **Views group**, click the **View** button to display the form in Form view.

c. On the Quick Access Toolbar, click the **Save** button. In the **Save As** dialog box, type **Award Students Form** and then click **OK**.

d. At the bottom of the form, click the **New (blank) record** button, and then add the following records, using your own first name and last name in the last record.

Firstname	Lastname	Address	City	State	ZIP	Phone Number	Award Area
Sergio	Bergan	948 Highland Oak Dr	St. Petersburg	FL	33709	727-555-0239	Architecture Design
Brendon	Gallager	4509 E Giddens Ave	St. Petersburg	FL	33702	727-555-0216	Aviation
Firstname	Lastname	11 Clayridge Dr	St. Petersburg	FL	33714	727-555-5632	Accounting

4. On the **Create tab**, in the **Reports group**, click the **Report Wizard** button. In the **Report Wizard** dialog box, verify that the **Award Students** table is selected. Under **Available Fields**, double- click the fields **Firstname, Lastname, Phone Number**, and **Award Area**, and then click **Next** two times.

a. Under **What sort order do you want for your records?**, click the **sort box arrow**, and then click **Lastname**. Click **Next**.

b. Under **Orientation**, click **Landscape**, and then click **Next**.

c. Under **What title do you want for the report?**, select the existing text, type **Lastname Firstname Award Students Report** and then click **Finish**.

d. Click the **File tab**, and then click **View and edit database properties**. In the **Properties** dialog box, on the **Summary tab**, in the **Subject** box, type your course name and section number. In the **Author** box, type your firstname and lastname, and then in the **Keywords** box, type **awards, contact info** Click **OK** to close the dialog box, and then click the **Print tab**.

e. Right-click the **Lastname Firstname Award Students Report**, and then on the shortcut menu, click **Close All**. If a message box displays to save the changes to the design of the report, click **Yes**. **Close** Access.

5. With your certificate displayed, click the **Mailings tab**. In the **Start group**, click the **Mail Merge button arrow**, and then click **Step by Step Mail Merge Wizard**.

a. In the **Mail Merge** task pane, under **Create recipient list**, verify that the **Use an existing list** option button is selected. At the bottom of the task pane, click **Next: Create or connect to a recipient list**.

b. In the **Select Data Source** dialog box, navigate to your **Integrated Projects Chapter 6** folder, select the Access file **Lastname_Firstname_6C_Students_Information**, and then click **Open**.

c. In the **Mail Merge Recipients** dialog box, under **Refine recipient list**, click **Sort**. In the **Filter and Sort** dialog box, click the **Sort by arrow**, and then click **Award Area**. Verify that the **Ascending** option is selected, and then click **OK**. In the **Mail Merge Recipients** dialog box, click **OK**.

Integrating Publisher and Access

d. In the publication, select the text *Name of recipient*. In the **Mail Merge** task pane, under **Prepare your publication**, click **Firstname**, and then press [Spacebar]. Under **Prepare your publication**, click **Lastname**.

e. Click in the paragraph that begins **In recognition of**. Press [Ctrl] + [A] to select all the text in the text box. On the **Home tab**, click the **Font Size button arrow**, and then click **14**. In the **Paragraph group**, click the **Center** button. In the same text box, click at the end of the paragraph—after the word *the*, and then press [Spacebar]. In the **Mail Merge** task pane, under **Prepare your publication**, click **Award Area**, press the [Spacebar], and then type **area Save** the publication.

6. In the **Mail Merge** task pane, under **Step 2 of 3**, click **Next: Create merged publication**. Under **Create merged publication**, click **Merge to a new publication**.

a. On the **Insert tab**, in the **Header & Footer group**, click the **Footer** button. In the footer, double- click the word **Awards**, and then type **Merged** On the **Master Page tab**, in the **Close group**, click the **Close Master Page** button.

b. In the **Mail Merge** task pane, under **Merged publication pages**, click **Save this publication**. In the **Save As** dialog box, navigate to your **Integrated Projects Chapter 6** folder. In the file name box, type **Lastname_Firstname_6C_Merged_Certificates** and then click **Save**.

c. Click the **File tab**, and then click the **Info tab**. Click **Publication Properties**, and then click **Advanced Properties**. In the **Properties** dialog box, on the **Summary tab**, in the **Subject** box, type your course name and section number. In the **Author** box, type your firstname and lastname, and then in the **Keywords** box, type **certificates, merged** Click **OK** to close the dialog box, and thenclick the **Home tab**.

d. **Close** the **Lastname_Firstname_6C_Merged_Certificates** publication. With the **Lastname_Firstname_6C_Awards_Certifcates** publication displayed, click **Save**, and then **Close** Publisher.

e. Submit your printed or electronic files as directed by your instructor.

You have completed Project 6C

Apply 6B skills from these Objectives:

5. Set Field properties in an Access Table
6. Create a Publication Using a Publisher Template
7. Modify the Layout of a Publication

In the following Skills Review, using an Access database and a Publisher template, you will create flyers for students regarding housing on the campus of Florida Port Community College. Your completed files will look similar to Figure 6.41.

Project Files

For Project 6D, you will need the following files:

New blank Access database
New blank Publisher publication
i06D_Housing_Logo

You will save your files as:

Lastname_Firstname_6D_FPCC_Students
Lastname_Firstname_6D_Residents_Flyer
Lastname_Firstname_6D_Campus_Flyer

Project Results

Figure 6.41

1. **Start** Access. Under **Available Templates**, verify **Blank database** is selected. In the right portion of the screen, click the **Browse** button. In the **File New Database** dialog box, navigate to your **Integrated Projects Chapter 6** folder. In the **File Name** box, type **Lastname_Firstname_6D_FPCC_Students** click **OK**, and then click **Create**.

    a. At the top of the second column, click the text *Click to Add*. In the list of data types, click **Text**, and then with *Field1* selected, type **Firstname** and then press ⏎.

    b. In a similar manner add the following fields to the table.

Lastname
Address
City
State
ZIP
Phone Number
Birth Date
Housing

    c. Click the **Birth Date** field. On the **Fields tab**, in the **Formatting group**, click the **Data Type box arrow**, and then click **Date/Time**. Click the **ID** field. On the **Fields tab**, in the **Formatting group**, click the **Data Type box arrow**, and then click **Text**.

    d. On the **Fields tab**, in the **Views group**, click the **View** button. In the **Save As** dialog box, type **Student Housing** and then click **OK**.

2. In **Design View**, under **Field Name**, click **Phone Number**. In the **Field Properties** area, click the **Input Mask** property box, and then click the **Build** button. In the **Input Mask Wizard** dialog box, under **Input Mask**, verify that **Phone Number** is selected, and then click **Finish**.

    a. Under **Field Name**, click **ID**, and then in the **Field Properties** area, click the **Input Mask** properties box. Type **77-0000000** and then press ⏎.

    b. Under **Field Name**, click **State**, and then in the **Field Properties** area, click the **Default Value** property box. Type **FL** and then press ⏎.

    c. Under **Field Name**, click **Birth Date**, and then in the **Field Properties** area, click the **Format** property box. Click the **Format arrow**, and then click **Short Date**.

    d. Change the **Field Size** of the following fields.

Field Name	Field Size
Firstname	30
Lastname	30
Address	60
City	50
ZIP	10
Housing	5

e. In the **City** field, under **Data Type**, click the **Text** data type, click the **Data Type arrow**, and then click **Lookup Wizard**. In the **Lookup Wizard** dialog box, select the option *I will type in the values I want*, and then click **Next**. Verify that the **Number of columns** is **1**, and then press Tab . Type **St. Petersburg** and then press Tab . Type **Tampa** and then click **Finish**.

f. Right-click the **Student Housing table tab**, and then on the shortcut menu, click **Close**. In the message box, click **Yes** to save the table.

3. In the **Navigation Pane**, click the **Student Housing** table name. On the **Create tab**, in the **Forms group**, click the **Form** button.

   a. On the **Home tab**, in the **Views group**, click the **View** button. Enter the following records. In the last record use your own first name and last name. The State field name is not listed below because all students are from Florida.

ID	Firstname	Lastname	Address	City	ZIP	Phone Number	Birth Date	Housing
0135766	Dave	Demoura	1512 Sunnyhills Dr	St. Petersburg	33702	7275550033	4/17/94	No
1182543	Johnnie	Borello	820 Mabry Hwy	St. Petersburg	33714	7275550783	11/4/93	Yes
1851332	Jennifer	Tham	513 Tanager Rd	St. Petersburg	33713	7275550119	6/18/92	No
5219083	Tamra	Alix	1201 7th Ave	St. Petersburg	33713	7275550892	3/17/94	Yes
5720555	Firstname	Lastname	222 Melody Ln	Tampa	33621	8135555831	8/26/92	Yes

   b. On the **Quick Access Toolbar**, click **Save**. In the **Save As** dialog box, under **Form Name**, type **Student Housing Form** and then click **OK**.

4. On the **Create tab**, in the **Reports group**, click the **Blank Report** button. If necessary, on the **Design tab**, in the **Tools group**, click the **Add Existing Fields** button to display the Field List pane.

   a. In the **Field List** pane, click **Show all tables**, and then click the plus sign (+) next to **Student Housing**. In the **Field List** task pane, double-click the fields **Firstname**, **Lastname**, **Phone Number**, and **Housing**.

   b. On the **Design tab**, in the **Grouping & Totals group**, click the **Group & Sort** button. Click the **Add a group** button, and then click **Housing**. Click the **Add a sort** button, and then click **Lastname**. On the **Design tab**, in the **Grouping & Totals group**, click the **Group & Sort** button. **Close** the Field List pane.

   c. On the **Design tab**, in the **Tools group**, click the **Property Sheet** button. In the report, click the **Firstname** field name, hold down Ctrl , and then click the field names **Lastname** and **Phone Number**. In the **Property Sheet** pane, in the **Width** box, select the number, type **1.5** and then press Enter . **Close** the Property Sheet pane.

   d. On the Quick Access Toolbar, click **Save**. In the **Save As** dialog box, type **Lastname Firstname 6D Housing Report** and then click **OK**. On the **Design tab**, in the **Header/Footer group**, click the **Title** button.

e. On the **Design tab**, in the **Themes group**, click the **Themes** button. In the **Themes** gallery, under **Built-In**, in the fourth row, click the third theme—**Equity**.

f. From **Backstage** view, click **View and edit database properties**. In the **Properties** dialog box, on the **Summary** tab, in the **Subject** box, type your course name and section number. In the **Author** box, type your firstname and lastname, and then in the **Keywords** box, type **housing report** Click **OK** to close the dialog box, and then click the **Home tab**. Right-click the **Lastname Firstname 6D Housing Report tab**, and then click **Close All**. In the message box, click **Yes** to save the changes, and then **Close** Access.

5. **Start** Publisher. From **Backstage** view, under **Available Templates**, with **Installed and Online Templates** displayed, click the arrow, and then click **Installed Templates**. Under **More Templates**, click **Flyers**, and then under **Event**, click **Brocade**. Under **Customize**, click the **Color scheme box arrow**, and then click **Marine**. Click **Create**.

a. Click the **File tab**, and then click the **Save As tab**. In the **Save As** dialog box, navigate to your **Integrated Projects Chapter 6** folder, and then save the file as **Lastname_Firstname_6D_Residents_Flyer**

b. Click the **Insert tab**, and then in the **Header & Footer group**, click the **Footer** button. In the **Footer** text box, type **Lastname Firstname 6D Residents Flyer** and then on the **Master Page tab**, in the **Close group**, click the **Close Master Page** button.

c. On the **Insert tab**, in the **Text group**, click the **Business Information** button, and then near the bottom of the list, click **Edit Business Information**. If the Create New Business Information Set dialog box does not display, in the Business Information dialog box, under Select a Business Information Set, click New.

d. In the **Create New Business Information Set** dialog box, type the following information.

Individual name	Salvador Shames
Job position	Housing Director
Organization name	Florida Port Community College
Address	2745 Dartmouth Ave N St. Petersburg, FL 33713
Phone Number	727-555-0030
Fax	727-555-0031
E-mail	housing@FloridaPortCC.edu
Tagline or motto	Campus Housing

e. Click the **Add logo** button. Navigate to your data files, select the file **i06D_Housing_Logo**, and then click **Insert**.

f. In the **Business Information set name** box, select the text, type **Shames** and then click **Save**. In the **Business Information** dialog box, click **Update Publication**.

6. Point to the logo, and then drag the logo down and to the right until the top middle sizing handle is at **4 inches on the horizontal ruler** and at **9.25 inches on the vertical ruler**.

a. With the logo selected, change the **Shape Height** to **1** and then change the **Shape Width** to **2**

b. At the top of the page, click the heading **Product/Service Information**, and then type **Tips for Living on the FPCC Campus**

c. Click in the blank area immediately below the title. In the displayed text box, right-click the text box border, and then on the shortcut menu, click **Cut**.

d. Click the **Insert tab**, and then in the **Illustrations group**, click the **Clip Art** button. In the **Clip Art** task pane, verify that *All media file types* displays. In the **Search for** box, type **apartments** and then click **Go**. Locate the image as shown in Figure 6.41, and then click the image.

e. Move the image so that the top middle sizing handle is approximately at **6.5 inches on the horizontal ruler** and at **1.5 inches on the vertical ruler**.

7. On the **Mailings tab**, in the **Start group**, click the **Mail Merge button arrow**, and then click **Step by Step Mail Merge Wizard**.

a. In the **Mail Merge** task pane, under **Create recipient list**, verify that the **Use an existing list** option button is selected. Click **Next: Create or connect to a recipient list**. In the **Select Data Source** dialog box, navigate to your **Integrated Projects Chapter 6** folder, select your Access file **Lastname_Firstname_6D_FPCC_Students**, and then click **Open**.

b. In the **Mail Merge Recipients** dialog box, under **Refine recipient list**, click **Filter**. In the **Filter and Sort** dialog box, click the **Field arrow**, and then click **Housing**. Verify that the **Comparison** box contains **Equal to**. Click in the **Compare to** box, type **Yes** and then click **OK**. In the **Mail Merge Recipients** dialog box, click **OK**.

c. Click the text box with the paragraph that begins *Place text here*. On the upper edge, point to the middle sizing handle, and then drag up to **3.5 inches on the vertical ruler**. With the text selected, on the **Home tab**, change the **Font Size** to **16**. In the **Mail Merge** task pane, under **Prepare your publication**, click **Firstname**, press Spacebar, click **Lastname**, and the press Enter.

d. Type **We are providing this flyer to each FPCC student with a campus housing room key. Living on campus with other students can be a wonderful experience if you are properly prepared. We want you to know that our Web site had a number of pages regarding housing issues such as Rules and Regulations, Roommate Relations, Swimming Pools, Residents' Web Sites, and Maintenance Requests. If you have any questions regarding living on the FPCC campus, please feel free to contact the Campus Housing office. Someone is there to answer the phone 24/7. Welcome to campus, and have a great year!**

8. In the **Mail Merge** task pane, under **Step 2 of 3**, click **Next: Create merged publication**, and then under **Created merged publication**, click **Merge to a new publication**.

a. Click the **Insert tab**, and then in the **Header & Footer group**, click the **Footer** button. In the footer, double-click the word **Residents**, and then type **Campus** On the **Master Page tab**, in the **Close group**, click the **Close Master Page** button.

b. In the **Mail Merge** task pane, under **Merged publication pages**, click **Save this publication**. Navigate to your **Integrated Projects Chapter 6** folder. In the **File name** box, delete the existing text, type **Lastname_Firstname_6D_Campus_Flyer** and then click **Save**. Close the **Mail Merge** task pane.

c. Click the **File tab**, and then click the Info tab. Click **Publication Properties**, and then click **Advanced Properties**. In the **Properties** dialog box, on the **Summary** tab, in the **Subject** box, type your course name and section number, in the **Author** box, type your firstname and lastname, and then in the Keywords box, type **housing flyer merged** Click OK to close the dialog box.

d. Click the Home tab, Save your changes, and then Close the publication. Save the **Lastname_Firstname_6D_Residents_Flyer** publication, and then Close Publisher.

e. Submit your printed or electronic files as directed by your instructor.

You have completed Project 6D

Apply 6A skills from these Objectives:

1. Construct a Newsletter in Publisher
2. Format a Newsletter
3. Use Mail Merge to Insert Names from an Access Table into a Publication
4. Insert Access Data Fields into a Publication

Mastering Integration | Project 6E Registration Flyer

In the following Mastering Integration project, you will complete a flyer for the Florida Port Community College registration department listing the various fees students may be charged. Your completed documents will look similar to Figure 6.42.

Project Files

For Project 6E, you will need the following files:

i06E_Registration_Flyer
i06E_Student_Fees

You will save your files as:

Lastname_Firstname_6E_Registration_Flyer
Lastname_Firstname_6E_Student_Fees
Lastname_Firstname_6E_Merged_Flyer

Project Results

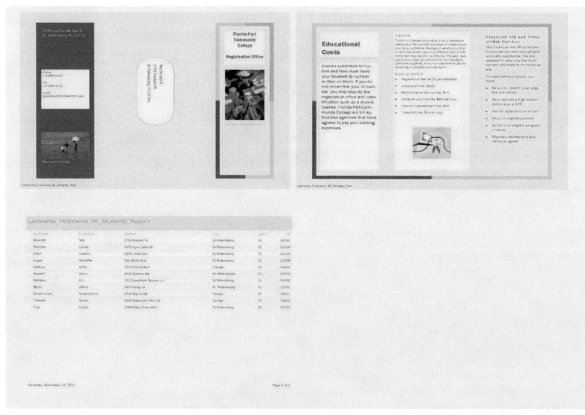

Figure 6.42

Integrating Publisher and Access

1. **Start** Publisher. Locate and open the data file **i06E_Registration_Flyer**. **Save** the file in the **Integrated Projects Chapter 6** folder as **Lastname_Firstname_6E_Registration_Flyer** Type the file name in the footer, and then **Close** the footer. Apply the color scheme **Technic**, and then apply the font scheme **Economy**. At the top left of **Page 1**, select the paragraphs that begin *Your Address*, and then change the **Font Size** to 12. Type **2745 Dartmouth Ave N** press Enter, and then type **St. Petersburg, FL 33713** In the next text box, delete the phone number, and then type **727-555-0030** Delete the fax number, and then type **727-555-0031** Delete the e-mail address, and then type **registration@FloridaPortCC.edu**

2. At the top right of **Page 1**, select the text *Organization name*, type **Florida Port Community College** and then press Enter two times. Type **Registration Office** Select all the text in the text box, apply the style **Title 3**, and then **Center** the text. Click in the middle of **Page 1**. On the **Insert tab**, in the **Building Blocks group**, click the **Page Parts** button, and then under **Pull Quotes**, click **Portal**. Position the text box so that the top middle sizing handle is approximately at **3 inches on the vertical ruler** and **5.5 inches on the horizontal ruler**. In the text box, select the text, change the **Font Size** to **12**, and then click the **Italic** button. On **Page 2**, select the heading *Main Inside Heading*, and then type **Educational Costs**

3. In the middle text box, select the text *Secondary Heading*, and then type **Tuition** Select the text *Heading*, and then type **Fees at FPCC** On the **ClipArt** task pane, search for *businessmen, technology*, and then insert the first image as shown in Figure 6.42. Change the text wrapping to **Top and Bottom**, change the **Shape Height** of the image to **1.5** inches, and then position the clip art in the middle text box, so that the top left corner is approximately at **5.5 inches on the vertical ruler** and **4.75 inches** on the horizontal ruler.

4. Select all the text in the right text box, and then change the **Font Size** to **12**. On **the Page Design tab**, in the **Page Background group**, display the **Background** gallery, click the background **30% tint of Accent 2**, and then **Apply to All Pages**. **Save** the publication.

5. **Start** Access. Open the file **i06E_Student_Fees**. From **Backstage** view, click **Save As**, and then save the file in the **Integrated Projects Chapter 6** folder as **Lastname_Firstname_6E_Student_Fees** Create a new form based on the **Students** table, and then **Save** the form with the name **Students Form** Enter the following records using your name in the last record.

Firstname	Lastname	Address	City	State	ZIP	Phone Number	Degree
Mara	Monell	4621 Duhme Rd	St. Petersburg	FL	33714	727-555-5351	Architecture Design
Nello	Mallory	1550 102nd Ave	Tampa	FL	33605	813-555-5832	Criminal Justice
Adrea	Rhyn	503 Trinity Ln	St. Petersburg	FL	33701	727-555-0894	Architecture Design
Firstname	Lastname	4716 Bay St NE	Tampa	FL	33621	813-555-0303	Accounting

6. Create a report using the **Report Wizard**. From the **Students** table, add the fields **Firstname, Lastname, Address, City, State**, and **ZIP**. **Sort** by the **Lastname** field, use **Landscape** orientation, and title the report **Lastname_Firstname 6E Students Report** **Close** all open objects. Display the **Properties** dialog box. In the **Subject** box, type your course name and section number, in the **Author** box, type your firstname and lastname, and then in the **Keywords** box, type **contact info** **Close** Access.

7. In your publication, on the **Mailings tab**, open the **Step by Step Mail Merge Wizard**. Connect to your Access file **Lastname_Firstname_6E_Student_Fees** as the recipient list. **Sort** the students by the **Lastname** field. On **Page 1** of your publication, click the **Pull Quote** text box that begins *To catch*, and then select all the text. Under **More items**, insert the **Address block**. Click the border of the text box, and then click the **Drawing Tools Format tab**. In the **Arrange group**, click the **Rotate button arrow**, and then click **Rotate Right 90°**. **Merge to a new publication**. **Save** the merged publication in your **Integrated Projects Chapter 6** folder as **Lastname_Firstname_6E_Merged_Flyer** Change the footer to display the file name.

8. Display the **Properties** dialog box. In the **Subject** box, type your course name and section number, in the **Author** box, type your firstname and lastname, and then in the **Keywords** box, type **students, merged** **Save** your changes, and then **Close** the publication. With your **Lastname_Firstname_6E_Registration_Flyer** displayed, click **Save**, and then **Close** Publisher. Submit your printed or electronic files as directed by your instructor.

You have completed Project 6E

5. Set Field
    properties in an
    Access Table
6. Create a
    Publication
    Using a
    Publisher
    Template
7. Modify the
    Layout of a
    Publication

Mastering Integration | Project 6F FPCC Clubs

In the following Mastering Integration project, you will create and modify an Access database, create a newsletter from a Publisher template, and then use the Mail Merge feature to create personalized flyers that will be sent to students interested in the golf club. Your completed files will look similar to Figure 6.43.

Project Files

For Project 6F, you will need the following files:

New blank Access database
New blank Publisher publication
i06F_Clubs_Logo

You will save your files as:

Lastname_Firstname_6F_FPCC_Clubs
Lastname_Firstname_6F_Campus_Clubs
Lastname_Firstname_6F_Merged_Clubs

Project Results

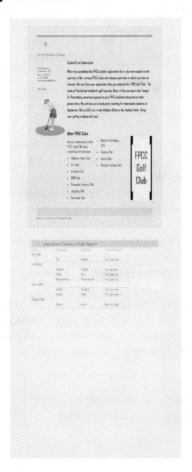

Figure 6.43

Integrating Publisher and Access

1. **Start** Access. **Create** a **Blank Database. Save** the database in the **Integrated Projects Chapter 6** folder as **Lastname_Firstname_6F_FPCC_Clubs** In the new **Table1, Save** the table as **Student Clubs** Insert the following fields, data types, and properties.

Field Name	Data Type	Field Size	Other Properties
ID	Text	10	Input Mask: 51-0000000
Firstname	Text	30	
Lastname	Text	30	
Address	Text	60	
City	Text	50	Lookup Wizard: St. Petersburg and Tampa
State	Text	2	Default Value: FL
ZIP	Text	10	
Phone Number	Text	10	Input Mask: Phone Number
Club	Text	50	

2. **Save** and **Close** the **Student Clubs** table. Create a form based on the **Student Clubs** table. **Save** the form with the name **Student Clubs Form** and then enter the following student records. In the last record, type your first name and last name.

ID	Firstname	Lastname	Address	City	ZIP	Phone Number	Club
4209863	Skylar	Weiden	8465 Flagstone Dr	St. Petersburg	33714	7275555937	Swim Club
2085626	Naomi	Deford	4776 Cove Cir	St. Petersburg	33708	7275554927	Golf Club
0172079	Vic	Fowler	421 W Denver Ave	St. Petersburg	33713	7275550230	Art Club
5504826	Chet	Lee	221 Mount Piney Ave	St. Petersburg	33713	7275550215	Golf Club
3093543	Karen	Jones	1102 Pinellas Dr	Tampa	33621	8135550993	Tennis Club
0992709	Kelley	Zeck	5904 Rosemary Dr	St. Petersburg	33709	7275555930	Swim Club
0977548	Firstname	Lastname	3526 Iris St	St. Petersburg	33708	7275550032	Golf Club

3. Use the **Blank Report** tool to create a report. Add the field names **Firstname, Lastname, Phone Number,** and **Club. Group** by the **Club** field, and then **Sort** by the **Lastname** field. Display the **Property Sheet** pane, and then change the **Width** of all report columns to **1.5 Save** the report as **Lastname Firstname Clubs Report**, and then add the **Title** to the report. Display the **Themes** gallery, and then apply the **Built-In** theme **Flow. Close** all open objects.

4. Display the **Properties** dialog box. In the **Subject** box, type your course name and section number, in the **Author** box, type your firstname and lastname, and then in the **Keywords** box, type **students, clubs Close** the Properties dialog box, click the **Home tab**, and then **Close** Access.

5. **Start** Publisher. Click the **Newsletters** publication type, and then under **Installed Templates**, click the **Arrows** design. Apply the **Sunrise** color scheme, and then, under **Options**, change the **Page Size** to **One-page spread. Create** the publication. **Save** the publication in your **Integrated Projects Chapter 6** folder as **Lastname_Firstname_6F_Campus_Clubs** Type the file name in the footer, and then click **Close Master Page.**

6. Delete **Page 1, Page 2,** and **Page 3.** Create a new business information set for Marcus Simmons using the following information. The logo is located in your data files.

Integrating Publisher and Access

Individual name	Marcus Simmons
Job position	FPCC Athletic Director
Organization name	Florida Port Community College
Address	2745 Dartmouth Ave N St. Petersburg, FL 33713
Phone Number	727-555-0030
Fax	727-555-0031
E-mail	Clubs@FloridaPortCC.edu
Tagline	FPCC Clubs
Logo	i06F_FPCC_Clubs_Logo
Business Information set name	Simmons

7. **Save** the business data set as **Simmons** and then click **Update Publication**. Open the **Clip Art** task pane, and then search for **golf, females** and insert the image as shown in Figure 6.43. On the **Format tab**, in the **Arrange group**, click the **Wrap Text** button, and then click **Tight**. Move the clip art so the top left corner is approximately at 4 **inches on the vertical rules** and the **0.5 inches on the horizontal ruler**. In the lower right corner of the page, **Cut** the image, and then in the same location, **Cut** the text box.

8. Locate the text box containing the text *We're on the Web*, select the text, and then type **FPCC Golf Club Center** the text in the text box, and then drag the text box to the lower right corner. Adjust the size of the text box so the top edge is approximately at **6 inches on the vertical ruler** and the lower edge is approximately at **9.5 inches on the vertical ruler**. Click the heading *Back Page Story Headline*, and then type **Other FPCC Clubs** Select the heading, and then change the **Font Size** to **16**. Click the text box with the paragraph that begins *This story can fit*, and then change the **Font Size** to **14**. Type **Are you interested in other FPCC clubs? We have something for everyone.** and then press Enter. Type the names of the following clubs, pressing Enter after each club name except the last one.

Alligator Swim Club
Art Club
Aviation Club
BBQ Club
Computer Science Club
Juggling Club
Lacrosse Club
Medical Technology Club
Running Club
Tennis Club
Ultimate Frisbee Club

9. Select the club names, and then apply **Bullets**. Click in a blank area of the page. Display the **Background** gallery, and then under **Solid Background**, in the second row, click the second background—**30% tint of Accent 2**.

10. Open the **Mail Merge** task pane. Use your file **Lastname_Firstname_6F_FPCC_Clubs** as the recipient list. **Filter** the recipient list to display only students interested in the **Golf Club**. Click the top right text box with the paragraph beginning *This would be*. Resize the text box so the lower border is at **5.5 inches on the vertical ruler**. Select the text, and then change the **Font Size** to **14**. From the **Mail Merge** task pane, insert the **Firstname** field, press Spacebar, insert the **Lastname** field, and then press Enter. Type **When you completed the FPCC student application form, you were asked to**

Integrating Publisher and Access

indicate any of the various FPCC clubs and campus activities in which you have an interest. We see from your application that you selected the FPCC Golf Club. The state of Florida has wonderful golf courses. Many of the courses in the Tampa/St. Petersburg area have agreed to give FPCC students discounts on their greens fees. We will have an introductory meeting for interested students on September 9th at 6:00 pm in the Athletic Office in the Student Union. Bring your golfing buddies with you! **Save** the publication.

11. Complete the **Merge to a new publication**. **Save** the publication in your **Integrated Projects Chapter 6** folder as **Lastname_Firstname_6F_Merged_Clubs** In the footer, double- click **Campus**, and then type **Merged** Display the **Properties** dialog box. In the **Subject** box, type your course name and section number, in the **Author** box, type your firstname and lastname, and then in the **Keywords** box, type **golf, merged** **Save** your changes, and then **Close** the publication. **Save** the **Lastname_Fistname_6F_Campus_Clubs** publication, and then **Close** Publisher. Submit your printed or electronic files as directed by your instructor.

You have completed Project 6F

Rubric

The following outcomes-based assessments are open-ended assessments. That is, there is no specific correct result; your result will depend on your approach to the information provided. Make Professional Quality your goal. Use the following scoring rubric to guide you in how to approach the problem and then to evaluate how well your approach solves the problem.

The *criteria*—Software Mastery, Content, Format and Layout, and Process—represent the knowledge and skills you have gained that you can apply to solving the problem. The *levels of performance*—Professional Quality, Approaching Professional Quality, or Needs Quality Improvements—help you and your instructor evaluate your result.

	Your completed project is of Professional Quality	Your completed project is of Approaching Professional Quality	Your completed project Needs Quality Improvements if you:
1-Software Mastery	Chooses and applies the most appropriate skills, tools, and features and identifies efficient methods to solve the problem.	Chooses and applies some appropriate skills, tools, and features, but not in the most efficient manner.	Chooses inappropriate skills, tools, or features, or is inefficient in solving the problem.
2-Content	Constructs a solution that is clear and well organized, containing content that is accurate, appropriate to the audience and purpose, and complete. The solution contains no errors of spelling, grammar, or style.	Constructs a solution in which some components are unclear, poorly organized, inconsistent, or incomplete. May misjudge the needs of the audience. May contain some errors in spelling, grammar, or style, but the errors do not detract from comprehension.	Constructs a solution that is unclear, incomplete, or poorly organized, containing some inaccurate or inappropriate content. May contain many errors of spelling, grammar, or style. May fail to solve the problem.
3-Format and Layout	Formats and arranges all elements to communicate information and ideas, clarify function, illustrate relationships, and indicate relative importance.	Applies appropriate format and layout features to some elements, but not others. Or, overuses features, causing minor distraction.	Applies format and layout that fails to communicate information or ideas or clearly. May fail to use format and layout features to clarify function, illustrate relationships, or indicate relative importance. Or, may use available features excessively, causing distraction.
4-Process	Uses an organized approach that integrates planning, development, self-assessment, revision, and reflection.	Demonstrates an organized approach in some areas, but not others. Or, uses an insufficient process of organization throughout.	Does not use an organized approach to solve the problem.

<table>
<tr><td>Apply a combination of the 6A and 6B skills.</td><td></td></tr>
</table>

GO! Think | **Project 6G Field Trip**

Project Files

For Project 6G, you will need the following files:

New blank Publisher publication
i06G_Field_Trip

You will save your files as:

Lastname_Firstname_6G_Field_Trip
Lastname_Firstname_6G_Trip_Flyer
Lastname_Firstname_6G_Merged_Flyer

Florida Port Community College offers field trips for their students. You have been asked to create a one-page flyer announcing upcoming trips.

Save the Access file i06G_Field_Trip with the file name **Lastname_Firstname_6G_Field_Trips** Adjust the field size property to a smaller size for all fields. Create a default value for the State field. Create a form based on the Student table, and then add the following students. Use your first name and last name for the last record.

Firstname	Lastname	Address	City	State	ZIP	Phone Number
Morgan	Woelfel	6232 Oak Cluster Cir	St. Petersburg	FL	33702	727-555-0973
Landon	Heidemann	5621 Samter Ct	St. Petersburg	FL	33702	727-555-0992
First name	Last name	2241 20th St	St. Petersburg	FL	33713	727-555-5351

Create a report with your choice of fields and title. Group the data by one field, and then sort by another field. Use a Publisher template to create a flyer. Add the file name to the footer, and then save the publication with the file name **Lastname_Firstname_6G_Trip_Flyer** Add information in the various text boxes about the different types of field trips that are available. Add appropriate titles and headings to the text boxes. Insert and format appropriate images. Apply a color scheme and font scheme. Use the Mail Merge feature to insert the student recipient names and address in the publication. Save the file. Complete the merge to a new publication. Save the new merged publication as **Lastname_Firstname_6G_Merged_Flyer** and then update the footer. Add appropriate document properties to all three files. Submit your printed or electronic files as directed by your instructor.

You have completed Project 6G

Integrating Publisher and Access

Integrating Publisher and Access

GO! Think | **Project 6H Construction Management**

Project Files

For Project 6H, you will need the following files:

New blank Publisher publication
i06H_Construction_Management
i06H_CM_Logo

You will save your files as:

Lastname_Firstname_6H_Construction_Management
Lastname_Firstname_6H_Construction_Conference
Lastname_Firstname_6H_Merged_Conference

In past years, Florida has been hit hard by hurricanes and other bad weather. The construction industry, working with Florida Port Community College, has put a renewed emphasis on training the Construction Management students to build structures that meet current building codes. You have been asked to create a flyer inviting all Construction Management students to attend a conference.

Save the Access file i06H_Construction_Management with the file name **Lastname_Firstname_6H_Construction_Management** Create a form based on the Students table, and then add the following student records. Use your first name and last name for the last record.

Firstname	Lastname	Address	City	State	ZIP	Phone Number	Degree
Kayla	Crumm	1171 54th Ave	St. Petersburg	FL	33714	727-555-0032	Construction Management
Ryan	Ingerson	2501 W Isabel St	St. Petersburg	FL	33708	727-555-5832	Information Systems
Alyssa	Maden	5304 Cypress St	St. Petersburg	FL	33701	727-555-0362	Construction Management
First Name	Last Name	2513 Frierson Ave	St. Petersburg	FL	33701	727-555-0186	Construction Management

Create a report using the Report Wizard that includes the fields Firstname, Lastname, Phone Number, and Degree. Group the data by Degree and sort the data by Lastname. Create a new publication based on a Publisher template of your choice. Save the file as **Lastname_Firstname_6H_Construction_Conference** and then insert the file name in the footer. In a text box, add information about the Construction Management conference. In another text box, list Florida cities that have had damage due to hurricanes. Insert and format appropriate clip art. Create a business set for Mr. Fasone using the following information.

Individual name	Taylor Fasone
Job position	Director, Construction Management Program
Organization name	Florida Port Community College
Address	2745 Dartmouth Ave N St. Petersburg, FL 33713
Phone Number	727-555-0030

Fax	727-555-0031
E-mail	construction@FloridaPortCC.edu
Tagline	Building a better Florida
Logo	i06H_CM_Logo
Business Information set name	Fastone

Start Mail Merge and connect to your Access file Lastname_Firstname_6H_Construction_Management. Filter the recipients to show only the Construction Management students. Insert the student's name and mailing address. Save the publication. Complete the merge to a new publication. Save the merged publication as **Lastname_Firstname_6H_Merged_Conference** and then update the footer. Add appropriate document properties to all three files. Submit your printed or electronic files as directed by your instructor.

You have completed Project 6H

GO! Think | **Project 6I Student Orientation**

Project Files

For Project 6I, you will need the following files:

New blank Access database
New blank Publisher publication

You will save your files as:

Lastname_Firstname_6I_Student_Orientation
Lastname_Firstname_6I_Orientation_Sessions
Lastname_Firstname_6I_Merged_Sessions

The FPCC Registration Office has decided to offer a New Student Orientation session for all incoming students. In this project, you will create a new Access database listing the students who will be attending the orientation sessions. You will create a publication providing the students with information regarding the orientation.

Create a new blank Access database, and save it with the file name **Lastname_Firstname_6I_Student_Orientation** Create a student table, and then enter the student records using the data below. Use your first name and last name for the last record. Include a State field with the default value FL—the state is the same for all records. In the ID field, add an input mask to include 38 as the first two digits. In the Phone Number field, add the Phone Number input mask.

ID	Firstname	Lastname	Address	City	ZIP	Phone Number	Degree
38-5355842	Shawn	Steinback	1807 E 15th Ave	St. Petersburg	33701	7275555333	Health Information Technology
38-5145839	Ethan	Bizier	5027 Woods Ave	St. Petersburg	33713	7275550993	Health Information Technology
38-5235763	Wyatt	Lebedev	2604 Marconi St	Tampa	33605	8135555352	Business Administration
38-6049584	Jorge	Brouhard	6803 Navin Ave	Tampa	33605	8135554773	Communications
38-2414986	First Name	Last Name	1529 W Pond Dr	St. Petersburg	33714	7275554831	Accounting

Create a report. Add the fields Firstname, Lastname, Degree, and at least one other field of your choice. Sort by Degree and apply Landscape orientation. Create a new one-page publication based on a Publisher template of your choice. Save the file with the file name

Integrating Publisher and Access

353

Lastname_Firstname_6I_Orientation_Sessions Insert the file name in the footer. In a text box, add a list of topics covered in the student orientation—such as meet one-on-one with an academic advisor, select correct courses, academic support services, student involvement, recreational opportunities, and a campus tour. Insert and format an object from the Borders & Accents gallery. Use the Mail Merge feature to insert the Firstname, Lastname, and Degree fields in a text box. Save the publication as **Lastname_Firstname_6I_Merged_Sessions** and then update the footer. Add appropriate document properties to all three files. Submit your printed or electronic records as directed by your instructor.

You have completed Project 6I

Integrating Word, Excel, Access, and PowerPoint

OUTCOMES
At the end of this chapter you will be able to:

OBJECTIVES
Mastering these objectives will enable you to:

PROJECT 7A
Create a Word template, an Excel PivotTable report, and an Excel PivotChart report.

1. Create and Save a Template in Word
2. Insert a Combo Box and an Option Group in an Access Form
3. Create a PivotTable Report and a PivotChart Report in Excel
4. Import Data into a PowerPoint Presentation

PROJECT 7B
Insert functions in Excel and insert a cover page and table of contents in a Word document.

5. Use Excel Functions
6. Create a Report in Word Using Data from Other Applications

In This Chapter

Olexa/Shutterstock

In this chapter, you will use Word, Excel, Access, and PowerPoint to take advantage of the way the applications work with one another in a software suite. By using the most appropriate application to complete the work with the data you have, you can create graphics or input data in one application and then export the data to another application without having to take the time to recreate or retype the graphic or data. It is important to identify the most suitable software to produce the desired solutions and to best utilize the features in the various applications.

The projects in this chapter relate to **Select National Properties Group**, a diversified real estate company that develops, builds, manages, and acquires a wide variety of properties nationwide. Among the company's portfolio of properties are shopping malls, mixed-use town center developments, high-rise office buildings, office parks, industrial buildings and warehouses, multi-family housing developments, educational facilities, and hospitals. Residential developments are mainly located in and around the company's hometown, Chicago; commercial and public buildings in the portfolio are located nationwide. The company is well respected for its focus on quality and commitment to the environment and economic development of the areas where it operates.

From Chapter 7 of *GO! with Microsoft® Office 2010 Integrated Projects Comprehensive*, First Edition, Shelley Gaskin, Carol L. Martin. Copyright © 2012 by Pearson Education, Inc. Published by Pearson Prentice Hall. All rights reserved.

Project 7A Property Presentation

Project Activities

In Activities 7.01 through 7.16, you will use Word, Access, Excel, and PowerPoint to create a variety of files to share information with customers and employees regarding the property portfolio of Select National Properties Group. Your completed files will look similar to Figure 7.1.

Project Files

For Project 7A, you will need the following files:

New blank Word document
New blank Excel workbook
i07A_Property_Data
i07A_Property_Presentation

You will save your files as:

Lastname_Firstname_7A_Leasing_Fax
Lastname_Firstname_7A_Midtown_Developers
Lastname_Firstname_7A_Property_Data
Lastname_Firstname_7A_Property_PivotTable
Lastname_Firstname_7A_Property_Presentation

Project Results

Figure 7.1
Project 7A Property Presentation

Objective 1 | Create and Save a Template in Word

In previous chapters, you have used templates in Access, PowerPoint, and Publisher; templates are also available for Word. A Word template determines the basic structure for a document and contains document settings such as fonts, page layout, and styles. You can create a customized template so that you do not have to recreate the basic document every time it is needed.

Activity 7.01 | Creating a Fax Template

Paul Stancill, the Leasing Manager, would like to send a fax to all new leasing customers, to let them know that their business is appreciated and that he is available to assist them. In this activity, you will create a template that he can reuse for each new customer.

1 **Start** Word. From **Backstage** view, click the **New tab**. Under **Available Templates**, click **Sample templates**. Under **Available Templates**, scroll toward the bottom of the window, and then click **Urban Fax**. Verify that *Urban Fax*—not *Urban Merge Fax*—is selected.

Notice that a preview of the *Urban Fax* template displays on the right.

2 Below the *Urban Fax* preview, click the **Template** option button, and then click the **Create** button. Compare your screen with Figure 7.2.

A new template based on the Urban Fax template is created. Notice in the title bar that the document name Template1, not Document1, displays. To the right of FROM, the user name displays—your name will differ.

Figure 7.2

Template1 in title bar

Template based on Urban Fax template

Name to the right of *FROM* will differ

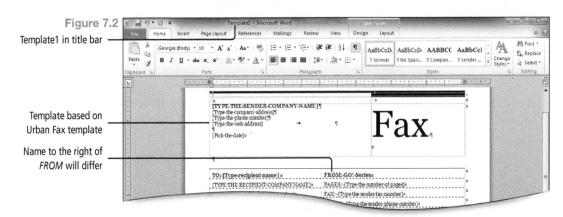

3 On the **Quick Access Toolbar**, click the **Save** button. In the **Save As** dialog box, notice that the location is the Templates folder on your computer and the *Save as type* is Word Template.

4 In the **Save As** dialog box, navigate to the location where you are saving your files, click the **New folder** button, type **Integrated Projects Chapter 7** and then press [Enter] two times. In the **File name** box, delete the existing text, type **Lastname_Firstname_7A_ Leasing_Fax** and then press [Enter].

Activity 7.02 | Changing Data in a Template

You can customize an installed template to better serve your needs. In this activity, you will modify the *content controls* to add the company name and company information. A content control is an area in a template indicated by placeholder text that can be used to add text, pictures, dates, or lists.

1 At the top of the page, locate and click the content control *TYPE SENDER COMPANY NAME*, type **Select National Properties Group** and then press Tab to select the content control *Type the company address*. Type **321 North Michigan Avenue, Suite 700, Chicago, IL 60601** and then press Tab. With the content control *Type the phone number* selected, type **312-555-0070** and then press Tab. With the content control *Type the web address* selected, type www.SelectNationalProp.com

> The template defines the font format of the content controls. In this case, the first content control displays the company name in all uppercase letters.

2 To the right of **FROM**, click the content control, on the left side of the content control, click the content control tab, and the press Del. Type **Paul Stancill, Leasing Manager**

> Text typed in the Author content control will display in the Author box of the Document Information Panel. For purposes of this instruction, because you will be entering different information in the Author box, it is necessary to delete the content control and simply type the text.

Note | Displaying the User Name

The FROM content control can automatically display the user name from the computer you are working at.

---

3 To the right of **PAGES**, click the content control *Type the number of pages*, and then type **1 of 1**

4 Below the **PAGES** heading, to the right of **FAX**, click the content control *Type the sender fax number*, and then type **312-555-0071** Below the text you just typed, to the right of **PHONE**, click the content control *Type the sender phone number*, and then type **312-555-0080**

5 To the right of **CC**, select the content control *Type text*, and then type **Shaun Walker, President**

6 To the right of **RE**, select the content control *Type text*, and then type **New Lease Agreement** Compare your screen with Figure 7.3.

> The data you are entering in the template will remain the same for all customers. You are not entering recipient data because those content controls will change for each recipient.

Figure 7.3

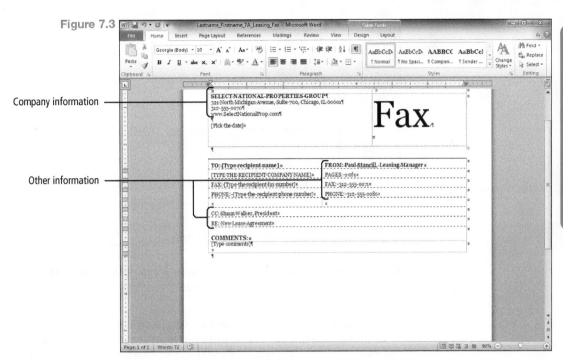

Company information

Other information

7 Below **Comments**, click the content control *Type comments*, and then type **I am pleased to hear from my sales team that you have decided to lease property from the Select National Properties Group. I want you to know that I am here to create and maintain a good working relationship with you and your company. In case you didn't know, our portfolio of properties includes:** and then press Enter.

8 On the **Home tab**, in the **Paragraph group**, click the **Bullets** button ▾. Type each of the following property types, pressing Enter after each type.

> **Shopping Malls**
>
> **Mixed-use Town Center Developments**
>
> **High-rise Office Buildings**
>
> **Office Parks**
>
> **Industrial Buildings and Warehouses**
>
> **Multi-family Housing Developments**
>
> **Educational Facilities**
>
> **Hospitals**

9 On the **Home tab**, in the **Paragraph group**, click the **Bullets** button ▾ to turn it off. Type **If you have any questions, please don't hesitate to contact any of us on the leasing team.**

10 On the **Home tab**, in the **Paragraph group**, click the **Line and Paragraph Spacing** button ▾, and then click **Add Space Before Paragraph**. Compare your screen with Figure 7.4.

Paragraph spacing of 12 pt is inserted above the paragraph.

Figure 7.4

Bulleted items

12 pt. spacing before
paragraph

11 Click the **Review tab**, and then in the **Proofing group**, click the **Spelling & Grammar** button. Check the spelling of the document, correct any misspelled words, and verify that you spelled the names correctly.

12 Display **Backstage** view, with the **Info tab** selected, click **Properties**, and then click **Show Document Panel**. In the **Document Information Panel**, in the **Author** box, type your firstname and lastname, in the **Subject** box, type your course name and section number, and then in the **Keywords** box, type new lease agreement **Close** ☒ the Document Information Panel. If you are instructed to submit your files electronically, go to Step 14.

13 To print your document, from **Backstage** view, click the **Print tab**, and then click **Print**.

14 **Save** 🖫 your document, and then **Close** ☒ Word.

Activity 7.03 | Creating a New Document from a Template

1 On the taskbar, click the **Windows Explorer** button 🖼. Navigate to the **Integrated Projects Chapter 7** folder, and then locate the file **Lastname_Firstname_7A_Leasing_Fax**. To the left of the file name, notice that the icon has a yellow stripe at the top, indicating that the file is a Word template, not a Word document. Compare your screen with Figure 7.5.

Figure 7.5

Template icon with
yellow stripe

2 Double-click the **Lastname_Firstname_7A_Leasing_Fax** file name to start Word and to open a new document based on the template.

In the title bar, notice that the document name is Document1. If you have other documents open, the number in the document name may vary.

3 Click the **Save** button 🖫. In the **Save As** dialog box, navigate to the **Integrated Projects Chapter 7** folder, and then save the document as **Lastname_Firstname_7A_Midtown_Developers**

Integrated Projects | Integrating Word, Excel, Access, and PowerPoint

4 Near the top of the document, click the content control *Pick the date*. Click the **content control arrow**, and then click **Today**.

> The current date displays in the content control.

5 To the right of **TO**, click the content control *Type recipient name*, and then type **David Riley** Below **TO**, click the content control *TYPE THE RECIPIENT COMPANY NAME*, and then type **Midtown Developers** To the right of **FAX**, click the content control *Type the recipient fax number*, and then type **312-555-5939** To the right of **PHONE**, click the content control *Type the recipient phone number*, and then type **312-555-5949**

6 On the **Insert tab**, in the **Header & Footer group**, click the **Footer** button, and then click **Edit Footer**. On the **Design tab**, in the **Insert group**, click the **Quick Parts** button, and then click **Field**. Under **Field names**, click **FileName**, and then click **OK**. On the **Design tab**, in the **Close group**, click the **Close Header and Footer** button.

7 From **Backstage** view, with the **Info tab** selected, click **Properties**, and then click **Show Document Panel**. In the **Document Information Panel**, in the **Author** box, delete the existing text, and then type your firstname and lastname. In the **Keywords** box, delete the existing text, and then type **fax, Midtown Close** ⊠ the Document Information Panel. If you are instructed to submit your files electronically, go to Step 9.

8 To print your document, from **Backstage** view, click the **Print tab**, and then click **Print**.

9 **Save** 🔲 your document, and then **Close** ⊠ Word. **Close** ⊠ Windows Explorer.

Objective 2 | Insert a Combo Box and an Option Group in an Access Form

In an Access form, a **form control** is an object that displays data, performs an action, and lets the user view and work with information. Form controls include text boxes, labels, check boxes, and subform controls.

Activity 7.04 | Adding a Combo Box to an Access Form

Recall that a form is a database object that is used to enter, edit, or display data from a table or query. A **combo box** is a form control that combines a drop-down list with a text box, providing a more compact way to present a list of choices. A combo box gives the user the ability to select a value from a list or to enter a value that is not listed.

1 **Start** Access, and then click **Open**. In the **Open** dialog box, navigate to the location where the student data files are located, and then open the database **i07A_Property_Data**. From **Backstage** view, click **Save Database As**. In the **Save As** dialog box, navigate to the **Integrated Projects Chapter 7** folder, and then **Save** the database as **Lastname_Firstname_7A_Property_Data**

2 On the **Message Bar**, click the **Enable Content** button.

3 In the **Navigation Pane**, click the **Property List** table name to select it. Click the **Create tab**, and then in the **Forms group**, click the **Form** button. On the **Design tab**, in the **Views group**, click the **View button arrow**, and then click **Design View**.

4 In the form, under **Detail**, click the **Property Type** label control—the control on the extreme left of the form. Hold down Ctrl and then click the **Property Type** text box control, the **Salesperson ID** label control, and the **Salesperson ID** textbox control. With all four controls selected, press Del.

> All four controls are deleted from the form. A *label control* is a control on a form or report that contains descriptive information, typically a field name. A *text box control* is the graphical object on a form or report that displays the data from the underlying table or query.

5 On the **Design tab**, in the **Controls group**, click the **More** button ⏷, and verify the **Use Control Wizards** button 🔧 is selected (orange).

6 In the **Controls** gallery, click the **Combo Box** button 🔲. At the bottom of the form, move the pointer below the **Facility Cost** text box control, where you deleted the Property Type text box control, and then click one time. Compare your screen with Figure 7.6.

> The combo box control, including a corresponding label control, is inserted on the form and the Combo Box Wizard dialog box displays. A *combo box control* is the graphical object on a form or report that displays a list from the underlying table or query.

Alert! | Does the Combo Box Wizard not display?

If the Combo Box Wizard dialog box does not display, on the Quick Access Toolbar, click the Undo button. Repeat Steps 5 and 6, being careful to click only one time to insert the combo box control; double-clicking will insert the control but cause the Combo Box Wizard not to display.

Figure 7.6

Combo Box Wizard dialog box

Label control (your number may differ)

Combo Box control

7 In the **Combo Box Wizard** dialog box, click the **I will type in the values that I want** option button, and then click **Next**. Verify that the **Number of columns** is **1**, and then press Tab. Type the following list of property types, pressing Tab after each property type except the last list item.

> **Educational Facility**
> **High-rise Office Building**
> **Hospital**
> **Industrial Building**
> **Mixed-use Town Center Development**
> **Multi-family Housing Development**
> **Office Park**
> **Shopping Mall**
> **Warehouse**

> **Note** | Moving Back in a Wizard
>
> If you accidentally press Enter instead of Tab, the next screen of the wizard will display. To return to the list, click the Back button.

---

8 Click **Next**. Click the **Store that value in this field** option button, and then click the **arrow**. In the field list, click **Property Type**, and then click **Next**. Under *What label would you like for your combo box?*, type **Property Type** and then click **Finish**.

> When data is entered in the form, the selected combo box list item will be stored in the Property Type field.

9 On the **Design tab**, in the **Views group**, click the **View** button to change to Form View.

10 With *Record 1* displayed, click the **Property Type combo box arrow**, and notice that all entries do not fully display. Press Esc to close the **Property Type** combo box list.

11 On the **Home tab**, in the **Views group**, click the **View button arrow**, and then click **Design View**. Click the **Property Type** label control (on the left), point to the middle left sizing handle to display the ⟷ pointer, and then drag to the right until the control is left-aligned with the other label controls. Click the **Property Type** combo box control, point to the middle right sizing handle to display the ⟷ pointer, and then drag to the right to **4 inches on the horizontal ruler**. Compare your screen with Figure 7.7.

Figure 7.7

Label control left-aligned
Combo Box control widened

Project 7A: Property Presentation | **Integrated Projects**

12 Under **Form Header**, click in the **Title** text box control, and then click to the left of the text **Property List** to position the insertion point. Using your own name, type **Lastname Firstname** and then press Spacebar. Click in a blank area of the form to deselect the control.

13 On the **Design tab**, in the **Views group**, click the **View button arrow**, and then click **Form View**. Click the **Property Type combo box arrow**, and notice that all property types are fully displayed. Press Esc to close the **Property Type** combo box list.

14 On the **Quick Access Toolbar**, click the **Save** button 🖫. In the **Save As** dialog box, type **Lastname Firstname Property List Form** and then click **OK**. Right-click the **Lastname Firstname Property List Form tab**, and then on the shortcut menu, click **Close**.

Activity 7.05 │ Adding a Relationship

Recall that a relationship is an association that is established between two tables using common fields. You will create a relationship between the Salesperson ID field in the Property List table and the Salespeople table.

1 Double-click the **Salespeople** table name to open the table in Datasheet view.

The Salespeople table displays showing two fields—the *Salesperson ID* field and the *Salesperson* field.

2 In the **Navigation Pane**, double click the **Property List** table name to open the table. Scroll to the right to view the **Salesperson ID** field.

The Salesperson ID is a number that identifies each salesperson. The name of each salesperson does not display in the Property List table.

3 Right-click the **Property List table tab**, and then on the shortcut menu, click **Close All**.

4 Click the **Database Tools tab**, and then in the **Relationships group**, click the **Relationships** button. If the *Show Table* dialog box does not display, on the **Design tab**, in the **Relationships group**, click the **Show Table** button.

5 In the **Show Table** dialog box, on the **Tables tab**, click the **Salespeople** table name, and then click **Add**. Click the **Property List** table name, and then click **Add**. **Close** 🗙 the **Show Table** dialog box.

6 Position your mouse point over the lower right corner of the **Property List** field list to display the 🗘 pointer, and then drag down until all fields are displayed.

7 In the **Salespeople** field list, point to the **Salesperson ID** field name, hold down the left mouse button, and then drag to the right to the **Property List** field list until the 🗘 pointer is on top of the **Salesperson ID** field name. Release the mouse button.

The Edit Relationships dialog box displays.

8 In the **Edit Relationships** dialog box, verify that *Salesperson ID* displays under both **Table/Query** and **Related Table/Query**. If not, click **Cancel**, and then repeat Step 7.

9 In the **Edit Relationships** dialog box, select the **Enforce Referential Integrity** option, and then click **Create**. Compare your screen with Figure 7.8.

A one-to-many relationship is created. Recall that a one-to-many relationship is a relationship between two tables where one record in the first table corresponds to many records in the second table. In this case, the Salesperson ID can only appear one time in the Salespeople table, but it can appear many times in the Property List table.

Figure 7.8

Property List field
list expanded

One-to-many relationship

10 Save 🖫 the relationship. On the **Design tab**, in the **Relationships group**, click the **Close** button.

Activity 7.06 | Adding an Option Group to an Access Form

An *option group* is an object on a form or report that displays a limited set of alternatives where only one option can be selected at a time. An option group consists of a group frame and a set of check boxes, toggle buttons, or option buttons. When an option button is selected, a number is stored in the Access table. The value of an option group can only be a number, not text.

1 In the **Navigation Pane**, double-click the **Salespeople** table name. To the left of *Salesperson ID 1*—Kaylee Behrns—click the **Expand** button ⊞. Compare your screen with Figure 7.9.

All of the 31 properties that Kaylee Behrns is responsible for are displayed. This is the result of creating a relationship between the Property List table and the Salespeople table. In this table, each salesperson has a unique ID number.

Figure 7.9

Salespeople table

Kaylee Behrns
record expanded

2 In the **Navigation Pane**, double-click the **Property List** table name. Scroll to the right until the **Salesperson ID** field is displayed.

Because of the one-to-many relationship, in this table, the Salesperson ID can be entered many times, instead of only one time in the Salesperson table.

3 Right-click the **Property List table tab**, and then on the shortcut menu, click **Close All**.

4 In the **Navigation Pane**, right-click the **Lastname Firstname Property List Form** name. On the shortcut menu, click **Design View**. **Close** « the **Navigation Pane**.

5 On the **Design tab**, in the **Controls group**, click the **More** button ⏷, and then verify that the **Use Control Wizards** button is selected. Click the **Option Group** button. Point to the form below the **Property Type** text box control, and then click one time. Compare your screen with Figure 7.10.

> The Option Group Wizard dialog box displays.

Figure 7.10

Option Group Wizard
dialog box

Option Group frame
(your number may differ)

6 In the **Option Group Wizard** dialog box, under **Label Names**, type **Kaylee Behrns** and then press ⟨Tab⟩. Type **Jenna Betts** press ⟨Tab⟩, type **Tyrone Mitchell** and then click **Next**.

7 Under **Do you want one option to be the default choice?**, click the **No, I don't want a default** option button, and then click **Next**.

8 Under **What value do you want to assign to each option?**, verify the value for Kaylee is *1*, Jenna is *2*, and Tyrone is *3*, and then click **Next**.

> Recall that the value of an option group must be a number, not text. In this form, when an option button is selected for a salesperson, the number 1, 2, or 3 will be stored in the Property List table, and then because of the relationship between the two tables the name of the salesperson can be queried.

9 Under **What do you want to do with the value of a selected option?**, click the **Store the value in this field** option button. Click the **arrow**, and then click the **Salesperson ID** field name. Click **Next**.

10 Under **What type of controls do you want in the option group?**, verify that **Option buttons** is selected. Under **What style would you like to use?**, click the **Shadowed** option button, and then click **Next**.

11 Under **What caption do you want for the option group?**, type **Salesperson Name** and then click **Finish**.

12 Click the border of the **Salesperson Name option group** control. With the entire control selected, not an individual name box, point to the border to display the ⌖ pointer. Drag the option group control so that the control is left-aligned with the **Property Type** combo box control, and the Salesperson Name caption displays below the Property Type combo box control.

Figure 7.11

Option Group control left aligned with combo box control

Option buttons

13 On the **Design tab**, in the **Views group**, click the **View** button, and then compare your screen with Figure 7.11.

14 **Save** 🖫 the changes to the form.

Activity 7.07 | Entering Data Using a Combo Box and an Option Group

1 At the bottom of the form, click the **New (blank) record** button ▶. Add the following record:

Property ID	**WY2709**
Property Name	**Rock Springs IB**
Address	**100 Linden Ln**
City	**Rock Springs**
State	**WY**
ZIP	**82901**
Land Cost	**150000**
Facility Cost	**407800**

2 In the **Property Type** combo box control, click the **arrow**, and then click **Industrial Building**. In the **Salesperson Name** option group, click the **Tyrone Mitchell** option button, and then compare your screen with Figure 7.12.

Project 7A: Property Presentation | **Integrated Projects**

Figure 7.12

Completed form

3 Press Enter to display a new blank record. Using the same technique, add the following records. Be careful to enter the data accurately.

Property ID	Property Name	Address	City	State	ZIP	Land Cost	Facility Cost	Property Type	Salesperson
WV7101	Woodland Daycare Center	320 Green St	Frankford	WV	24938	250600	450100	Educational Facility	Kaylee Behrns
IA3624	Broaddus Warehouse	145 Tudor Dr	Waterloo	IA	50112	140500	215400	Warehouse	Jenna Betts
MI5189	Kite Subsystems Cos	8692 Technology Blvd	Berkeley	MI	48708	290100	980550	Warehouse	Tyrone Mitchell

4 Verify that you have 80 records. If you are instructed to submit your files electronically, go to Step 6.

5 To print one record, from **Backstage** view, click the **Print tab**, and then click the **Print Preview** button. On the **Print Preview tab**, in the **Page Layout group**, click the **Landscape** button. On the **Print Preview tab**, in the **Close Preview group**, click the **Close Print Preview** button. Below the form, in the navigation area, click the **Last record** button ▶. With Property ID **WY2709** displayed, from **Backstage** view, click the **Print tab**, and then click the **Print** button. In the **Print** dialog box, under **Print Range**, click the **Selected Record(s)** option button. Click **OK** to close the dialog box.

6 Right-click the **Lastname Firstname Property List Form tab**, and then on the shortcut menu, click **Close**.

Integrated Projects | Integrating Word, Excel, Access, and PowerPoint

Activity 7.08 | Creating an Access Query

In the previous activity, when you entered the property records and selected the Salesperson option button, a number was stored in the Salesperson ID field in the Property List table. In order to see which salesperson is responsible for each property, you will create a query that includes fields from both tables in the database.

1 On the **Create tab**, in the **Queries group**, click the **Query Wizard** button. In the **New Query** dialog box, verify that **Simple Query Wizard** is selected, and then click **OK**.

2 Under **Tables/Queries**, verify that **Table: Property List** displays. Under **Available Fields**, double-click the field names **Property Name**, **Address**, **City**, **State**, **ZIP**, **Land Cost**, **Facility Cost**, and **Property Type**.

3 Under **Tables/Queries**, click the **arrow**, and then click the **Salespeople** table name. Under **Available Fields**, double-click the field name **Salesperson**. Compare your screen with Figure 7.13.

The selected field names from both tables display under Selected Fields.

Figure 7.13

Salespeople table name

Selected fields from both tables

4 Click **Next** two times.

5 Under *What title do you want for your query?*, type **Lastname Firstname Property List Query** and then click **Finish**.

6 Scroll to the right and notice the names of the salespeople display in the Salesperson field.

The names of the salespeople come from the Salesperson field in the Salespeople table. All of the other fields come from the Property List table. Because the tables are related, you can display any field from either table in a query.

7 From **Backstage** view, at the right, click **View and edit database properties**. In the **Properties** dialog box, on the **Summary tab**, in the **Subject** box, type your course name and section number, in the **Author** box, type your firstname and lastname, and then in the **Keywords** box, type **form controls, query** Click **OK** to close the dialog box, and then click the **Home tab**.

8 Right-click the **Lastname Firstname Property List Query tab**, and then on the shortcut menu, click **Close**. **Close** [×] Access.

Objective 3 | Create a PivotTable Report and a PivotChart Report in Excel

Although Access is generally the best application to use for storing data, you can import the data into Excel to manipulate it using features such as the *PivotTable report* and the *PivotChart report*.

A PivotTable is an interactive, cross-tabulated Excel report that summarizes and analyzes data. In a PivotTable, you can *pivot*—move a row to a column or a column to a row—to see different views and summaries of the source data. You can display the details for areas of interest, or calculate the different summaries such as averages. Use a PivotTable when you want to analyze related totals or compare several facts about each value, especially when you have a long list of figures to sum.

A PivotChart is a graphical representation of the data in a PivotTable. The advantage of creating a PivotChart instead of a standard Excel chart is that you can pivot the data displayed in the PivotChart just as you can in a PivotTable.

Activity 7.09 | Importing Access Data into Excel

Paul Stancill, the Leasing Manager, is preparing a presentation to upper management. He has asked you to use Excel's PivotTable report and PivotChart report features to analyze the data in the Access database so that he can use the information in his presentation.

1 **Start** Excel. Click the **Data tab**, and then in the **Get External Data group**, click the **From Access** button. In the **Select Data Source** dialog box, navigate to the **Integrated Projects Chapter 7** folder. Click the Access file **Lastname_Firstname_7A_Property_Data**, and then click **Open**. In the **Select Table** dialog box, verify **Lastname Firstname Property List Query** is selected, and then click **OK**.

2 In the **Import Data** dialog box, under *Select how you want to view this data in your workbook*, click the **PivotTable Report** option button.

3 Under *Where do you want to put the data?*, verify that the **Existing worksheet** option button is selected and that =$A$1 displays in the box. Click **OK**. Compare your screen with Figure 7.14.

The *PivotTable Field List*, on the right side of your screen, enables you to move fields to different areas in the PivotTable or PivotChart. The *Field Section*—the upper portion of the task pane—contains the available field names you can add to the *Area Section*. The Area Section—the lower portion of the task pane that contains four quadrants where field names are placed to determine how the report will display. The graphic at the left of your screen is replaced with the PivotTable when you select fields in the task pane.

Figure 7.14

PivotTable Field
List task pane

PivotTable 1 graphic
(your number may differ)

Field Section

Area Section

Alert! | Does your PivotTable Field List layout differ?

If the PivotTable report has been used previously on your computer, the arrangement of the Field Section and the Area Section of the PivotTable Field List may display in a different layout. To change to the layout shown in this instruction, near the top of the task pane, to the right of Choose fields to add to report, click the button, and then click Field Section and Area Section Stacked.

---

4 On the **Quick Access Toolbar**, click the **Save** button. In the **Save As** dialog box, navigate to the **Integrated Projects Chapter 7** folder, and then save the file as **Lastname_Firstname_7A_Property_PivotTable**

Note | Addressing a Security Warning

When you import Access data into Excel, you are linking the two files. If you close and then reopen your linked Excel file, a Security Warning may display alerting you that the file is linked. Click the Enable Content button, and then click OK.

Activity 7.10 | Creating a PivotTable

To create a PivotTable, you will add the fields from the PivotTable Field List. Within the PivotTable, you can display the level of detail, create calculations, and sort or filter the data.

1 In the **PivotTable Field List** task pane, under **Choose fields to add to report**, drag the **Salesperson** field name to the **Row Labels** box at the bottom of the task pane. Compare your screen with Figure 7.15.

The Salesperson data is placed on the worksheet in column A as a *Row Label*. Row Labels are fields that are assigned a row orientation in a PivotTable and become the row headings. When a field is added to the Area Section of the task pane, a check mark displays to the left of the field name in the Field Section.

Project 7A: Property Presentation | **Integrated Projects**

Integrated Projects

Figure 7.15

Content of Salesperson
field displays in column A

Salesperson field
check mark

Salesperson field in
Row Labels box

2 In the **PivotTable Field List** task pane, drag the **Property Type** field to the **Column Labels** box.

> *Column Labels* are fields that are assigned a column orientation in a PivotTable and become the column headings.

3 In the **PivotTable Field List** task pane, drag the **Land Cost** field to the **Values** box. Compare your screen with Figure 7.16.

> The *Values* area contains the cells in a PivotTable that summarize quantitative data. The default is to sum the figures, but you can display the values in a variety of other ways, such as the average, maximum, or minimum.

Figure 7.16

Grand Total for each
salesperson

Sum of Land Cost
displays in cell A1

Grand Total for each
property type

Property Type field in
Column Labels box

Sum of Land Cost
in Values box

4 On the **Options tab**, in the **Active Field group**, click the **Field Settings** button. In the **Value Field Settings** dialog box, at the bottom left, click **Number Format**. In the **Format Cells** dialog box, under **Category**, click **Currency**. Click the **Decimal places spin box down arrow** two times to display **0**. Verify that the **Symbol** is **$** and then click **OK**. In the **Value Field Settings** dialog box, click **OK**, and then compare your screen with Figure 7.17.

Figure 7.17

Numbers display as
currency with 0
decimal places

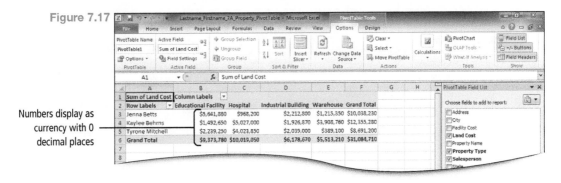

5 Click cell **A10**.

The PivotTable Field List task pane and the PivotTable contextual tabs no longer display because the PivotTable is not selected.

6 Click cell **A1** to select the PivotTable and to display the PivotTable Field List task pane.

7 Save 🖫 the workbook.

Activity 7.11 | Pivoting the PivotTable Report

To view different summaries of the source data, you can pivot a row to a column or a column to a row.

1 In the **PivotTable Field List** task pane, drag the **State** field to the **Column Labels** box, and then drop the **State** field so it displays under the **Property Type** field. Compare your screen with Figure 7.18.

The Property Types display in row 2 of the PivotTable and the States display in row 3.

Figure 7.18

Property types display in row 2

States display in row 3

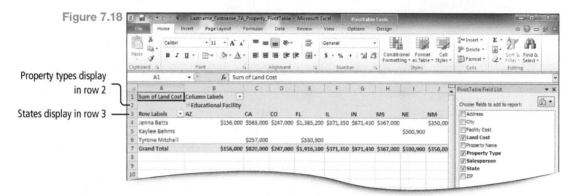

2 In the **Column Labels** box, click the **State arrow**, and then click **Move Up**. Compare your screen with Figure 7.19.

In the PivotTable, the States display in row 2 and the Property Types display in row 3.

Figure 7.19

States display in row 2

Property types display in row 3

State and Property Type fields in Column Labels box

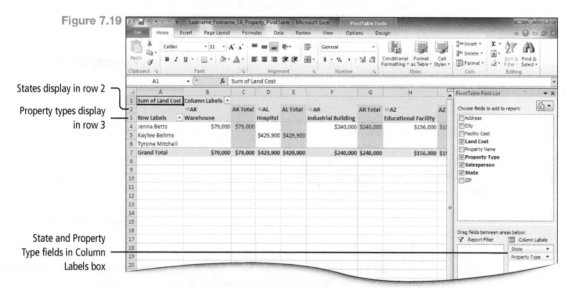

3 From **Backstage** view, click the **Print tab**. Below the **Print Preview**, in the navigation area, click the **Next Page** button ▶ to view the pages.

There are 15 pages in the report. One reason to use a PivotTable is that you can present the data in a concise manner. This report does not meet that requirement.

4 Click the **Home tab**. In the **Column Labels** box, click the **State arrow**, and then click **Move to Row Labels**. If necessary, drag the State field so that it displays below the Salesperson field. Compare your screen with Figure 7.20.

> In the PivotTable, the State field is pivoted—changed from a column label to a row label. In the Row Labels box, the State field displays below the Salesperson field.

Figure 7.20

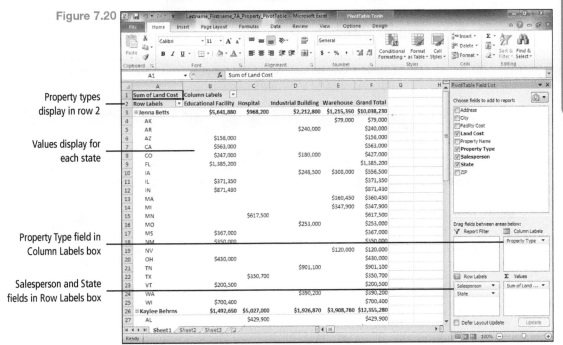

Property types display in row 2

Values display for each state

Property Type field in Column Labels box

Salesperson and State fields in Row Labels box

5 From **Backstage** view, click the **Print tab**. Below the **Print Preview**, in the navigation area, click the **Next Page** button ▶ to view the second page.

> There are two pages in the report. By pivoting the fields, the same data is presented in a more concise manner—a two-page report instead of a 15-page report.

6 Click the **Home tab**. In cell **A3**, to the left of the name *Jenna Betts*, click the **Collapse** button ⊟. Scroll down, and then in cell **A28**, to the left of the name *Tyrone Mitchell*, click the **Collapse** button ⊟.

> Only the details for the salesperson Kaylee Behrns are displayed. The details are hidden for Jenna Betts and for Tyrone Mitchell, but the totals for these two salespeople are displayed.

7 Right-click the **Sheet1 sheet tab**, and then on the shortcut menu, click **Rename**. Type **Behrns Detail** and then press Enter.

8 Press Ctrl + Home. **Save** 🖬 the workbook.

Activity 7.12 | Filtering the PivotTable Report

Recall that filtering is the process of displaying only a subset of data. In this activity, you will use the *Report Filter* area to display the information for only one salesperson at a time. The Report Filter is the area on a PivotTable that is used to restrict the data that displays.

1 Right-click the **Behrns Detail sheet tab**, and then on the shortcut menu, click **Move or Copy**. In the **Move or Copy** dialog box, click **(move to end)**, and then select the **Create a copy** check box. Click **OK**.

A new Behrns Detail (2) sheet is created and selected. You would normally use the same worksheet to filter data in various ways. For purposes of this instruction, however, you are creating copies of worksheets and applying filters.

2 In the **PivotTable Field List** task pane, in the **Row Labels** box, click the **Salesperson arrow**, and then click **Move to Report Filter**. Compare your screen with Figure 7.21.

In the PivotTable, the Salesperson field displays in row 1 above all the other fields. In cell B1, the term *(All)* and the field filter arrow indicate that the Salesperson field is not filtered—data for all salespersons is displayed.

Figure 7.21

Salesperson field name displays in cell A1

(All) displays in cell B1

Field filter arrow

Salesperson field in Report Filter box

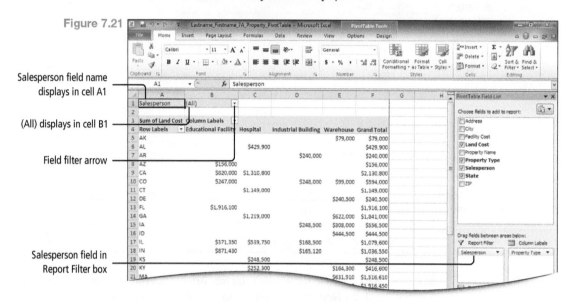

3 In cell **B1**, click the **Salesperson filter arrow** ⏷, click **Tyrone Mitchell**, and then click **OK**. Compare your screen with Figure 7.22.

Only the data for Tyrone Mitchell displays. The totals do not display for the other salespeople. The filter icon in cell B1 informs the user that the PivotTable has a filter applied.

Figure 7.22

Tyrone Mitchell displays in cell B1

Filter icon displays in cell B1

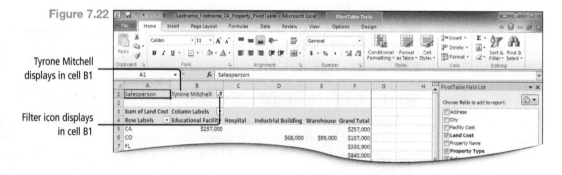

Integrated Projects | Integrating Word, Excel, Access, and PowerPoint

Another Way

Double-click the sheet tab to select the sheet name, type the new sheet name, and then press Enter.

4 Right-click the **Behrns Detail (2) sheet tab**, and then on the shortcut menu, click **Rename**. Type **Mitchell Detail** and then press Enter.

5 Right-click the **Mitchell Detail sheet tab**, and then on the shortcut menu, click **Move or Copy**. In the **Move or Copy** dialog box, click **(move to end)**, and then select the **Create a copy** check box. Click **OK**.

A new Mitchell Detail (2) sheet is created and selected.

6 In cell **B1**, click the **Salesperson filter arrow** [▼], click **Jenna Betts**, and then click **OK**.

Only the data for Jenna Betts displays.

7 Right-click the **Mitchell Detail (2) sheet tab**, and then on the shortcut menu, click **Rename**. Type **Betts Detail** and then press Enter.

8 Save [💾] the workbook.

Activity 7.13 | Using a Drill-Down Indicator

One of the features of a PivotTable is the *drill-down indicator*—a feature that shows the detailed records of a PivotTable total. Paul Stancill has asked you to create a new PivotTable report to display the Facility Cost by Property Type and by State, and then use the drill-down indicator to show the detailed records for the state of Illinois. Because upper management wants to determine in which state the company has the most investments in hospitals, you will sort the PivotTable by hospitals and then display the detailed records for the state of California.

1 Click the **Sheet2 sheet tab** to make it the active worksheet.

2 Click the **Data tab**, and then in the **Get External Data group**, click the **From Access** button. In the **Select Data Source** dialog box, navigate to the **Integrated Projects Chapter 7** folder. Click the Access file **Lastname_Firstname_7A_Property_Data**, and then click **Open**. In the **Select Table** dialog box, verify **Lastname Firstname Property List Query** is selected, and then click **OK**.

3 In the **Import Data** dialog box, under *Select how you want to view this data in your workbook*, click the **PivotTable Report** option button.

4 Under *Where do you want to put the data?*, verify that the **Existing worksheet** option button is selected, and then click **OK**.

A new PivotTable report displays.

> **Note** | Creating a New PivotTable Report
>
> Every time you create a new PivotTable report, Excel will automatically number the report—PivotTable1, PivotTable2, and so on. Your PivotTable names may vary depending on how many reports you have created. Generally, you can pivot the same PivotTable to present the data in various ways. In order to submit all of your work to your instructor, you imported the Access data again to create a new PivotTable report.

5 Double-click the **Sheet2 sheet tab**, type **Facility Cost by State** and then press Enter.

6 In the **PivotTable Field List** task pane, under **Choose fields to add to report**, drag the **State** field name to the **Row Labels** box.

7 In the **PivotTable Field List** task pane, drag the **Property Type** field to the **Column Labels** box, and then drag the **Facility Cost** field to the **Values** box. Compare your screen with Figure 7.23.

The States are listed in column A and the Property Types display in row 2.

Project 7A: Property Presentation | **Integrated Projects**

Figure 7.23

States display in column A

Facilities display in row 2

Property Type field in Column Labels box

State field in Row labels box

Sum of Facility Cost field in Values box

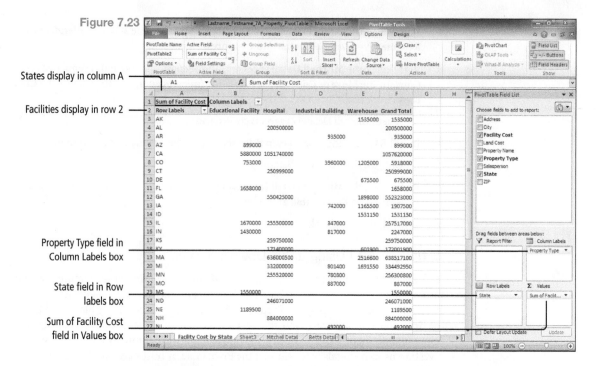

8 On the **Options tab**, in the **Active Field group**, click the **Field Settings** button. In the **Value Field Settings** dialog box, at the bottom left, click **Number Format**. In the **Format Cells** dialog box, under **Category**, click **Currency**. Click the **Decimal places spin box down arrow** two times to display **0**. Verify that the **Symbol** is **$**, and then click **OK**. In the **Value Field Settings** dialog box, click **OK**.

The numbers in the PivotTable are formatted as currency with 0 decimal places.

9 Click cell **F15**. Verify that cell F15 represents the Grand Total for the state of Illinois (IL).

Alert! | **Is your Grand Total different?**

If the Grand Total for the state of Illinois does not display in cell F15, return to Activity 7.7, Step 3, and verify that you entered the Access data accurately.

---

10 Double-click cell **F15**, and then click cell **A6** to deselect the table. Compare your screen with Figure 7.24.

A new Sheet6 is created, and the detailed records of the Illinois properties are displayed. Your sheet number may differ.

Figure 7.24

Three records display with State field IL

Integrated Projects | Integrating Word, Excel, Access, and PowerPoint

11 Right-click the **Sheet6 sheet tab**, and then on the shortcut menu, click **Rename**. Type **IL Detail** and then press (Enter).

12 Click the **Facility Cost by State sheet tab**. Click any cell in **column C**—the Hospital property type field. On the **Home tab**, in the **Editing group**, click the **Sort & Filter** button, and then click **Sort Largest to Smallest**. Compare your screen with Figure 7.25.

> Column C is sorted in descending order.

Figure 7.25

CA displays in cell A3

Column C sorted in descending order

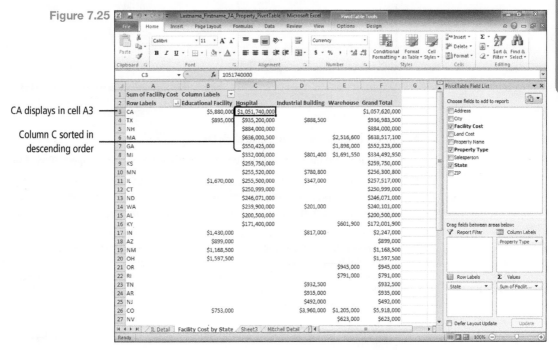

13 Double-click cell **C3**.

> A new Sheet7 is created, and the detailed records of the hospitals in California (CA) are displayed.

14 Right-click the **Sheet7 sheet tab**, and then from the shortcut menu, click **Rename**. Type **CA Hospitals** and then press (Enter).

15 **Save** 🖫 the workbook.

Activity 7.14 | Creating and Modifying a PivotChart Report

A PivotChart is based on a PivotTable, and the two are interactive. If you change the way the data displays on the PivotChart, it changes the display of the same data on the related PivotTable. Morgan Bannon-Navarre, the Select National Properties Group CFO, has asked you to create a PivotChart showing the average cost of investments the company has for industrial buildings and warehouses.

1 Click the **Facility Cost by State sheet tab**. Click the **Options tab**, and then in the **Tools group**, click the **PivotChart** button. In the **Insert Chart** dialog box, verify that **Column** is selected, and then in the first row, click the fourth style—**3-D Clustered Column**. Compare your screen with Figure 7.26.

Figure 7.26

Insert Chart dialog box

3-D Clustered Column chart style

2 In the **Insert Chart** dialog box, click **OK**.

A chart and the field buttons Sum of Facility Cost, State, and Property Type display.

3 On the **Design tab**, in the **Location group**, click the **Move Chart** button. In the **Move Chart** dialog box, click the **New Sheet** option button, in the **New Sheet** box, type **Average Cost Chart** and then click **OK**. Compare your screen with Figure 7.27.

The PivotChart displays on a new Average Cost Chart sheet. The names of the boxes in the Area Section of the PivotTable Field List task pane change. The *Legend Fields (Series)* are the fields—in this case, the Property Type field—that are assigned to the columns that display in a column PivotChart report. The *Axis Fields (Categories)* are the fields—in this case, the States field—that are assigned to the categories that display on the horizontal axis in a column PivotChart.

Figure 7.27

PivotChart report

Legend Fields (Series) box

Axis Fields (Categories) box

Integrated Projects | Integrating Word, Excel, Access, and PowerPoint

4 Above the **Legend**, click the **Property Type** field button. Click the **Educational Facility** check box, and then click the **Hospital** check box.

> The check boxes for Educational Facility and Hospital are cleared. The check boxes for Industrial Building and Warehouse are selected.

5 Click **OK**. Click the **Analyze tab**, and then in the **Show/Hide group**, click the **Field List** button and the **Field Buttons** button. Compare your screen with Figure 7.28.

> The PivotChart is filtered to display facility costs only for only the Industrial Building and Warehouse property types. The PivotTable Field List task pane and the PivotChart Field Buttons are toggled off and no longer display.

Figure 7.28

Field Buttons and Field List buttons toggled off

Industrial Building and Warehouse display in legend

States display on horizontal axis

6 Click the **Facility Cost by State sheet tab**. Notice in **row 2** that only the Industrial Building and Warehouse property types are displayed.

> Recall that the PivotChart and the PivotTable are interactive. Because you filtered the PivotChart to display only the Industrial Building and Warehouse property types, the related PivotTable is also filtered.

7 Scroll down to **row 29**, and then notice the Grand Total values. If necessary, click anywhere in the table. Click the **Options tab**, and then in the **Active Field group**, click the **Field Settings** button. In the **Value Field Settings** dialog box, under **Summarize value field by**, click **Average**, and then click **OK**. Notice that the Grand Totals are lower numbers because they are averages and not totals. Scroll up to view cell **A1**, and notice that the heading is changed to *Average of Facility Cost*. Compare your screen with Figure 7.29.

Project 7A: Property Presentation | **Integrated Projects**

Figure 7.29

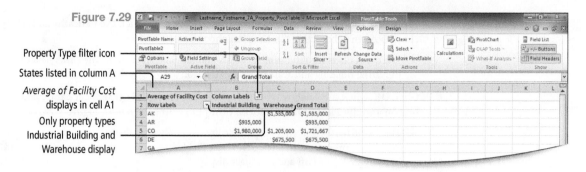

Property Type filter icon

States listed in column A

Average of Facility Cost
displays in cell A1
Only property types
Industrial Building and
Warehouse display

8 On the **Options tab**, in the **Show group**, click the **Field List** button. In the **PivotTable Field List** task pane, drag the **Salesperson** field name down to the **Row Labels** box, and then drop it so that it displays above the **State** field name.

The fields are pivoted to display the Average of Facility Cost for each salesperson.

9 Click the **Average Cost Chart** sheet tab.

The PivotChart reflects the changes made in the PivotTable. Columns are grouped by the name of the salesperson. Within each group, the states display in alphabetical order.

10 **Close** ☒ the **PivotTable Field List** task pane.

11 Click the **Layout tab**. In the **Labels group**, click the **Chart Title** button, and then click **Above Chart**. Type **Average Cost of Industrial Buildings and Warehouses** and then click in a blank area of the chart.

12 On the **Layout tab**, in the **Labels group**, click the **Legend** button, and then click **Show Legend at Top**. Click the **Legend** to select it. Click the **Home tab**, and then in the **Font group**, click the **Increase Font Size** button Aˆ two times. In the **Font group**, click the **Bold** button B .

13 Right-click the **Sheet3 sheet tab**, and then on the shortcut menu, click **Delete**.

14 Right-click the active sheet tab—*Mitchell Detail*—and then on the shortcut menu, click **Select All Sheets**. Click the **Insert tab**, and then in the **Text group**, click the **Header & Footer** button. On the **Design tab**, in the **Navigation group**, click the **Go to Footer** button. In the **Footer** area, click the box just above the word **Footer**, and then in the **Header & Footer Elements group**, click the **File Name** button. Click any cell in the worksheet to exit the footer.

15 On the right side of the status bar, click the **Normal** button ▦ , and then press Ctrl + Home to make cell **A1** the active cell. Right-click any sheet tab, and then on the shortcut menu, click **Ungroup Sheets**.

16 From **Backstage** view, click **Properties**, and then click **Show Document Panel**. In the **Information Document Panel**, in the **Author** box, type your firstname and lastname, in the **Subject** box, type your course name and section number, and then in the **Keywords** box, type **costs, PivotTable, PivotChart Close** ☒ the **Document Information Panel**.

17 **Save** 🖫 the workbook.

Objective 4 | Import Data into a PowerPoint Presentation

PowerPoint is an application that enables you to present data to a group of people in a straightforward manner. Recall that all of the applications in an office suite work well together. This means you can import data from the other applications into PowerPoint to create a high-quality presentation.

Activity 7.15 | Copying Data into a PowerPoint Presentation

1 **Start** PowerPoint. From **Backstage** view, click **Open**. In the **Open** dialog box, navigate to the location of the student data files, and then open **i07A_Property_Presentation**. From **Backstage** view, click **Save As**. In the **Save As** dialog box, navigate to the **Integrated Projects Chapter 7** folder, and then **Save** the presentation as **Lastname_Firstname_7A_Property_Presentation** If necessary, to display the rulers, on the View tab, in the Show group, select the Ruler check box.

2 Click the **Insert tab**, and then in the **Text group**, click the **Header & Footer** button. In the **Header and Footer** dialog box, on the **Notes and Handouts tab**, select the **Footer** check box. Type **Lastname Firstname 7A Property Presentation** and then click **Apply to All**.

3 **Start** Word. Navigate to the **Integrated Projects Chapter 7** folder, and then open the document **Lastname_Firstname_7A_Midtown_Developers**. Under **Comments**, select the list of eight property types. On the **Home tab**, in the **Clipboard group**, click the **Copy** button 🖹.

4 On the taskbar, click the **PowerPoint** button to make the **Lastname_Firstname_7A_Property_Presentation** window active. Click **Slide 2**. Click the **Home tab**, and then in the **Clipboard group**, click the **Paste** button. With the placeholder border selected, point to the middle left sizing handle to display the 🖾 pointer, and then drag the placeholder to approximately **4 inches left of 0 on the horizontal ruler**.

The eight property types from the Word document are pasted in Slide 2.

5 Click anywhere in the placeholder, and then press Ctrl + A to select all the text in the placeholder. On the **Home tab**, in the **Font group**, click the **Font Size button arrow** 44 ▾, and then click **24**. On the **Home tab**, in the **Paragraph group**, click the **Bullets button arrow** ▤ ▾, and then click **Filled Round Bullets**. Click in a blank area of the slide and then compare your screen with Figure 7.30.

Figure 7.30

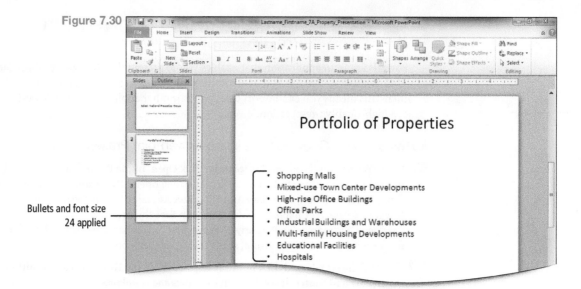

Bullets and font size
24 applied

6 On the taskbar, click the **Excel** button to make the **Lastname_Firstname_7A_ Property_PivotTable** window active. Click the **Average Cost Chart sheet tab**. Click in a blank area of the chart, and then verify that the entire chart is selected. On the **Home tab**, in the **Clipboard group**, click the **Copy** button.

7 On the taskbar, click the **PowerPoint** button to make the **Lastname_Firstname_7A_ Property_Presentation** window active. Click **Slide 3**. On the **Home tab**, in the **Clipboard group**, click the **Paste** button.

   The Excel PivotChart report Average Cost of Industrial Buildings and Warehouses is pasted on Slide 3.

Activity 7.16 | Modifying the PowerPoint Presentation

1 On the **Home tab**, in the **Slides group**, click the **New Slide button arrow**, and then click **Title and Content**. On the new slide, Slide 4, click the **Title** placeholder, and then type **Contact Us**

2 Click the bottom placeholder, type **312-555-0070** and then press Enter. Type www. SelectNationalProp.com and then press Ctrl + A. On the **Home tab**, in the **Paragraph group**, click the **Bullets** button to remove the bullets. In the **Paragraph group**, click the **Center** button.

3 Click **Slide 1**. On the **Design tab**, in the **Themes group**, click the **More** button. In the **Themes** gallery, under **Built-in**, in the first row, click the fifth theme—**Apothecary**.

4 Click the **Transitions tab**, and then in the **Transition to This Slide group**, click the **Fade** transition. In the **Timing group**, click the **Apply To All** button.

5 Click the **Slide Show tab**. In the **Start Slide Show group**, click the **From Beginning** button, and then view your presentation, clicking the mouse to advance through the slides. When the black slide displays, click the mouse one more time to display the presentation in Normal view.

6 From **Backstage** view, verify the **Info tab** is selected, click **Properties**, and then click **Show Document Panel**. In the **Document Information Panel**, in the **Author** box, type your firstname and lastname, in the **Subject** box, type your course name and section number, and then in the **Keywords** box, type **properties, portfolio Close** the Document Information Panel.

Integrated Projects | Integrating Word, Excel, Access, and PowerPoint

7 **Save** 💾 the presentation. If you are instructed to submit your files electronically, go to Step 5. To print your PowerPoint presentation, from **Backstage** view, click the **Print tab**. Under **Settings**, click the **Full Page Slides arrow**, under **Handouts**, click **6 Slides Horizontal**, and then click **Print**.

8 **Close** ❎ PowerPoint. If you are instructed to submit your files electronically, go to Step 7.

9 To print selected Excel worksheets, click the **Average Cost Chart sheet tab**, hold down Ctrl, and then click the **Facility Cost by State** and **Betts Detail** sheet tabs. From **Backstage** view, under **Settings**, verify **Print Active Shee**ts displays, and then click **Print**.

10 **Close** ❎ Excel, and then **Close** ❎ Word.

11 Submit your electronic or printed Word, Excel, PowerPoint, and Access files as directed by your instructor.

End **You have completed Project 7A**

Project 7B Retail Report

In Activities 7.17 through 7.22, you will import data from Access into Excel, and then use Excel functions to help determine loan information. Morgan Bannon-Navarre, the Select National Properties Group CFO, is considering the purchase of several retail stores and has asked you to analyze the data. Your completed files will look similar to Figure 7.31.

Project Files

For Project 7B, you will need the following files:

New blank Excel worksheet
i07B_Retail_Stores
i07B_Retail_Report

You will save your files as:

Lastname_Firstname_7B_Store_Payments
Lastname_Firstname_7B_Retail_Report

Project Results

Figure 7.31
Project 7B Retail Report

Recall that a function is a predefined formula—a formula that Excel has already built for you—that performs calculations by using specific values—*arguments*—in a particular order. An argument is any value that the function uses to perform operations or calculations. Common arguments used with functions include numbers, text, cell references, and names.

Activity 7.17 | Inserting the PMT Function

Morgan Bannon-Navarre, the company CFO, is considering the purchase of several retail stores. He has created a list of stores and their purchase prices in an Access database, and needs to decide if the company should purchase any of these properties. To purchase any stores, he knows the company would borrow the money for 20 years at an annual interest rate of 6 percent. Excel's *PMT function* calculates the payment for a loan based on constant payments and a constant interest rate. In the following activity, you will import the retail store data into Excel, and then use the PMT function to calculate the monthly payment for each store.

1 Start Excel. Click the **Data tab**, and then in the **Get External Data group**, click the **From Access** button. In the **Select Data Source** dialog box, navigate to the location of your student data files. Click the Access file **i07B_Retail_Stores**, and then click **Open**.

Because there is only one table in the database, Excel automatically selects the table and displays the Import Data dialog box.

2 In the **Import Data** dialog box, under *Select how you want to view this data in your workbook*, verify that the **Table** option button is selected.

3 Under *Where do you want to put the data?*, verify that the **Existing worksheet** option button is selected, and then click **OK**. Compare your screen with Figure 7.32.

The data from the Access table—the ID, Store and Purchase Price fields—displays as a table in the worksheet.

Figure 7.32

Purchase Price data in column C

Store names in column B

ID in column A

4 On the **Quick Access Toolbar**, click the **Save** button 🖫. In the **Save As** dialog box, navigate to the **Integrated Projects Chapter 7** folder, and then **Save** the file as **Lastname_Firstname_7B_Store_Payments**

5 Click cell **D1**. Type **Monthly** and then hold down [Alt] and press [Enter]. Type **Payment** and then press [Enter].

> Pressing [Alt] + [Enter] causes the heading *Monthly Payment* to display on two lines in cell D1. The heading format from the table is automatically applied to the new Monthly Payment heading.

6 Verify that cell **D2** is the active cell. On the **Formula Bar**, click the **Insert Function** button 𝑓ₓ. Click the **Or select a category arrow** to view a list of function categories.

7 Press [Esc] to close the category list. Under **Search for a function**, select the text, type **PMT** and then click **Go**. Under **Select a function**, verify that **PMT** is selected, and then near the bottom left of the dialog box, click **Help on this function**.

> The Excel Help window opens, and an explanation of the PMT function displays.

8 Read the information about the PMT function, and then **Close** [✕] the **Excel Help** window.

9 In the **Insert Function** dialog box, click **OK** to display the Function Arguments dialog box. If necessary, move the Function Arguments dialog box so that the data in columns A:C is visible.

Note | Function Arguments

The Function Arguments dialog box separates the different arguments of the function so that you can input the arguments one by one. As you click each argument box, an explanation of the argument displays at the bottom of the dialog box. Argument names that display in bold are required for the function. Argument names that are not bolded are optional. When you complete the arguments and click OK, the structure of the function will automatically be entered in the active cell.

---

10 In the **Function Arguments** dialog box, in the **Rate** argument box, type **6%/12** and then press [Tab].

> The monthly interest rate of 0.005 displays to the right of the Rate argument box. The 6% interest rate is an annual interest rate, but you want to calculate a monthly payment. In order to determine a monthly interest rate, you need to divide the annual rate by 12—the number of months in a year.

11 In the **Nper** argument box, type **20*12** and then press [Tab].

> The number 240 displays to the right of the Nper argument box. The loan is for 20 years, but you want the PMT function to calculate a monthly payment. To determine how many months you will be paying back the loan, you need to multiply the number of years by 12—the number of months in one year.

12 Verify that the insertion point is in the **Pv** argument box, and then click cell **C2**. Compare your screen with Figure 7.33.

> 159000 displays to the right of the Pv argument box. This is the present value of how much money the company would need to borrow to purchase the Remembrances store. Because the PMT function will be copied to the remaining cells in column D, you use a cell reference instead of typing the actual dollar amount. Below the Type argument box, -1139.125383—the amount of the monthly payment—displays.

Figure 7.33

Monthly rate

Rate argument

Number of monthly
payments

Present value

Monthly payment

13 Delete all of the text in the **Pv** argument box. Type a minus sign (-), and then click cell **C2**.

> Notice -159000 displays to the right of the Pv argument box. In order to display the monthly payment amount as a positive number, in the Pv argument box, it is necessary to type the minus sign before clicking cell C2.

14 In the **Function Arguments** dialog box, click **OK**.

> The monthly payment for each row displays in column D. Recall that, in an Excel table, a calculated column uses a single formula that adjusts for each row of the column.

15 **Save** the workbook.

Activity 7.18 | Inserting the IF Function

The **IF function** uses a logical test to check whether a condition is met, and then returns one value if true, and another value if false. Morgan Bannon-Navarre has decided that the company will purchase a store if the monthly payment is less than $2000.

1 Click cell **E1**. Type **Purchase** and then hold down Alt and press Enter. Type **Store?** and then press Enter.

> The heading *Purchase Store?* displays on two lines in cell E1.

2 Verify cell **E2** is the active cell. On the **Formula Bar**, click the **Insert Function** button *fx*. Click the **Or select a category arrow**, and then click **Logical**. Under **Select a function**, click **IF**, and then click **OK**.

3 In the **Function Arguments** dialog box, in the **Logical_test** argument box, type **D2<2000** and then press Tab. Compare your screen with Figure 7.34.

> The logical test is the condition that you are determining is TRUE or FALSE. In this case, you want to determine if the monthly payment in cell D2 is less than 2000. TRUE automatically displays to the right of the Logical_test argument box because the value in cell D2 is less than 2000. Because the IF function will be copied to the remaining cells in column E, you are using a cell reference.

Figure 7.34

Logical test argument

Logical test TRUE

4 In the **Value_if_true** argument box, type **Yes** and then press Tab.

To the right of the Value_if_true argument box, Yes displays in quotes. Text in an argument must be in quotation marks; Excel automatically puts the quotation marks around the text.

5 In the **Value_if_false** argument box, type **No** and then click **OK**.

The result of the IF statement for each row displays in column E.

6 At the top of the **Purchase Store?** column—column E—click the **AutoFilter arrow**. Select the **No** check box to toggle it off, and then click **OK**. Compare your screen with Figure 7.35.

Only the rows with Yes in column E display. The AutoFilter icon displays in cell E1 to indicate that the column is filtered.

Figure 7.35

Purchase Store?
AutoFilter icon

Column E displays
only Yes results

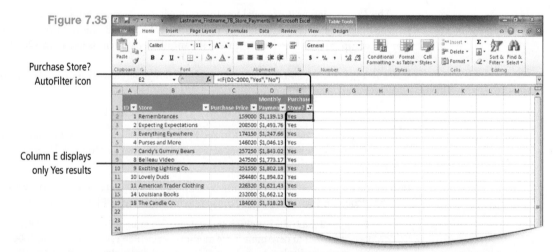

7 Select **column C**. On the **Home tab**, in the **Number group**, click the **Number Format button arrow** General, and then click **Currency**. Select **columns A:E**. Point to the line between the headings A and B until the ⊞ pointer displays, and then double-click.

The columns are widened to display all data.

Integrated Projects | Integrating Word, Excel, Access, and PowerPoint

8 Click the **Sheet2 sheet tab**. Hold down [Shift], and then click the **Sheet3 sheet tab**. Right-click the **Sheet3 sheet tab**, and then on the shortcut menu, click **Delete**. Right-click the **Sheet1 sheet tab**, and then on the shortcut menu, click **Rename**. Type **Retail Stores** and then press [Enter].

9 Click the **Insert tab**, and then in the **Text group**, click the **Header & Footer** button. On the **Design tab**, in the **Navigation group**, click the **Go to Footer** button. In the **Footer** area, click the box just above the word **Footer**, and then in the **Header & Footer Elements group**, click the **File Name** button. Click any cell in the worksheet to exit the footer.

10 On the right side of the status bar, click the **Normal** button 🏢, and then press [Ctrl] + [Home] to make cell **A1** the active cell.

11 Display **Backstage** view. With the **Info tab** selected, click **Properties**, and then click **Show Document Panel**. In the **Author** box, type your firstname and lastname, in the **Subject** box, type your course name and section number, and then in the **Keywords** box, type **PMT, IF functions Close** ☒ the Document Information Panel.

12 **Save** 🖫 the workbook. If you are instructed to submit your files electronically, go to Activity 7.19.

13 To print your workbook, display **Backstage** view, and then click the **Print tab**. Under **Settings**, verify **Print Active Sheets** is selected, and then click the **Print** button.

More Knowledge | Using Comparison Operators

You can compare two values using a variety of comparison operators.

Comparison Operator	Meaning
=	Equal to
>	Greater than
<	Less than
>=	Greater than or equal to
<=	Less than or equal to
<>	Not equal to

Objective 6 | Create a Report in Word Using Data from Other Applications

Word has many features that help you produce professional-looking documents. For example, you can create a report that includes a cover page and a table of contents. Importing data from other applications allows you to complete a report quickly.

Activity 7.19 | Inserting a Cover Page

A *cover page* is the first page of a complex document that provides introductory information. Word contains a gallery of predesigned cover pages with content controls that enable the user to fill in information, such as the title, author, and date.

1 **Start** Word. From **Backstage** view, click **Open**. In the **Open** dialog box, navigate to the student data files, and then open **i07B_Retail_Report**. Click the **File tab**, and then click the **Save As tab**. In the **Save As** dialog box, navigate to the **Integrated Projects Chapter 7** folder, and then save the file as **Lastname_Firstname_7B_Retail_Report** If necessary, display formatting marks.

2 On the **Insert tab**, in the **Header & Footer group**, click the **Footer** button, and then click **Edit Footer**. On the **Design tab**, in the **Insert group**, click the **Quick Parts** button, and then click **Field**. Under **Field names**, click **FileName**, and then click **OK**. Press (Tab) two times. On the **Design tab**, in the **Header & Footer group**, click the **Page Number** button, click **Current Page**, and then under **Simple**, click **Plain Number**.

> In the footer, the file name is left-aligned and the page number—1—is right-aligned. When you use the Page Number feature, Word automatically numbers all pages of the document.

3 Double-click in the document to close the footer. On the **Insert tab**, in the **Pages group**, click the **Cover Page** button. In the **Cover Page** gallery, scroll down, and then click **Sideline**. Compare your screen with Figure 7.36.

> A cover page, which includes content controls, is inserted at the beginning of the document. Because it is a cover page, Word does not assign it a page number. Depending on your computer settings, content controls may automatically display a company name or user name.

Figure 7.36

Cover page —

Content controls —

4 In the **Company content control**, with the text selected, type **Select National Properties Group** and then press (Tab) to select the text in the Title content control.

5 With the text in the **Title content control** selected, type **Retail Business Opportunities** and then press (Tab) to select the Subtitle content control.

6 In the **Subtitle content control**, with the text selected, click the tab **Subtitle**, and then press (Del) to delete the content control. Type **A list of retail businesses available for purchase**

> Text typed in the Subtitle content control will display in the Subject box of the Document Information Panel. For purposes of this instruction, because you will be entering different information in the Subject box, it is necessary to delete the content control and simply type the text.

7 At the bottom of the page, in the text box, select the first line of text. In the **Author content control**, using your name type **Firstname Lastname** and then press (Tab) to select the Date content control.

> The name you type will automatically display in the Document Information Panel in the Author box.

Integrated Projects | Integrating Word, Excel, Access, and PowerPoint

8 Click the **Date content control arrow**, and then click **Today**.

9 **Save** 🖫 your document.

Activity 7.20 | Inserting a Table of Contents

A *table of contents* is a list of a document's headings and subheadings marked with the page numbers where those headings and subheadings occur.

1 On **Page 2** of the document, select the paragraph *Advantages and Disadvantages of Buying an Existing Business*. Click the **References tab**. In the **Table of Contents group**, click the **Add Text** button, and then click **Level 1**.

A Level 1 heading style is applied to the paragraph.

2 Select the paragraph *Advantages*. Hold down Ctrl, and then select the paragraph *Disadvantages*. On the **References tab**, in the **Table of Contents group**, click the **Add Text** button, and then click **Level 2**. Click to deselect the paragraphs, and then compare your screen with Figure 7.37.

A Level 2 heading style is applied to the selected paragraphs.

Figure 7.37

Level 1 heading

Level 2 headings

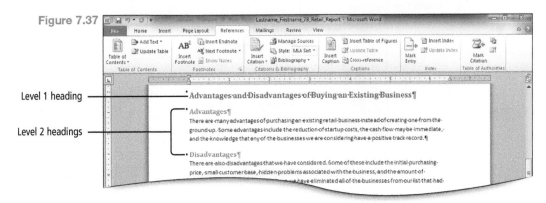

3 Scroll down, and then select the paragraph *Business Documents We Have Reviewed*. On the **References tab**, in the **Table of Contents group**, click the **Add Text** button, and then click **Level 1**.

4 Select the paragraph *Contracts*. Hold down Ctrl, and then select the paragraphs *Financial Statements*, *Tax Returns*, *Appraisals*, and *Other Documents*. On the **References tab**, in the **Table of Contents group**, click the **Add Text** button, and then click **Level 2**.

5 Using the technique you just practiced, format the paragraphs *Government Requirements* and *Other Considerations* as **Level 1** text. Format the paragraphs *Licenses*, *Zoning Requirements*, *Environmental Concerns*, *Tax Concerns*, *Location*, *Local Economy*, and *Quality* as **Level 2** text.

6 At the top of **Page 2** of the document, click to the left of the paragraph beginning *Select National Properties Group* to position the insertion point. Click the **Insert tab**, and then in the **Pages group**, click **Blank Page**.

A new blank page is inserted as Page 2 of the document.

7 At the top of the blank **Page 2**, click to the left of the paragraph mark to position the insertion point, and then click the **References tab**. In the **Table of Contents group**, click the **Table of Contents** button, and then click **Automatic Table 2**. If necessary, scroll up to view the table of contents, and then compare your screen with Figure 7.38.

> The table of contents is inserted with all Level 1 and Level 2 paragraph headings displaying on the left and the corresponding page numbers (based on the page number in the footer) displaying on the right.

Figure 7.38

8 **Save** the document.

Activity 7.21 | Inserting Data from Other Applications

1 Press Ctrl + End to move to the end of the document.

2 Click the **Insert tab**, and then in the **Pages group**, click the **Blank Page** button.

> A new blank page—Page 6—is added at the end of the document.

3 Type **List of Retail Businesses Available for Purchase** and then press Enter.

4 On the taskbar, click the **Excel** button to make the **Lastname_Firstname_7B_Store_Payments** window active. Select cells **B1:D19**, and then on the **Home tab**, in the **Clipboard group**, click the **Copy** button.

5 On the taskbar, click the **Word** button to make the **Lastname_Firstname_7B_Retail_Report** window active.

6 Click the **Home tab**, and then in the **Clipboard group**, click the **Paste** button to insert the Excel data in the document. Compare your screen with Figure 7.39.

Integrated Projects | Integrating Word, Excel, Access, and PowerPoint

Figure 7.39

Typed heading

Inserted Excel data

7 Click any cell in the table. Click the **Layout tab**, and then in the **Table group**, click the **Properties** button. In the **Table Properties** dialog box, on the **Table tab**, under **Alignment**, click **Center**, and then click **OK**. On the **Layout tab**, in the **Cell Size group**, click the **AutoFit** button, and then click **AutoFit Contents**.

8 Save 🖫 the document.

Activity 7.22 | Updating the Table of Contents

Whenever you make changes in a document, such as adding or removing headings and modifying text, you should update the table of contents to reflect those changes.

1 Select the paragraph that begins *List of Retail Businesses*. Click the **References tab**, in the **Table of Contents group**, click the **Add Text** button, and then click **Level 1**.

2 On the **References tab**, in the **Table of Contents group**, click the **Update Table** button.

3 In the **Update Table of Contents** dialog box, click the **Update entire table** option button, and then click **OK**. Scroll up to view the table of contents, and then compare your screen with Figure 7.40.

The paragraph that begins List of Retail Business is added to the table of contents. The page number 5 represents the page number that displays in the footer on the last page of the document.

Figure 7.40

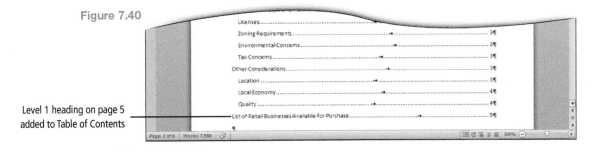

Level 1 heading on page 5 added to Table of Contents

4 Press `Ctrl` + `Home`. Display **Backstage** view, verify the **Info tab** is selected, click **Properties**, and then click **Show Document Panel**. In the **Document Information Panel**, in the **Author** box, notice your firstname and lastname display. In the **Subject** box, type your course name and section number, and then in the **Keywords** box, type **cover page, TOC Close** ☒ the Document Information Panel.

5 **Save** 🖫 the document. If you are instructed to submit your files electronically, go to Step 7.

6 To print your document, display **Backstage** view, click the **Print tab**, and then click the **Print** button.

7 **Close** 🗙 Word, and then **Close** 🗙 Excel. If a message box displays asking if you want to save changes, click **Yes**.

8 Submit your printed or electronic files as directed by your instructor.

End **You have completed Project 7B** ————————————————

Content-Based Assessments

Summary

It is a common task to work with Access data in an Excel workbook in order to take advantage of the data analysis and charting features, the flexibility in data arrangement and layout, and the many features that are not available in Access. The main advantage of importing and exporting data between applications is that you can work with the best features of each of the applications—Word, Excel, Access, and PowerPoint—without retyping or recreating the data; this can save time and improve accuracy.

Key Terms

Area Section	Cover page	Legend Fields (Series)	PMT function
Argument	Drill-down indicator	Option group	Report Filter
Axis Fields (Categories)	Field Section	Pivot	Row Label
Column Labels	Form control	PivotChart report	Table of contents
Combo box control	IF Function	PivotTable Field List	Text box control
Content control	Label control	PivotTable report	Values area

Matching

Match each term in the second column with its correct definition in the first column by writing the letter of the term on the blank line in front of the correct definition.

_____ 1. In an Access form, an object that displays data, performs actions, and lets the user view and work with information.

_____ 2. A form control that combines a drop-down list with a text box, providing a more compact way to present a list of choices.

_____ 3. A control on a form or report that contains descriptive information, typically a field name.

_____ 4. A graphical object on a form or report that displays the data from the underlying table or query.

_____ 5. An object on a form or report that displays a limited set of alternatives where only one option can be selected at a time.

_____ 6. A graphical representation of the data in a PivotTable.

_____ 7. A location in the PivotTable Field List task pane containing the available field names that you can add to the Area Section.

_____ 8. The location in the PivotTable Field List task pane that contains four quadrants where field names are placed to determine how the report will display.

_____ 9. Fields that are assigned a column orientation in a PivotTable and become the column headings.

_____ 10. The cells in a PivotTable report that summarize quantitative data.

_____ 11. The area on a PivotTable that is used to restrict the data that displays.

A Area Section

B Axis Fields (Categories)

C Column labels

D Combo box control

E Cover page

F Field Section

G Form control

H Label control

I Legend Fields (Series)

J Option group

K PivotChart report

L Report Filter

M Table of contents

N Text box control

O Values area

_____ 12. The fields that are assigned to the columns that display in a column PivotChart report.

_____ 13. The fields that are assigned to the categories that display on the horizontal axis in a column PivotChart report.

_____ 14. The first page of a complex document that provides introductory information.

_____ 15. A list of a document's headings and subheadings, marked with the page numbers where those headings and subheadings occur.

Multiple Choice

Circle the correct answer.

1. In a template, an area indicated by placeholder text that can be used to add text, pictures, dates, or lists is called a:
   - **A.** content control
   - **B.** form control
   - **C.** report control

2. An interactive, cross-tabulated Excel report that summarizes and analyzes data is called a:
   - **A.** Pivot report
   - **B.** PivotChart report
   - **C.** PivotTable report

3. An Excel feature that enables you to move fields to different areas in the PivotTable or PivotChart report is the:
   - **A.** PivotTable dialog box
   - **B.** PivotTable Field List
   - **C.** Excel Field List

4. Fields that are assigned a row orientation in a PivotTable report and become the row headings are called:
   - **A.** cell labels
   - **B.** field labels
   - **C.** row labels

5. A PivotTable feature that shows the detailed records of a PivotTable total is the:
   - **A.** Drill-down indicator
   - **B.** Field Expander
   - **C.** Total Filter

6. Any value that an Excel function uses to perform operations or calculations is called the:
   - **A.** argument
   - **B.** operator
   - **C.** variable

7. An Excel function that calculates the payment for a loan based on constant payments and constant interest rate is the:
   - **A.** NPV function
   - **B.** PMT function
   - **C.** RATE function

8. An Excel function that uses a logical test to check whether a condition is met, and then returns one value if true, and another value if false is the:
   - **A.** FALSE function
   - **B.** IF function
   - **C.** TRUE function

9. In a predesigned cover page, text typed in the Subtitle content control will automatically display in the Document Information Panel in the:
   - **A.** Author box
   - **B.** Subject box
   - **C.** Title box

10. When changes are made to a document, such as adding or removing headings and modifying text, you should reflect those changes by updating the:
    - **A.** cover page
    - **B.** document properties
    - **C.** table of contents

Apply 7A skills from these Objectives:

1. Create and Save a Template in Word
2. Insert a Combo Box and an Option Group in an Access Form
3. Create a PivotTable Report and a PivotChart Report in Excel
4. Import Data into a PowerPoint Presentation

Skills Review | Project 7C Atlanta Warehouses

In the following Skills Review, you will create a letter template to thank the new tenants of the Atlanta warehouses that the Select National Properties Group owns. You will import Access data into Excel, create a Pivot Chart report, and then import it into a PowerPoint presentation. Your completed files will look similar to Figure 7.41.

Project Files

For Project 7C, you will need the following files:

New blank Word document
New blank Excel workbook
i07C_Atlanta_Warehouses
i07C_Warehouse_Presentation

You will save your files as:

Lastname_Firstname_7C_Lease_Template
Lastname_Firstname_7C_Cromen_Lease
Lastname_Firstname_7C_Atlanta_Warehouses
Lastname_Firstname_7C_Warehouse_PivotTable
Lastname_Firstname_7C_Warehouse_Presentation

Project Results

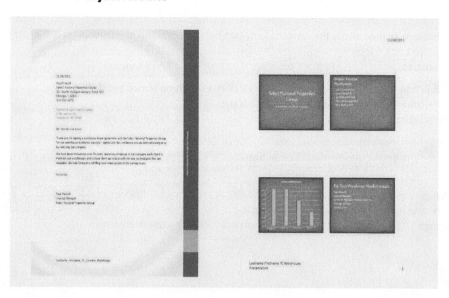

Figure 7.41

Integrating Word, Excel, Access, and PowerPoint

1. **Start** Word. From **Backstage** view, click the **New tab**. Under **Available Templates**, click **Sample templates**. Under **Available Templates**, click **Equity Letter**. Click the **Template** option button, and then click **Create**.

   a. On the **Quick Access Toolbar**, click the **Save** button. In the **Save As** dialog box, navigate to the **Integrated Projects Chapter 7** folder, and then **Save** the file as **Lastname_Firstname_7C_Lease_Template**

   b. Immediately below the date content control, delete the content control, and then type **Paul Stancill**. Click in the content control *Type the sender company name*, type **Select National Properties Group** and then press ⒯ᵃᵇ. In the content control *Type the sender company address*, type **321 North Michigan Avenue, Suite 700** and then press Ⓔⁿᵗᵉʳ. Type **Chicago, IL 60601** press Ⓔⁿᵗᵉʳ, and then type **312-555-0070**

   c. Click the content control *Type the salutation*, and then type **RE: Warehouse Lease**

   d. Below the salutation, click the content control that begins *On the Insert tab*, and then type **Thank you for signing a warehouse lease agreement with the Select National Properties Group for our warehouse in Atlanta, Georgia. I appreciate the confidence you are demonstrating in us by selecting our company.** Press Ⓔⁿᵗᵉʳ, and then type **We have been in business over 30 years, and every employee in our company works hard to maintain our warehouses and to keep them up to date with the new technologies that are available. We look forward to fulfilling your expectations in the coming years.**

   e. Click the content control *Type the closing*, and then type **Sincerely,** Below the closing, delete the content control, and then type **Paul Stancill** Click the content control *Type the sender title*, and then type **Leasing Manager**

   f. Display **Backstage** view. Click **Properties**, and then click **Show Document Panel**. In the **Author** box, type your firstname and lastname, in the **Subject** box, type your course name and section number, and then in the **Keywords** box, type **letter, lease** Close the Document Information Panel, **Save** your changes, and then **Close** Word.

2. On the taskbar, click the **Windows Explorer** button. Navigate to the **Integrated Projects Chapter 7 folder**, and then double-click the file **Lastname_Firstname_7C_Lease_Template**. Click the **Save** button. In the **Save As** dialog box, navigate to the **Integrated Projects Chapter 7** folder, and then save the document as **Lastname_Firstnae_7C_Cromen_Warehouse**

   a. Near the top of the document, click the content control *Pick the date*, click the **content control arrow**, and then click **Today**.

   b. Click the content control *Type the recipient name*, and then type **Cromen & Egert Manufacturing** c. Click the content control *Type the recipient address*, type **1706 Lamson Rd** and then press Ⓔⁿᵗᵉʳ. Type **Henderson, NV 89014**

   c. On the **Insert tab**, in the **Header & Footer group**, click the **Footer** button, and then click **Edit Footer**. On the **Design tab**, in the **Insert group**, click the **Quick Parts** button, and then click **Field**. Under **Field names**, click **FileName**, and then click **OK**. On the **Design tab**, in the **Close group**, click the **Close Header and Footer** button.

Integrating Word, Excel, Access, and PowerPoint

d. Display **Backstage** view. Click **Properties**, and then click **Show Document Panel**. In the **Author** box, type your firstname and lastname, in the **Subject** box, type your course name and section number, and then in the **Keywords** box, type **Cromen, lease** Close the Document Information Panel, **Save** your changes, and then **Close** Word.

3. **Start** Access, and then click **Open**. In the **Open** dialog box, navigate to the data files, and then open the file **i07C_Atlanta_Warehouses**. From **Backstage** view, click the **Save Database As tab**. In the **Save As** dialog box, navigate to the **Integrated Projects Chapter 7** folder, and then save the file as **Lastname_Firstname_7C_Atlanta_Warehouses** In the **Message Bar**, click the **Enable Content** button. In the **Navigation Pane**, click **Warehouses:Table**.

   a. On the **Create tab**, in the **Forms group**, click the **Form** button. On the **Design tab**, in the **Views group**, click the **View button arrow**, and then click **Design View**. In the form, under **Detail**, click the **Address** label control, hold down Ctrl, and then click the **Address** text box control, the **Monthly Rent** label control, and the **Monthly Rent** text box control. Press Del.

   b. On the **Design tab**, in the **Controls group**, click the **More** button, and then verify that the **Use Control Wizards** button is selected. In the **Controls** gallery, click the **Combo Box** button. At the bottom of the form, move the pointer below the **Tenant** text box control, and then click one time. In the **Combo Box Wizard** dialog box, click the **I will type in the values that I want** option button, and then click **Next**. Verify that the **Number of columns** is **1**, and then press Tab. Type the following list of addresses, pressing Tab after each address except the last list item.

| 208 E Central Ave |
| 2445 East 51st St |
| 403 Industrial Blvd |
| 8692 Technology |
| 8851 Skyline Ave |

   c. Click **Next**. Click the **Store that value in this field** option button, and then click the **arrow**. In the field list, click **Address**, and then click **Next**.

   d. Under *What label would you like for your combo box?*, type **Address:** and then click **Finish**.

   e. On the right side of the **Address** combo box control, point to the middle sizing handle, and then drag to the right to **3 inches on the horizontal ruler**.

4. On the **Design tab**, in the **Controls group**, click the **Option Group** button. In the form, below **Detail**, point below the **Address** combo box, and then click one time.

   a. In the **Option Group Wizard** dialog box, under **Label Names**, type the following list, pressing Tab after each number except the last list item.

| $4500 |
| $5000 |
| $5500 |
| $6000 |

Integrating Word, Excel, Access, and PowerPoint

b. Click **Next**. Under **Do you want one option to be the default choice?**, click the **No, I don't want a default** option button, and then click **Next**. Under **What value do you want to assign to each option?**, type the following list of values next to each Label Name, and then click **Next**.

Label Names	Values
$4500	4500
$5000	5000
$5500	5500
$6000	6000

c. Under **What do you want to do with the value of a selected option?**, click the **Store the value in this field** option button, click the **arrow**, and then click the **Monthly Rent** field name. Click **Next**.

d. Under **What type of controls do you want in the option group?**, verify that **Option buttons** is selected. Under **What style would you like to use?**, click the **Raised** option button, and then click **Next**.

e. Under **What caption do you want for the option group?**, type **Monthly Rent** and then click **Finish**.

5. On the **Design tab**, in the **Views group**, click the **View** button.

a. On the **Quick Access Toolbar**, click the **Save** button. In the **Save As** dialog box, type **Warehouses Form** and then click **OK**.

b. At the bottom of the form, click the **New (blank) record** button, and then add the following records.

Tenant	Address	Monthly Rent
Cromen & Egert Manufacturing	208 E Central Ave	$5500
AMS Fulfillment Services	8692 Technology Blvd	$6000

c. Right-click the **Warehouse Form tab**, and then on the shortcut menu, click **Close**.

d. From **Backstage** view, click **View and edit database properties**. In the **Properties** dialog box, on the **Summary** tab, in the **Subject** box, type your course name and section number, in the **Author** box, type your firstname and lastname, and then in the **Keywords** box, type **form controls** Click **OK** to close the dialog box, and then **Close** Access.

6. **Start** Excel. On the **Data tab**, in the **Get External Data group**, click the **From Access** button. In the **Select Data Source** dialog box, navigate to the **Integrated Projects Chapter 7** folder, click the Access file **Lastname_Firstname_7C_Atlanta_Warehouses**, and then click **Open**.

a. In the **Import Data** dialog box, under *Select how you want to view this data in your workbook*, click the **PivotTable Report** option button. Under *Where do you want to put the data?*, verify that the **Existing worksheet** option button is selected and that =$A$1 displays in the box. Click **OK**.

Integrating Word, Excel, Access, and PowerPoint

b. On the **Quick Access Toolbar**, click the **Save** button. In the **Save As** dialog box, navigate to your **Integrated Projects Chapter 7** folder, and then save the file as **Lastname_Firstname_7C_Warehouse_PivotTable**

c. In the **PivotTable Field List** task pane, under **Choose fields to add to report**, drag the **Tenant** field name to the **Row Labels** box. Drag the **Address** field to the **Column Labels** box. Drag the **Monthly Rent** field to the **Values** box.

d. On the **Options tab**, in the **Active Field group**, click the **Field Settings** button. In the **Value Field Settings** dialog box, click **Number Format**. In the **Format Cells** dialog box, under **Category**, click **Currency**. Click the **Decimal places spin box down arrow** two times to display **0**. Verify the symbol is **$**, and then click **OK**. In the **Value Field Settings** dialog box, click **OK**.

e. In the **PivotTable Field List** task pane, in the **Column Labels** area, click the **Address field arrow**, and then click **Move to Report Filter**. In cell **B1**, click the **Address filter arrow**, click **403 Industrial Blvd**, and then click **OK**.

7. On the **Options tab**, in the **Tools group**, click the **PivotChart** button. In the **Insert Chart** dialog box, verify that **Column** is selected, and then in the second row, click the first style—**Clustered Cylinder**. Click **OK**.

a. On the **Design tab**, in the **Location group**, click the **Move Chart** button. In the **Move Chart** dialog box, click the **New Sheet** option button, in the **New Sheet** box, type **403 Industrial Blvd Chart** and then click **OK.**

b. On the **Layout tab**, in the **Labels group**, click the **Legend** button, and then click **None**. Click the **Chart Title**, select the text, type **403 Industrial Blvd Tenants** and then click in a blank area of the chart.

c. Right-click any sheet tab, and then from the shortcut menu, click **Select All Sheets**.

d. On the **Insert tab**, in the **Text group**, click the **Header & Footer** button. On the **Design tab**, in the **Navigation group**, click the **Go to Footer** button. In the **Footer** area, click the box just above the word **Footer**, and then in the **Header & Footer Elements** group, click the **File Name** button. Click any cell to exit the footer, and then on the status bar, click the **Normal** button. Press ⌈Ctrl⌉ + ⌈Home⌉. Right-click any sheet tab, and then on the shortcut menu, click **Ungroup Sheets**.

e. Display **Backstage** view. Click **Properties**, and then click **Show Document Panel**. In the **Author** box, type your firstname and lastname, in the **Subject** box, type your course name and section number, and then in the **Keywords** box, type **PivotChart** Close the Document Information Panel, and then **Save** your workbook.

8. **Start** PowerPoint. From **Backstage** view, click **Open**. In the **Open** dialog box, navigate to the data files, and then open the file **i07C_Warehouse_Presentation**. From **Backstage** view, click **Save As**. In the **Save As** dialog box, navigate to the **Integrated Projects Chapter 7** folder, and then save the file as **Lastname_Firstname_7C_Warehouse_Presentation**

a. On the **Insert tab**, in the **Text group**, click the **Header & Footer** button. On the **Notes and Handouts tab**, select the **Footer** check box. Type **Lastname Firstname 7C Warehouse Presentation** and then click **Apply to All**.

Integrating Word, Excel, Access, and PowerPoint

b.   Click **Slide 2**. On the **Home tab**, in the **Slides group**, click the **New Slide button arrow**, and then click **Blank**. On the taskbar, click the **Lastname_Firstname_7C_Warehouse_PivotTable** button to display the Excel window. Click the **403 Industrial Blvd Chart sheet tab**. Click in a blank area of the chart. On the **Home tab**, in the **Clipboard group**, click the **Copy** button.

c.   On the taskbar, click the **Lastname_Firstname_7C_Warehouse_Presentation** button to make the PowerPoint window active. Verify that **Slide 3** is the active slide. On the **Home tab**, in the **Clipboard group**, click the **Paste** button.

d.   On the **Design tab**, in the **Themes group**, click the **More** button, and then click **Paper**. Click **Slide 1**.

e.   From Backstage view, click Properties, and then click Show Document Panel. In the Author box, type your firstname and lastname, in the Subject box, type your course name and section number, and then in the Keywords box, type PivotChart Close the Document Information Panel, Save your changes, and then Close PowerPoint. Close Excel.

f.   Submit your printed or electronic files as directed by your instructor.

You have completed Project 7C

Integrating Word, Excel, Access, and PowerPoint

Apply 7B
skills from
these
Objectives:
5. Use Excel
    Functions
6. Create a Report
    in Word Using
    Data from Other
    Applications

Skills Review | Project **7D Tenant Owners**

In the following Skills Review, you will import data form an Access database into an Excel workbook. You will determine monthly payments for a lease-to own contract for tenants of a facility owned by the Select National Properties Group. You will import the Excel data into a Word report. Your completed files will look similar to Figure 7.42.

Project Files

For Project 7D, you will need the following files:

> Excel workbook
> i07D_Tenant_Owners
> i07D_Tenant_Report

You will **save your files as:**

> Lastname_Firstname_7D_Tenant_Owners
> Lastname_Firstname_7D_Tenant_Report

Project Results

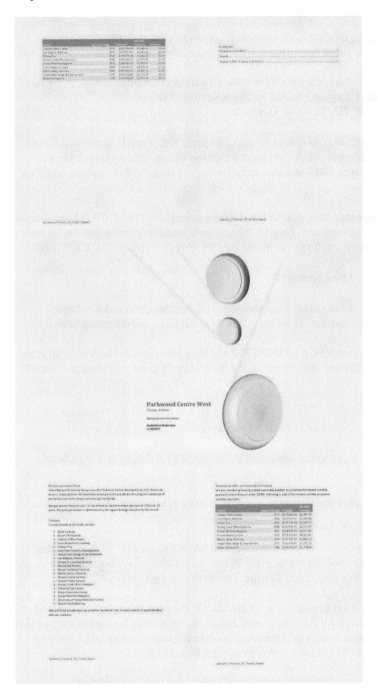

Figure 7.42

1. **Start** Excel. On the **Data tab**, in the **Get External Data group**, click the **From Access** button. In the **Select Data Source** dialog box, navigate to your data files. Click the Access file **i07D_Tenant_Owners**, and then click **Open**.

   a. In the **Import Data** dialog box, under *Select how you want to view this data in your workbook*, verify that the **Table** option button is selected, and then click **OK**.

   b. On the **Quick Access Toolbar**, click the **Save** button. In the **Save As** dialog box, navigate to the **Integrated Projects Chapter 7** folder, and then **Save** the file as **Lastname_Firstname_7D_Tenant_Owners**

   c. Click cell **D1**. Type **Monthly** hold down ⌷Alt⌷, and then press ⌷Enter⌷. Type **Payment** and then press ⌷Enter⌷. On the **Formula Bar**, click the **Insert Function** button. Under **Search for a function**, select the text, type **PMT** and then click **Go**. Verify that PMT is selected, and then click **OK**.

   d. In the **Function Arguments** dialog box, in the **Rate** argument box, type **7.5%/12** and then press ⌷Tab⌷. In the **Nper** argument box, type **15*12** and then press ⌷Tab⌷. Verify that the insertion point is in the **Pv** arugment box. Type the minus sign (-), and then click cell **C2**. Click **OK**.

2. Click cell **E1**. Type **Discount** and then press ⌷Enter⌷.

   a. On the **Formula Bar**, click the **Insert Function** button. Click the **Or select a category arrow**, and then click **Logical**. Under **Select a function**, click **IF**, and then click **OK**

   b. In the **Logical_test** argument box, type **D2>5000** and then press ⌷Tab⌷. In the **Value_if_true** argument box, type **D2*2%** and then press ⌷Tab⌷. In the **Value_if_false** argument box, type **0** and then click **OK**.

   c. Select cells **C2:C21**. Hold down ⌷Ctrl⌷, and then select cells **E2:E21**. On the **Home tab**, in the **Number group**, click the **Number Format button arrow**, and then click **Currency**.

   d. Select the **columns A:E**. Point to the line between the headings A and B, and then double-click.

   e. At the top of **column E**, click the **Discount AutoFilter arrow**, select the **$0.00** check box, and then click **OK**.

3. Click the **Sheet2 sheet tab**. Hold down ⌷Shift⌷, and then click the **Sheet3 sheet tab**. Right click the **Sheet3 sheet tab**, and then on the shortcut menu, click **Delete**. Right-click the **Sheet1 sheet tab**, and then on the shortcut menu, click **Rename**. Type **Tempe Tenants** and then press ⌷Ctrl⌷.

   a. On the **Insert tab**, in the **Text group**, click the **Header & Footer** button. On the **Design tab**, in the **Navigation group**, click the **Go to Footer** button. In the **Footer** area, click the box just above the word **Footer**, and then in the **Header & Footer Elements group**, click the **File Name** button. Click any cell in the workbook to exit the footer.

   b. On the right side of the status bar, click the **Normal** button, and then press ⌷Ctrl⌷ + ⌷Home⌷ to make cell **A1** the active cell.

Integrating Word, Excel, Access, and PowerPoint

c. Display **Backstage** view. Click **Properties**, and then click **Show Document Panel**. In the **Author** box, type your firstname and lastname, in the **Subject** box, type your course name and section number, and then in the **Keywords** box, type **PMT, IF functions** Close the Document Information Panel, and then **Save** your changes.

4. **Start** Word, and then open the file **i07D_Tenant_Report. Save** the file in the **Integrated Projects Chapter 7** folder as **Lastname_Firstname_7D_Tenant_Report**

a. On the **Insert tab**, in the **Header & Footer group**, click the **Footer** button, and then click **Edit Footer**. On the **Design tab**, in the **Insert group**, click the **Quick Parts** button, and then click **Field**. Under **Field name**, click **FileName**, and then click **OK**. Double-click in the document.

b. On the **Insert tab**, in the **Pages group**, click the **Cover Page** button. In the **Cover Page** gallery, scroll down, and then click **Mod**. Select the **Title content control**, type **Parkwood Centre West** and then press ⒯ᵃᵇ. In the **Subtitle content control**, type **Tempe, Arizona** and then press ⒯ᵃᵇ. In the **Abstract content control**, type **Making tenants into owners** and then press ⒯ᵃᵇ. In the **Author content control**, using your name type **Firstname Lastname** and then press ⒯ᵃᵇ. Click the **Date content control arrow**, and then click **Today**.

5. On **Page 2**, select the paragraph *Parkwood Centre West*. Hold down Ⓒᵗʳˡ, and then click the paragraph *Tenants*. On the **References tab**, in the **Table of Contents group**, click the **Add Text** button, and then click **Level 1**.

a. At the top of **Page 2**, place the insertion point to the left of the paragraph beginning *Parkwood Centre West*. On the **Insert tab**, in the **Pages group**, click **Blank Page**.

b. Move to the top of the blank **Page 2**. On the **References tab**, in the **Table of Contents group**, click the **Table of Contents** button, and then click **Automatic Table 1**.

c. Press Ⓒᵗʳˡ + ᴱⁿᵈ. Place the insertion point to the left of the paragraph beginning *We are considering*. On the **Insert tab**, in the **Pages group**, click the **Page Break** button. Type **Tenants to Offer an Ownership Position** and then press ᴱⁿᵗᵉʳ.

d. Select the paragraph T*enants to Offer an Ownership Position*. On the **References tab**, in the **Table of Contents group**, click the **Add Text** button, and then click **Level 1**.

6. On the taskbar, click the **Lastname_Firstname_7D_Tenant_Owners** button. Select cells **A1:D17**, and then on the **Home tab**, in the **Clipboard group**, click the **Copy** button.

a. On the taskbar, click the **Lastname_Firstname_7D_Tenant_Report** button. Press Ⓒᵗʳˡ + ᴱⁿᵈ. On the **Home tab**, in the **Clipboard group**, click the **Paste** button. Click any cell in the table. On the **Layout tab**, in the **Cell Size group**, click the **AutoFit** button, and then click **AutoFit Contents**. Press Ⓒᵗʳˡ + ᴴᵒᵐᵉ.

b. On the **References tab**, in the **Table of Contents group**, click the **Update Table** button. In the **Update Table of Contents** dialog box, click the **Update entire table** option button. Display **Backstage** view. Click **Properties**, and then click **Show Document Panel**. In the **Keywords** box, type **cover page, TOC** Close the Document Information Panel, and then **Save** your changes.

Integrating Word, Excel, Access, and PowerPoint

c. **Close** Word, and then **Close** Excel.

d. Submit your printed or electronic files as directed by your instructor.

You have completed Project 7D

Apply 7A skills from these Objectives:
1. Create and Save a Template in Word
2. Insert a Combo Box and an Option Group in an Access Form
3. Create a PivotTable Report and a PivotChart Report in Excel
4. Import Data into a PowerPoint Presentation

In the following Mastering Integration project, you will create and modify an Access form. You will export the facility records to Excel, where you will create a PivotTable report and a PivotChart report. You will import the Pivot Chart into a PowerPoint presentation. Your completed files will look similar to Figure 7.43.

Project Files

For Project 7E, you will need the following files:

New blank Excel workbook
i07E_Texas_Facilities
i07E_Facilities_Presentation

You will save your files as:

Lastname_Firstname_7E_Texas_Facilities
Lastname_Firstname_7E_Facilities_PivotTable
Lastname_Firstname_7E_Facilities_Presentation

Project Results

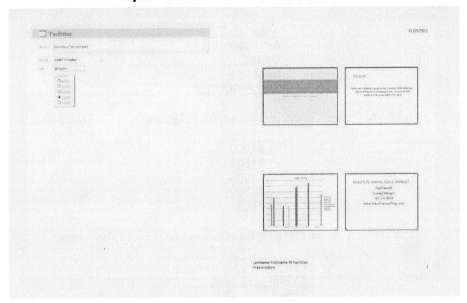

Figure 7.43

Integrating Word, Excel, Access, and PowerPoint

411

1. **Start** Access. Navigate to your data files, and then open the database **i07E_Texas_Facilities**. From **Backstage** view, click the **Save Database As tab**, and then save the file in your **Integrated Projects Chapter 7** folder as **Lastname_Firstname_7E_Texas_Facilities** On the **Message Bar**, click **Enable Content**.

2. Create a form based on the **Facilities** table. In **Design View**, delete the **Facility**, **City**, and **Utilities** form controls. Under the **Tenant** form control, insert a **Combo Box**. In the **Combo Box Wizard** dialog box, click the **I will type in the values that I want** option button, and then click **Next**. Type the following list of facilities, and then store the value in the **Facility** field, and label the combo box **Facility:**

Crosby Complex
Lantana Center
Lydell Complex
Meridian Park IV
Parkwood Complex South
Rancho Bernardo Multiplex
Spyglass Center
Traders Pointe

3. Below the *Facility* combo box control, insert a **Combo Box**. In the **Combo Box Wizard** dialog box, click the **I will type in the values that I want** option button, and then click **Next**. Type the following list of cities, and then store the value in the **City** field and label the combo box **City:**

Amarillo
Arlington
Dallas
Lubbock
San Antonio

4. Below the *City* combo box control, insert an **Option Group**. Type the following Label Names.

$1000
$1500
$2000
$2500
$3000

5. Do not set a default choice. Type the following list of values next to each Label Name.

Label	Values
$1000	1000
$1500	1500
$2000	2000
$2500	2500
$3000	3000

6. Store the value in the **Utilities** field, use **option buttons**, apply the **Raised** style, and then in the option group caption, type Utilities: If necessary move the form controls on the form to line up with the other

Integrating Word, Excel, Access, and PowerPoint

form controls. Resize the form controls so all data can be read. **Save** the form as **Facilities Form**
Add the following records.

Tenant	Facility	City	Utilities
THG Medical Records	Crosby	Amarillo	$3000
Broaddus Technologies	Lydell Complex	Amarillo	$2500

7. From **Backstage** view, display the **Properties** dialog box. In the **Subject** box, type your course name and section number, in the **Author** box, type your firstname and lastname, and then in the **Keywords** box, type **form controls Close** the **Properties** dialog box, **Close All** object tabs, and then **Close** Access.

8. **Start** Excel. **Import** the Access file **Lastname_Firstname_7E_Texas_Facilities** as a **PivotTable Report. Save** the Excel file in the **Integrated Projects Chapter 7** folder as **Lastname_Firstname_7E_Facilities_PivotTable** Add the **Facility** field name to the **Row Labels** box. Add the **City** field to the **Column Labels** box. Add the **Utilities** field to the **Values** box. Format the **Values Field Settings** to **Currency** with **0 decimal places**. Rename **Sheet1** as **Utilities** Create a **Copy** of the **Utilities** sheet, and then rename the new sheet **Amarillo Utilities** Filter the **City** field to display only *Amarillo*. Double-click cell **C3**—the grand total for the Crosby Complex. Rename the new sheet **Crosby Complex** and then widen the columns so that all data displays.

9. On the **Utilities** sheet, create a **Clustered Column PivotChart** report based on the PivotTable. Move the chart to a new sheet named **Utilities Chart** Pivot the chart so the **City** field is in the **Axis Fields** box and the **Facility** field is in the **Legend Fields** box. Above the chart, insert a **Chart Title** with the text **Utilities by City** Delete *Sheet2* and *Sheet3*. Insert the file name as field in the footer of all worksheets. **Ungroup** the worksheets, and then return to **Normal** view. **Close** the PivotTable Field List task pane and the PivotChart Filter Pane. Display the Document Information Panel. In the **Author** box, type your firstname and lastname, in the **Subject** box, type your course name and section number, and then in the **Keywords** box, type **Crosby, PivotChart Close** the Document Information Panel, and then **Save** your changes.

10. **Start** PowerPoint, and then open the data file **i07E_Facilities_Presentation. Save** the file in the **Integrated Projects Chapter 7** folder as **Lastname_Firstname_7E_Facilities_Presentation** In the handouts, insert the footer **Lastname Firstname 7E Facilities Presentation** and then **Apply to All**. Apply the design theme **Equity** to all slides. In the Excel file, on the **Utilities Chart** worksheet, **Copy** the **Utilities by City** PivotChart to a new blank **Slide 3** of the presentation. Insert a new **Slide 4** with the layout **Title and Content**. Add the title **Need Information About Utilities?** In the lower placeholder, type the following information.

Paul Stancill
Leasing Manager
312-555-0070
www.SelectNationalProp.com

11. In the lower placeholder, toggle off the bullet points, **Center** the paragraphs, and then change the **Font Size** to **36**. Display the Document Information Panel. In the **Author** box, type your firstname and lastname, in the **Subject** box, type your course name and section number, and then in the **Keywords** box, type **PivotChart Close** the Document Information Panel, and then **Save** the presentation. **Close** PowerPoint, and then **Close** Excel. Submit your printed or electronic files as directed by your instructor.

You have completed Project 7E

Mastering Integration | **Project 7F Office Parks**

In the following Mastering Integration project, you will import a list of office parks into Excel. You will use the SUM, PMT, and IF functions, and then import the data into a Word report. The report will be made available to customers of the Select National Properties Group. Your completed files will look similar to Figure 7.44.

Project Files

For Project 7F, you will need the following files:

New blank Excel workbook
i07F_Office_Parks
i07F_Parks_Report

You will save your files as:

Lastname_Firstname_7F_Parks_Data
Lastname_Firstname_7F_Parks_Report

Project Results

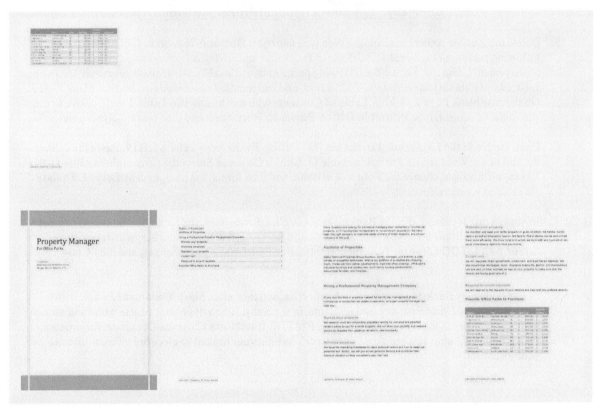

Figure 7.44

Integrating Word, Excel, Access, and PowerPoint

1. **Start** Excel. Import the data from the Access file **i07F_Office_Parks** into an Excel table. **Save** the Excel file in the **Integrated Projects Chapter 7** folder as **Lastname_Firstname_7F_Parks_Data**

2. In cell **G1**, type **Total Cost** In cell **G2**, insert the **SUM** function to add cells **E2:F2**. In cell **H1**, type **Monthly Payment** so that it displays on two lines. In cell **H2**, insert the **PMT** function to calculate the monthly payment. The rate is 7%, the loan is for 25 years, and the present value is the Total Cost. (Your result should display as a positive number). In cell **I1** type **Purchase?** In cell **I2**, insert the **If** function. If the Monthly Payment is less that $5500, *Yes* should display, otherwise, *No* should display. Filter **column I** to only display the cells that contain *Yes*.

3. Format **columns E:H** using **Accounting Number Format** with **0** decimals. Adjust the width of the columns to display all data. Hide **columns D:F** and **column I**. **Delete** *Sheet2* and *Sheet3*. **Rename** Sheet1 as **Office Parks** and then insert the file name in the footer as a field. Return to **Normal** view, and then **Save** the workbook.

4. **Start** Word, and then open the file **i07F_Parks_Report**. **Save** the file in the **Integrated Projects Chapter 7** folder as **Lastname_Firstname_7F_Parks_Report** Insert the file name in the footer. Insert the **Pinstripes** cover page. Type the following information in the content controls.

Title	Property Manager
Subtitle	For Office Parks
Date	Today
Company	Select National Properties Group

5. Delete the **Author** content control, and then type **Morgan Bannon-Navarre, CFO** Format the following paragraphs as **Level 1**: *Portfolio of Properties* and *Hiring a Professional Property Management Company*. Format the following paragraphs as **Level 2**: *Market your property*, *Minimize vacancies*, *Maintain your property*, *Collect rent*, and *Respond to tenant requests*. Insert a blank Page 2. On the new blank **Page 2**, insert a **Table of Contents** with the **Automatic Table 2** style. Move to the end of the document, type **Possible Office Parks to Purchase** and then press [Enter] two times.

6. From the Excel file **Lastname_Firstname_7F_Office_Parks**, copy cells **A1:H19**. **Paste** the cells at the end of the Word report. Format the table to AutoFit Contents. Select the paragraph **Possible Office Parks to Purchase**, change the **Font** to **Verdana**, and then format the paragraph as **Level 1**. **Update** the table of contents. Press [Ctrl] + [Home]

7. In your Word document, display **Backstage** view, click **Properties**, and then click **Show Document Panel**. In the **Author** box, type your firstname and lastname, and then in the **Keywords** box, type **cover page, TOC** Close the Document Information Panel, **Save** your changes, and then **Close** Word.

8. In Excel, display **Backstage** view, click **Properties**, and then click **Show Document Panel**. In the **Author** box, type your firstname and lastname, in the **Subject** box, type your course name and section number, and then in the **Keywords** box, type **PMT, IF functions** Close the Document Information Panel, **Save** your changes, and then **Close** Excel. Submit your printed or electronic files as directed by your instructor.

You have completed Project 7F

Integrating Word, Excel, Access, and PowerPoint

Rubric

The following outcomes-based assessments are open-ended assessments. That is, there is no specific correct result; your result will depend on your approach to the information provided. Make Professional Quality your goal. Use the following scoring rubric to guide you in how to approach the problem and then to evaluate how well your approach solves the problem.

The *criteria*—Software Mastery, Content, Format and Layout, and Process—represent the knowledge and skills you have gained that you can apply to solving the problem. The *levels of performance*— Professional Quality, Approaching Professional Quality, or Needs Quality Improvements—help you and your instructor evaluate your result.

	Your completed project is of Professional Quality	Your completed project is of Approaching Professional Quality	Your completed project Needs Quality Improvements
1-Software Mastery	Chooses and applies the most appropriate skills, tools, and features and identifies efficient methods to solve the problem.	Chooses and applies some appropriate skills, tools, and features, but not in the most efficient manner.	Chooses inappropriate skills, tools, or features, or is inefficient in solving the problem.
2-Content	Constructs a solution that is clear and well organized, containing content that is accurate, appropriate to the audience and purpose, and complete. The solution contains no errors of spelling, grammar, or style.	Constructs a solution in which some components are unclear, poorly organized, inconsistent, or incomplete. May misjudge the needs of the audience. May contain some errors in spelling, grammar, or style, but the errors do not detract from comprehension.	Constructs a solution that is unclear, incomplete, or poorly organized, containing some inaccurate or inappropriate content. May contain many errors of spelling, grammar, or style. May fail to solve the problem.
3-Format and Layout	Formats and arranges all elements to communicate information and ideas, clarify function, illustrate relationships, and indicate relative importance.	Applies appropriate format and layout features to some elements, but not others. Or, overuses features, causing minor distraction.	Applies format and layout that fails to communicate information or ideas or clearly. May fail to use format and layout features to clarify function, illustrate relationships, or indicate relative importance. Or, may use available features excessively, causing distraction.
4-Process	Uses an organized approach that integrates planning, development, self-assessment, revision, and reflection.	Demonstrates an organized approach in some areas, but not others. Or, uses an insufficient process of organization throughout.	Does not use an organized approach to solve the problem.

Integrating Word, Excel, Access, and PowerPoint

GO! Think | **Project 7G Educational Facilities**

Project Files

For Project 7G, you will need the following files:

New blank Excel workbook
i07G_Facilities_Data
i07G_Educational_Report

You will save your files as:

Lastname_Firstname_7G_Educational_Facilities
Lastname_Firstname_7G_Educational_Report

The Select National Properties Group is considering selling some of its educational facilities. The facilities have been tracked in an Access database. Shaun Walker, the President of the company, has asked you to prepare a report. Import the Access data in the file i07G_Facilities_Data as a table into Excel. Using the PMT function, calculate the monthly payments the company could expect. The company would charge an 8% rate over 10 years. The result should be a positive number. Mr. Walker also asked you to calculate an extra processing fee for monthly loan payments using the IF function. If a monthly loan payment is less than $6000, the company would charge a processing fee of $150; otherwise, there would be no processing fee. Filter the rows to display only those facilities where there is a $0 processing fee. Save the Excel file as **Lastname_Firstname_7G_Educational_Facilities**

Open the Word document i07G_Educational_Report, and then save the file as **Lastname_Firstname_7G_Educational_Report** Add a cover page of your choice, and then complete the content controls on the cover page. In the report, format headings as Level 1 or Level 2, and then insert a table of contents on a new page. Copy the Excel data into the Word document, and then add an appropriate heading. Format the new heading as Level 1, and then update the table of contents. In each file, insert the file name as a field in the footer, and then add appropriate document properties. Submit your printed or electronic files as directed by your instructor.

You have completed Project 7G

Integrating Word, Excel, Access, and PowerPoint

Apply a combination of the 7A and 7B skills.

GO! Think | **Project 7H Hospital Properties**

Project Files

For Project 7H, you will need the following files:

New blank Excel workbook
i07H_Hospital_Properties
i07H_Hospitals_Presentation

You will save your files as:

Lastname_Firstname_7H_Hospital_Properties
Lastname_Firstname_7H_Hospitals_PivotTable
Lastname_Firstname_7H_Hospitals_Presentation

The Select National Properties Group is concerned about the maintenance and utility costs of the hospitals they own. Hugh Duden, the Hospital
Property Manager, has been tracking the annual costs in an Access database.

Open the Access database i07H_Hospital_Properties, and then save the database as
Lastname_Firstname_7H_Hospital_Properties Create a form based on the Hospitals table. Insert an
option group for the Utilities field. Insert a combo box for the Administrator field. Add the following
record

Hospital	Address	City	State	ZIP	Maintenance	Utilities	Administrator
Arroyo Grande Rehabilitation Hospital	500 NW Cheyenne	Salem	NH	03079	$755,200	$200,000	Miranda Hevey
Community Hospital West	33 Herman Ave	Concord	MA	01742	$562,750	$150,000	Mary Brady

Insert appropriate document properties, and then close Access. Start Excel and import the Access data as a
PivotTable report. Create a PivotTable report utilizing fields of your choice. Copy the worksheet, and
then pivot the PivotTable report on the new worksheet. Use the drill- down indicator on a total of your
choice. Create a PivotChart report. Delete any blank worksheets, and then rename the remaining
worksheets. Save the file as **Lastname_Fistname_7H_Hospitals_PivotTable** Add the file name
as a field to all worksheets, and then insert appropriate document properties. Open the PowerPoint
presentation i07H_Hospitals_Presentation, and then save the file as
Lastname_Firstname_7H_Hospitals_Presentation Insert a new slide, and then import the
PivotChart from the Excel file. Add the file name as a footer on the Notes page. Apply a design theme,
and then add appropriate document properties. Submit all printed or electronic files as directed by your
instructor.

You have completed Project 7H

Integrating Word, Excel, Access, and PowerPoint

<table>
<tr><td>

Apply a combination of the 7A and 7B skills.

</td><td>

Project Files

For Project 7I, you will need the following files:

</td></tr>
</table>

New blank Word document
New blank Excel workbook
i07I_Office_Tenants

You will save your files as:

Lastname_Firstname_7I_Tenants_Template
Lastname_Firstname_7I_Tenant_Jones
Lastname_Firstname_7I_Tenants_Data
Lastname_Firstname_7I_Tenants_Presentation

The Cypress Lake Office Park at 11301 Fourth Street in Grant, Florida, is one of the office parks owned by the Select National Properties Group. Paul Stancill, the Leasing Manager, would like to send each new tenant a letter explaining the various expenses they will incur. Mr. Stancill has been tracking the tenant expenses in an Access database.

In Word, select a Letter template. Create a letter from Mr. Stancill. Include the company name and address: 321 North Michigan Avenue, Suite
700, Chicago, IL 60601. Complete the template by typing appropriate text explaining anticipated expenses. Include a list of expenses that the tenant will pay—such as taxes, insurance, telephone, water, electricity, gas, management fees, and maintenance fees. Include a sentence telling the tenant to contact him with any questions. Mr.Stancill's phone number is 312-555-0070. Save the template as **Lastname_Firstname_7I_Tenants_Template** Open a new document, based on the template, and then send the letter to Clay Jones, 4334 North Orange Blvd, Grant, Florida 32949. Save the letter as **Lastname_Firstname_7I_Tenant_Jones** In both documents, insert the file name in the footer, add appropriate document properties, and save your changes.

Import the data from the Access database i07I_Office_Tenants into an Excel workbook as an Excel table. Save the workbook as **Lastname_Firstname_7I_Tenants_Data** Insert the heading **Insurance** in cell F1. In column F, use the IF function to determine the amount of insurance each tenant pays. If the square footage is greater than 3000 feet, the tenant pays insurance of $5750; otherwise, the tenant pays $3500. Insert the heading **Total Expenses** in cell G1. In column G, total the expenses for each tenant. Adjust column widths to display all data. Rename the worksheet, and then delete any blank worksheets. Insert the file name as a field in the footer. Add appropriate document properties. Open the PowerPoint presentation i07I_Tenants_Presentation. Add a new slide, and then insert the list of expenses from your Word document. Move and resize the list as need and add a slide title. Add a new slide, and then insert the Excel table. Apply a design theme, and then insert the file name as a footer on the Notes page. Add appropriate document properties, and save your changes. Submit your printed or electronic files as directed by your instructor.

You have completed Project 7I

Integrating Word, Excel, Access, and PowerPoint

Integrating Word, Excel, and Access

OUTCOMES

In this capstone case you will:

Create a form and enter records in an Access database, export the data into an Excel workbook, copy Excel data into a Word document, and use Mail Merge to generate letters and envelopes.

Patricia Malina/Shutterstock

Adamantine Jewelry

Adamantine Jewelry is based in Milan, Italy, one of the world's leading centers for fashion and design. The company's designers take inspiration from nature, cultural artifacts, and antiquities to produce affordable, fashionable jewelry that is sold through major retailers in the United States. With a 40-year history, the company is well respected among its retail customers and has expanded to online and television retailers in recent years. In addition to women's bracelets, rings, and earrings, the company also produces sport and fashion watches for men and women.

From Capstone Case 1 of *GO! with Microsoft® Office 2010 Integrated Projects Comprehensive*, First Edition, Shelley Gaskin, Carol L. Martin. Copyright © 2012 by Pearson Education, Inc. Published by Pearson Prentice Hall. All rights reserved.

Content-Based Assessments

GO! Solve It | Capstone Case **1** Jewelry Sale

Project Files

For Capstone Case 1, you will need the following files:

New blank Excel workbook
i01cc_Jewelry_Customers
i01cc_Sale_Invitation

You will save your files as:

Lastname_Firstname_1cc_Jewelry_Customers
Lastname_Firstname_1cc_Jewelry_Discount
Lastname_Firstname_1cc_Phoenix_Invitations
Lastname_Firstname_1cc_Phoenix_Envelopes

Jennifer Bernard, the Adamantine Jewelry U.S. Sales Director, has been planning a sale with the manager of the Phoenix retail store. If the sale goes well at the Phoenix store, she would like to use the same promotion at the other Adamantine Jewelry store locations.

Ms. Bernard maintains an Access database **i01cc_Jewelry_Customers** that lists customer information. She has written a draft of an invitation letter in the Word document **i01cc_Sale_Invitation**. Navigate to the location where you are saving your files, and create a new folder named **Integrated Projects Capstone Cases** Open the file **i01cc_Jewelry_Customers**. Save the database in your **Integrated Projects Capstone Cases** folder with the file name **Lastname_Firstname_1cc_Jewelry_Customers**

In the Jewelry Customers table, add a text field **Jewelry Preference** Create a form based on the Jewelry Customers table. Add a combo box to the form that lists the following types of jewelry: Bracelets, Earrings, Fashion watches, Necklaces, Rings, and Sport watches. Store the value in the Jewelry Preference field, and then label the combo box **Preference** Using the form, add a jewelry preference to all customer records, using each jewelry type at least one time. Add the following records, using your first name and last name for the last record. Save the form as **Lastname Firstname Jewelry Customers Form**

First Name	Last Name	Address	City	State	ZIP	Jewelry Preference
Miranda	Hevey	500 NW Cheyenne	Salem	NH	03079	Necklaces
Allison	Plasek	33 Herman Ave	Concord	MA	01742	Rings
Firstname	Lastname	4126 Mercer Ln	Phoenix	AZ	85009	Sport watches

Create an Access report that contains all the fields from the Jewelry Customers table. Group the report by the Jewelry Preferences field, and then sort the data by the City field. Title the report **Lastname Firstname Jewelry Preferences Report**

Open a new blank Excel workbook. Import the Access table Jewelry Types as an Excel table. In column C, add the title **Discount** and then insert the IF function to calculate a 20% discount on jewelry that costs greater than $15,000. Format columns B and C using the Currency format and zero decimal places. Filter the table to display only the jewelry that displays a discount amount other than zero in column C. Save the Excel workbook in your **Integrated Projects Capstone Cases** folder as **Lastname_Firstname_1cc_Jewelry_Discount**

Open the file **i01cc_Sale_Invitation**. Apply a paragraph style to the four paragraphs listing the company name, address, and phone number. Insert the current date below the company phone number. Apply a theme to the document. Insert a text box that includes the statement **What a perfect time to shop for a Mother's Day gift!** Position the text box so your document has a professional appearance. In the Excel workbook, copy the filtered data and paste it at the end of the Word document. Center the table in the document.

Use the mail merge feature to merge the letter with the Access customer list. Insert the Address Block below the date. Filter the recipients for only the Phoenix customers. At the end of the

(Capstone Case 1 Jewelry Sale continues on the next page)

Content-Based Assessments

GO! Solve It | Capstone Case **1** Jewelry Sale (continued)

paragraph that begins *We see from your*, insert the merge field Jewelry Preferences, and then type a period. Preview the document and make any necessary changes. Complete the merge, and then save the new document to your **Integrated Projects Capstone Cases** folder as **Lastname_Firstname_1cc_Phoenix_Invitations** Use mail merge to create envelopes for the Phoenix customers. In the return address, type your first name and last name, and then use the Adamantine Jewelry address from the top of the letter to complete the return address. Save the merged envelopes as **Lastname_Firstname_1cc_Phoenix_Envelopes**

In your two Word files and your Excel file, insert the file name as a field in the footer. In all four of your files, insert appropriate document properties.

Submit all files as directed by your instructor.

		Performance Level		
		Exemplary: You consistently applied the relevant skills	**Proficient:** You sometimes, but not always, applied the relevant skills	**Developing:** You rarely or never applied the relevant skills
Performance Element	Add a combo box to a form	A combo box is added to the form and displays appropriately.	A combo box is added to the form but does not display appropriately.	A combo box is not added to the form.
	Create a report	The report is created and all data displays appropriately.	The report is created but either the data is not grouped or it is not sorted.	The report is not created.
	Insert the IF function and apply a filter	The IF function is inserted and the data is filtered correctly.	The IF function is inserted but the data is not filtered correctly.	The IF function is not inserted.
	Insert and position a text box	The text box is inserted and positioned appropriately.	The text box is inserted but is not positioned appropriately.	The text box is not inserted.
	Filter an Access data source	The data source is filtered using the correct field and value.	The data source is filtered but does not use the correct field or does not use the correct value.	The data source is not filtered.
	Insert text and merge fields in a letter and in an envelope	Text and merge fields are inserted appropriately.	At least one item is not inserted appropriately.	No items are inserted appropriately.

End You have completed Capstone Case 1 ————————

Integrating Word, Excel, and PowerPoint

OUTCOMES

In this capstone case you will:

Create an outline in Word, create an Excel chart, create a PowerPoint presentation that includes data imported from a Word document, and link an Excel chart to the presentation.

Skyline Bakery & Café

Skyline Bakery & Café is a chain of casual dining restaurants and bakeries based in Boston. Each restaurant has its own in-house bakery, which produces a wide variety of high-quality specialty breads, breakfast sweets, and desserts. Breads and sweets are sold by counter service along with coffee drinks, gourmet teas, fresh juices, and sodas. The full-service restaurant area features a menu of sandwiches, salads, soups, and light entrees. Fresh, high-quality ingredients and a professional and courteous staff are the hallmarks of every Skyline Bakery & Café.

From Capstone Case 2 of *GO! with Microsoft® Office 2010 Integrated Projects Comprehensive*, First Edition, Shelley Gaskin, Carol L. Martin. Copyright © 2012 by Pearson Education, Inc. Published by Pearson Prentice Hall. All rights reserved.

Content-Based Assessments

Apply a combination of the Chapters 1–7 skills.

GO! Solve It | Capstone Case 2 Specialty Coffees

Project Files

For Capstone Case 2, you will need the following files:

New blank PowerPoint presentation
i02cc_Coffee_Types
i02cc_Coffee_Sales

You will save your files as:

Lastname_Firstname_2cc_Coffee_Types
Lastname_Firstname_2cc_Coffee_Sales
Lastname_Firstname_2cc_Coffee_Presentation

Nancy Goldman, Chief Baker at Skyline Bakery & Café, has been researching the possibility of adding specialty coffees to the restaurant menu. She has listed different coffees in a Word document and projected annual sales in an Excel workbook. Ms. Goldman's contact information is 37 Newbury Street, Boston, MA 02116, 617-555-0037, www.skylinebakery.biz.

If necessary, navigate to the location where you are saving your files and create a new folder **Integrated Projects Capstone Cases** Open the file **i02cc_Coffee_Types**. Save the document in your **Integrated Projects Capstone Cases** folder as **Lastname_Firstname_2cc_Coffee_Types** Insert the file name in the footer. In Outline view, promote to Level 1 the headings Coffees, Coffee Definitions, and the names of each of the different types of coffee. Demote to Level 2 each of the paragraphs located after each of the Level 1 headings. Move the headings, and related subheadings—Espresso Con Panna, Espresso Granita, and Espresso Romano—so they display after Espresso. Add appropriate document properties.

Open the file **i02cc_Coffee_Sales**. Save the workbook in your **Integrated Projects Capstone Cases** folder as **Lastname_Firstname_2cc_Coffee_Sales** Insert the SUM function in row 14 and in column F and apply an appropriate number format. Add appropriate titles in cells A14 and F3. Merge and center the title and subtitle, and apply a cell style. Apply a cell style to the headings in cells A4:A14 and cells B3:F3. Insert a column chart that shows all coffee types and quarters. The chart should display on a new sheet named **Projected Sales Chart** Change the chart style and add an appropriate title. Rename the Sheet 1 tab as **Projected Coffee Sales** and delete any blank worksheets. All worksheets should have a professional appearance. Insert the file name in the footer of all worksheets and add appropriate document properties.

In a new blank PowerPoint presentation, import the Word outline to create the slides. Save the presentation in your **Integrated Projects Capstone Cases** folder as **Lastname_Firstname_2cc_Coffee_Presentation** On Slide 1, add the title **Skyline Bakery & Café** and subtitle **New Specialty Coffees**. On a new slide following the last slide of the presentation, link the chart from the Excel workbook. Following the chart slide, on a new slide, insert the contact information for Nancy Goldman. Insert a picture that displays a female chef. Insert at least two more appropriate pictures or clip art images on other slides in the presentation and adjust them to create a pleasing effect. Add a design theme and apply a transition to all slides. Apply a WordArt style to all slide titles except on the first slide. Insert the date and the file name in the footer so that the footer displays on all notes and handouts. Add appropriate document properties.

Submit all files as directed by your instructor.

(Capstone Case 2 Specialty Coffees continues on the next page)

Content-Based Assessments

	Performance Level		
	Exemplary: You consistently applied the relevant skills	**Proficient:** You sometimes, but not always, applied the relevant skills	**Developing:** You rarely or never applied the relevant skills
Apply outline levels	Paragraphs are assigned appropriate levels.	At least one paragraph is not assigned an appropriate level.	No levels are assigned to paragraphs.
Insert the SUM function	The SUM function is inserted and all values display correctly.	The SUM function is inserted but not all values display correctly.	The SUM function is not inserted.
Apply cell styles	All title and heading cells have cell styles applied.	At least one title or heading cell does not have a cell style applied.	No title or heading cells have cell styles applied.
Create a column chart	The chart is created and displays appropriately.	The chart is not a column chart or does not have a chart style applied.	The chart is not created.
Create a presentation from an outline	The information displays appropriately on all slides.	Not all information displays or at least one slide is not created.	The presentation is not created.
Insert and format objects	All objects are inserted and formatted appropriately.	At least one object is not inserted or it is not formatted appropriately.	No objects are inserted in the presentation.

(left vertical label: **Performance Element**)

End You have completed Capstone Case 2

Integrating Access, PowerPoint, and Publisher

OUTCOMES

In this capstone case you will:

Set Access field properties, create a PowerPoint presentation using a template, create a publication using a template, and use Mail Merge to generate postcards.

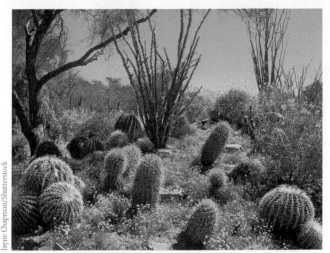

Jayne Chapman/Shutterstock

Southwest Gardens

The southwest style of gardening is popular in many areas of the country, not just in the yards and gardens of Arizona and New Mexico. The stylish simplicity and use of indigenous, hardy plants that are traditional in the Southwest United States make for beautiful, environmentally friendly gardens in any part of the country. Produced by Media Southwest Productions, the television show *Southwest Gardens* is broadcast nationwide. The show and its Web site provide tips and tricks for beautiful gardens and highlight new tools and techniques. The show's hosts present tours of public and private gardens that showcase the southwest style.

From Capstone Case 3 of *GO! with Microsoft® Office 2010 Integrated Projects Comprehensive*, First Edition, Shelley Gaskin, Carol L. Martin. Copyright © 2012 by Pearson Education, Inc. Published by Pearson Prentice Hall. All rights reserved.

GO! Solve It | Capstone Case 3 Cooking Show

Project Files

For Capstone Case 3, you will need the following files:

New blank Publisher publication
New blank PowerPoint presentation
i03cc_Cooks_Data
i03cc_Tang_Logo

You will save your files as:

Lastname_Firstname_3cc_Cooks_Data
Lastname_Firstname_3cc_Cooks_Presentation
Lastname_Firstname_3cc_Cooks_Postcard
Lastname_Firstname_3cc_Merged_Postcard

David Tang, Marketing Manager for Southwest Gardens, wants to add a cooking segment to the television broadcast. He has created an Access database that lists cooks who are interested in demonstrating their recipes. He has asked you to create a PowerPoint presentation that he can use to help persuade the show's co-hosts, Vicky Aurelias and Phillip Miel, as well as the show's executives, that the cooking segment is a good idea. Because Mr. Tang is confident that the cooking segment will be approved, he has also asked you to create a postcard in Publisher that can be mailed to each of the cooks. David Tang's business information is 41122 N 23rd St., Phoenix, AZ 85022, 602-555-0030, www.southwestgardens.tv.

If necessary, navigate to the location where you are saving your files and create a new folder **Integrated Projects Capstone Cases** Open the file **i03cc_Cooks_Data**. Save the file in your **Integrated Projects Capstone Cases** as **Lastname_Firstname_3cc_Cooks_Data** Add a default value to a field, and then add an input mask to another field. Create a form based on the Cooks table, and then enter the following data—the City field is **Phoenix** and the State field is **AZ** for all five records. Use your own name in the last record.

First Name	Last Name	Address	ZIP	Phone	Recipe
Miranda	Hevey	2409 Voltaire Ave.	85016	480-555-0185	Spicy Roasted Red Pepper Dip
Mary	Brady	4221 Ray Rd.	85255	480-555-5832	Salmon with Chile-Honey Glaze
Anita	Delgado	8343 Tonto Ln.	85208	480-555-5332	Spinach, Avocado, and Papaya Salad
Zachary	Plasek	126 Mercer Blvd.	85297	480-555-5351	Grilled Salmon Burrito
Firstname	Lastname	2103 Sapium Way	85208	480-555-2081	Green Chile Stew

Save the form as **Lastname Firstname Cooks Form** Add appropriate database properties.

Start PowerPoint and open any template that is appropriate for a persuasive presentation. Save the presentation to your **Integrated Projects Capstone Cases** folder as **Lastname_Firstname_3cc_Cooks_Presentation** On one slide create a SmartArt graphic that includes a list of fresh fruits that might be used in recipes. On another slide, create a SmartArt graphic that includes a list of fresh vegetables. Insert appropriate pictures or clip art. Insert a slide mentioning that Toni Jones is President of Media Southwest Productions. On the same slide, insert a note reminding the speaker to thank Toni Jones for attending and to introduce the two summer interns, Karen Galvin and Henry Cavazos, who have been working with the cooks. Add at least two additional slides with text that could help persuade the audience to support Mr. Tang's idea. Insert additional text and images to create a professional appearance. Insert the file name in a footer to display on all notes and handouts pages. Add appropriate document properties.

Open a Publisher template that is suitable for a postcard to be sent to cooks participating in the cooking segment. Save the publication in your **Integrated Projects Capstone Cases** folder as **Lastname_Firstname_3cc_Cooks_Postcard** Create a business information set for Mr. Tang. Add a tag line and the logo **i03cc_Tang_Logo** from your student files. In a text box, thank the cook for

(Capstone Case 3 Cooking Show continues on the next page)

Content-Based Assessments

GO! Solve It | Capstone Case **3** Cooking Show (continued)

participating and mention that Mr. Tang is looking forward to tasting the recipe. Copy one of the SmartArt graphics listing fresh fruit and vegetables from your PowerPoint presentation, and then paste it in the publication. Apply a color scheme and a font scheme, and add a design accent. Modify the publication to create a professional appearance. Use mail merge and the Access database to insert the Recipe field in the paragraph you typed. Add the address block at the appropriate place in the publication. Filter the data to include only cooks with the ZIP field 85208. Save your changes, and then complete the merge. Save the new merged publication as **Lastname_Firstname_3cc_Merged_Postcard** Insert the file name in the footer and add appropriate document properties.

Submit all files as directed by your instructor.

		Performance Level	
	Exemplary: You consistently applied the relevant skills	**Proficient:** You sometimes, but not always, applied the relevant skills	**Developing:** You rarely or never applied the relevant skills
Add default value and input mask properties	A default value and an input mask are added appropriately.	Either a default value or an input mask is not added appropriately.	Neither a default value nor an input mask is added appropriately.
Create SmartArt graphics	Two SmartArt graphics are created and display appropriate information.	One SmartArt graphic is not created or does not display appropriate information.	No SmartArt graphics are created.
Insert a note on a slide	The note is inserted on the appropriate slide and does not contain spelling or grammar errors.	The note is not inserted on the appropriate slide or the note contains spelling or grammar errors.	The note is not inserted.
Create and format a postcard	The postcard contains appropriate text and objects and is formatted to create a professional appearance.	Some text is inappropriate, at least one object is missing, or the formatting does not create a professional appearance.	The postcard is not created.
Insert merge fields from a filtered data source	The merge fields are inserted and the data source is filtered using the correct field.	Not all merge fields are inserted or the data source is not filtered using the correct field.	No merge fields are inserted and the data source is not filtered.

Performance Element

End **You have completed Capstone Case 3**

Integrating Word, Excel, Access, and PowerPoint

OUTCOMES

In this capstone case you will:

Import Excel data into an Access database, create an Access report, create PivotTable and PivotChart reports, use Mail Merge to generate letters and envelopes, and create a PowerPoint presentation that includes a linked PivotChart.

Midwest HVAC Manufacturer

Midwest HVAC Manufacturer is one of the country's largest suppliers of heating, ventilation, and air conditioning (HVAC) equipment. The company delivers high-performance climate control parts and systems primarily to wholesale customers. Because of the growing popularity of do-it-yourself projects, they also have two local retail stores. Two times each year, Midwest HVAC Manufacturer updates its parts catalog, which includes supplies such as fans, motors, heating and cooling coils, filter units, and dehumidification and humidification units. It designs and manufactures all of its own products and has won several engineering and product awards.

From Capstone Case 4 of *GO! with Microsoft® Office 2010 Integrated Projects Comprehensive*, First Edition, Shelley Gaskin, Carol L. Martin. Copyright © 2012 by Pearson Education, Inc. Published by Pearson Prentice Hall. All rights reserved.

Apply a combination of the Chapters 1–7 skills.

GO! Solve It | Capstone Case **4** Advertising Letter

Project Files

For Capstone Case 4, you will need the following files:

New blank Access database
i04cc_HVAC_Customers
i04cc_HVAC_Savings
i04cc_Advertising_Letter
i04cc_Maintenance_Presentation

You will save your files as:

Lastname_Firstname_4cc_HVAC_Customers
Lastname_Firstname_4cc_HVAC_Savings
Lastname_Firstname_4cc_Advertising_Letter
Lastname_Firstname_4cc_Merged_Letters
Lastname_Firstname_4cc_Merged_Envelopes
Lastname_Firstname_4cc_Maintenance_Presentation

Lecia Beecroft, Marketing Director at Midwest HVAC Manufacturer, is planning to send an advertising letter to current customers in an effort to increase the number of customers who participate in the company's preventive maintenance program. She would also like to make a presentation available to interested customers. Ms. Beecroft's contact information is Marketing Manager, 4437 Harney St., Omaha, NE 68179, 402-555-0707.

If necessary, navigate to the location where you are saving your files, and then create a new folder named **Integrated Projects Capstone Cases** Open a blank Access database and save it in your **Integrated Projects Capstone Cases** folder as **Lastname_Firstname_4cc_HVAC_Customers** Import the data from the Excel workbook **i04cc_HVAC_Customers**. Create a form based on the HVAC Customers table, and then enter the following records. The State field for all records is AZ. Enter your name in the last record.

First Name	Lastname	Address	City	ZIP	Phone	Model
Collin	Plasek	5048 E Via Montoya	Phoenix	85016	480-555-0185	OMH036B LE
Jake	Kettler	4126 Mercer Ln	Gilbert	85297	480-555-2256	OMH038C ME
Nathaniel	Plasek	1847 S 28th St	Chandler	85226	480-555-2778	OMH044B HE
Sidney	Paolino	3002 W 49th Way	Mesa	85208	480-555-3113	OMH048C LE
Firstname	Lastname	488 Carol Way	Phoenix	85009	480-555-8827	OMH070B LE

Save the form as **Lastname Firstname HVAC Customers Form** Create a report that groups the data by the Model field and sorts the data by the Lastname field. Do not include the ID field in the report. Make any necessary changes to the layout to create a professional appearance. Save the report as **Lastname Firstname HVAC Customers Report** Add appropriate database properties.

Open the file **i04cc_HVAC_Savings**. Save the file in your **Integrated Projects Capstone Cases** folder as **Lastname_Firstname_4cc_HVAC_Savings** Create a PivotTable report that displays the Power field as a column, the Height field as a row, and the Weight field as the value. Rename the worksheet **Height** Create similar PivotTable reports for the Width and Length fields, and rename the worksheets appropriately. From the HVAC Units worksheet, create a PivotChart that reflects the savings from the maintenance program based on the Power and Heating BTU fields. Move the chart to a new sheet and make any design changes to give the chart a professional appearance. Delete any blank worksheets. Adjust the layout of all worksheet pages to print on one page. For all worksheets, insert the file name in the footer, and then add appropriate document properties.

Open the file **i04cc_Advertising_Letter**. Save the document in your **Integrated Projects Capstone Cases** folder as **Lastname_Firstname_4cc_Advertising_Letter** Format the company address so it displays as a letterhead. Format the document using Word features—such as themes,

(Capstone Case 4 Advertising Letter continues on the next page)

Advertising Letter | **Integrated Projects**

GO! Solve It | Capstone Case **4** Advertising Letter (continued)

page colors, and page borders—to create a letter with a professional appearance. Below the company address, insert the current date. Use mail merge and your Access database to insert the address block, and adjust paragraph spacing. Apply a filter for those customers who have purchased the OMH070B LE model. Complete the merge. Save the new document as **Lastname_Firstname_ 4cc_Merged_Letters** Insert the file name in the footer, and add appropriate document properties. Create envelopes for the OMH070B LE customers. Use your name in the return address and the Midwest HVAC Manufacturer company address. Save the merged envelopes in the Integrated Projects Capstone Cases folder as **Lastname_Firstname_4cc_Merged_Envelopes** Insert appropriate document properties.

Open the file **i04cc_Maintenance_Presentation**. Save the file in your **Integrated Projects Capstone Cases** folder as **Lastname_Firstname_4cc_Maintenance_Presentation** Insert the file name to display in the footer on all notes and handouts pages. In a new slide at the end of the presentation, link the Excel PivotChart report. In a new final slide, add the contact information for Lecia Beecroft. Adjust any slide elements to create a professional appearance. Add a design theme and apply a transition to all slides. Add appropriate document properties.

Submit all files as directed by your instructor.

Performance Element	Performance Level		
	Exemplary: You consistently applied the relevant skills	**Proficient:** You sometimes, but not always, applied the relevant skills	**Developing:** You rarely or never applied the relevant skills
Import Excel data to an Access database	All data is imported to an Access table and displays appropriately.	Some data is not imported to the Access table or the data does not display appropriately.	No data is imported to the Access table.
Create a report	The report is created and all data is grouped and sorted appropriately.	The report is created but either the data is not grouped or it is not sorted.	The report is not created.
Create PivotTable and PivotChart reports	All PivotTable and PivotChart reports are created and display appropriately.	At least one PivotTable or PivotChart report is not created or does not display appropriately.	No PivotTable or PivotChart reports are created.
Filter an Access table	The table is filtered using the correct field and value.	The table is filtered but does not use the correct field or does not use the correct value.	The table is not filtered.
Insert text and merge fields in a letter and in an envelope	Text and merge fields are inserted appropriately.	At least one item is not inserted appropriately.	No merge fields are inserted.
Link a PivotChart report in a slide	A PivotChart report is linked in a slide and displays appropriately.	A PivotChart report is linked in a slide but does not display appropriately.	A PivotChart report is not linked in a slide.

End You have completed Capstone Case 4

Integrating Word, Excel, and PowerPoint

OUTCOMES

In this capstone case you will:

Create and filter an Excel table, create a SmartArt graphic, and create a PowerPoint presentation that includes pasted objects.

Sportstock/Shutterstock

Board Anywhere Surf and Snowboard Shop

College classmates Dana Connolly and J. R. Kass grew up in the sun of Orange County, California, but they also spent time in the mountain snow. After graduating with business degrees, they combined their business expertise and their favorite sports to open Board Anywhere Surf and Snowboard Shop. The store carries top brands of men's and women's apparel, goggles and sunglasses, and boards and gear. The surfboard selection includes both classic and the latest high-tech boards. Snowboarding gear can be purchased in packages or customized for the most experienced boarders. Connolly and Kass are proud to count many of Southern California's extreme sports games participants among their customers.

From Capstone Case 5 of *GO! with Microsoft® Office 2010 Integrated Projects Comprehensive*, First Edition, Shelley Gaskin, Carol L. Martin. Copyright © 2012 by Pearson Education, Inc. Published by Pearson Prentice Hall. All rights reserved.

Content-Based Assessments

GO! Solve It | Capstone Case 5 Helicopter Jumps

Project Files

For Capstone Case 5, you will need the following files:

i05cc_Jumps_Presentation
i05cc_Jump_Dates
i05cc_Jump_Flyer

You will save your files as:

Lastname_Firstname_5cc_Jump_Dates
Lastname_Firstname_5cc_Jump_Flyer
Lastname_Firstname_5cc_Jumps_Presentation

Dana Connolly and J. R. Kass, the owners of Board Anywhere Surf and Snowboard Shop, have decided to add adventure traveling to their offerings—specifically helicopter jumps for snowboarders. They have started a flyer in Word that will be printed and available at the local ski resorts. An Excel workbook contains the dates and costs for the helicopter jumps. The owners also plan to run a PowerPoint presentation in their retail store.

If necessary, navigate to the location where you are saving your files, and create a new folder named **Integrated Projects Capstone Cases** Open the file **i05cc_Jump_Dates**. Save the workbook in your **Integrated Projects Capstone Cases** folder as **Lastname_Firstname_5cc_Jump_Dates** Copy the Instructors worksheet to a new worksheet. In the new worksheet, create an Excel table and apply a table style. Filter the table to display only data related to instructor Sarah Begren. Rename the worksheet as **Begren** On the Instructors worksheet, insert a new row 1, and then type the company name. Merge and center the text so it displays above all the columns containing data. The headings in row 1 and row 2 should display on all pages when the worksheet is printed. Sort the list by date. For the last date, insert a comment that mentions that more dates may be added. Format the worksheet using cell styles. Adjust column widths as necessary to create a professional appearance. Delete any blank worksheets. Insert the file name in the footer on all worksheets, and then add appropriate document properties.

Open the file **i05cc_Jump_Flyer**. Save the file in your **Integrated Projects Capstone Cases** folder as **Lastname_Firstname_5cc_Jump_Flyer** and then insert the file name in the footer. Insert a SmartArt graphic listing the five instructors. Paste the Excel table displaying the dates for Sarah Begren in the Word document. Format the document using Word features—such as text effects, font styles, themes, and page borders—to create a flyer with a professional appearance. Adjust any text, spacing, margins, or objects so the document displays on one page. Add appropriate document properties.

Open the PowerPoint presentation **i05cc_Jumps_Presentation**. Save the file in your **Integrated Projects Capstone Cases** folder as **Lastname_Firstname_5cc_Jumps_Presentation** Insert the file name in the footer on all pages of the notes and handouts. Add text to each slide to answer the question in the title. On the slide at the end of the presentation, insert the reservation information **949-555-0049** and **www.boardanywhere.biz** Insert a new slide at the end of the presentation, and then paste the SmartArt graphic from the Word document. Insert a picture or clip art on at least three slides. Add a design theme and apply a transition to all slides. Make any adjustments so the presentation has a professional appearance. Add appropriate document properties.

Submit all files as directed by your instructor.

(Capstone Case 5 Helicopter Jumps continues on the next page)

Content-Based Assessments

GO! Solve It | Capstone Case **5** Helicopter Jumps (continued)

	Performance Level		
	Exemplary: You consistently applied the relevant skills	**Proficient:** You sometimes, but not always, applied the relevant skills	**Developing:** You rarely or never applied the relevant skills
Create and filter a table	The table is created and filtered correctly.	The table is created but is not filtered correctly.	The table is not created.
Insert a comment	A comment is inserted in the correct cell.	A comment is inserted but is not in the correct cell.	A comment is not inserted.
Create a SmartArt graphic	A SmartArt graphic is created and all names display.	A SmartArt graphic is created but at least one name does not display.	A SmartArt graphic is not created.
Format a document	The document is formatted appropriately and displays on one page.	The document is not formatted appropriately or does not display on one page.	The document is not formatted appropriately.
Add text to a presentation	Appropriate text is added and is free from spelling and grammar errors.	Some text is inappropriate or contains at least one spelling or grammar error.	Text is not inserted.
Format a presentation	A design theme and transition are applied to all slides.	A design theme or a transition is not applied to all slides.	A design theme and a transition are not applied.

(left column label: Performance Element)

End You have completed Capstone Case 5 ——————

Integrating Word, Excel, Access, and PowerPoint

OUTCOMES

In this capstone case you will:

> Create a PivotTable, import Excel data into an Access database, group and sort data to create an Access report, and paste a PivotTable in a Word document and in a PowerPoint presentation.

Florida Port Community College

Florida Port Community College is located in St. Petersburg, Florida, a coastal port city located near the Florida High-Tech Corridor. With 60 percent of Florida's high-tech companies and a third of the state's manufacturing companies located in the St. Petersburg and Tampa Bay areas, the college partners with businesses to play a vital role in providing a skilled workforce. The curriculum covers many areas, including medical technology, computer science, electronics, aviation and aerospace, and simulation and modeling. The college also serves the community through cultural, athletics, and diversity programs and adult basic education.

From Capstone Case 6 of *GO! with Microsoft® Office 2010 Integrated Projects Comprehensive*, First Edition, Shelley Gaskin, Carol L. Martin. Copyright © 2012 by Pearson Education, Inc. Published by Pearson Prentice Hall. All rights reserved.

Apply a combination of the Chapters 1–7 skills.

GO! Solve It | Capstone Case **6** FPCC Graduation

Project Files

For Capstone Case 6, you will need the following files:

New blank Access database
i06cc_Graduation_Report
i06cc_Graduating_Students
i06cc_Graduation_Presentation

You will save your files as:

Lastname_Firstname_6cc_Graduation_Report
Lastname_Firstname_6cc_Graduating_Students
Lastname_Firstname_6cc_Students_Data
Lastname_Firstname_6cc_Graduation_Presentation

Leyla Barwari, Vice President of Academic Affairs at Florida Port Community College, wants to provide information for graduating students. Students who have graduation questions can contact the Advisement and Counseling Office at 727-555-0030 or visit the Web site FloridaPortCC.edu. Ms. Barwari would like to provide a report to students who are close to earning a degree and need information regarding graduation. She has created a list of graduating students in an Excel worksheet, but thinks it would be easier to maintain the list in an Access database. She would also like a PowerPoint presentation that will run in the Student Union.

If necessary, navigate to the location where you are saving your files, and then create a new folder named **Integrated Projects Capstone Cases** Open the file **i06cc_Graduation_Report**. Save the document in your **Integrated Projects Capstone Cases** folder as **Lastname_Firstname_6cc_Graduation_Report** and then insert the file name in the footer. Following the paragraph referring to the deans, insert a table, and enter the following data:

Dean	College Department
Henry Krasnow	Adult Education
Caitlin Freeman	Aviation & Aerospace
Richard Plasek	Business & Information Technology
Mary George	Humanities
Ella Hall	Mathematics

Apply a table style and center the table on the page. Insert a cover page, including a graphic and contact information, and then create a table of contents.

Open the file **i06cc_Graduating_Students**. Save the workbook in your **Integrated Projects Capstone Cases** folder as **Lastname_Firstname_6cc_Graduating_Students** Create a PivotTable report on a new worksheet that shows the total fees due from the students for each college department. Rename the worksheet with an appropriate name, and then delete any blank worksheets. Insert the file name in the footer on all worksheets. Add appropriate document properties.

Open a new blank Access database, and then save the database in your **Integrated Projects Capstone Cases** folder as **Lastname_Firstname_6cc_Students_Data** From Excel, import the Graduating Students worksheet Create an Access report listing the fields First Name, Last Name, College Department, and Fees Due. Group the report by College Department, and sort by Last Name. Title the report **Lastname Firstname Graduating Students** Create a query that displays the fields First Name Last Name, Address, City, State, and ZIP and displays only the Humanities students. Save the query as **Humanities Students Query** Create a report based on the query, sort the report by Last Name, and then save the report as **Lastname Firstname Humanities Students** Add appropriate database properties.

(Capstone Case 6 FPCC Graduation continues on the next page)

GO! Solve It | Capstone Case 6 FPCC
Graduation (continued)

Open the file **i06cc_Graduation_Presentation**. Save the presentation to your **Integrated Projects Capstone Cases** folder as **Lastname_Firstname_6cc_Graduation_Presentation** Insert the file name in the footer to display on all notes and handouts pages. Insert appropriate pictures or clipart on at least three slides. Format the graphics by adding effects—for example, reflections or glows. Insert a new blank slide and paste the PivotTable report from Excel, and then modify the column headings. Paste the Word table listing the college deans in a new slide. At the end of the presentation, insert a slide listing the contact information for students who have graduation questions. Apply a design theme to all slides, and then add appropriate document properties.

In your Word document, in the body text, above the Graduate with Honors heading, type the heading **Fees Due by College Department** Under the heading, paste the PivotTable report from Excel, and then modify the column headings. Format the document to create a professional appearance using features such as themes, page colors, or page borders, or page layouts. Update the table of contents.

Submit all files as directed by your instructor.

	Performance Level		
	Exemplary: You consistently applied the relevant skills	**Proficient:** You sometimes, but not always, applied the relevant skills	**Developing:** You rarely or never applied the relevant skills
Insert a cover page and table of contents	The cover page and table of contents are inserted appropriately.	Either the cover page or the table of contents is not inserted appropriately.	Neither the cover page nor the table of contents is inserted.
Create a PivotTable report	The PivotTable report is created and displays the correct data.	The PivotTable report is created but not all data displays correctly.	The PivotTable report is not created.
Create an Access report from a table	The report is created and all data is grouped and sorted correctly.	The report is created but either the data is not grouped or the data is not sorted.	The report is not created.
Create a report from a query	The report is created and displays only the filtered data.	The report is created but the data is not filtered appropriately.	The report is not created.
Insert objects in a presentation	All objects are inserted and display appropriately.	At least one item is not inserted or does not display appropriately.	No items are inserted.
Insert a Word table and a PivotTable report	The Word table and a PivotTable report are inserted correctly.	The Word table or the PivotTable report is not inserted correctly.	The Word table and the PivotTable report are not inserted.

(Performance Element — row label on left side)

End You have completed Capstone Case 6 ————————

Integrating Word, Excel, Access, and PowerPoint

OUTCOMES

In this capstone case you will:

Insert a function in Excel, create and filter an Excel table, create queries and reports in Access, export an Access table to a Word document, and link Excel data to a Word document and a PowerPoint presentation.

Olexa/Shutterstock

Select National Properties Group

Select National Properties Group is a diversified real estate company that develops, builds, manages, and acquires a wide variety of properties nationwide. Among the company's portfolio of properties are shopping malls, mixed-use town center developments, high-rise office buildings, office parks, industrial buildings and warehouses, multi-family housing developments, educational facilities, and hospitals. Residential developments are mainly located in and around the company's hometown, Chicago; commercial and public buildings in the portfolio are located nationwide. The company is well respected for its focus on quality and commitment to the environment and economic development of the areas where it operates.

From Capstone Case 7 of *GO! with Microsoft® Office 2010 Integrated Projects Comprehensive*, First Edition, Shelley Gaskin, Carol L. Martin. Copyright © 2012 by Pearson Education, Inc. Published by Pearson Prentice Hall. All rights reserved.

Content-Based Assessments

GO! Solve It | Capstone Case **7** Sale Properties

Project Files

For Capstone Case 7, you will need the following files:

New blank Word document
New blank Access database
New blank PowerPoint presentation
i07cc_Sale_Properties

You will save your files as:

Lastname_Firstname_7cc_Sale_Properties
Lastname_Firstname_7cc_SNPG_Properties
Lastname_Firstname_7cc_Killgorn_Letter
Lastname_Firstname_7cc_Sales_Presentation

Tate Plasek, Sales Manager, has an Excel workbook listing properties for sale. If a property is sold, Select National Properties Group will finance the property loan for 30 years at 7.5% interest. If the monthly payment of a property is greater than $300,000, the company will give the buyer a 1% discount of the selling price. Lisa Killgorn is interested in purchasing the Harvest Properties Warehouse, one of the company's properties. She lives at 2231 University Drive, Tempe, AZ 85280.

If necessary, navigate to the location where you are saving your files, and create a new folder named **Integrated Projects Capstone Cases** Open the file **i07cc_Sale_Properties**, and then save the workbook in your **Integrated Projects Capstone Cases** folder as **LastnameFirstname_ 7cc_Sale_Properties** Copy the Properties worksheet to a new worksheet, and then rename the worksheet as **Payments** In the Payments worksheet, convert the data to a table. In column G, insert a calculated column using the PMT function to calculate the monthly payment for each of the properties. In column H, insert a calculated column using the IF function to determine whether the property qualifies for a discount. Determine the totals for columns F:H. Apply conditional formatting to cells with a selling price between $40,000,000 and $70,000,000. Copy the Payments worksheet to a new worksheet, and then rename the new worksheet as **Harvest Properties** Filter the table to display only the data for the Harvest Properties Warehouse. Delete any blank worksheets. Insert the file name in the footer so that it displays on all worksheets. Add appropriate document properties.

Create a blank Access database, and then save it in your **Integrated Projects Capstone Cases** folder as **Lastname_Firstname_7cc_SNPG_Properties** Import the data from the Properties worksheet. Create a query that displays all fields, except the ID field, for properties located in Florida and Georgia. Save the query as **Lastname Firstname FL GA Query** Export the query result as an RTF file to your **Integrated Projects Capstone Cases** folder. Create another query that displays all fields, except the ID field, for all properties with selling prices less than $1,000,000. Save the query as **Lastname Firstname Price Query** For each query, create and format a report. Save each report with the name as the query, substituting the word **Report** for **Query** Add appropriate database properties.

Create a letter using a Word template of your choice. Save the document in your **Integrated Projects Capstone Cases** folder as **Lastname_Firstname_7cc_Killgorn_Letter**. Insert the file name in the footer. Insert the current date, and then insert Lisa Killgorn's name and address. Type a paragraph introducing the company, using information at the beginning of this case. Type a second paragraph letting Ms. Killgorn know that Select National Properties Group is willing to finance the purchase of Harvest Properties Warehouse. From Excel, on the Harvest Properties worksheet, link cells F1:G2 to the Word document. Type another paragraph informing Ms. Killgorn that we understand that she is interested in property in either Florida or Georgia. In the paragraph, include the number of properties that are available in those states. Under the paragraph, insert the RTF file listing the Florida and Georgia properties. End the letter with a paragraph thanking Ms. Killgorn for her interest. The letter is from Mr. Plasek, 321 North Michigan Avenue, Suite 700, Chicago, IL 60601, 312-555-0070. Format the document to create a professional appearance. Add appropriate document properties.

(Capstone Case 7 Sale Properties continues on the next page)

Integrated Projects | Integrating Word, Excel, Access, and PowerPoint

GO! Solve It | Capstone Case **7** Sale Properties (continued)

Create a PowerPoint presentation using a template of your choice; the presentation will be shown to prospective buyers attending a sales conference. Save the presentation to your **Integrated Projects Capstone Cases** folder as **Lastname_Firstname_7cc_Sales_Presentation** Insert the file name in the footer to display on all pages of the notes and handouts. Modify the slides to help persuade buyers to purchase property from Select National Properties Group. On one slide, inform the audience that the company sells many properties. On the same slide, link the cell from the Excel Payments worksheet that displays the total selling price. On a new slide, insert a SmartArt graphic that lists some of the different types of properties that the company develops and manages. At the end of the presentation, insert a slide that contains the contact information for Mr. Plasek. Insert additional text, pictures, and clip art to enhance the presentation. Format any text or other objects to create a professional appearance. Add appropriate document properties.

Copy the SmartArt graphic from your presentation to the letter, changing text wrapping and resizing as necessary to display the letter in a professional manner.

Submit all files as directed by your instructor.

	Performance Level		
	Exemplary: You consistently applied the relevant skills	**Proficient:** You sometimes, but not always, applied the relevant skills	**Developing:** You rarely or never applied the relevant skills
Insert PMT and IF functions	The PMT and IF functions are inserted and the correct values display.	The PMT function or IF function is not inserted or all values do not display correctly.	The PMT function and the IF function are not inserted.
Create two reports from queries	The reports are created and display the correct data.	One report is not created or some data in either report does not display correctly.	Neither report is created.
Insert text and objects in a letter	All text and objects are inserted appropriately.	At least one item is not inserted appropriately.	No items are inserted appropriately.
Create a SmartArt graphic	The SmartArt graphic is created and displays the correct information	The SmartArt graphic is created but not all information is correct.	The SmartArt graphic is not created.
Insert text and objects in a presentation.	All text and objects are inserted appropriately.	At least one item is not inserted appropriately.	No items are inserted appropriately.

(left margin label) **Performance Element**

End You have completed Capstone Case 7 ————————————

Glossary

Absolute cell reference A cell reference that refers to cells by their fixed position in a worksheet; an absolute cell reference remains the same when a formula is copied to other cells.

Accounting Number Format The Excel number format that applies a thousand comma separator where appropriate, inserts a fixed U.S. dollar sign aligned at the left edge of the cell, applies two decimal places, and leaves a small amount of space at the right edge of the cell to accommodate a parenthesis for negative numbers.

Action query A query that changes the data in the data source or creates a new table.

Animation A visual or sound effect that is added to an object or text on a slide.

Append query A query that adds a set of records from one or more source tables to one or more destination tables.

Area Section The location in the PivotTable Field List task pane that contains four quadrants where field names are placed to determine how the report will display.

Argument Any value that an Excel function uses to perform operations or calculations.

Ascending order Text is arranged in alphabetical order (A to Z) or numbers from the lowest to the highest value.

AutoExpansion An Excel table feature in which a new column is automatically included as part of the existing table.

AutoFill An Excel feature that extends values into adjacent cells based on the values of selected cells.

AutoFilter An Excel feature where only a portion of the data (a subset) that meets the criteria you specify is displayed; the data that does not meet the criteria is hidden—not deleted.

AutoFit A Word feature that adjusts the width of the columns in a table to fit the cell content of the widest cell in each column.

AutoSum Another name for the SUM function.

Axis Fields (Categories) The fields that are assigned to the categories that display on the horizontal axis in a column PivotChart report.

Black slide A slide that displays at the end of a PowerPoint presentation indicating that the slide show is over.

Blank Report tool An Access tool with which you can create a report from scratch by adding the fields you designate in the order you want them to display.

Bound A term that describes objects and controls that are based on data stored in one or more tables or queries in the database.

Building blocks Reusable pieces of content—for example, borders, text boxes, logos, and calendars—that are stored in galleries.

Business information set A customized group of information—including items such as a company name, address, phone number, e-mail address, and logo—that can be used to quickly fill in appropriate places in a publication.

Calculated column An Excel feature that uses a single formula that adjusts for each row of a column in a data table.

Calculated field A field that stores the value of a mathematical expression.

Category axis The area along the bottom of a chart that identifies the categories of data; also referred to as the x-axis.

Cell A small box formed by the intersection of a column and a row.

Cell address Another name for *cell reference*.

Cell reference The identification of a specific cell by its intersecting column letter and row number.

Character spacing An Office feature that allows you to increase or decrease the space between characters.

Chart layout The combination of chart elements that can be displayed in a chart such as a title, legend, labels for the columns, and the table of charted cells.

Chart Layouts gallery A group of predesigned chart layouts that you can apply to an Excel chart.

Chart sheet A workbook sheet that contains only a chart and is useful when you want to view a chart separately from the worksheet data.

Chart style The overall visual look of a chart in terms of its graphic effects, colors, and backgrounds; for example, you can have flat or beveled columns, colors that are solid or transparent, and backgrounds that are dark or light.

Chart Styles gallery A group of predefined chart styles that you can apply to an Excel chart.

Clip art Predefined graphics included with Microsoft Office or downloaded from the Internet.

Color scheme A predefined set of harmonized colors that can be applied to text and objects.

Column chart A chart in which the data is arranged in columns. It is useful for showing data changes over a period of time or for illustrating comparisons among items.

Column Labels Fields that are assigned a column orientation in a PivotTable and become the column headings.

Combo box control A form control that combines a drop-down list with a text box, providing a more compact way to present a list of choices.

Comma Style The Excel number format that inserts thousand comma separators where appropriate, applies two decimal places, and leaves space at the right of the cell to accommodate a parenthesis for negative numbers.

Comment A note that can be added from the Review tab and is generally not printed.

Comparison operators Symbols that evaluate each field value to determine if it is the same (=), greater than (>), less than (<), or in between a range of values as specified by the criteria.

Conditional format A format that changes the appearance of a cell—for example, by adding cell shading or changing font color—based on a condition; if the condition is true, the cell is formatted based on that condition, if the condition is false, the cell is *not* formatted.

Content control In a template, an area indicated by placeholder text that can be used to add text, pictures, dates, or lists.

Contextual spelling A Word feature that marks words that are spelled correctly but used incorrectly with a wavy blue underline.

Contextual tabs Tabs that are added to the Ribbon when a specific object, such as a table, is selected and that contain commands relevant to the selected object.

Cover page The first page of a complex document that provides introductory information.

From the Glossary of *GO! with Microsoft® Office 2010 Integrated Projects Comprehensive*, First Edition, Shelley Gaskin, Carol L. Martin. Copyright © 2012 by Pearson Education, Inc. Published by Pearson Prentice Hall. All rights reserved.

Criteria The conditions in a query that identify the specific records for which you are looking.

Data marker A column, bar, area, dot, pie slice, or other symbol in a chart that represents a single data point.

Data point The value that originates in a worksheet cell and that is represented in a chart by a data marker.

Data series The related data points represented by data markers.

Data source A list of variable information, such as names and addresses, that is merged with a main document to create customized form letters, envelopes, or labels.

Data type The characteristic that defines the kind of data that can be entered into a field, such as numbers, text, or dates.

Database An organized collection of facts about people, events, things, or ideas related to a particular topic or purpose.

Datasheet view The Access view that displays data organized in columns and rows similar to an Excel worksheet.

Date Picker A calendar control that is used to select a date.

Decimal tab stop A tab stop in which the text aligns with the decimal point at the tab stop location.

Default value The value that is automatically entered in a new record.

Default value (property) In Access, the data that is automatically entered in a field.

Descending order Text is arranged in reverse alphabetical order (Z to A) or numbers from the highest to the lowest value.

Design Checker A Publisher feature that automatically reviews a publication for a range of design and layout flaws and provides options to fix any identified problems.

Design grid The lower pane of the Advanced Filter window that displays the design of the filter.

Design view An Access view that displays the detailed structure of a table, query, form, or report and the view in which some tasks must be performed.

Destination file The file where the linked data or object is inserted.

Document Inspector A Microsoft Office feature that enables you to find and remove hidden data and personal information in a file.

Drill-down indicator A PivotTable feature that shows the detailed records of a PivotTable total.

Embedded chart A chart that displays as an object within a worksheet.

Excel table A series of rows and columns that contains related data that is managed independently from the data in other rows and columns of the worksheet.

Explode The action of pulling out one or more pie slices from a pie chart for emphasis.

Field A placeholder that displays preset content, such as the current date, the file name, a page number, or other stored information.

Field (Access) A single piece of information that is stored in every record and formatted as a column in a database table.

Field list A list of the field names in a table.

Field property Characteristics of a field that control how the field displays and how data can be entered in the field.

Field Section A location in the PivotTable Field List task pane containing the available field names that you can add to the Area Section.

Field size The maximum number of characters you can enter in a field.

Fill handle A small black square located in the lower right corner of a selected cell.

Filtering The process of displaying only a portion of the data based on matching a specific value to show only the data that meets the criteria you specify.

Font scheme A predefined set of fonts that is associated with a publication, where a primary font and a secondary font are specified.

Foreign key The field that is included in the related table so the field can be joined with the primary key in another table for the purpose of creating a relationship.

Form A database object used to enter data, edit data, or display data from a table or query.

Form control In an Access form, an object that displays data, performs actions, and lets the user view and work with information.

Form view The Access view in which you can view the records, but you cannot change the layout or design of the form.

Formula A mathematical expression that contains functions, operators, constants, and properties, and returns a value to a cell.

Formula Bar An element in the Excel window that displays the value or formula contained in the active cell and permits you to enter or edit the values or formulas.

Freeze Panes A command that enables you to select one or more rows and columns and freeze (lock) them into place; the locked rows and columns become separate panes.

Function A predefined formula that performs calculations by using specific values in a particular order.

Gallery An Office feature that displays a list of potential results instead of just the command name.

Grouping An Access report feature that enables you to separate groups of records visually and to display introductory and summary data for each group in a report.

Hyperlinks Text, buttons, pictures, or other objects that, when clicked, access other sections of the current file, another file, or a Web page.

IF function An Excel function that uses a logical test to check whether a condition is met, and then returns one value if true and another value if false.

Input mask A set of literal characters and placeholder characters that control what can and cannot be entered in an Access field.

Join line In the Relationships window, the line joining two tables that visually indicates the related field and the type of relationship.

Label control A control on a form or report that contains descriptive information, typically a field name.

Layout guides Nonprinting lines that mark the margins, columns, rows, and baselines and are used to align the text, pictures, and other objects so that the publication has balance and uniformity.

Layout view The Access view in which you can make changes to a form or to a report while the object is running—the data from the underlying data source displays.

Legend A chart element that identifies patterns or colors that are assigned to the categories in the chart.

Legend Fields (Series) The fields that are assigned to the columns that display in a column PivotChart report.

Linking The process of inserting information from a source file into a destination file, while maintaining the connection between the two files.

Live Preview A technology that shows the result of applying an editing or formatting change as the pointer is moved over the results presented in the gallery.

Lookup Wizard An Access feature that creates a list box to look up a value in another table, a query, or a list of values.

Mail merge A Microsoft Word feature that joins a main document and a data source to create customized letters, envelopes, or labels.

Main document In a mail merge, the document that contains the text or formatting that remains constant.

Margin guides Nonprinting lines on the top, bottom, left, and right sides of the page that are used to define the page margins.

Mark as Final A Microsoft Office feature that changes the file to a read-only file—typing and editing commands are turned off.

Master page The page that contains the design and layout elements, including headers and footers, that you want to repeat on multiple pages of your publication.

Merge & Center A command that joins selected cells into one large cell and then centers the contents in the new cell.

Message Bar The area directly below the Ribbon that displays information such as security alerts when there is potentially unsafe, active content in an Office 2010 document that you open.

Mini toolbar A small toolbar containing frequently used formatting commands that displays as a result of selecting text or objects.

Minus outline symbol A formatting mark that indicates there are no subordinate heading or body text paragraphs.

Name Box An element of the Excel window that displays the name of the selected cell, table, chart, or object.

Navigation Pane The area of the Access window that displays and organizes the names of the objects in a database; from here, you can open objects for use.

Normal view The primary editing view in PowerPoint where you write and design your presentation.

Normal view (Excel) A screen view that maximizes the number of cells visible on your screen and keeps the column letters and row numbers close to the columns and rows.

Notes Page view A view where you can work with notes in a full page format.

Notes pane A PowerPoint element that displays below the Slide pane and allows you to type notes regarding the active slide.

Objects The basic parts of a database that you create to store your data and to work with your data; for example, tables, forms, queries, and reports.

One-to-many relationship A relationship between two tables where one record in the first table corresponds to many records in the second table—the most common type of relationship in Access.

Option Group An object on a form or report that displays a limited set of alternatives where only one option can be selected at a time.

Outline symbol A small gray circle that identifies heading and body text paragraphs in an outline.

Outline view A document view that shows headings and subheadings, which can be expanded or collapsed.

Overflow Text that does not fit within a text box.

Page Layout view (Excel) A screen view in which you can use the rulers to measure the width and height of data, set margins for printing, hide or display the numbered row heading and lettered column heading, and change the page orientation.

Pane In Excel, a portion of a worksheet bounded by and separated from other portions by vertical and horizontal bars.

Parameter query A query that prompts you to supply the criteria when the query is run.

Pie chart A chart that shows the relationship of each part to a whole.

Pivot The action of moving a row to a column or a column to a row in an Excel PivotTable or PivotChart.

PivotChart report A graphical representation of the data in a PivotTable.

PivotTable Field List An Excel feature that enables you to move fields to different areas in the PivotTable or PivotChart report.

PivotTable report An interactive, cross-tabulated Excel report that summarizes and analyzes data.

Placeholder A slide element that reserves a portion of a slide and serves as a container for text, graphics, and other slide elements.

Plus outline symbol A formatting mark that indicates there are subordinate heading or body text paragraphs.

PMT function An Excel function that calculates the payment for a loan based on constant payments and a constant interest rate.

Populate The action of filling a database table with records.

Primary key A field that uniquely identifies a record in a table.

Print Layout view A view of a document that looks like a sheet of paper and displays margins, headers, footers, and graphics.

Print Preview A view of a document that displays information exactly as it will print based on the options that are selected.

Property Sheet A list of characteristics—properties—for fields or controls on a form or report in which you can make precise changes to each property associated with the field or control.

Query A database object that retrieves specific data from one or more database objects—either tables or other queries—and then, in a single datasheet, displays only the data you specify.

Quick Tables A selection of preformatted tables.

Record All of the categories of data pertaining to one person, place, thing, event, or idea, and which is formatted as a row in a database table.

Record source The tables or queries that provide the underlying data for a report.

Referential integrity A set of rules that Access uses to ensure that the data between related tables is valid.

Relational database A sophisticated type of database that has multiple collections of data within the file that are related to one another.

Relationship An association that you establish between two tables based on common fields.

Relative cell reference The address of a cell based on the relative position of the cell that contains the formula and the cell referred to.

Report A database object that summarizes the fields and records from a table (or tables) or from a query in an easy-to-read format suitable for printing.

Report Filter The area on a PivotTable that is used to restrict the data that displays.

Report header Information—such as logos, titles, and dates—printed once at the beginning of a report.

Report tool An Access feature that creates a report with one mouse click, which displays all the fields and records from the record source that you select.

Report Wizard An Access feature with which you can create a report by answering a series of questions; Access designs the report based on your answers.

Rich Text Format (RTF) A universal document format that can be read by nearly all word processing programs and that retains most text and paragraph formatting.

Row Labels Fields that are assigned a row orientation in a PivotTable report and become the row headings.

Ruler guide A nonprinting horizontal or vertical line that can be aligned to any position on the ruler.

Run The process in which Access searches the records in the table(s) included in a query design, finds the records that match the specified criteria, and then displays those records in a datasheet.

Select query A type of Access query that retrieves (selects) data from one or more tables or queries, displaying the selected data in a datasheet.

Shortcut menu A context-sensitive menu that displays commands and options relevant to the selected object.

Sizing handles The small squares or circles that display on each corner and in the middle of each side of a chart or graphic.

Slide pane A PowerPoint screen element that displays a large image of the active slide.

Slide Show view A view where the slides fill the computer screen, which enables you to view the presentation the way your audience will see it.

Slide Sorter view A presentation view that displays thumbnails of all of the slides in a presentation.

Slide transitions The motion effects that occur in Slide Show view when you move from one slide to the next during a presentation.

Slides/Outline pane A PowerPoint screen element that displays either the presentation outline (Outline tab) or all of the slides in the form of thumbnails (Slides tab).

SmartArt A designer-quality representation of your information that you can create by choosing from the many different layouts to effectively communicate your message or ideas.

Sorting The process of arranging data in a specific order based on the value in each field.

Source file The file where the data or object is created.

Speaker's notes Notes that are printed for the speaker to refer to as a presentation is being delivered.

Status bar A horizontal bar at the bottom of the presentation window that displays the current slide number, number of slides in a presentation, the applied theme, View buttons, Zoom slider, and Fit slide to current window button.

Subset A portion of the total records available in a table.

SUM function A predefined formula that adds all the numbers in a selected range of cells.

Tab stop A specific location on a line of text, marked on the Word ruler, to which you can move the insertion point by pressing the Tab key, and which is used to align and indent text.

Table A format for information that organizes and presents text and data in columns and rows.

Table (Access) The object that is the foundation of an Access database.

Table area The upper pane of the Advanced Filter window that displays the field lists for tables that are used in the filter.

Table of contents A list of a document's headings and subheadings marked with the page numbers where those headings and subheadings occur.

Table Style A predefined set of formatting characteristics, including font, alignment, and cell shading.

Template A preformatted database designed for a specific purpose.

Text box A movable, resizable container for text or graphics.

Text box control A graphical object on a form or report that displays the data from the underlying table or query.

Text link A hyperlink applied to a selected word or phrase.

Text Pane A SmartArt element where text that displays in the graphic can be entered and edited.

Text wrapping The manner in which text displays around an object, such as a picture or clip art.

Theme A predefined set of colors, fonts, lines, and fill effects that are professionally designed.

Thumbnails In PowerPoint, miniature images of presentation slides.

Underlying formula The formula that is entered in a cell and visible only on the Formula Bar.

Update query A query that adds or changes data in one or more existing records.

Validation rule Criteria that limit or control what users can enter in a field.

Value axis A numerical scale on the left side of a chart that shows the range of numbers for the data points; also referred to as the y-axis.

Values area The cells in a PivotTable report that summarize quantitative data.

View buttons A set of commands that control the look of the presentation window.

Wizard A feature in Microsoft Office that walks you step by step through a process.

WordArt A gallery of text styles with which you can create decorative effects, such as shadowed or 3-D text.

x-axis Another name for the *category axis*.

y-axis Another name for the *value axis*.

Zooming The action of increasing or decreasing the viewing area on the screen.

Index

Page references followed by "f" indicate illustrated figures or photographs; followed by "t" indicates a table.

A

Access 2007
  mastering, 115, 173, 289, 355
Action query, 198, 443
active content, 118, 445
Active slide, 66-67, 239, 445-446
Adamantine Jewelry, 2, 421-422
Add Space Before Paragraph, 359
Alignment
  clip art and, 295
Animation effects
  definition, 94, 265, 330
Application software
  commercial, 355
Apply to All option, 72
Area Section, 371, 443-444
AutoExpansion, 178, 443
AutoFilter
  Custom, 177-178
Axis Fields (categories), 380, 443

B

.biz, 86, 254, 425, 434
Blank Report, 317, 443
Blank Report tool, 317, 443
Board Anywhere, 227, 433-434
Boolean operators
  AND filter, 205
Brightness button, 296
Browsers, Web
  graphical, 445
Bullet points
  converted to SmartArt graphic, 248
Business Information dialog box, 323-324
buttons
  Comma Style, 443

C

Calculated eld(s)
  queries and, 439
Calendar control, 312, 444
Category axis, 229, 443
Center on page, 14, 181
central processing units (CPUs)
  performance, 173, 432
Change button, 25
Character spacing, 76, 443
Character Spacing button, 78
Chart Layouts gallery, 230, 443
Chart Styles gallery, 230, 443
chart(s) (Excel)
  animating, 247
Choose a SmartArt Graphic dialog box, 83-84, 252
Civic theme, 78
Close Print Preview button, 128, 190-191, 368
colors
  sheet tab, 264
columns
  freezing, 260-261
Commands
  Freeze Panes, 265-266, 444
commands
  Page Setup, 14
Comments
  Show All, 263
Computer sales analysis exercise
  Nationwide, 439
computer-aided instruction (CAI)
  flaws, 331
Confirm File Rename message, 136
Content controls

date picker, 330, 444
contextual spelling, 24-25, 443
Convert button, 89
Copy button, 10, 82-83, 238, 383-384
Cost by Facility query, 362
Create New Business Information set dialog box, 322

D

Data
  warehouses, 355
data bars
  applying conditional formatting, 179
Data types
  field option, 183, 363
data validation
  Combo Box and, 355
databases (Access)
  security alerts, 118, 445
Decrease List Level button, 238
deleting
  table columns, 20
Del.icio.us, 83-84
Design Checker, 299-300, 444
desktop publishing (DTP)
  technology, 289
Detail section
  Layout View in, 150
dialog box
  Save Export Steps, 129
  Update Table of Contents, 395
dialog boxes
  Business Information Set, 322-324, 443
  Choose a SmartArt Graphic, 83-84, 252
  Create New Business Information set, 322
  Data Analysis, 397
  Field Settings, 373
  New from Existing Presentation, 77
  PivotChart, 370, 443-444
  Value Field Settings, 373
Document Information category, 382
Document Information Panel, 14, 134, 181, 237, 358
Document Inspector, 227, 444
document(s) (Word)
  text inserted from another, 6
documents (Word 2007)
  cell shading, 38, 201
Drill-down indicator, 377, 444

E

Edit Business Information Set dialog box, 324
editing
  headers and footers, 445
  logos, 445
  numbers in cells, 26
  speaker's notes, 94-95, 446
.edu, 298-299
education
  high-tech, 227, 289, 433, 436
  mathematics, 437
Effects gallery, 248
Enforce Referential Integrity check box, 196
Excel
  comparison operators, 205-206, 391, 443
Exporting
  data between applications, 397

F

Field List pane, 317-319, 364-365
Field lists, 185, 446
Field Section, 371, 444
Field Settings button, 373
Field Size property box, 313
Field(s)
  PivotTable, 370-372, 445-446
fields
  placeholders for, 301

fields (database tables)
  Field1, 310
  ID numbers, 311
  innermost sort, 186-187
  outermost sort, 186-187
File menu
  commands in, 296
File New Database dialog box, 117, 182, 310
Filter by Form, 183
Filtering
  recipients, with mail merge, 327
Filter(s)
  report with, 188, 440, 445
Finish & Merge button, 142
Fixed date option, 73
Florida Port Community College, 289-291, 436-437
Font Color button arrow, 23, 89, 131-132, 180, 320
Font schemes, 292
Fonts
  button arrow, 70, 293
Form controls
  identification of, 443
  list box, 313, 445
  textbox, 362
Form letters, 136, 444
Format contextual tab, 69, 294
Format property, 312
Formatting
  slide elements, 94, 445
Formatting with conditional format
  newsletter background, 298
  numbers and text, 2
Freezing, Excel rows, 260
Future Value (FV) function
  arguments of, 388

G

galleries
  Shape, 132
  Shape Styles, 132
General tab, 136
Group & Sort button, 318-319
Grow Font button, 132
Guides
  margin, 326
  ruler, 323, 446

H

Horizontal Title, 30
Horizontally check box, 14

I

ID field, 119-120, 189, 310-312, 364-366, 431, 440
Ignore Once button, 25
Input Mask
  property box, 311-314
  Wizard dialog box, 311
Insert Chart dialog box, 239, 379-380
Insert Columns, 21
Insert Object button, 130
Insert Picture from File button, 86
Inserting absolute cell reference
  lookup field, 309
  text, from another Word document, 5
Installed Templates, 115, 322
ISNUMBER function
  IF function and, 423

K

key terms
  chapter 1, 6

L

Layout
  Data Sheet, 233
Layout guide, 330